"Through combining the 'mobilities turn' in the social sciences with the new interest in the material dimensions of social worlds, *Material Mobilities* offers eye-opening perspectives on the everyday world, its infrastructural landscapes, and the power-dimensions of mobilities. Reading this book will leave you sensing, feeling, and moving through your own social world with renewed curiosity."
 - **Prof Mimi Sheller,** *Director of the Center for Mobilities Research & Policy, Drexel University, USA*

"That social theory would turn back to reflect on its development in the contradictions of mobilities was predictable; but nothing could have prepared us for Jensen, Lassen, Lange and their colleagues' extraordinary engagement with the discourse of materialities. This collection is absolutely indispensable."
 - **Prof Anthony Elliott,** *Executive Director of the Hawke EU Jean Monnet Centre of Excellence, University of South Australia*

Material Mobilities

Material Mobilities explores the material dimension of various forms of mobilities and its implications for society, politics and everyday experiences as well as investigates how materials themselves are on the move. Together the different contributions and perspectives on material mobilities illustrate how materialities are critical components within mobilities but also shape how mobilities are produced and consumed within contemporary mobile societies. This insight may potentially influence the ways disciplines of mobilities understand and approach mobilities in the future.

This book exemplifies how the 'new mobilities turn' may profit from foregrounding materials, the material, and materiality as a common pivot for social analysis. During the last decade of research affiliated to the new mobilities turn, the societal repercussions of intensive mobilities has been in focus. The 'turn' has documented the social, environmental, economic, and cultural effects of the contemporary patterns of movement of people, vehicles, goods, data, and information. In parallel with this work new ideas and concepts about the human/non-human and the 'material dimension' of the social world has surfaced within a wide array of fields such as philosophy, anthropology, and cultural studies.

Material Mobilities offers a materially sensitive and focused attention to the new mobilities turn. The 'turn to the material' opens up a new set of research questions related to how artefacts and technologies facilitating and affording mobilities are being designed, constructed, and instituted. The new material interest furthermore points at new ways of comprehending the political and the power-dimensions of mobilities and infrastructural landscapes. The turn to the material furthermore problematizes the Modern binary distinctions between humans and non-humans, subjects and objects, and culture and nature.

Ole B. Jensen is Professor, Deputy Director, and Co-Founder of the Centre for Mobilities and Urban Studies (C-MUS), Aalborg University. His main research interests are Urban Mobilities, Mobilities Design, and Networked Technologies. He has published more than 200 academic publications on cities, mobilities, and design.

Claus Lassen is Associate Professor and Director of the Centre for Mobilities and Urban Studies (C-MUS) at Aalborg University. His research analyses changing social relations in the light of international air travel, and he has published a number of articles and book chapters on business travel, aeromobilities, and airports.

Ida Sofie Gøtzsche Lange is Assistant Professor and board member at the Centre for Mobilities and Urban Studies (C-MUS), Aalborg University. Her main research interests are Urban Mobilities, Port–City Relationships, Urban Design, Planning, Place theory, and Mobilities Design.

Changing Mobilities
Series Editors: Monika Büscher, Peter Adey

This series explores the transformations of society, politics and everyday experiences wrought by changing mobilities, and the power of mobilities research to inform constructive responses to these transformations. As a new mobile century is taking shape, international scholars explore motivations, experiences, insecurities, implications and limitations of mobile living, and opportunities and challenges for design in the broadest sense, from policy to urban planning, new media and technology design. With world citizens expected to travel 105 billion kilometres per year in 2050, it is critical to make mobilities research and design inform each other.

Dialogues on Mobile Communication
Adriana de Souza e Silva

Elite Mobilities
Edited by Thomas Birtchnell, Javier Caletrío

Bicycle Utopias
Imagining Fast and Slow Cycling Futures
Cosmin Popan

Cycling
A Sociology of Vélomobility
Peter Cox

Sea Log
Indian Ocean to New York
May Joseph

Material Mobilities
Edited by Ole B. Jensen, Claus Lassen and Ida Sofie Gøtzsche Lange

For a full list of titles in this series, please visit www.routledge.com/Changing-Mobilities/book-series/CHGMOB.

Material Mobilities

Edited by Ole B. Jensen, Claus Lassen
and Ida Sofie Gøtzsche Lange

LONDON AND NEW YORK

First published 2020
by Routledge
2 Park Square, Milton Park, Abingdon, Oxon OX14 4RN

and by Routledge
605 Third Avenue, New York, NY 10017

First issued in paperback 2020

Routledge is an imprint of the Taylor & Francis Group, an informa business

© 2020 selection and editorial matter, Ole B. Jensen, Claus Lassen and Ida Sofie Gøtzsche Lange individual chapters, the contributors

The right of Ole B. Jensen, Claus Lassen and Ida Sofie Gøtzsche Lange to be identified as the authors of the editorial material, and of the authors for their individual chapters, has been asserted in accordance with sections 77 and 78 of the Copyright, Designs and Patents Act 1988.

All rights reserved. No part of this book may be reprinted or reproduced or utilised in any form or by any electronic, mechanical, or other means, now known or hereafter invented, including photocopying and recording, or in any information storage or retrieval system, without permission in writing from the publishers.

Trademark notice: Product or corporate names may be trademarks or registered trademarks, and are used only for identification and explanation without intent to infringe.

British Library Cataloguing-in-Publication Data
A catalogue record for this book is available from the British Library

Library of Congress Cataloging-in-Publication Data
A catalog record has been requested for this book

ISBN 13: 978-0-367-72667-6 (pbk)
ISBN 13: 978-0-367-18821-4 (hbk)
ISBN 13: 978-0-429-19849-6 (ebk)

Typeset in Times New Roman
by Wearset Ltd, Boldon, Tyne and Wear

Contents

List of illustrations	ix
Notes on contributors	xi
Foreword	xiv
MIKKEL BILLE	

1 **Material mobilities**   1
OLE B. JENSEN, CLAUS LASSEN AND
IDA SOFIE GØTZSCHE LANGE

2 **From structure to infrastructuring?**
On transport infrastructures and socio-material
ordering   16
TOBIAS RÖHL

3 **The cathedrals of automobility: how to read a motor show**   31
RICHARD RANDELL

Interlude 1: Immaterial immobilities and the
Infrastructuring of Mobile Utopia   49
INTERVIEW WITH MONIKA BÜSCHER

4 **Relating movement to information in consumer**
mobilities, using Space Syntax   59
ZOFIA BEDNAROWSKA AND JAMIE O'BRIEN

5 **"It's going to be very slippery": snow, space and mobility**
while learning cross-country skiing   77
PAUL MCILVENNY

6 **Moving forward – left behind: asynchrone experiences. The**
use of mobile media technologies when young people leave   101
IDA WENTZEL WINTHER AND RUNE BUNDGAARD

7	**Mapping unknown knowns of transit infrastructures** ELISA DIOGO SILVA, DITTE BENDIX LANNG AND SIMON WIND	118
	Interlude 2: Five ways to make design and mobility political INTERVIEW WITH ALBENA YANEVA	139
8	**Designing places for experiences: a study of architectural practices** JØRGEN OLE BÆRENHOLDT AND ANITA SCHOU KJØLBÆK	147
9	**A material review of Costa Rica's attempt to carbon neutrality: assembling heterogeneous actor-networks of emissions, mobilities and calculations** YAMIL HASBUN	166
10	**Acupunctural mobilities design 'from below': reflecting on uneven material mobilities in the Global South, the Caracas a pie case** ANDREA V. HERNANDEZ BUENO AND DITTE BENDIX LANNG	185
	Interlude 3: Material mobilities – 'keynote interlude' INTERVIEW WITH OLE B. JENSEN	203
11	**Moving *with*: molecular mobilities and our connective tissue fascia** DOERTE WEIG	210
12	**Mobile work, space and processes of transition** HANNE VESALA AND SEPPO TUOMIVAARA	223
13	**Dwelling on the move** CECILIE BREINHOLM CHRISTENSEN	240
	Index	256

Illustrations

Figures

2.1	Varieties of structures according to Reckwitz (1997)	17
3.1	Photograph of one of the halls in the Palais des Expositions et des Congrès de Genève	35
4.1	Example Space Syntax map of sampled area rendered in greyscale for normalised integration values at 5 km radial scale. Road segments have been rendered in light-to-dark gradation to represent high-to-low integration values respectively. The area sampled represents the extent of consumer journeys described by the workshop participants	67
4.2	Participants working on their consumer maps at the workshops. Lancaster, UK, April 2016	70
4.3	Some of the participants' maps showing their consumer journeys in Lancashire. They used colours to mark different types of journeys as well as dots or stars for marking stops or destinations. Lancaster, UK, April 2016	72
5.1	Virgin site on Day 1	81
5.2	Testing the snow's slipperiness	85
5.3	Arrival at the site on Day 1	89
5.4	Building the loop track	90
5.5	A practical infrastructure for learning to ski	91
6.1	Najaaraq shows where she lives to her family at home (to the left) and virtual containing (to the right)	108
6.2	Family photographs back home	110
6.3	Everyday life at the halls of residence	111
6.4	Everyday life at the halls of residence	112
6.5	Home to the serious conversation	113
7.1	Berlin public transport infrastructures	118
7.2	The journey through the city centre of Berlin: A story told through embodied experiences – and emojis	126

x *Illustrations*

7.3	Four stations, four mapping moments taken from: The journey through the city centre of Berlin: A story told through embodied experiences – and emojis	127
7.4	An A to B auto-ethnographic mapping of Berlin	129
8.1	Second Rødby design meeting (27.05.2016, 14:07)	154
8.2	First Houens Odde design meeting, overview (04.05.2016, 17:06)	156
8.3	First Houens Odde design meeting, discussion on topography (04.05.2016, 17:19)	157
8.4	First Houens Odde design meeting, model in mess (04.05.2016, 18:01)	158
8.5	Second Houens Odde design meeting, references being handled (09.05.2016, 16:34)	159
9.1	Evolution of Costa Rica's motorized fleet, according to vehicle type	174
10.1	Caracas urban mobilities from focalized places in the west (Catia) and east (Chacao). Libertador and Chacao Municipalities	191
10.2	'Anthropological mappings' example (Carvajal, 2016). *Caracas a pie: Y sin embargo se mueve ('Walking Caracas: But it moves'* – our translation from Spanish). *Caracas a pie, 2012. El Nacional publications*	194
10.3	Three cases: From experiencing and imagining the city to urban action	197

Excerpts

5.1	Excerpt 1 – Day 2/arrival	83
5.2	Excerpt 2 – Day 5/loop 6b	86
5.3	Excerpt 3 – Day 1/arrival	87–88
5.4	Excerpt 4 – Day 1/loop 2	92
5.5	Excerpt 5 – Day 2/loop 2	92
5.6	Excerpt 6 – Day 4/arrival	94
5.7	Excerpt 7 – Day 5/arrival	95
5.8	Excerpt 8 – Day 1/loop 4	95
5.9	Excerpt 9 – Day 3/loop 1	95
5.10	Excerpt 10 – Day 5/loop 2	96

Contributors

Jørgen Ole Bærenholdt is Professor of Human Geography, Department of People and Technology, Roskilde University, also teaching Spatial Designs and Society. He is interested in tourist place design and social mobilization for tourism in peripheries. Further research interests are heritage, spatial design, design processes, mobility, regional development and the circular economy. Books in English include *Performing Tourist Places* (2004), *Space Odysseys* (2004), *Coping with Distances* (2007), *Mobility and Place* (2008) and *Design Research* (2010).

Zofia Bednarowska is a Regionalist and Computational Social Scientist. Her PhD research identified and explained spatial exclusion in consumption space. Zofia completed research fellowships at the State University of New York at Buffalo (2015) and at CeMoRe at the University of Lancaster (2016, 2017). She is a graduate of the GEOSTAT Summer School and Essex Summer School in Social Science Data Analysis. Zofia holds an MA degree in Political Science, a BA in Interfaculty Studies in Humanities and an MA in Social Research and Data Analysis.

Andrea Victoria Hernandez Bueno is an architect and urban designer, and currently a PhD student at Aalborg University in the department of Architecture, Design and Media Technology. Her special interest is the democratization of urban areas by improving urban mobilities and public spaces through design.

Rune Bundgaard is an educational anthropologist. He has a background in Greenland as a boarding school teacher, educational consultant and ethnographical filmmaker. Through a number of projects he has studied Greenlandic youth, focusing on the links and clashes between everyday life on the one side and school and dorm life on the other. The main focal points of his work are communication, shyness, home, mobility and teaching concepts.

Cecilie Breinholm Christensen holds an MA in architecture, a minor in psychology and is currently her PhD on Mobilities Design, unfolding mobile embodied situations as they are staged by architecture and design in Copenhagen Municipality by use of new tracking technologies. She is affiliated with the

Department of Architecture, Design and Media Technology, Aalborg University, and has a general research interest in 'dwelling' and human aspects of architecture and urban design.

Yamil Hasbun is a tenured Associate Professor in Environmental Design at the National University of Costa Rica. His current research focuses on the use of Actor-Network Theory for analysing the construction of 'nature' embodied in ecocertifications, standards and 'green' discourses based on politically charged technoscientific calculations and rhetorics. He is currently at the concluding stages of his PhD candidacy at the chair of Urban Design and Urbanization at the Technical University of Berlin.

Anita Schou Kjølbæk (cand.scient in human geography) is a project manager within Copenhagen Municipality. She works in the field of urban development on large-scale projects and is experienced with both newly developed neighbourhoods and the transformation of older areas. She is interested in planning processes, spatial designs, city planning and the circular economy. She is a former research assistant at the Department of People and Technology, Roskilde University, where she worked with tourist place design, heritage and cultural planning.

Ditte Bendix Lanng is Associate Professor in Urban Design and Mobilities with a focus on mobilities design and democratic agencies at the Department of Architecture, Design and Media Technology, Aalborg University, Denmark. She is an urban designer by training and holds a PhD in urban mobilities design.

Paul McIlvenny is Professor in the Department of Culture and Global Studies, as well as Director of the Centre for Discourses in Transition (C-DiT) and a member of the board of the Centre for Mobilities and Urban Studies (C-MUS), at Aalborg University. His current research interests include the everyday practices of vélomobility and skimobility, the mobility practices and micro-politics of prefigurative protest movements, and zoo-mobility practices in nature tours.

Jamie O'Brien (Dr) is a specialist in design research in the built environment, focusing on the spatial contexts of problems in design and planning. He holds a doctorate in design from UCL's Bartlett School of Architecture, and has published widely in academic journals. He is author of the book *Spatial Complexity in Urban Design Research*, (Routledge, 2019). Dr O'Brien is a Fellow of the Royal Geographical Society and Fellow of the Higher Education Academy.

Richard Randell is a faculty member in the Department of Psychology, Sociology & Professional Counseling at Webster University Geneva. He received his PhD in sociology from the University of Wisconsin-Madison.

Tobias Röhl (Dr) is a sociologist and ethnographer interested in socio-material approaches, microsociology and practice theory. Currently, he works at the

Collaborative Research Centre 'Media of Cooperation' at the University of Siegen as a postdoctoral researcher in a project investigating how different actors deal with disruptions in public transport. Previously, he has conducted ethnographic research on the development and use of technologies in education.

Elisa Diogo Silva is an architect (M.Arch) and urban designer (MSc). Her special interests are mobilities design, the intricate relationship between people and the urban space, sustainable urban transformations and exploring future scenarios for our cities and society.

Seppo Tuomivaara (Psychologist and PhD) works as a Specialist Researcher at the Finnish Institute of Occupational Health. His research activities have been focused on human–ICT relations at work, work development practices, implementation of ICT systems, and perceived ICT competence. He has also studied well-being at work in ICT use at leadership activity (ERP) and telework arrangements. Dr Tuomivaara has worked as a leader in several research and development projects and published research in scientific outlets.

Hanne Vesala is a PhD student at the University of Tampere, Finland, Faculty of Social Sciences. Her dissertation examines how workplace flexibility can enhance creativity and well-being at work. She has worked in several research projects at the Finnish Institute of Occupational Health (FIOH) studying mobile and telework, international business travel, sustainable work and employee-sharing. Her research interests include, *inter alia*, changing work values and careers, and natural and therapeutic work environments.

Doerte Weig's fascination is to uncover how the different facets of human physicality relate to understanding mobilities and socio-political transformation. Doerte has a PhD in Social Anthropology and research experience ranging from working with hunter-gatherers to contemporary dancers to smart citizens. Inspired by Posthumanism, Doerte believes that we cannot think through the future of mobilities and societies without taking our moving-sensing bodies more into account. In her workshops, Doerte combines readings with movement exercises.

Simon Wind is a mobility planner with special focus on urban traffic and mobility planning and design at the City of Aarhus, Denmark. He holds a BA in Architecture & Design, an MA in Urban Design and a PhD in Urban Mobilities Studies from Aalborg University, Denmark.

Ida Wentzel Winther, HoD, is Associate Professor in the Department of Educational Anthropology at the University of Aarhus. She trained as a cultural sociologist, and has for many years worked in the spheres of mobility, everyday life, home, family transformations and the importance of space and place. She focuses on the ordinary and the obvious: small items, and gaps in-between time and in-between space. She works on the levels of the theoretical, methodological and practical associated with visual anthropology and culture phenomenology.

Foreword

Mikkel Bille

Turn after turn. The material turn, the spatial turn, the affective turn, the linguistic turn, the mobility turn. Each turn has its own legitimacy and academic logic enabling it to be branded as such. Yet the most inspiring moments are often when these turns engage with one another with an open mind, rather than in opposition. Such engagement should not aim to establish a new "new", leaving a trail of previous turns now "unfashionable", before any intellectual depth can actually be accomplished. Rather, it should allow something to be brought forth that has perhaps lain as an undercurrent in both "turns". This may then strengthen the analytical potential of both approaches, help develop the accompanying methodological toolbox, and deepen the theoretical and conceptual understanding.

Material mobilities may just prove to offer one such means of fruitful engagement. Material culture studies, the field in which I mainly roam, as well as science and technology studies, have always been engaged with aspects of mobility. Likewise, mobilities research has always engaged in material objects such as trains, planes and buses. However, it has not been until recently, e.g. in the journal *Mobilities* or John Urry and Mimi Sheller's (2006) classic article on the new mobility paradigm, that questions have consistently been raised about the very materiality of such mobility infrastructure and the human activity of being mobile – both physically and virtually.

Despite their overlaps, the two approaches also differ in that each perspective explores, respectively, mobility and material objects as a way of understanding social worlds. To mobility studies, this often means outlining how larger systems of infrastructure enable the worlds of moving people, and ideas and goods, to unfold, and the politics of this. Material culture studies, in contrast, highlight the interwoven meaning-making processes of engaging with a vibrant and active materiality, engaging senses, matter and textures. As the book also illustrates, the combination of the two may go beyond simply an epistemological question of "access", with two different entry points to understanding the central issue: "social life". Rather, the combination may illuminate the core features of mobility or materiality itself. That is, mobility in the sense of giving access to a better understanding of materiality, and vice versa, and the effect this then may have on understanding whatever is meant by "the social".

It may seem obvious to point out that mobilities involve material objects. Luckily, this is not the point of this book either. Rather, combining the two "turns" offers, for instance, the opportunity to reach a deeper understanding of how human sentiments, such as uncertainty, fear, joy and comfort, are shaped through the vibrancy of both mobility and materiality. By merging the materiality and mobility foci, the role of place, matter, architecture and politics of such sentiments are not simply given, but also designed with more or less hidden agendas and human consequences. This includes materializing the surveillance and segregation of people, as well as the sustainability and liveability of modern life as residents, commuters and travellers. This is, to me at least, where it becomes even more interesting, since it shows that materiality and mobility – together or apart – shape something "more" that humans, as sentient and meaning-making beings, are entangled in. This "more" may not be measurable or clearly defined, but rather simply sensed as an ephemeral geography with weather, atmospheres and affordances; yet it is nonetheless real.

Attending more actively to the mobility aspects of material objects, and the material aspects of mobility, highlights how a vast plethora of objects – and the systems behind the making and maintaining of such objects – undergirds even the most common practices in modern human lives. Focusing on the role of the material world in such mobility practices or systems (or "networks" and "assemblages" as they are framed in an actor-network theory approach), renders common preconceptions of the clear distinctions between human and non-human increasingly untenable. Instead, it opens up questions about how mobility shapes social lives, by empirically demonstrating the processes whereby humans and material objects appear separated or entangled: Who or what is doing what, when, why and with what effect?

Promoting *Material Mobilities* requires a very keen eye on the methodological challenges of investigating how, why and when people and things move and are being moved in physical and virtual ways. This means exploring the impact of, and on, the very materiality of the objects soliciting such mobility. Is the standard ethnographic toolbox of interviews and observations the preferred approach, or is mappings or discourse analysis the best option? Or do we need new methodologies to actually get to the core of such a combined focus on matter and mobility? The methodological issue is one of the future challenges for the editors of this volume and the people taking up their call, not least in terms of making a broader societal impact.

In all its broad academic scope, one of the key promises of the book is that it raises the issue about how framing the right questions and methods can offer answers to societal challenges, for instance, new sustainable mobility systems, where the dominance of technical or quantitative measures do not suffice. The book demonstrates that a more qualitative understanding of how material objects and mobility are entangled is necessary to deal with future mobility challenges.

1 Material mobilities

*Ole B. Jensen, Claus Lassen and
Ida Sofie Gøtzsche Lange*

Introduction

Modern societies are increasingly on the move. It is estimated that over 1 billion passenger cars travel the streets and roads of the world (OICA 2016). Worldwide, 2.1 billion passengers travelled the seas on ferries in 2018 (Interferry 2019), and annual air passenger numbers exceeded four billion in 2017 for the first time; airlines now connect over 20,000 city pairs with regular services and there is on average more than 9,700 planes in the sky carrying almost 1.3 million people at any given time (Avakian 2017; IATA 2018). In addition, there are more than a billion bicycles in the world, and billions of people walk every day (Bathurst 2011).

These various forms of mobilities are highly material and closely related to a number of immobile material systems (Sheller and Urry 2006). The world's road network is more than 64 million kilometres in length (CIA 2018). The world's biggest road network in the US exceeds a total of 6.58 million kilometres, of which approximately 4.3 million kilometres are paved roads (Praveen 2014). Worldwide there are 1,148,186 km of railway tracks, 41,820 airports and 2,293,412 km of navigable rivers, canals and other inland bodies of water (CIA 2018). More than 7,806,142,681 mobile phones are under water, and there are over 420 submarine cables stretching over 1.1 million km connecting the world (Routley 2017). Materials and objects are also themselves on the move (Urry 2007:34), and 10.7 billion tons of goods were loaded worldwide in 2017 (HBS 2018). Moreover, mobilities also have a number of very material consequences. Transport energy use represents nearly one quarter of global primary energy (Moriarty and Honnery 2016:1), and almost a quarter of the total global CO_2 emissions from fuel combustion are produced by the transportation sector (Planète Energies 2017). Materialities and mobilities seem in many ways to be 'hybrid systems' that combine objects, technologies and socialities (Sheller and Urry 2006:214). This book focuses on such material mobilities.

During the last two decades, research affiliated to the 'new mobilities turn' has focused on the societal repercussions of intensive mobilities (see Urry 2007). This 'turn' towards mobilities has documented the social, environmental, economic and cultural effects of the contemporary patterns of movement of people, vehicles, goods, data and information. In parallel with this work, new ideas and concepts about the human/non-human and the 'material dimension' of the social world have surfaced within a wide array of fields such as philosophy, anthropology and cultural studies (see Bille and Sørensen 2019). The 'turn to the material' opens up a new set of research questions related to how artefacts and technologies facilitating and affording mobilities are being designed, constructed and instituted. Furthermore, the new material interest points at new ways of comprehending the political and the power-dimensions of mobilities and infrastructural landscapes. The turn to the material further problematizes the modern binary distinctions between humans and non-humans, subjects and objects, and culture and nature.

In this book, we focus on this intellectual shift and enquire how the new turn towards the material may affect insights within the mobilities turn research communities.[1] This focus offers materially sensitive and focused attention on the new mobilities turn. It exemplifies how this research perspective may profit from foregrounding materials, the material, and materiality as a common pivot for social analysis. In the book we argue, through a variety of perspectives on material mobilities, that understanding the new mobile world is also about understanding new forms of materialities and that the perspective on material mobilities enables a deeper understanding of the uncertain, and at times insecure, life conditions of contemporary societies.

Before the structure of the book is presented, we first detail some of the aspects of the mobilities turn and show some examples of how materialities are critical components within mobilities that shape how the latter are produced and consumed within contemporary mobile societies.

The mobilities turn

The various contributions to the material mobilities presented in this book are meta-theoretically grounded in the 'mobilities turn' (see Urry 2000, 2007; Kaufmann 2002; Creswell 2006; Adey 2010; Jensen 2015). One of the most important characteristics of this mobilities turn is the placement of mobility at the heart of understanding the 'social', with a particular focus on how mobility forms and reforms social life (Lassen 2019). Movement should here be understood not only as mobility but rather as various forms of mobilities. Urry (2007:47) identifies five interdependent mobilities that, he argues, produce social life:

- The *corporeal* travel of people for work, leisure, family life, pleasure, migration and escape, organized in terms of contrasting time-space modalities (from daily commuting to once-in-a-lifrganized in terms oetime exile)
- The physical movement of *objects* to producers, consumers and retailers; as well as the sending and receiving of presents and souvenirs
- The *imaginative* travel effected through the images of places and people appearing on and moving across multiple print and visual media

- *Virtual* travel, often in real time, thus transcending geographical and social distance
- The *communicative* travel though person-to-person messages via messages, texts, letters, telegraph, telephone, fax and mobile

In relation to this, Urry stresses 'that social research typically focuses on one of these separate mobilities and its underlying infrastructures and then generalizes from its particular characteristics' (Ibid.:48). Opposite to this, he argues that mobilities research must by contrast focus on the complex assemblage between these different mobilities and the interconnections between them. Such various forms of mobilities are connected with, and depend on, systems of material worlds (Ibid.:54, see also above). After all, 'Mobility is always located and materialised and occurs through mobilisations of locality and rearrangements of the materiality of places' (Sheller, 2004 in Sheller and Urry 2006:210). However, so far the material perspective seems to be an insufficiently researched area within mobilities research. Already, in 2006, Sheller and Urry raised the question in their classic article on the new mobility paradigm: 'Is there (or should there be) a new relation between "materialities" and "mobilities" in the social sciences?' (Ibid.:212). This was later followed up by Jensen (2013), who concludes that there seems to be unfulfilled potential to be found in opening up the 'mobilities turn' much more to material-orientated and design-orientated perspectives.

The 'turn to the material'

During the last decade or so, a 'new material turn' has emerged alongside the many other 'turns' within the cultural sciences. In this short introduction, we cannot present the full landscape of this turn, but we can indicate the borders and the rough contours of the topography. Elsewhere, Jensen has argued for the high relevance of connecting mobilities research to this emerging 'new materialities' literature (Jensen 2017). In particular, he points to positions such as Actor-Network-Theory (ANT), Non-representational Theory (NRT), the Nonhuman Turn, and Object-Oriented-Ontologies (OOO) (e.g. see Law 2002; Latour 2005; Anderson and Wylie 2009; Bennett 2010; Bryant 2011; Bryant *et al*. 2011; Bille and Sørensen 2019; Bogost 2012; Cole 2013; Kimbell 2013; Grusin 2015). The interesting dimension across these diverse thinkers is the increased sensitivity toward the material, or what we might term a new 'material imagination':

> Textures and densities, liquidities and radiances, thus act as sets of imperatives within and through which movement and sensation are inspired and performed ... materiality, in this reading, is multiple: the term connotes forces and processes that exceed any one state (solid, liquid, gas), and are defined ultimately in terms of movement and processes rather than stasis.
> (Anderson and Wylie 2009:326)

In this quote, we see a call for a much more open-minded and wide-ranging understanding of materialities within the mobilities turn. Moreover, we are inspired by the focus on technologies, artefacts and things as, for example, illustrated by Latour (2005). The associations of human and non-human entities into potent networks of agency render a material understanding that transgresses Cartesian dualisms if fully necessary. Part of the 'promise' of the turn to materialities is, in other words, a pragmatic approach to overcoming fixed ideas of subjects standing in front of objects, as well as the primacy of the former. The turn to materialities is teaching us to see mobilities on the ground as made up of complex assemblages of people, vehicles, infrastructures, technologies, legal frameworks, ideas of the good life and much else. These 'mobile assemblages' (Jensen 2013) of the contemporary mobilities landscapes are, furthermore, much better understood in light of the so-called symmetry thesis advocated by Latour (2005). By this it is meant an awareness of the fact that mobile practices are not about human subjects 'in control' over 'inferior' infrastructures and artefacts. Rather, we (as subjects) are enrolled into complex networks of distributed agency. The other key element for why the mobilities turn might benefit from engaging with the new materialities is seen in the emerging research field connecting the mobilities turn to the area of urban design and architecture. The emerging field of 'mobilities design' is surely an example of how a material turn within mobilities research may be articulated (Jensen and Lanng 2017).

The material turn within mobilities research

In the discussion of the overlapping research agendas of the new material turn and the mobilities turn, a number of themes are identified (Jensen 2017):

- To create further conceptual and theoretical explorations that seek more coherence and to challenge the avoidance of 'human exceptionalism' which seems embedded in the various versions of phenomenology and multisensorial analysis.
- To engage things and artefacts from new perspectives, taking the point of departure to be things rather than humans.
- To make an active connection to experimental methods and performative interventions from design and art practice.
- To engage in public acts of co-design, co-creation, participatory design and 'speculative design'.
- To explore notions of 'design justice' and differential mobilities through an investigation of how power and social exclusion manifest themselves through material design decisions and interventions.
- To address the process of designing for differential abilities and disabilities.

These (and many others) are dimensions of the ways in which the material turn may affect the mobilities turn. To illustrate some elements of how the new turn towards the material may affect insights within the mobilities turn research communities, we initially exemplify this.

First, let us discuss the example of a simple concrete tunnel. In the suburb of Aalborg East, the separated traffic systems of the post-war garden city typology stand as a testament to Modernist urban planning (Jensen and Lanng 2017). As planners aimed to create safe traffic journeys for pedestrians and cyclists, they separated the fast from the slow traffic in a complex network of streets and paths. There is nothing conspicuous or aesthetically interesting in the architecture of this 'transport machine'. It is seen by contemporary planners and designers as 'non-places' (Augé 1995) of the conform suburb. However, the research conducted as mobilities design research combined 'designerly ways of thinking', mobilities theories and ethnographic approaches, only to render a very different understanding of the infrastructural landscapes of the suburb. By meticulous ethnographic field studies combined with 'designerly questions' (for example questioning the understanding of the mono-functionality of infrastructure) and the agenda of the mobilities turn to look for 'more than A to B', these spaces and their meaning to people were put in an altogether different light. The specific concrete tunnel was a case in point. The network caters for the slow mobilities mode (bike, pedestrian, skateboarding) by offering them underpasses via concrete tunnels in the whole neighbourhood. The tunnel that was explored was of concrete, and the investigation explored the acoustics dimension (the classic 'tunnel eco') as well as the visual light-conditions in the day time and night time (these tunnels are dark 'holes' to walk into in the daytime and are so over-lit at night that one is almost blinded when moving out of the tunnel – hence the concerns in relation to perceived lack of safety). Besides exploring the material layout of the concrete walls and how the multi-sensorial inhabitation of this tunnel de facto took place, the research explored the tunnel as a meeting point and nexus of social interaction. It is not appropriate to go into detail here, but the point is clear. By utilizing the analytical capacities of the mobilities turn and the material sensitivity in both 'designerly ways of thinking' and the new material turn, the research showed that the tunnel indeed was a place! The critical-creative potential for opening up the understanding of this unconscious artefact (a leftover from the Modernist urban planning discourse trying to enhance speed and safety) is a vivid illustration of and testament to the potential of connecting mobilities and materialities thinking.

Second, through a study of light rail projects in two mid-sized European cities, Bergen and Angers, Olesen and Lassen (2016) focus on the many complex relations between materialities and mobilities. They challenge the paradox that despite the fact light rail projects in many cases have poorer socio-economic returns than other similar modes, such as bus rapid transit systems, they continue to be built. This showcases that the implementation of a new light rail mobilities system (Urry 2007) in cities is not just a matter of creating capacity and reducing travel time. Instead, it is also the visions and patterns of meaning associated with the specific materialities and spatial layout of the light rail projects that make them valuable and relevant in a strategic urban development perspective. Olesen and Lassen analyse more specifically how the different visions and meanings have materialized in various 'light rail scapes':

> [...] the term 'scape' then defines the visions and rationalities that have been incorporated into an object; the design and planning of infrastructure trigger certain ways of enacting the social world. A light rail holds a vision of the world that is inscribed in its material and spatial construction; a specific scape can be the colour of the light rail vehicles, or the segregation of the tracks, the placing and design of stations, or any element important to the way this infrastructure interacts with the city and its users.
>
> (Olesen and Lassen 2016)

Following this approach, the analysis illustrates that in the cities of Bergen and Angers, the choice of mobilities technology also can be considered a physical manifestation. In the corridors of the light rail, the physical and mental presence of light rail tracks provides 'mental potential' for mobility where the tracks create a mental map (Lynch, 1960) of a new path in the city, and, as such, a visual alternative to the car. Based on findings of such various material impacts and relations, Olesen and Lassen argue that it is not only the city that shapes the light rail project, 'but light rail also alters and shapes urban structures and planning practices because of its materiality and spatial interaction with the city' (2016:374). In this way, there exist a number of invisible and unexplored relations between the making of light rail mobilities systems and the various forms of the new and old materialities within cities. Consequently, light rail projects in research, policy and praxis therefore need to be rethought as complex urban development projects instead of merely simple 'pieces of infrastructure'. Decision-making processes of mobilities systems are not only a matter of technology, but are also related to the type of service, its image and material impacts.

Third, a mixed-methods case study of the Danish port town of Hirtshals (Lange 2016) has revealed how the materialization of distinct mobilities visions back in 1919 has worked as the DNA of the town for an entire century. The study includes document analysis, interviews, surveys, register data and physical-spatial place analysis, and the mixture of these different methods allows the case to be studied from many angles, and investigates the past, present and future prospects of the town. Hirtshals is a planned town that was established due to a strategical desire on a national level to build a fishing port at this specific site at the Danish west coast. Thus, an architectural competition was launched, and the winning plan for a whole new town was organized around a simple traffic diagram, arguing that where road, rail and port traffic would meet, a town would flourish. The plan was clearly inspired by English Garden City planning ideas, and much emphasis was put on the qualities of wide roads providing direct connections between A and B, and the segregation of city functions to prevent pollution and the spread of diseases, and to provide space for air and people to easily circulate. The physical planning ideas of frictionless transportation of people and goods via road, rail and waterways have been frozen into the material structures of a whole town. These material mobilities have been so influential on the development of the port and the town that they can been described as roots that anchor the local identities of the town even today, 100 years after the town plan was drawn.

Even though the town did not grow up until the 1990s, today the town is challenged by a critically decreasing number of inhabitants, a low socio-economic status and the shutting down of city functions, and the study shows that the open town structure does not provide inviting urban spaces for stay. The port, on the other hand, is still growing and expanding in land size, and so today the geographical dimensions exceed the area of the town. In this regard Hirtshals can be understood as a Terminal Town (Lange 2020a), a word play suggesting that not only is this place orchestrating the transportation between roads/rails and ferries/ships, but that it is also a place that is at risk of dying. Mobilities planning is thus not only about the efficient transportation of people and goods, but also about visual appearance and physical appeal towards (future) citizens and potential tourists. Strategies that seem logic and beneficial in terms of growth on a municipal, regional and national political agenda materialize in infrastructure projects that come with local consequences and that can be experienced as barriers not only physically but also socially/mentally (Lange 2020b).

From these admittedly very different examples, we have sketched out some of the rough dimensions of a new material interest within the mobilities research field. Obviously, much more detail and exemplification is needed. However, this should be adequate for the ambition of framing the theme of this book. Rather than writing theory frames ourselves, we want to invite the reader to explore the many different entries that such a general framing lead to. Therefore, the content of the book is what we turn to now.

Framing infrastructures and imaginaries

This book is divided into four parts that all focus on 'material mobilities' by exploring the material dimension of various forms of mobilities and its implications for society, politics and everyday experiences as well as exploring how materials themselves are on the move. The parts are divided by three interludes, written via the key notes at the C-MUS Conference 2016 with the theme 'material mobilities'. Together, the different contributions and perspectives on material mobilities illustrate how materialities are critical components within mobilities but also shape how mobilities are produced and consumed within contemporary mobile societies. The ambition of the book is that this insight may potentially influence the methods by which disciplines of mobilities understand and approach mobilities in the future.

The first part of the book addresses how highly material systems and infrastructures frame 'regimes' and social ordering for mobilities practices and means of transport within contemporary societies. This shows that researching transport infrastructures and mobilities systems brings a stronger socio-material awareness into the mobilities studies. The contributors in this first section therefore particularly reflect on socio-material aspects of infrastructures.

In *Chapter 2*, Tobias Röhl focuses on transport infrastructures and socio-material ordering. He argues that rather than the metaphysical notion of structures, we need to focus on concrete material infrastructures and their relationship with mobile practices instead. His underlying idea is that the understanding of railway lines and how they work may often tell us much more about social (mobile) life than trying to trace universal norms and values as regular and rule-bound systems which, in various ways historically, seems to have been a central concept across a number of sociological theories (such as Rational Choice, Marxism, Sociology, Structuralism, Functionalism and Symbolic Interactionism). Therefore, Röhl proposes in his conclusion a twofold praxeological shift away from supra-(structure) to infrastructuring.

In *Chapter 3*, Richard Randell provides us with a reading of the Geneva Motor Show. He offers us an alternative interpretation, a rewriting of text, by locating the motor show within the literature and discourse, drawing on contemporary automobilities studies that provide a set of analytical tools for locating the automobiles, the exhibitors, the visitors and the architectural space of the motor show. Through this approach, Randell directs our focus away from automobilities and invites us to think about the car as one component of a larger 'system' or 'regime' of automobility. Motor shows, Randell argues, contribute in unique ways to the cultural reproduction of automobility and in so doing they contribute to the continued and highly material capital accumulation prospects of automobile manufacturers and associated industries.

In *Interlude 1*, Monika Büscher stresses that alongside the lived materialities of the myriad of human mobilities, there are more imperceptible materialities of movement and stasis. Together, such lived, cumulative and hard-to-perceive (im)material (im)mobilities bring tremendous problems. Therefore, Büscher argues that material mobilities require post-disciplinary analysis, because they are generative of many of today's 'wicked problems' (problems without solutions). Here the mobilities paradigm, with its sensitivity on the fleeting, multiscalar, distributed nature of phenomena, their emergence from lived practice and their systemic complexities and fragilities, offers a much-needed analytical overview and agility which makes it possible to connect microscopically small material mobilities of antimicrobial resistance with human mobilities that cause climate change and refugee crises. Here, Büscher highlights the fact that theories are very often in search of explanations, and too often driven by a desire for solutions. However, today's problems are complex and wicked, and therefore research needs descriptions, paradigms, ethics, politics, methodologies of knowledge production, evaluation, experimentation and reversibility. However, this challenge, Büscher emphasizes, is mainly methodological. She argues that we need to develop a sense of crisis and ways of managing crises differently. For that, we need methodologies that can translate analytical insights and creative responses into action at the points that promise the greatest leverage. Following this, she suggests, as a methodological approach of change, asking 'What now?' when changes are taking effect, transformations are happening and unintended (perhaps unwanted, or unexpectedly positive) consequences emerge.

Approaches

The second part of the book focuses on how the new material sensitivity within mobilities studies calls for new approaches and involves mobile methods such as mapping-in-motion, mobile ethnography and more-than-representational anthropology to be able to more deeply investigate and understand material mobilities practices. It therefore focuses on different mobile methodologies that are used to unfold everyday (or seasonal/holiday) practices by examining mobile video ethnography, visual anthropology, and mapping operations/mapping-in-motion – all with a somewhat interactional mobility analytical approach.

In *Chapter 4*, Zofia Bednarowska and Jamie O'Brien introduce consumer mobility as a distinct extraction from the mobilities paradigm which describes how consumer journeys are based mostly on 'bricks and mortar' shopping. In the chapter, they develop a prototype method for mapping consumer journeys, also considering consumer's mental modelling and information gathering. The authors have coupled these observations with a model of urban network formation that underpins different scales of movement as well as different modalities of information-gathering. Bednarowska and O'Brien aim to observe how pathways at different scales overlay each other, so that functions of the network across a range of scale converge along the same road segments. They seek to observe how various forms of materialities for consumer behaviours are based on such 'affordances' for movement which are generative within urban environments as socio-technical domains.

In *Chapter 5*, Paul McIlvenny explores the ways in which a child learns to sense and move through a transient environment of recreational skiing within the context of familial social interaction. Using a mobile video ethnography and interactional mobility analysis approach, the chapter examines how snow, a complex, dynamic materiality that can afford spatial movement in its surface – is sensed, felt and made salient in spatio-interactional practices. MacIlvenny shows how the weather and snow surface conditions are a fundamental material resource for instructed mobile action. The wild but malleable snowscape is re(territorialized) by the participants making temporary tracks in the snow, and much time is spent at the site maintaining this practical spatial infrastructure for ski-mobility. Tracks can shape and habituate future mobile actions and immanent pedagogical activities within the practices of cross-country skiing that inculcate the child's feeling for an ephemeral geography of snow. In this way, the chapter delivers an important contribution to the study field on children's mobilities practices, both in relation to how children are made mobile and, equally importantly, to an increased understanding of the context in which children learn to be mobile in an adult world and what mobility means in the child's everyday life.

In *Chapter 6*, Ida Wentzel Winther and Rune Bundgaard focus on how young people in Greenland are often forced to move away from home, families, friends and familiar surroundings to get an education. The chapter describes some of the microprocesses of everyday life, with a focus on doing, feeling and practising mobility. Methodologically, the study draws on a filmed fieldwork conducted in one of the Greenlandic towns which offers upper secondary education and focuses on how young people deal with having to fend for themselves from a rather early age to show and describe the material and spatial universe in which the young people are situated. The analysis shows that while some enjoy life far away from their parents, others suffer severe homesickness; their families are, physically, far away but can be reached via different kinds of materialities (mobile media technologies, e.g. Skype and Facetime). The chapter is, as such, also a methodological attempt to intertwine sensory impressions and atmospheres, which can be captured in film, with the reflections of written language, along with the ambition of including the material dimension and a sensibility to mobile and educational research.

In *Chapter 7*, Elisa Diogo de Andrade Silva, Simon Wind and Ditte Bendix Lanng take their point of departure to be mobilities design (see above and Jensen, Interlude 3 of this book), an emerging research agenda focusing on identifying and examining critical issues in relation to the design of infrastructure (e.g. road networks, train stations, and bike parking facilities). Some dimensions of these infrastructures such as quantitative flows, materials, solid structures and others are relatively easy to map. However, the transit infrastructures are also important sites for people's everyday lives for more than their purpose of efficient transport. In these nodes and corridors, embodied mobilities are performed through everyday journeys, social and cultural encounters, emotions, atmospheres and resistance; they constantly materialize and dissolve, merge and separate. The chapter therefore argues that the design insight into transit infrastructures needs to include less representational dimensions of travellers' embodied 'drawling-in-motion' (Urry 2007). The authors emphasize that this insight is indispensable when designers seek to understand and explore the lived environment of infrastructures. The chapter therefore discusses a number of operational mapping tools that sensitize mobilities designers to less representational aspects of the interrelationship between embodied mobilities and physical infrastructure.

In *Interlude 2*, Albena Yaneva shifts the focus away from 'material' in mobilities, towards the mobile aspect of mobilities, i.e. those things and material arrangements that make us move. Embracing an STS- and ANT-inspired view on things and material arrangements that are commonly considered neutral, passive, immutable, she argues that we need to trace how social relations emerge as we interact with, stroll, inhabit and let ourselves be guided by these mundane artefacts and material arrangements. Moreover, we need to trace how they are shaped to become mobile, and how they are actively explored as mobile in the process of use or dwelling. According to Yaneva, methods thus need to take a step away from the traditionally dominant perspectivalism in architectural theory, and foreground the practicalities, materialities and events of buildings and mobile material arrangements. By this Yaneva wants architecture (as well as other fields) to move away from seeing the buildings as political symbols or embodiments of big political forces, but, rather, to consider what is done in design, renovation and dwelling. Therefore, we must formulate methods that both focus on things and material arrangements – that are commonly considered mute, neutral, passive, or immutable. Such methods must also focus on the practices of their makers (designers, engineers and architects, planners), which Yaneva terms as a 'ethnographic turn in architecture'. This holds a significant potential to dislodge the certainty of traditional architectural knowledge, the belief placed in the absolute authority of the historical archive, and the simplifications of its practitioners, who reduce, or even naturalize, architectural research to the production of critical discourse about practices.

Place and politics

In the third part of the book, place and politics are explored as important material dimensions of changing mobilities. The design of places and politics are, in a number of cases, a critical material component for creating new experiences, political movements, etc. while in others it seems more to be the missing materialization of global de-carbonizing policies that is the brake pad locally for achieving a 'greener' society. In a political framing, the chapters are, therefore, elaborating on destination development, cultural history, narratives, environmental governance and eco-tourism.

In *Chapter 8*, Jørgen Ole Bærenholdt and Anita Schou Kjølbæk focus on the 'creation' of attractive places from the perspective of the 'experience economy', whereby some architectural offices are increasingly specializing in designing destinations. Through the investigation of a new architectural office in Copenhagen which has specialized in destination development and with inspiration from the work of Yaneva (see Interlude 2 of this book), the chapter seeks to understand the company's architectural designs through the design practices that go on inside and outside the office. The aim is to understand how these practices have implications for the spatial design of experiential places. Based on observation notes, photographs and interviews, Bærenholdt and Kjølbæk show how there is a certain kind of material semiotic at play. The chapter argues that narratives, multiplicity and fellowship are held together through the devices of models in designing and through designs with inherent narratives more than practical functions. A story is told not merely through its symbolic representation, but through its manifestation as spatial environment (Lonsway 2009:51). Mobile subjects, objects and situations are important components that tie together the various elements of such design processes. Designers are frequently 'on the move' to meetings, with clients often 'bringing their design models with them', and 'walking and talking at the location' with customers, users and project participants, and using the car as a mobile workspace for professional talks 'in a good atmosphere … on the long car journey from the site back to the office'.

In *Chapter 9*, Yamil Hasbun focuses on the specific case of Costa Rica from an ANT-perspective, more precisely on the country's aim to become one of the first 'carbon neutral' nations. He seeks to shed new light on the mechanism of calculation, displacement and stabilization of certain mobilized socio-technical constructions of nature(s) found in regulatory frameworks of environmental governance, in particular those embodied in the process of 'de-carbonizing' economies as a new trend to consolidate greater competitiveness in increasingly globalized markets. Hasbun argues that the ambitious goal of Costa Rica has not been backed up by sound on-the-ground implementations and strategies relating to the country's severely collapsed transportation and infrastructure. Hasbun further contends that the 'Carbon-Neutrality' goal has not been assembled heterogeneously because its non-material 'discourses' and its material 'practices' have not been conceived as integral actants of the same process of translation, and henceforth the gap between the network's materiality and its inscriptions will irremediably cause the network to break down. At a more general level, the chapter points towards how the various 'experts' enrolled in these post-industrial 'green' networks assemble and mobilize heterogeneous 'de-carbonizing' calculation in order to legitimize techno-scientific claims which set out to both silence any uncooperative or unaligned actors and ultimately render 'nature' governable.

In *Chapter 10*, Andrea Bueno and Ditte Bendix Lanng explore how urban mobility affects the economic, social and cultural aspects of a place by focusing on the case of Caracas in Venezuela, which, under extreme political, social and economic circumstances, works to improve its urban mobilities, connectivity and continuity. The chapter focuses on practices of acupunctural design as an alternative for designing urban mobility in Caracas, using walking as a method for unfolding the case. They show how ordinary walking or crossing the street is often a difficult practice in Caracas. Bueno and Lanng argue that to facilitate such practices, not only are overarching urban transformation plans needed, but also focalized 'acupunctural' interventions at particular places that target, for example, 'legal' materialization of pedestrians crossing and incorporation of public spaces to help create the continuity and imaginary of the city as a whole from the pedestrian point of practising embodied mobilities. Bueno and Lanng therefore call for new ways of engaging and understanding the city from the simple, yet imperative practices and experiences 'on the move' that can result in the design of mobilities alternatives.

In *Interlude 3*, Ole B. Jensen stresses that the turn to materialities is not fully new, however; it has moved from an abstract notion of 'the material' towards a much more sensitive and detailed understanding of the material condition of human and non-human existence. In particular, Jensen is inspired by the 'designerly ways of thinking'. The design way of thinking as a method, as well as the choices of materials, the physical composition of spaces and infrastructural landscapes leads quite easily to a material mobilities design agenda. However, Jensen does not consider any methods to be particularly 'mobile', but instead he argues for a pragmatic viewpoint on methods. The relevant methods for mobilities researchers are the ones they use because of their usefulness and not because they are defined as 'mobile methods'. In Jensen's own work, this pragmatic approach means a combination of more technologically oriented methods as a supplement to the more 'classic' ones, such as qualitative research interviews and ethnographic observations. Through a methodological dialogue with Büscher (see Interlude 1 of this book), he recommends a double research strategy when approaching material mobilities: first, posing the utopian 'What if...?' question that opens up to critically creative speculations about possible futures; and second, the equally important 'What now...?' question that brings matters 'down to earth' as it were, forcing us to ask questions about ethics, hard choices, policy dilemmas and power. It is, according to Jensen, in such a 'double' methodological approach that the key to 'a designerly ways of thinking' within material mobilities research must be found!

Bodies on the move

Finally, the fourth part of the book addresses the relations between the material world and our embodied performances on a micro level. This part shows – with points of departures in phenomenology and psychology and particularly by exploring bodies on the move in mobile practices such as commuting, mobile work and moving-with – how a stronger material sensitivity changes the way elements such as urban space, transition and dwellings are understood.

In *Chapter 11*, Doerte Weig explores the question of how moving with one another takes new shapes in today's culturally blurred urban spaces is central to urban design in a post-automobile world. The chapter combine concepts of temporality inherent in mobility and process philosophy with the physiology of fascia, which advances conceptualizations of movement and mobility practices to correlate with corporal realities. Weig argues that, with fascia, our bodily connective tissue and quality of 'tensional responsiveness' gives us new vocabularies relevant to sustainable urban planning and future mobilities. Moreover, fascia offers us methodological and theoretical inspirations, materializing the temporal move from knowledge of motion to knowledge in motion.

In *Chapter 12*, Hanne Vesala and Seppo Tuomivaara focus on mobile work. The chapter stresses that this topic has mainly been approached as a technical challenge of dealing with contingent and unfamiliar infrastructure, but its personal and affective dimensions are less well known. Supplementary to such a perspective, Vesala and Tuomivaara show how the work period in the alternative environment created an experience of time that is more owned and authentic than the rhythm of the everyday environment. This more authentic time enables mindful concentration and reflections of one's personal past and future. Therefore, Vesala and Tuomivaara argue that mobile work enables processes of transition, particularly in spaces where one can feel 'at home' and simultaneously experience a rupture in the everyday environment.

In *Chapter 13*, Cecilie Breinholm Christensen presents observations and considerations on the everyday commute by train between Copenhagen and Odense in Denmark. Mobile practices are observed on the material, social and bodily level (see Jensen 2013). The chapter focuses on how 'people' preserve psychological and personal coherence during everyday mobilities, and how this relates to the ability and possibility of 'dwelling on the move'. Christensen investigates this by viewing identity formation as a bodily practice, where a coherent sense of self is obtained by 'homing' the surrounding environment. In relation to this, the chapter questions whether it is possible to maintain a coherent sense of self in a world of mobilities. Drawing on a psychological and critical theory perspective, the chapter highlights that the constant pressure for self-development, for being 'on the move', may have psychological consequences for the individual. Christensen therefore emphasizes that we shouldn't overlook the importance of physical settings when being on the move. We invite readers to move with us!

Note

1 This book gathers the inputs from the International Conference held at the Centre for Mobilities and Urban Studies (C-MUS) in Aalborg, November 2016.

References

Adey, P. (2010), *Mobility*. London: Routledge.
Anderson, B. and Wylie, J. (2009), 'On geography and materiality'. *Environment & Planning A* 41:318–335.
Augé, M. (1995), *Non-places. Introduction to an Anthropology of Supermodernity*. London: Verso.
Avakian, T. (2017), Here's How Many Planes Are in the Air at Any Moment. *Travel + Leisure* magazine. Available at www.travelandleisure.com/airlines-airports/number-of-planes-in-air.
Bathurst, B. (2011), *The Bicycle Book*. London: HarperCollins Publishers.
Bennett, J. (2010), *Vibrant Matter. A Political Ecology of Things*. Durham: Duke University Press.
Bille, M. and Sørensen, T. F. (2019), *Materialized*. En indføring i kultur, identitet og teknologi (Materiality. An introduction to culture, identity and technology). Copenhagen: Samfundslitteratur.
Bogost, I. (2012), *Alien Phenomenology, or What's It Like to be a Thing?* Minneapolis: University of Minnesota Press.
Bryant, L. (2011), *The Democracy of Objects*. Ann Arbor: Open Humanities Press.
Bryant, L., Srnicek, N. and Harman, G., eds (2011), *The Speculative Turn. Continental Materialism and Realism*. Melbourne: re.press.
Cole, A. (2013), The Call of Things. A Critique of Object-Oriented Ontologies. *Minnesota Review* 80: 106–118.
CIA (2018), *The World Factbook*. Virginia: Central Intelligence Agency. Available at: www.cia.gov/library/publications/the-world-factbook/.
Cresswell, T. (2006), *On the Move: Mobility in the Modern Western World*. London: Routledge.
Grusin, R., ed. (2015), *The Nonhuman Turn*. Minneapolis: University of Minnesota Press.
HBS (2018), The UNCTAD Handbook of Statistics 2018. Geneva: Development Statistics and Information Branch UNSTAD. Available at: https://stats.unctad.org/handbook/MaritimeTransport/WorldSeaborneTrade.html.
IATA (2018), Traveller Numbers Reach New Heights. Press Release No. 516. The International Air Transport Association. Available at www.iata.org/pressroom/pr/Pages/2018-09-06-01.asp.
Interferry (2019), Ferry Industry Facts. Available at: https://interferry.com/ferry-industry-facts/?

Jensen, O. B. (2013), *Staging Mobilities*. London and New York: Routledge,
Jensen, O. B., ed. (2015), *Mobilities*, Vols 1–4. London: Routledge.
Jensen, O. B. (2017), Urban design for mobilities – towards material pragmatism. *Urban Development Issues* 56: 5–11.
Jensen, O. B. and Lanng, D. B. (2017), *Mobilities Design: Urban designs for mobile situations*. London, Routledge.
Kaufmann, V. (2002), *Re-thinking Mobility: Contemporary sociology*. Aldershot: Ashgate.
Kimbell, L. (2013), The object strikes back: an interview with Graham Harman. *Design and Culture* 5(1):103–117.
Lange, I. S. G. (2016), *Transit eller leveby. Et casestudie af Hirtshals som et stærkt mobilitetspåvirket sted i Gennemfartsdanmark'*. PhD edn. Aalborg University.
Lange, I. S. G. (2020a), Terminal towns. In: Jensen, O. B., Lassen, C., Kaufmann, V., Freudendal-Pedersen, M. and Lange, I. S. G., eds. *The Routledge Handbook of Urban Mobilities*. London: Routledge.
Lange, I. S. G. (2020b), The paradox of a transit hub – Hirtshals as case of local life and global flow. In: Lassen, C., Laursen, L. L. H. and Larsen, G. R., eds. *Mobilities and Place Management: Scandinavian Contexts*. London: Routledge.
Lassen, C. (2019), How one book and one meeting shaped my aeromobilities research. In Jensen, O. B., Kesselring, S. and Sheller, M., eds, *Mobilities and Complexities*. London: Routledge.
Latour, B. (2005), *Reassembling the Social*. Oxford: Oxford University Press.
Law, J. (2002), *Aircraft Stories. Decentering the Object in Technoscience*. Durham: Duke University Press.
Lonsway, B. (2009), *Making Leisure Work: Architecture and the Experience Economy*. London: Routledge.
Lynch, K. (1960), *The Image of the City*. Cambridge MA.: MIT Press.
Moriarty, P. and Honnery, D. (2016), Global transport energy consumption. In Lehr, J. H. and Keeley, J., eds, *Alternative Energy and Shale Gas Encyclopedia*. New York: John Wiley and Sons. Available at: www.researchgate.net/publication/301650630_Global_Transport_Energy_Consumption.
OICA (2016), World Vehicles in Use. Statistic. The International Organization of Motor Vehicle Manufacturers. Available at www.oica.net/category/vehicles-in-use/.
Olesen, M. and Lassen, C. (2016), Rationalities and materialities of light rail scapes. *Journal of Transport Geography* 54(June):373–382.
Planète Energies (2017), *The Global Transportation Sector: CO_2 Emissions on the Rise*. Planète Energies. Available at www.planete-energies.com/en/medias/close/global-transportation-sector-co2-emissions-rise.
Praveen, D. (2014), The World's Biggest Road Networks. Road Traffic Technology. Web-article. Available at: www.roadtraffic-technology.com/features/featurethe-worlds-biggest-road-networks-4159235/.
Routley, N. (2017), The World's Network of Submarine Cables. Web-article. Visual Capitalist. 24 August. Available at: www.visualcapitalist.com/submarine-cables/.
Sheller M. (2004), Automotive emotions: feeling the car. *Theory, Culture and Society* 21:221–242.
Sheller, M. and Urry, J. (2006), The new mobilities paradigm. *Environment and Planning A* 38:207–226.
Urry, J. (2000), *Sociology Beyond Societies*. London: Routledge.
Urry, J. (2007), *Mobilities*. Cambridge: Polity Press.

2 From structure to infrastructuring

On transport infrastructures and socio-material ordering

Tobias Röhl

Introduction

The material turn in mobilities studies entails an interest in the infrastructures and "mobility-systems" (Urry, 2007, pp. 12–16) that *"enable* the movement of people, ideas and information from place to place, person-to-person" (Ibid., 12). Mobile practices rest on a number of (rather immobile) material infrastructures – for example, railways rely on train stations and tracks and many other infrastructural components. Consequently, researching transport infrastructures provides insights into the dialectical relation between mobility and immobility (Adey, 2006; Hannam *et al.*, 2006). In this chapter I will, however, make a further claim. Bringing together mobilities studies, social research on infrastructures and practice theory, this chapter reconceptualises the problem of social order. Instead of talking about the rather metaphysical notion of structures we should talk about concrete (transport) infrastructures and their relationship with (mobile) practices instead. To put it very bluntly and also provocatively: the idea is that understanding railway lines and how they work might often tell us more about social life than trying to trace (immaterial) universal norms and values as regular and rule-bound systems. This results in a concept of social order that is in line with practice theories: social order becomes something to be understood as processual, socio-material, and integral to observable practices. In other words: Instead of looking up to metaphysical heaven, we should look towards the things beneath and amidst us. The notion of material mobilities advanced by this volume thus not only offers new ways of thinking about mobilities but also facilitates reformulating concepts in social theory.

I will develop my arguments by using transport infrastructures as an example. First, I will outline the prototypical notion of structure and its shortcomings from a praxeological perspective. Following this critique I will argue that one can remain ontologically flat and still describe large-scale phenomena. One way to do this is to follow (transport) infrastructures in their relation to (mobile) practices. In my conclusion I propose a twofold praxeological shift from (supra-)structure to infra-structuring opened up by the material turn in mobilities studies.

Supra-structures and praxeological critique

The concept of structure can be seen as one of the central concepts in the social sciences. As Andreas Reckwitz (1997) argues, most strands of sociology seek to find and describe patterns, rules and regularity in the seemingly chaotic variety of social life. They differ, however, in their focus and aims along two dimensions: (1) The first dimension concerns the nature of structures directly. While some focus on structures as regularity, others focus on structures as rules; (2) the second dimension pertains to the question where structure is located and what it governs. Structures can either be seen as inhabiting and governing whole systems, or be described as being part of individual interactions and actions. Consequently, four different ways of conceptualising structure can be distinguished and linked to different approaches (Figure 2.1).

Typically, structure is associated with approaches in field number 4 of the list – not surprisingly the prototypical proponents of this type all bear structure in their name: structuralism and Parson's Structural Functionalism (Parsons, 1991). Following Durkheim's notion of "social fact" (Durkheim, 2014) structures are seen as rather persistent, collective, and immaterial entities that appear as objective reality beyond individual idiosyncrasies. In terms of their content, social structures then consist of universal rules, norms and values that externally govern what people do. As such they are situated above and outside of concrete interactions and social situations.

It is this notion of structure as a supra-structure that was and still is criticised by various authors in the heterogeneous field of practice theory and its precursors. Three connected points of critique can be identified:

1. *Ontological*: Structures are relegated to a plane which is both different from and distant to the practices observed (Latour, 2005). They are positioned in a metaphysical realm which itself is disconnected from practice and describes a sphere of bodiless and immaterial ideas.
2. *Epistemological*: The epistemological critique harks back to Wittgenstein's notion of rules (1963: §§ 143–242; cf. Lynch, 1992). Like the concept of rules, structures are not to be understood as something that can explain how things are (for example, how social practices come to be the way they are).

	Action	System	
Regular	Rational Choice	Marxism, Sociology	Structural
Rule-bound	Ethnomethodology, Symbolic Interactionism	Structuralism, Functionalism	Structural

Figure 2.1 Varieties of structures according to Reckwitz (1997).

Instead, it can only be something that one arrives at by trying to make sense of practice. Structures are, however, not to be mistaken for the cause of practice; they are merely a "scholastic" theory distanced from practice (Bourdieu, 1990).

3   *Anthropological*: Harold Garfinkel's notion of the "judgemental" or "cultural dope" (1967, p. 67f.) points to the negative anthropology of such a structuralist view on practice:

> By 'cultural dope' I refer to the man-in-the-sociologist's-society who produces the stable features of the society by acting in compliance with preestablished and legitimate alternatives of actions that the common culture provides. [...] The common feature in the use of these 'models of man' is the fact that courses of common sense rationalities of judgement which involve the person's use of common sense knowledge of social structures over the temporal 'succession' of here and now situations are treated as epiphenomenal.
>
> (Ibid., p. 68)

Human action is seen as a mere fulfilment of rules. How rules, norms, and values are enacted and interpreted in practice is left unclear. Instead, common sense notions about structure are used implicitly to account for practices in a given situation. This argument can also be found in Pierre Bourdieu's critique of structuralism (1977) with its timeless rule-systems that fail to account for the time-sensitive strategies that actors use in practice – it is, for example, important *when* to return a favour or gift, even though structuralism views that as a timeless system of gift exchange.

To sum it up: Ontologically, adherents of supra-structures subscribe to a platonic perspective on reality. They position structures on another plane of existence akin to the platonic realm of ideas. From this perspective structures appear as the real force working behind our backs. Epistemologically, structures are within this way of thinking therefore used to explain why things are the way they are. Anthropologically, they are seen as powerful entities that govern human action. How metaphysical supra-structures are linked to concrete practices cannot sufficiently be explained.

Flat ontologies and large-scale phenomena

On the other hand, microsociological strands of social theory (Garfinkel, 1967; Goffman, 1990) have often been accused of being confined to local situations and not being able to describe phenomena that extend single sites (Fuchs, 1989): for example, changes in class relations in a society or the emergence and dispersion of new practices in society. How can one trace large-scale phenomena without referring to some disconnected, immaterial, and almighty entity-like structure? The challenge is to remain "ontologically flat" (Latour, 1996; Schatzki, 2016) while at the same time tracing such phenomena (Nicolini, 2017).

Transport infrastructures and ordering 19

"Flat ontologies" promise to tackle this issue. Three common features of flat ontologies can be identified:

1 Flat ontologies are *posthumanist* and turn towards material entities in order to account for social order. Adopting a socio-material perspective, materiality is seen as not merely mediating practices but constitutive to them – the material and social are entangled and cannot be separated from each other (Gherardi, 2006). In Schatzki's case this means to start among human activities and look at the material arrangements of bodies, organisms, materials, and things, amidst which practice transpires (Schatzki, 2016).
2 Flat ontologies are also *anti-reductionist*. They assume that there is only one plane of existence and do not distinguish between a macro and micro order of the social (Schatzki, 2016). Every notion of a higher order has to be explained by solely referring to particular practices and their connections with other practices. There is, for example, social class, and there is German society and culture. They are, however, produced in concrete practice with mundane technologies: There is no special place reserved for them. Such notions also cannot be used to explain how things are but can only be traced back to places where they are brought about. Accordingly, macrosociology is seen as "a sociology for impatient people" (Nicolini, 2017, p. 101).
3 Finally, flat ontologies are r*elational* and reject essentialist notions of agency. Consequently, they are in line with other "new materialisms" (Coole and Frost, 2010; Kalthoff *et al.*, 2016b) in opposing deterministic views of materiality. Even though material entities are an important part of practice, they have to be viewed in relation to other elements of practice (material arrangements, competences, understandings, etc.) and not in isolation.

One way to do justice to a flat ontology is to follow actual links between situations. Situations have never been self-contained but are linked to other situations via bodies, artefacts, texts, and, of course, infrastructures. Through this "texture" (Gherardi, 2006) of socio-material connections social order is perpetuated (Schatzki, 2005). Because there are transport infrastructures, for example, people can collectively participate in practices of commuting. Social order is consequently not to be found in a world of ideas but in concrete doings and sayings, and also in material arrangements that connect a given situation to other situations. It can thus be described as an accomplishment that is constantly brought about and revised by activities at various interrelated sites (Röhl, 2015). And these activities are linked by material entities. These entities have a social history and future reaching beyond the given situation. They are made and configured before we encounter them; they are – in some way – remade and reconfigured in a given situation; and they leave a site changed, often bearing marks of situated practices – some of them intentional (e.g. texts as documents of a situation), some of them unintentional (e.g. wear and tear on bodies and objects alike).

From the perspective of such a "connected situationalism" (Nicolini, 2017, p. 101) two types of connections can be distinguished:

1   **Intersituative connections** (Knorr-Cetina, 2009; Hirschauer, 2014) make something absent present by mediating *between* situations. As such they establish "relations of mediation" (Verbeek, 2005, p. 123ff.), i.e. more or less transparent systems of exchange between participants – either by embodying something else or by representing it symbolically. Bodily presence is substituted by mere "response presence" in which "the interacting party is not or need not be physically present but is accountable for responding without inappropriate delay to an incoming attention or interaction request" (Knorr-Cetina, 2009, p. 74). Examples include "scopic systems" (Knorr-Cetina, 2009) of global financial markets, but also letters, phones, screens, and any other means of communication in which the participant ascribes the presence of another participant to signs and sights.
2   **Transsituative connections** (Nicolini, 2017) point to dispersed practices *across* many situations. While intersituative connections explicitly open up a presence of something absent for the participants involved, transsituative connections often remain implicit. What all the things, bodies, and texts around us do to us, whom they include and exclude, what actions they "invite" or "inhibit" (Verbeek, 2005, p. 171ff.) is seldom thematically made relevant, although they play an important part in perpetuating (or destabilising) order (Schatzki, 2005). Latour's shepherds are not made explicitly present via the fences installed by them – they are, however, implicitly present via their attempt at ordering their herd practically enacted by the fence (Latour, 1996). And all kinds of infrastructures are, of course, an important part of this transsituative establishment of social order. We are connected to and synchronised with a faceless collective of people doing similar things by using electrical appliances (Walker, 2014), or by entering a ferry (Stäheli, 2012).

Following the first type of connections does not necessarily require the researcher to take the infrastructure of exchange into account. One can, for example, gain insights into telephone communication by treating the telephone and the lines connecting its speakers as a black box. In this vein conversation analysts could show important features of telephone communication such as the technologically modified distribution of summons, answers, and greetings (Schegloff, 1979). In contrast, with the second type of connections one has to look for the implicit and practical ways that an artefact, a body, a text, or an infrastructure is relevant for the observed situations and their participants. Yet, thinking about these two types of connections does not entail an *a priori* categorisation. Instead, they are two strategies to think about socio-material connections. An infrastructural perspective is, however, better suited to a transsituative research stance on social order. In this vein, I argue that by following transport infrastructures one can see how modern life is ordered without referring to an unattainable structure. Researching intersituative and transsituative connections also entails not staying put as a researcher but becoming increasingly mobile (Schubert and Röhl, 2017). Such "mobile methods" (Urry, 2007, p. 39ff.; Büscher *et al.*, 2010) call for researchers not only following people, but also objects, data, media, and so forth. Following these material entities allows the researcher to trace social order in the practical making beyond isolated situations.

Infrastructures and infrastructuring: towards a more modest notion of structure

Unlike the concept of supra-structure, the concept of infrastructure is much more modest and mundane. If we go back to its etymological origins, this becomes especially apparent: As Ashley Carse (2017) points out, the term infrastructure originated in nineteenth-century French and was solely used in the realm of engineering. When the term was introduced into the English language in the early twentieth century, it simply referred to the work required before railroad tracks could be built and which was situated beneath the tracks (e.g. a roadbed of substrate material). In the course of the twentieth century the term was widely adapted to other areas and soon received its common meaning of an underlying built system providing some common good or supporting an activity – there are, for example, transport, communication, energy, political and economic infrastructures.

This common notion of infrastructure already offers some clues on how to rethink the concept of structure in the social sciences. Infrastructures are concrete (and not abstract/ideal); they are beneath our feet, in our walls; they surround us and entangle our daily lives; they are even up in the sky or in earth's orbit (but not in metaphysical heaven). As such they can – at least potentially – be grasped empirically. Nevertheless, infrastructures and their workings are often overlooked (Star, 1999). One reason for this "invisibility" is that they are "infra" in the narrow sense of the word: They are built "beneath" or "below" other built structures. Getting hold of them might in some cases require substantial work: e.g. digging up ground by following construction and maintenance workers around to trace the networks of cables that enable the use of modern appliances, or at least acquiring plans, maps and diagrams showing us these networks in idealised form. Another reason can be found in a more metaphorical interpretation of "infra": They are "beneath" our immediate awareness. Phenomenologically speaking they are part of "background relations" (Ihde, 1990, p. 108ff.) in which material entities like our heating systems are involved in the ways we experience the world, but are themselves "transparent". As Susan Leigh Star once put it, researching infrastructures means in a way "to study boring things" (1999, p. 377). They are part of routine practices in which their workings are taken for granted. Yet, they are often an integral part of many dispersed practices at once (Shove *et al.*, 2015).

Infrastructures and the configuration of practices

Infrastructures are consequently not only supporting but also shaping (mobile) practices (Niewöhner, 2015). Like other material entities, infrastructures are not a neutral means but are themselves involved in practice. This can be illustrated with a few examples from the literature on the history of the railway. These examples show how transport infrastructures configure practice and thus bring about social order. When railways were introduced in many European countries in the course of the nineteenth century, two things happened from the perspective of practice theory: (1) around the new technology and its infrastructure new practices emerged and well-established practice were reconfigured, (2) these changes affected areas well beyond the immediate environment of the infrastructure.

When people started to travel by train in the nineteenth century, they experienced journeys differently than travelling in horse carriages (Schivelbusch, 2014, p. 52ff.). They saw themselves as "parcels" that were transported from place A to B as part of an industrial activity (Thrift, 1996, p. 266). Instead of experiencing the countryside through which they travelled with all their senses, they only had a fleeting visual glimpse of an ever-changing landscape. Travellers first had to learn not to focus on objects in their proximity but on distant things, resulting in a panoramic view of the landscape (Schivelbusch, 2014, p. 59ff.). In other words: a new practice of turning towards the land appeared in the wake of this new form of travelling. Consequently, "land" turned into "landscape", as something to be experienced solely visually (Urry, 2007, p. 102).

Sometimes practices are not necessarily new but recombined and reconfigured. In the case of railway journeys, reading became an activity during travelling (Schivelbusch, 2014, p. 64ff.; Bradley, 2016, p. 118ff.). Before the railway became the main mode of transport those who could afford it travelled in horse-drawn carriages. On the surface, compartmental coaches of the European railway and those of horse-drawn carriages have much in common. And indeed, European first- and second-class coaches drew on the design of horse-drawn carriages and their coaches. Yet, travellers experienced the proximity of their fellow travellers differently on trains than in horse carriages. In horse carriages one spent a prolonged time together and shared a destination. Consequently, others were perceived as being on the same journey and conversations with each other were the norm. On trains, however, fellow travellers changed more often and the proximity of strangers was perceived as unpleasant. Instead of talking to each other – at least in first- and second-class compartmental coaches in Europe – people widely started reading newspaper and literature (Schivelbusch, 2014, p. 64ff.). To meet the demands of this reconfigured practice of reading while travelling, booksellers started to populate the stations of Europe's railways (Richards and MacKenzie, 1986, pp. 298–303).

A new mode of mobility brought about a reconfiguration of practice: a new way of encountering the landscape emerged, and reading became one of the activities in travel practices. Like other infrastructures, mobility systems (Urry, 2007, pp. 12–16) are thus closely linked to concrete mobile practices and how they are performed.

The introduction of the railway also had wide-reaching effects beyond the journey. Many historians describe how the introduction of the railroad changed whole societies and made the modern state possible (Perkin, 1970; Beniger, 1989; Gall and Pohl, 1999; Bradley, 2016; Hylton, 2016). I will briefly refer to two well-known examples of this societal change.

Railways facilitated the standardisation of time, first nationally, and then on a global level (Zerubavel, 1982). In order to synchronise timetables across cities, railway companies needed a time that extended local time – railway time was established. Railways thus made visible the synchronicity (or the lack thereof) of distant places. Soon this was adapted by whole nations and facilitated modern states with their rationalised interlocking and synchronised organisations.[1] From the perspective of practice theory the railway is consequently not just a symbol for the rationalisation of modern society but directly involved in the process of rationalisation itself. Infrastructures are more than a manifestation of society; they are an actor in its manifold creation (Jensen and Morita, 2017). Another example is the geographic separation of classes in cities like London. With the rise of the railway in the nineteenth century, affluent factory owners could move even further away from their factories and thus also their workers – segregated suburbs could emerge (Hylton, 2016, p. 31). Again, transport infrastructures are not just an addendum to society but directly involved in it – in this case in the enactment of a class society and its spatial segregation. Similarly, the class system of coaches (Bradley, 2016, p. 54ff.) is not just a symbol of societal hierarchies but tied to a practice of travelling in which social differences are performed and visibly brought about.

The introduction of the railway thus not only brought forth new ways of travelling but also enacted a new society in which a new mode of transportation facilitated certain features and inhibited others. At the same time traditional ways of travelling were becoming less and less viable because the infrastructures on which they used to rely partly vanished. If one wanted, for example, to travel by horse-drawn carriages in the second half of the nineteenth century in Great Britain one would encounter problems because "chains of coaching inns with fresh horses no longer existed" (Ibid., p. 102). Once they reach a certain threshold newly established practices seem to perpetuate themselves because the infrastructures they rely on are extended and constantly maintained. At the same time other infrastructures are neglected in their favour. And since practices are not only interdependent with competences of their carriers but also with infrastructures and other material entities, certain practices can disappear when one of these elements is missing (Shove *et al.*, 2012).

Infrastructuring: practice theory and the relationality of infrastructures

Pointing out the ubiquity and importance of transport infrastructures for modern life does not, however, entail falling back to technological determinism. Infrastructures are to be understood as relational entities (Korn *et al.*, 2019). They are "part of multivalent sociotechnical relations" (Parks and Starosielski, 2015, p. 8) in which all elements temporarily receive their meaning because of their position in concrete practices.

Consequently, we have to look for the performative and relational dimension of infrastructures. Infrastructures need to be worked on and to be enacted in particular instances in order to have an effect. This involves a counterintuitive shift in our thinking. Because infrastructures are ubiquitous and mundane, their contribution to practice seems not only trivial but also fixed and given. Roads, power lines, and other infrastructures are seemingly simply there, once they are installed. This holds also true for infrastructures in the broader sense: technological artefacts, buildings, furniture, texts, bodies, and so on. An ecological perspective on infrastructure (Star and Ruhleder, 1996) aims to overcome this static view and reminds us of two things:

1 *relationality*: one person's infrastructure can be or become another person's focal object, and vice versa. For maintenance workers infrastructures can, of course, become their focal object thus leaving the thematic background (Denis et al., 2016).
2 *performativity*: in order to function properly, infrastructure needs ongoing situated work. This constant work is necessary to maintain and uphold infrastructure, but also to simply use and repurpose it.

Instead of looking at infrastructures as static and fixed entities one therefore has to look at their processual and dynamic dimension, i.e. the "infrastructuring" (Pipek and Wulf, 2009) surrounding them. Following infrastructuring not only means tracing processes of design, development, and installation but also (mobile) practices of use and repurposing of already-installed infrastructures (Dantec and DiSalvo, 2013; Wagenknecht and Korn, 2016). In line with a relational view on im/mobilities (Sheller, 2013), infrastructures are made and remade, perpetuated and contested in their practical relevance. By looking at infrastructures this way, social order is no longer seen as singular and stable, but as something that is mutually made, multiple and contested (Jarzabkowski and Pinch, 2013). This multiplicity and the contested nature of social order becomes especially visible when new infrastructures are planned and built. In this vein, Penny Harvey and Hannah Knox (2015) show the different visions of modernity and the nation state that collide during the construction of highways in South America. But this contested work does not stop after infrastructures are installed. Even such a seemingly simple and rather fixed infrastructure as the signage system of the Parisian Metro is in need of maintenance crews constantly cleaning, readjusting and rearranging signs and thus reworking the system (Denis and Pontille, 2010). In general, while usually backgrounded, such repair and maintenance practices are obviously vital for infrastructures to work properly (Dant, 2005; Graham and Thrift, 2007; Denis et al., 2016; Krebs, Schabacher and Weber, 2018).

When transport infrastructures are disrupted or break down, one usually does not encounter disorder but routine practices. As such, disruptions and breakdowns are "normal" events that are expected by transport companies and passengers alike (e.g. disruptions in baggage handling at airports; see Potthast, 2007).

Passengers in public transport, for example, are not surprised by delays or cancellation but expect a standardised way of being informed by transport companies (Röhl, 2019). In the case of disasters and accidents, things may, however, come to a rather permanent halt. When Iceland's volcano Eyjafjallajökull erupted in April and May 2010, mobile practices of travelling by plane became impossible for several days and people were stranded at airports and other places (Birtchnell and Büscher, 2011). But even in this and other cases, people are able to improvise and find "workarounds" (Brohm et al., 2017) when things are not working properly. In the case of Eyjafjallajökull's eruption, for example, people soon began to form informal networks to organise alternative modes of travel (Barton, 2011). And when trains arrive late or are cancelled, passengers resort to a fairly common repertoire of dealing with the event in question – for example, by starting a conversation with their fellow passengers (Pütz, 2017). Routines are in place to remedy and ultimately normalise disruptions (Vollmer, 2013). Infrastructures are thus actively relegated to the thematic background and turned into something beneath our awareness. This makes them at the same time powerful and inconspicuous. Yet, a lot of work is required to uphold this status quo of our infrastructure. Without this work things would not transpire the way they do.

Even when things are working properly, there is work to be done by those relying on infrastructures. Being a passenger is better described as an activity – "passengering" (Laurier et al., 2008). When entering trains or other means of transportations, passengers need to actively become a relatively immobile collective. Practices of mobility and immobility are thus closely related to each other (Büscher et al., 2016). This also entails adhering to unwritten rules of conduct – be it on airplanes (Schindler, 2015), on ferries (Hodson and Vannini, 2007; Stäheli, 2012), on buses (Kim, 2012), or in elevators (Hirschauer, 2005). In elevators or buses we need, for example, to minimise our bodily presence (for instance, by controlling our gaze) in order to uphold one important feature of public spheres: the "civil inattention" described by Goffman (1963, p. 83ff.) through which people systematically disengage from each other in public (Hirschauer, 2005; Kim, 2012).

Concluding remarks

In the preceding pages I have argued for a praxeological perspective on social order problematising the classic notion of structure as supra-structure. From this perspective social order has to be understood as a socio-material achievement in which practices interact with material entities. The concept of infrastructure (or infrastructuring) allows us to trace this work done by different actors at different sites. Drawing on Theodore Schatzki's concept of materiality, I propose to broaden the concept to include not only infrastructure in the classic sense but all kinds of material entities as part of "nexuses of practices and material arrangements" (2010, p. 129): materials (Ingold, 2007), substances (Hahn and Soentgen, 2011), bodies (Ihde, 2002; Mol, 2002), texts (Smith, 2001), and artefacts

(Latour, 1994; Harman, 2010), among others (see Kalthoff *et al.*, 2016a). Practices are constituted in their entanglement with these material entities and they are connected to each other via them.

Understood in this way, the concept of infrastructure (or infrastructuring) could provide an alternative take on the problem of social order – one that promises us to remain "ontologically flat" in the sense of practice theory while also letting us tackle phenomena usually located at the macro-level. While this might not necessarily entail abandoning the concept of structure in general, this alternative concept could at least supplement and empirically ground abstract notions of social order. As I have argued this involves two shifts: (1) from metaphysical supra-structure to concrete infrastructures; (2) from a material determinism of infrastructures to socio-material practices of infrastructuring.

The notion of material mobilities can consequently not only enlighten our perspective on transport infrastructures and mobilities but promises to offer new insights in social theory in general. This touches upon fundamental questions on how to conceptualise sociality beyond "sedentarist" (Sheller and Urry, 2006, p. 208) notions by mobilising hitherto immobile concepts. As mobility systems, infrastructures are thus not only the material and immobile side of mobilities; they are also themselves mobile and fluid, made and remade in mobile practices. As such they are not simply stabilising the social but part of practices of ordering. Materialising mobility does thus not provide so much as an answer as it raises new questions on how to approach mobile practices and their im/mobilities.

Acknowledgements

The work underlying this chapter is funded by the German Research Foundation (DFG) as part of the project "Normal breakdowns. Structure and change in transport infrastructures" (A04; PI: Jörg Potthast) at the Collaborative Research Centre "Media of Cooperation" (SFB 1187) at the University of Siegen. The chapter profited from comments made by Silvia Gherardi, Jörg Potthast, and Susann Wagenknecht.

Note

1 This process was, however, far from linear, but itself contested and asynchronous with different temporal regimes existing alongside each other (Ogle, 2015).

References

Adey, P., 2006. If Mobility Is Everything Then It Is Nothing: Towards a Relational Politics of (Im)mobilities. *Mobilities*, 1(1), pp. 75–94.

Barton, D., 2011. People and Technologies as Resources in Times of Uncertainty. *Mobilities*, 6(1), pp. 57–65.

Beniger, J., 1989. *The Control Revolution: Technological and Economic Origins of the Information Society*. Cambridge, MA: Harvard University Press.

Birtchnell, T. and Büscher, M., 2011. Stranded: An Eruption of Disruption. *Mobilities*, 6(1), pp. 1–9.
Bourdieu, P., 1977. *Outline of a Theory of Practice*. Cambridge: Cambridge University Press.
Bourdieu, P., 1990. The Scholastic Point of View. *Cultural Anthropology*, 5(4), pp. 380–391.
Bradley, S., 2016. *The Railways: Nation, Network and People*. London: Profile Books.
Brohm, H., Gießmann, S., Schabacher, G. and Schramke, S., eds., 2017. *Workarounds. Praktiken des Umwegs*. ilinx – Berliner Beiträge zur Kulturwissenschaft. Hamburg: Philo Fine Arts Stiftung.
Büscher, M., Sheller, M. and Tyfield, D., 2016. Mobility Intersections: Social Research, Social Futures. *Mobilities*, 11(4), pp. 485–497.
Büscher, M., Urry, J. and Witchger, K., 2010. *Mobile Methods*. 1st ed. London: Routledge.
Carse, A., 2017. Keyword: Infrastructure. How a Humble French Engineering Term Shaped the Modern World. In: P. Harvey, C.B. Jensen and A. Morita, eds., *Infrastructures and Social Complexity: A Routledge Companion*. London: Routledge, pp. 27–39.
Coole, D. and Frost, S., eds., 2010. *New Materialisms: Ontology, Agency, and Politics*. Durham NC; London: Duke University Press.
Dant, T., 2005. *Materiality and Society*. Maidenhead: Open University Press.
Dantec, C.A.L. and DiSalvo, C., 2013. Infrastructuring and the Formation of Publics in Participatory Design. *Social Studies of Science*, 43(2), pp. 241–264.
Denis, J. and Pontille, D., 2010. Placing Subway Signs: Practical Properties of Signs at Work. *Visual Communication*, 9(4), pp. 441–462.
Denis, J., Mongili, A. and Pontille, D., 2016. Maintenance & Repair in Science and Technology Studies. *TECNOSCIENZA: Italian Journal of Science & Technology Studies*, 6(2), pp. 5–16.
Durkheim, E., 2014. *The Rules of Sociological Method: And Selected Texts on Sociology and Its Method*. New York, NY: Simon and Schuster.
Fuchs, S., 1989. On the Microfoundations of Macrosociology: A Critique of Microsociological Reductionism. *Sociological Perspectives*, 32(2), pp. 169–182.
Gall, L. and Pohl, M., eds., 1999. *Die Eisenbahn in Deutschland: Von den Anfängen bis zur Gegenwart*. 1st ed. München: C.H. Beck.
Garfinkel, H., 1967. *Studies in Ethnomethodology*. Englewood Cliffs, NJ: Prentice Hall.
Gherardi, S., 2006. *Organizational Knowledge: The Texture of Workplace Learning*. Oxford: Blackwell.
Goffman, E., 1963. *Behavior in Public Places: Notes on the Social Organization of Gatherings*. New York, NY: The Free Press.
Goffman, E., 1990. *The Presentation of Self in Everyday Life*. New York, NY: Anchor.
Graham, S. and Thrift, N., 2007. Out of Order: Understanding Repair and Maintenance. *Theory, Culture & Society*, 24(3), pp. 1–25.
Hahn, H.P. and Soentgen, J., 2011. Acknowledging Substances: Looking at the Hidden Side of the Material World. *Philosophy & Technology*, 24(1), pp. 19–33.
Hannam, K., Sheller, M. and Urry, J., 2006. Editorial: Mobilities, Immobilities and Moorings. *Mobilities*, 1(1), pp. 1–22.
Harman, G., 2010. Technology, Objects and Things in Heidegger. *Cambridge Journal of Economics*, 34(1), pp. 17–25.
Harvey, P. and Knox, H., 2015. *Roads: An Anthropology of Infrastructure and Expertise*. Ithaca: Cornell University Press.

Hirschauer, S., 2005. On Doing Being a Stranger: The Practical Constitution of Civil Inattention. *Journal for the Theory of Social Behaviour*, 35(1), pp. 41–67.

Hirschauer, S., 2014. Intersituativität. Teleinteraktionen und Koaktivitäten jenseits von Mikro und Makro. *Zeitschrift für Soziologie*, Sonderheft "Interaktion-Organisation-Gesellschaft revisited. Anwendungen, Erweiterungen, Alternativen", pp. 109–133.

Hodson, J.N. and Vannini, P., 2007. Island Time: The Media Logic and Ritual of Ferry Commuting on Gabriola Island, BC. *Canadian Journal of Communication*, 32(2), pp. 261–275.

Hylton, S., 2016. *What the Railways Did for Us: The Making of Modern Britain*. Stroud: Amberley Publishing.

Ihde, D., 1990. *Technology and the Lifeworld. From Garden to Earth*. Bloomington, IN: Indiana University Press.

Ihde, D., 2002. *Bodies in Technology*. Minneapolis, MN: University of Minnesota Press.

Ingold, T., 2007. Materials Against Materiality. *Archaeological Dialogues*, 14(1), pp. 1–16.

Jarzabkowski, P. and Pinch, T., 2013. Sociomateriality Is "the New Black": Accomplishing Repurposing, Reinscripting and Repairing in Context. *Management (France)*, 16(5), pp. 579–592.

Jensen, C.B. and Morita, A., 2017. Infrastructures as Ontological Experiments. *Ethnos*, 82(4), pp. 1–12.

Kalthoff, H., Cress, T. and Röhl, T., 2016a. Einleitung: Materialität in Kultur und Gesellschaft. In: H. Kalthoff, T. Cress and T. Röhl, eds., *Materialität. Herausforderungen für die Kultur- und Sozialwissenschaften*. Paderborn: Fink, pp. 11–41.

Kalthoff, H., Cress, T. and Röhl, T., eds., 2016b. *Materialität. Herausforderungen für die Sozial- und Kulturwissenschaften*. Paderborn: Fink.

Kim, E.C., 2012. Nonsocial Transient Behavior: Social Disengagement on the Greyhound Bus: Nonsocial Transient Behavior. *Symbolic Interaction*, 35(3), pp. 267–283.

Knorr-Cetina, K., 2009. The Synthetic Situation: Interactionism for a Global World. *Symbolic Interaction*, 32(1), pp. 61–87.

Korn, M., Reißmann, W., Röhl, T. and Sittler, D., 2019. Infrastructuring Publics. A Research Perspective. In: M. Korn, W. Reißmann, T. Röhl and D. Sittler, eds., *Infrastructuring Publics*, Media of Cooperation. Wiesbaden: Springer VS.

Krebs, S., Schabacher, G. and Weber, H., eds., 2018. *Kulturen des Reparierens: Dinge – Wissen – Praktiken*. Edition Kulturwissenschaft. Bielefeld: Transcript.

Latour, B., 1994. Where Are the Missing Masses? The Sociology of a Few Mundane Artefacts. In: W.E. Bijker and J. Law, eds., *Shaping Technology. Building Society*. Cambridge, MA: MIT Press, pp. 225–258.

Latour, B., 1996. On Interobjectivity. *Mind, Culture, and Activity*, 3(4), pp. 228–245.

Latour, B., 2005. *Reassembling the Social. An Introduction to Actor-Network-Theory*. Oxford: Oxford University Press.

Laurier, E., Lorimer, H., Brown, B., Jones, O., Juhlin, O., Noble, A., Perry, M., Pica, D., Sormani, P., Strebel, I., Swan, L., Taylor, A.S., Watts, L. and Weilenmann, A., 2008. Driving and "Passengering": Notes on the Ordinary Organization of Car Travel. *Mobilities*, 3(1), pp. 1–23.

Lynch, M., 1992. Extending Wittgenstein: The Pivotal Move from Epistemology to the Sociology of Science. In: A. Pickering, ed., *Science as Practice and Culture*. Chicago: University of Chicago Press, pp. 215–265.

Mol, A., 2002. *The Body Multiple. Ontology in Medical Practice*. Durham, NC: Duke University Press.

Nicolini, D., 2017. Is Small the Only Beautiful? Making Sense of "Large Phenomena" from a Practice-Based Perspective. In: A. Hui, T. Schatzki and E. Shove, eds., *The Nexus of Practices. Connections, constellations, practitioners*. Oxon and New York, NY: Routledge, pp. 98–113.

Niewöhner, J., 2015. Infrastructures of Society, Anthropology of. In: J.D. Wright, ed., *International Encyclopedia of the Social & Behavioral Sciences* (Second Edition). Oxford: Elsevier, pp. 119–125.

Ogle, V., 2015. *The Global Transformation of Time: 1870–1950*. Cambridge, MA: Harvard University Press.

Parks, L. and Starosielski, N., 2015. Introduction. In: L. Parks and N. Starosielski, eds., *Signal Traffic: Critical Studies of Media Infrastructures*. Urbana: University of Illinois Press, pp. 1–28.

Parsons, T., 1991. *The Social System*. London: Routledge.

Perkin, H.J., 1970. *The Age of the Railway*. London: Panther.

Pipek, V. and Wulf, V., 2009. Infrastructuring: Toward an Integrated Perspective on the Design and Use of Information Technology. *Journal of the Association for Information Systems*, 10(5), pp. 447–473.

Potthast, J., 2007. *Die Bodenhaftung der Netzwerkgesellschaft. Eine Ethnografie von Pannen an Großflughäfen*. 1st ed. Bielefeld: Transcript.

Pütz, O., 2017. How Strangers Initiate Conversations: Interactions on Public Trains in Germany. *Journal of Contemporary Ethnography*, 47(4), pp. 426–453.

Reckwitz, A., 1997. *Struktur: Zur sozialwissenschaftlichen Analyse von Regeln und Regelmäßigkeiten*. Opladen: Westdeutscher Verlag.

Richards, J. and MacKenzie, J.M., 1986. *The Railway Station: A Social History*. Oxford: Oxford University Press.

Röhl, T., 2015. Transsituating Education. Educational Artefacts in the Classroom and Beyond. In: S. Bollig, M.-S. Honig, S. Neumann and C. Seele, eds., *MultiPluriTrans. Emerging Fields in Educational Ethnography*. Bielefeld and New York, NY: Transcript/Columbia University Press, pp. 143–161.

Röhl, T., 2019. Making Failure Public. Communicating Breakdowns of Public Infrastructures. In: M. Korn, W. Reißmann, T. Röhl and D. Sittler, eds., *Infrastructuring Publics*. Wiesbaden: Springer VS.

Schatzki, T.R., 2005. Peripheral Vision. The Sites of Organization. *Organization Studies*, 26(3), pp. 465–484.

Schatzki, T.R., 2010. Materiality and Social Life. *Nature and Culture*, 5(2), pp. 123–149.

Schatzki, T.R., 2016. Practice Theory as Flat Ontology. In: G. Spaargaren, D. Weenink and M. Lamers, eds., *Practice Theory and Research. Exploring the Dynamics of Social Life*. Oxon and New York, NY: Routledge.

Schegloff, E.A., 1979. Identification and Recognition in Telephone Conversation Openings. In: G. Psathas, ed., *Everyday Language. Studies in Ethnomethodology*. New York, NY: Irvington, pp. 23–78.

Schindler, L., 2015. The Flying Body: Wie Körper und Dinge sich gegenseitig und eine Flugreise hervorbringen. *Body Politics*, 3(6), pp. 285–308.

Schivelbusch, W., 2014. *The Railway Journey: The Industrialization of Time and Space in the Nineteenth Century*. Berkeley: University of California Press.

Schubert, C. and Röhl, T., 2017. Ethnography and Organisations: Materiality and Change as Methodological Challenges. *Qualitative Research*, 19(2), 164–181.

Sheller, M., 2013. Sociology After the Mobilities Turn. In: P. Adey, D. Bissel, K. Hannam, P. Merriman and M. Sheller, eds., *The Routledge Handbook of Mobilities*. London: Routledge, pp. 45–54.

Sheller, M. and Urry, J., 2006. The New Mobilities Paradigm. *Environment and Planning A: Economy and Space*, 38(2), pp. 207–226.

Shove, E., Pantzar, M. and Watson, M., 2012. *The Dynamics of Social Practice: Everyday Life and How It Changes*. London: Sage.

Shove, E., Watson, M. and Spurling, N., 2015. Conceptualizing connections: Energy demand, infrastructures and social practices. *European Journal of Social Theory*, 18(3), pp. 274–287.

Smith, D.E., 2001. Texts and the Ontology of Organizations and Institutions. *Studies in Cultures, Organizations and Societies*, 7(2), pp. 159–198.

Stäheli, U., 2012. Infrastrukturen des Kollektiven: alte Medien–neue Kollektive? *Zeitschrift für Medien- und Kulturforschung*, 2012(2), pp. 99–116.

Star, S.L., 1999. The Ethnography of Infrastructure. *American Behavioral Scientist*, 43(3), pp. 377–391.

Star, S.L. and Ruhleder, K., 1996. Steps Toward an Ecology of Infrastructure: Design and Access for Large Information Spaces. *Information Systems Research*, 7(1), pp. 111–134.

Thrift, N., 1996. *Spatial Formations*. London: Sage.

Urry, J., 2007. *Mobilities*. Cambridge: Polity Press.

Verbeek, P.-P., 2005. *What Things Do. Philosophical Reflections on Technology, Agency, and Design*. University Park, PA: Penn State Press.

Vollmer, H., 2013. *The Sociology of Disruption, Disaster and Social Change: Punctuated Cooperation*. Cambridge and New York, NY: Cambridge University Press.

Wagenknecht, S. and Korn, M., 2016. Hacking as Transgressive Infrastructuring: Mobile Phone Networks and the German Chaos Computer Club. In: *Proceedings of the 19th ACM Conference on Computer-Supported Cooperative Work and Social Computing*. [online] pp. 1102–1115. Available at: http://dl.acm.org/citation.cfm?doid=2818048.2820027 [Accessed 11 February 2017].

Walker, G., 2014. The Dynamics of Energy Demand: Change, Rhythm and Synchronicity. *Energy Research & Social Science*, 1, pp. 49–55.

Wittgenstein, L., 1963. *Philosophical Investigations*. 2nd ed. Oxford: Blackwell.

Zerubavel, E., 1982. The Standardization of Time: A Sociohistorical Perspective. *American Journal of Sociology*, 88(1), pp. 1–23.

3 The cathedrals of automobility
How to read a motor show

Richard Randell

Introduction

> Cars today are almost the exact equivalent of the great Gothic cathedrals: I mean the supreme creation of an era, conceived with passion by unknown artists, and consumed in image by a whole population which appropriates them as a purely magical object.
>
> (Roland Barthes, La nouvelle Citroën)

Roland Barthes (1972, pp. 88–90) in "La nouvelle Citroën" famously compared the automobile to Gothic cathedrals; each was, he wrote, "the supreme creation" of its respective era. Contemporary automobility studies have directed our focus away from automobiles to thinking about the car as one component of a larger "system" (Urry, 2004) or "regime" (Böhm *et al.*, 2006) of automobility. So conceptualized, a more appropriate comparison to Gothic cathedrals are the numerous motor shows that are regularly held across the planet. Within the automobile industry, the Detroit, Frankfurt, Geneva, Paris, and Tokyo motor shows are considered the most prestigious of these automobile expositions. It was at one of the five major motor shows, the 1955 *Salon de l'Automobile*, as the Paris Motor Show was then called, that the Citroën described by Barthes – the *DS, la Déesse*, the Goddess – was presented to the French automobile public. Lasting approximately two weeks, these modern cathedrals of automobility are as transitory and mobile as the automobile itself. Thirty-six motor shows are currently certified by the International Organization of Motor Vehicle Manufacturers (Organisation Internationale des Constructeurs D'Automobiles, 2014), a global lobbying organization based in Paris that represents the collective interests of automobile manufacturers.

Despite the importance attributed to motor shows within the automobile industry and the extensive coverage devoted to them on television, in newspapers and automobile magazines, on social media and elsewhere, apart from some historical research on automobile exhibitions (Gundler, 2013; Curts, 2015) there has been little discussion or analysis of motor shows within the automobility studies literature. One exception is a paper by Mimi Sheller (2007) based on participant observation at the Philadelphia International Auto Show. The focus of her research, however, was not the motor show itself but new car technologies, which for the purposes of Sheller's research questions were conveniently located in the single space that a motor show provides. While motor shows are experienced by the majority of visitors as interesting, entertaining and enjoyable events, for those critical of automobility, possibly the imagined reader (Iser, 1979, pp. 20–49) of this chapter, they are likely to be experienced as extraordinarily tedious events. One goal of this chapter is to demonstrate that motor shows and similar events deserve serious scholarly attention. They are theoretically and empirically interesting, and politically significant.

This chapter is based primarily on observations at the Geneva International Motor Show (*Salon international de l'automobile*, hereafter "Geneva Motor Show") over several years, some in the context of class excursions for an undergraduate course on automobility for which the author was the instructor at the Geneva campus of Webster University, and secondarily on observations at the Paris and Detroit motor shows. One peculiarity of the Geneva Motor Show is that, of the five major motor shows, it is the only one that is located in a country without a domestic automobile industry, although there are companies in Switzerland that produce automobile components and modified production cars. At the other four major motor shows, where domestic automobile manufacturers are represented, they typically occupy larger and more central exhibit spaces than do their non-domestic competitors. Across these motor shows there is, consequently, variation in the automobile manufacturers that are represented as well as the classes of automobiles that are exhibited. At the Detroit Motor Show, as might be expected, many of the exhibits are dominated by pickup trucks. At the Geneva Motor Show a larger number of luxury and sports vehicles are exhibited than at the other motor shows.

Participant observation at a motor show requires observing, experiencing and representing the motor show from the perspective of the visitors and engaging in the activities of visitors: walking, looking, stopping, taking photographs, touching and sitting in the cars – experiencing in oneself the automobility emotions the visitors feel. It also requires attending to aspects of the motor show that lie in the background and periphery of attention of visitors. This includes the architectural space, the arrangement of automobiles in company-specific exhibits, the salespeople and other employees, and the visitors themselves: who they are; how they move and observe as they serially encounter the succession of individual exhibits and automobiles while traversing the floor of the motor show; how they interact with others, and with the automobiles. It also includes much that is external to the physical location of the motor show. Although bound in space to the interior of the exhibition halls and in time to the calendar, from March 7–17 with press days on March 5 and 6 in the case of the 2019 Geneva Motor Show, motor shows exceed these two ostensibly distinct spatial and temporal boundaries. Before its official opening, the Geneva Motor Show is present in the mass media – in newspapers, radio and television, and in cyberspace through social media sites such as Facebook, Twitter and Instagram; and across Switzerland advertisements are posted in railway stations and on roadside billboards.

Theoretically uninformed participant observation does not, however, at least at an event such as this, get one very far. How, then, might such an event be read? What is a motor show? A trade show composed of a collection of car dealerships conveniently located, for both sellers and buyers, in one continuous space; an exhibition housing a collection of contemporary items of automobility technology akin to a transport museum; a celebration, spectacle and affirmation of automobility; something else or all of the above? This chapter provides a reading of the Geneva Motor Show informed by the automobility studies literature, a sub-field of "the mobilities turn" (Sheller and Urry, 2006; Cresswell, 2010); that literature provides a set of analytic tools for locating the automobiles, the exhibitors, the visitors, and the architectural space of the motor show, within the larger system of automobility.

Motor shows are significant in several respects. First, they provide an exemplary illustration of the central themes that have been addressed within the automobility literature. Secondly, they are politically significant: motor shows are cultural spectacles the primary purpose of which is to promote, legitimate and reproduce what John Urry (2004) has called "the system of automobility", or what Foucauldian scholars have called the "automobility regime" (Böhm *et al.*, 2006). Thirdly, as a spectacle and celebration of automobility, motor shows are significant components of the automobility imaginary; they contribute in unique ways to the continued legitimation, reproduction and expansion of automobility across the planet, and in so doing contribute to the continued capital accumulation prospects of automobile manufacturers and associated industries. In the following section, these themes are explored through an analysis of the Geneva Motor Show. I then turn to a consideration of the political-economic dimension of motor shows, in particular their relationship to the economic and political interests of automobile manufacturers. In the Conclusion, I take up Barthes' portrayal of the automobile as a "magical object". It is an image which should, I suggest, be taken more seriously and literally than Barthes possibly intended it to be taken.

A final introductory remark concerns the title of this chapter. If interpretation is understood not under the metaphor of "reading" but of "writing" in the Derridean sense of *écriture* (Derrida, 1978; see also Rorty, 1982; Fish, 1989, pp. 38–67), the interpretive challenge becomes not how to "read a motor show" but how to *write* a motor show. The representation of a motor show in textual format constitutes, both literally and metaphorically, not a reading but a textual reconstruction of a motor show. This applies not only and most obviously to the written text in hand, which provides a representation in textual format of the Geneva Motor Show as "read" through the hermeneutic of contemporary automobility studies, but to motor shows themselves. Like written texts, motor shows construct, albeit in a distinct material form, a particular narrative of automobility. It is a narrative that is constructed from the artefacts, technologies, objects and other material stuff of which a motor show is constructed. Motor shows are spaces of material mobility, but what is absent in that material mobility narrative is as important as what has been included. It is this narrative that requires deconstruction, not least to render visible the politics of these ostensibly apolitical events.

The Geneva Motor Show

Geneva does in fact have a Gothic cathedral, *La Cathédrale Saint-Pierre*, whose most famous preacher was none other than John Calvin. Unlike Geneva's Gothic cathedral, the Geneva Motor Show is a temporary construction that each year is assembled and disassembled inside the exhibition halls of the *Palais des Expositions et des Congrès de Genève* (Geneva Exhibition and Congress Centre, also known as Palexpo), which is adjacent to Geneva Airport, is several minutes' walk from the Geneva Airport railway station, and is accessible via a motorway connected to other Swiss cities and to major French autoroutes. According to the promotional materials on the Palexpo website, the largest of the six Palexpo exhibition halls is 662,000 cubic metres in volume, with a floor area of 27,000 square metres. The combined surface area of the seven exhibition halls of the Geneva Motor Show is 104,000 square metres (Palexpo SA, 2019). To provide some comparison, the Basilica of Saint Peter in the Vatican (which is the largest church in the world, although it is technically not a cathedral) has an interior floor area of 15,160 square metres. The largest hall, not to mention the exhibition in its entirety, dwarfs in size any cathedral, Gothic or otherwise.

These abstract mathematical dimensions of the exhibition halls do not, however, adequately convey the sense of size and space as experienced by the visitors (Figure 3.1). The exhibits, the miscellaneous equipment, and the people – visitors, employees, officials – are not simply "inside" the buildings but are components of an experiential, articulated equipmental totality (Heidegger, 1962, pp. 79, 97–100) that includes the space and the buildings. The height, length and breadth of the Palexpo halls constitute *in part* the architectural background of the motor show. That background, however, is transformed by the background noise of the visitors; the contents of the motor show, composed of the individual installations of each automobile manufacturer; the visitors themselves; and the walkways throughout the halls and through the individual installations, which enable and direct ways of moving and experiencing as one makes one's way through the motor show.

The Palexpo exhibition halls are on different levels, which makes it possible at some of the hall entrances and exits to view an entire hall from above. Seen from these vantage points, where visitors stop to take photographs, the motor show is impressive *qua* spectacle in two respects. First, in that the vast architectural space that is the Geneva Exhibition and Congress Centre is barely sufficient to contain a collection of something approximating the world's current range of automobiles (180 automobile *brands* were represented at the 2018 Geneva Motor Show, exhibiting over 900 automobiles). Secondly, in respect of the large and constantly moving crowd that winds its way through the floors and exhibits of the motor show (the 2018 Geneva Motor Show was attended by approximately 660,000 visitors). Of course, something similar could be said of other exhibitions that are held in the same structure, but each component of the combination of *architectural space, automobile exhibits* and *visitors* is recursively transformed in automobile-specific ways. It is this equipmental totality that is the focus of empirical interest of this chapter.

Figure 3.1 Photograph of one of the halls in the Palais des Expositions et des Congrès de Genève.

Source: Photograph taken by the author.

Public transportation

During the eleven days it is open to the general public, specially scheduled additional trains to the motor show are provided by the Swiss National Railways. There is limited onsite parking space (2,800 spaces) and limited freeway capacity for an event of this size; without public transportation, the lack of onsite parking and automobile congestion on the adjacent motorway would make it impossible for the current number of visitors to attend. There is considerable irony here in that the motor show is dependent on the provision of public transportation: the national railway systems of Switzerland and surrounding European countries, as well as the local Geneva public transportation system. It is one more example of the support of automobility by the state through the provisioning of automobility-related infrastructure (Paterson, 2007, pp. 91–120).

Trains provide not only transportation; employees of different automobile manufacturers work the trains that transport visitors to and from the motor show, handing out promotional literature. This is a further sense in which the boundaries of the Geneva Motor Show extend beyond the walls of the exhibition halls. On one of the specially scheduled extra trains that I took from Berne to the

Geneva Motor Show, young women walked through the carriages distributing literature for the Renault Clio which, the Renault brochure I received claimed, evinces *"sportliche Emotionen"* – "sport emotions". As a participant observer, it is emotions such as these that one hopes also to feel.

Gendered automobility

The composition of the railway passengers reflects, as one might expect, the demographic of the visitors inside the exhibition halls. Before one arrives at the Geneva Motor Show, it is clear it is very much a masculine event. In my carriage, there were approximately 100 passengers, among whom were two women, with most of the men travelling not individually but in groups. Similarly, throughout the floors of the motor show are numerous small and large all male groups of visitors. On weekends a significant number of fathers and sons visit the motor show, the latter being initiated into the secret men's business of automobility: esoteric knowledge regarding the functioning of automobiles and internal combustion engines and the meaning of technical specifications. There are occasionally men accompanied by wives and girlfriends (pondering, perhaps, the discrepancy between the attention bestowed on them by their partners to that bestowed on the automobiles) but few all-female groups. Among the motor show employees, it is primarily men, dressed conservatively in suit and tie, who are on hand to provide technical information regarding the automobiles. The women employees, in contrast to the men, are frequently presented as ornamental automobile accessories in what can only be described as clichés of automobile femininity: young, thin, dressed in short skirts, sometimes posing motionless next to, or leaning on, or sitting on the hood or trunk of, an automobile. Like all social occasions, motor shows are unexceptional in that they provide one more occasion where gender is routinely performed (West and Zimmerman, 1987). What is specific to motor shows is that they provide for the performing of specific modes of *automobile* masculinity and femininity wherein gender is intertwined with, and inseparable from, the automobile (Paterson, 2007, p. 134; Randell, 2017, p. 8).

Since its origins, automobility has been largely a domain of masculinity (Möser, 2003). In popular film and music, the automobile has been represented as both a literal and metaphorical *vehicle* for the refraction and reproduction of dominant cultural ideals of masculinity (Zimmerman, 1995, pp. 34–36). Similarly, automobile advertisements associate distinct types of automobiles – pickup trucks in the United States for example – with masculinity, while the very act of driving provides for the routine performance of masculinity (Connell and Pearse, 2015, p. 99; Randell, 2017, pp. 671–672). In the motor show, automobile masculinity and femininity are not only produced and reproduced, but celebrated, which celebration allows for the reproduction of forms of exemplary automobile dependent masculinity and femininity. It is through the routine micro-interactions on the floor of the motor show that automobile gender is done; at the individual installations of automobile manufacturer by employees and visitors through their interactions with each other and the automobiles.

Femininity is done by women employed as ornamental accessories to the automobiles; by women visitors through accompanying their male companions, who are the reason they are there; by sitting in *passenger* seats. Masculinity is done in the reading of technical specifications and the asking of technical questions, in opening hoods and inspecting engines, sitting in the *driver's* seat and pretending to drive, as Barthes (1972, p. 90) did at the Paris Motor Show, "with one's whole body".

Automobile desire

The production of automobile subjectivities through technologies of contemporary neoliberal governance has been a central theme in Foucauldian automobility scholarship. Questioning the assumption that anyone and everyone *naturally* desires automobility due to the intrinsic qualities of the object of desire – the automobile – and therefore this desire requires no further explanation, Foucauldian automobility scholarship has brought into theoretical relief the technologies of governance through which are produced subjects who desire the autonomy and freedom that automobility ostensibly provides (Böhm *et al.*, 2006; Paterson, 2007, pp. 91–120). Motor shows are doubly interesting in this respect. First, they are locations where both individual and collective automobile desire are observable. Secondly, motor shows are locations where automobile desire is reproduced and intensified. It is visible in newsreels of the Citroën DS – *la Déesse*, the Goddess, to translate into English this French pun on the model designation – described by Barthes at the 1955 Paris Motor Show (*Le salon de l'automobile*, 1955); in contemporary motor shows the same desire is rendered visible through the act of mass photography and its subsequent reproduction on social media sites, enabled by mobile telephones with video and photographic features. It is not, however, a generic and singular desire that motor shows elicit and render visible, but desires in the plural. As one makes one's way through the motor show it is experienced as a space of serial cathexis, transferred from one automobile to the next, each one of which belongs to a distinct category of automobile: Italian sports car, British luxury automobile, SUV, American pickup truck, etc. An interplay of subject and object, the generic automobile desire that each visitor brings to the motor show is brought into being and transformed by the qualities of each successive individual object of that desire.

Social class

Central to the construction and reproduction of desire at a motor show are the exhibits of luxury cars and iconic sports cars which, for the majority of visitors, are unaffordable. These are automobiles that the majority of visitors will never be able to possess, yet it is precisely these automobiles that attract the largest crowds. Unattainable objects of desire, they elicit a particular form of desire – envy, which English term evokes both similarity and difference from its French cognate, *envie*. It is through envy that automobiles and desire intersect with social class, both in terms of how the motor show is physically structured, and in respect of the social class of the visitors.

The exhibits of mass production automobiles – Ford, General Motors, Volkswagen, but also BMW, Mercedes-Benz, Jaguar and similar brands – are open for all visitors to enter; here the automobiles may be touched, their doors opened, and sat in by the visitors. If only in terms of accessibility for the purposes of the motor show, these exhibits might be described as democratic, available to all for close inspection – at least to all who have paid the relatively modest motor show entry price. In contrast, luxury brands such as Rolls-Royce and Bentley, and sports cars such as Ferrari, Aston Martin, McLaren and Lamborghini, are closed off to the general public with glass, metal and plastic barriers, and are not open for general entry. The barriers are both material and symbolic, separating those who are outside from those who are permitted inside. Enquiries at the Rolls-Royce exhibit, at the entrance to which a security guard was stationed, revealed that most of their visitors had received personal invitations. Many of the people inside these exclusive exhibits *appear* (and they so appear to the members of the public who are unable to enter) to be contemplating purchasing such an automobile. At the Ferrari exhibit, where the starting purchase price is around EUR 250,000, roughly the same as for a Rolls-Royce, there were several sets of well-dressed fathers with sons around 20 years of age, equally fashionably attired, who studiously examined the interior and exteriors of the automobiles and engaged in serious discussion with the salesmen (the gender-specific term here used purposely) presumably about details that would be entered into only with a prospective purchaser. They exhibit an embodied demeanour (Goffman, 1982), enabled by the possession of both economic capital and automobile cultural capital, signified through dress, movement and interaction with the salesmen and the automobiles, through which *distinction*, in the sense described by Pierre Bourdieu (1979), is made visible. It is a habitus rendered doubly visible by those few visitors allowed entry, who – signified by their contrasting demeanour, dress, movement and interaction, which indicate they are content to have been permitted entry to the restricted area – appear out of place, in possession of insufficient financial resources to purchase the automobiles. Whether the majority of the visitors to the enclosed exhibit areas who appear to have the financial resources to purchase these automobiles are, or are not able, to afford the automobiles is impossible to know from casual observation – and it is only casual observation that is available to the visitors. It is, however, I would suggest, irrelevant. What is significant is that available for all to see are credible public performances, even if performed by the impecunious. They appropriately exhibit, as Erving Goffman (1951, p. 300) has put it, "behaviours [that] involve matters of etiquette, dress, deportment, gesture, intonation, dialect, vocabulary [and] small bodily movements".

The restricted exhibits, the select automobiles on display, the barriers to entry, and the observable differences between those inside and outside the boundary, including access to exclusive, invitation only, bar areas serving that most socially distinguishing of beverages – champagne – represent a demarcation of social class and social status. The exhibits of the manufacturers of select automobiles, symbolically underscored by physical barriers manned by security personnel, render in materially visible form that some individuals are able to afford the automobiles on display, while the overwhelming majority of visitors cannot. Among exhibits that are open to the general public, social class is of course not absent, but is signified not through physical barriers to entry but by the purchase price of the automobiles. It is not social class in the abstract that is visible and performed; social class denies, or allows for, the performance not only of routine automobile masculinities but the exemplary automobile masculinity that expensive sports cars can provide.

Equally significant is the audience to these performances of social class and gender. Not only their presence but their demeanour, of utter seriousness (Goffman, 1956), is essential to the success of the performances. No one mocks or laughs at those inspecting the Italian sports cars with utter seriousness, or questions where or how the money to purchase them was obtained. The interactions between the pecunious and impecunious occur in a situation of taken-for-granted normality (Harvey, 2007): that the distribution of wealth and income outside the motor show – which the automobiles inside, albeit imperfectly, mirror – is right and just. In that visitors know how to act appropriately in the public place that is a motor show (see Goffman, 1963) is unremarkable, yet these displays of deference render normal not only inequality but automobility itself.

Decontextualized automobiles

Like photographs that portray persons of exceptional beauty and desirability, the motor show, wherein automobiles of exceptional beauty and desirability are exhibited, might be described as a form of automobile pornography – the term here employed in its widest sense – in material form. The additional benefit of the motor show is that visitors are permitted to take their own photographs. The automobiles being representations of what you yourself might own, or hope to own, they are no less signifiers than their corresponding representations in television advertisements and in glossy promotional brochures. Analogous to air-brushed and digitally modified photographs that allow for the removal of deficiencies to enhance the beauty and perfection of the signified and signifying object (Shelton, 2013, p. 12), imperfections are continually erased from the automobiles at the motor show. An important but barely visible class of employees who move through the background of the motor show are workers whose task is to keep the automobiles immaculately clean – to remove dust, fingerprints, and other disagreeable marks that have appeared on the automobiles. Equipped with feather dusters, cloths, sponges, and plastic bottles of cleaning fluid, they are kept ceaselessly busy. The perfectly presented and decontextualized automobiles belie the actually existing automobiles encountered on the road.

A second way in which automobiles are decontextualized is in their very mode of representation. Anger (see Katz, 1999), traffic congestion, car crashes, ambulances and hospital emergency centres, wheelchairs, funeral parlours, are markedly absent at the motor show, as is anything that might signify, even inadvertently, the alternative reality of actually existing contemporary automobility outside the motor show halls. (The sole exceptions are exhibits in one of the smaller halls where one can find, according to the Geneva Motor Show official brochure, "everything related to maintaining vehicles in a perfect condition": miscellaneous automobile accessories, garage maintenance and service equipment, and drive-in car-wash equipment.) Rather, the automobiles are presented on rotating raised daises, on carpets, marble and glass floors. The representation of the automobile at a motor show is analogous to car advertisements that present automobiles in scenes of natural beauty and on empty roads. Indeed, several exhibits display, on wall-sized screens, videos of their automobiles traversing pristine landscapes on traffic-free roads.

As one might assume as so obvious to not require comment, which visitors similarly assume as unremarkable, the engines of none of the automobiles are running. Neither the sound of idling engines nor that of accelerating sports cars is audible – nor of car horns, which have been disabled. There are no obnoxious and poisonous exhaust fumes within the motor show halls, only the scent of new cars. This is obviously for reasons of health and safety – that those at the motor show do not die from carbon monoxide poisoning. But this absence is precisely the point that needs to be underscored: the signifying automobile of the motor show is represented, as Barthes put it, "as a purely magical object" – not as the actually existing object that pollutes the world, causes illness, debilitating injury and death by disease and through car crashes, massively contributes to global warming, and which is responsible for other urban and rural environmental degradations. The very experience of everyday automobility, of noise, exhaust fumes, the ever-present danger that requires of us constant attention and must be navigated by all road users, above all by pedestrians and cyclists (Taylor, 2003; Urry, 2004, p. 29), is absent. All of this is occluded and effaced at a motor show.

Although the focus of this chapter is one specific motor show, neither the Geneva nor any other single motor show is an entirely unique event. At the conclusion of one motor show, many of the exhibits are packed up and are transported to the location of the next motor show at which they will be exhibited, where they are reinstalled. While some employees are hired on site for the duration of single motor shows, many hold permanent positions and travel from motor show to motor show. Each individual motor show, consequently, should be thought of as a location for the temporary display of a travelling collection of exhibits. Taken in its entirety, this travelling exhibition might be likened to a transport museum containing an extensive collection of items of contemporary automobility technology. So described, if one considers what could be included in such an event, what an alternative curator might choose to exhibit, such as displays that would address the themes and issues that are the subject of this chapter, the limited scope of the motor show becomes apparent (Shelton, 2013). The visions that are promoted, the themes that have been chosen, the objects that are exhibited, the context that has been created for their display, all without exception are entirely uncritical.

The motor show as spectacle and celebration

Although this chapter provides an alternative narrative of the motor show to that which the motor show itself provides, *qua* written text it can only aspire to be a supplement, not a substitute to attending a motor show. Although I have referred to the spectacularity of the Geneva Motor Show, text and photographs can only inadequately convey the spectacle of a contemporary motor show. Not only do the size of the exhibition halls, the excess of automobiles, and the size of the crowd contribute to the creation of the spectacle that is a motor show; as one traverses the floors of the exhibition halls one encounters automobile exhibits with dancers and accompanying music and wall-size video screens. Videos of the brand of automobile being promoted and accompanying music with extreme bass notes are ubiquitous. It is a carnival atmosphere that celebrates automobility across a variety of social dimensions: social class, masculinity, freedom, speed, power, fun, and so forth. The combined effect of this spectacular and entertaining celebration of automobility is to efface and occlude the externalities of everyday automobility through the construction within the internal space of the exhibition halls of nothing less than an automobile utopia (Jasanoff and Kim, 2015, p. 5).

The political economy of the motor show

The five major international motor shows, as well as many of the less prestigious motor shows, are certified by the International Organization of Motor Vehicle Manufacturers, known also under its French acronym, OICA, a global lobbying organization that describes itself on its website as "the voice speaking on automotive issues in world forums" (Organisation Internationale des Constructeurs d'Automobiles, 2019a). There is some empirical if not epistemological merit to this claim: the OICA is an accredited representative to the United Nations, and it is represented at global events such as the annual World Economic Forum in Davos, as are analogous national organizations. Its current president, Matthias Wissmann, previously federal minister for transportation (*Bundesminister für Verkehr*) in the government of Helmut Kohl, is also president of the German automotive industry association (*Verband der Automobilindustrie*). Recent presidents include Patrick Blain, a past president of the French automotive industry association (*Comité des Constructeurs Français d'Automobiles*) and David McCurdy, a past president of the Alliance of Automobile Manufacturers in the United States, former member of the US House of Representatives and former Chair of the House Intelligence Committee, and current president of the American Gas Association (Wikipedia, 2019). In short, officials at the highest levels of the governance structure of the OICA not only have access to, but are part of, the highest levels of national and global governance. The OICA is a major political actor and lobbying organization in the global political economy (Phillips and Robinson, 2018).

OICA's membership is comprised of vehicle manufacturers and national trade associations. Its remit is to support and expand automobility. Of course, the different automobile manufacturers compete with each other for sales, but they are united in their support of automobility, in particular the defence and expansion of the components of what Urry (2004) has called "the system of automobility", such as freeway infrastructure, oil supplies, and government regulations. Motor shows are a location where this unified will to automobility may be observed. Indeed, motor shows, in particular the Detroit, Frankfurt, Geneva, Paris and Tokyo motor shows, may be described as significant world forums in their own right, through which motor vehicle manufacturers speak and through which they promote and, as they brazenly put it on their web site, "defend the interests of the vehicle manufacturers, assemblers and importers". Motor shows, in short, are events where power is exercised.

"The voice speaking on automotive issues in world forums" is the same voice that "defends the interests of the vehicle manufacturers, assemblers and importers". With no apparent irony, the home page of OICA's website announces that: "Through our autos, we connect people, products and services to enhance quality of life and sustainable automobility" (Organisation Internationale des Constructeurs d'Automobiles, 2019b). This voice that defends the interests of the vehicle manufacturers, assemblers and importers, in simultaneously describing itself as *the voice* speaking on automotive issues in world forums, is a claim to possession of politically neutral expert knowledge (Rose, 1993, p. 297), in virtue of which expertise that voice claims to articulate nothing less than the general automotive interests of humanity. It is an echo of the claim by Charles Wilson, CEO of General Motors and United States Secretary of Defense in the Eisenhower administration, that what was good for GM was good for America. In this age of globalization, the new slogan might be "What's good for automobile manufacturers is good for the planet".

I would here underscore that other voices exist. Contemporary automobility studies constitute one alternative voice to that of the International Organization of Motor Vehicle Manufacturers and similar national organizations, such as the Alliance of Automobile Manufacturers in the United States, the *Verband der Automobilindustrie* in Germany, the *Comité des Constructeurs Français d'Automobiles*, or the Japan Automobile Manufacturers Association. While not possessing anything approaching the means of persuasion that is a motor show, automobility studies is one of the few voices that challenges the voice of motor vehicle manufacturers, who have arrogated for themselves the grammatical singular definite article "the" in claiming they are "*the* voice speaking on automotive issues in world forums" (Organisation Internationale des Constructeurs d'Automobiles, 2019a, b). For those who would like to see alternative and sustainable forms of mobility and question the continuing expansion of automobility across the planet and its associated death, injury and environmental destruction (Urry, 2004, p. 26; Böhm et al., 2006; Lamont, 2012; Lindegaard, 2016, p. 83), motor shows are one of the last places one is likely to visit. They are, however, politically significant, as are other spectacular automobility-related events, such as Formula 1 and production-car racing. As material and architectural spectacles (Ritzer, 2010), motor shows are extraordinary rhetorical events, and what they aim to persuade their visitors to engage in is automobility. It seems to me that politically effective critical automobility studies must wrest the definite article "the" from the interests of those that motor shows represent, car manufacturers in particular, such that an alternative voice that is able to articulate interests other than those of motor vehicle manufacturers might become "*the* voice speaking in world forums", including forums such as the United Nations and other "intergovernmental and international bodies" (Organisation Internationale des Constructeurs d'Automobiles, 2019a, b).

Conclusion

Motor shows, I have argued in this chapter, are significant in several respects. First, they illustrate in an exemplary fashion many of the central themes discussed in the automobility literature. Secondly, they are important components of what Urry (2004) has called the "system of automobility", or what Foucauldian scholars have called the "automobility regime" (Böhm *et al.*, 2006). Thirdly, they contribute in unique ways to the cultural reproduction of automobility (Paterson, 2007, pp. 91–120) and in so doing they contribute to the continued capital accumulation prospects of automobile manufacturers and associated industries.

While it is the individual automobiles that are the ostensible centre of the spectacle that is a motor show, it is the motor show in its entirety that is spectacular. It is not only the automobile but automobility, of which the automobile is one component, that is celebrated. Among those components are gender, social class and automobility subjectivities. Their celebration occurs on the floor of the motor show, and the successful performance of that celebration occurs through the active participation of the visitors. It is not automobility *simpliciter* that is celebrated, but automobility in its myriad variations: the automobility masculinity that is celebrated at the exhibits of Italian sports cars and American pickup trucks; social class that is performed at the exhibits of luxury automobiles but equally, if less visibly, at the exhibits of cheaper mass-produced cars. While motor shows are events where the central themes of the automobility literature are observable, such as gender and social class, such themes are performed and amplified in the motor show in ways that further promote automobility.

Foucault (1994, p. xvi) once observed that "commentary questions discourse as to what it says and intended to say; ... in other words, in stating what has been said, one has to restate what has never been said". As a form of commentary, the automobility studies literature provides the possibility to restate what motor shows themselves do not articulate – what has never been said – in order to identify what is in fact articulated by and within the motor show. If described under the metaphor of a text, motor shows provide a forum for the transmission of the voice that has authorized itself to speak on automotive issues. This chapter provides an alternative interpretation, a rewriting of the material text that is a motor show, by locating the motor show within the literature and discourse of contemporary mobility studies.

If motor shows may be described as cathedrals of automobility, the automobile showrooms that litter the peripheries of modern cities might be likened to parish churches. But to which god, or goddess, do we pray when we enter these places of worship? To which religion do they belong? "Whole populations", Barthes suggested in "La nouvelle Citroën", have appropriated the car as a magical object. For Calvin, the preacher in Geneva's other – Gothic – cathedral, the sacraments of Catholicism were nothing more than forms of magic and superstition: the belief that the words of the priest can absolve the believer of his or her sins. Calvinism, Weber (2001, p. 61) observed, was a consistent and rational theodicy that had entirely removed magic from the world. "The spirit of modern capitalism ... rational conduct on the basis of the idea of the calling," Weber (Ibid., pp. 122–123) argued, "was born ... from the spirit of Christian asceticism." That asceticism required, Weber wrote, citing the Presbyterian Richard Baxter, that "the care for external goods should lie on the shoulders of the 'saint like a light cloak, which can be thrown aside at any moment'". "But fate decreed," he added in what has become the most famous passage in *The Protestant Ethic and the Spirit of Capitalism*, "that the cloak should become an iron cage." That iron cage, which can no longer be thrown aside at any moment, is the "material goods [that] have gained an increasing and finally an inexorable power over the lives of men as at no previous period in history". One of those material goods is the automobile, which Urry (2004, p. 28) has aptly described as nothing less than Weber's metaphorical iron cage of modernity in literal material form.

Yet the automobile does not appear to us as an iron cage; at least, it does not so appear to those unfamiliar with Urry's (2006) portrayal of it as an iron cage, the "steel-and-petroleum car". Barthes suggested that the automobile's magical properties come into existence through its appropriation by an entire population. What kind of magical object is it? The increasing rationalization and concomitant disenchantment of the world that Weber saw assumed a traditional understanding of magic as supernatural power, which existed either in the person of the magician or in an object. Contemporary depictions of magic of this sort are *The Lord of the Rings* and the series of Harry Potter books and films. Ludovico Ariosto's *Orlando Furioso*, published between 1516 and 1532, contains a similar compendium of magical persons, beings and objects: wizards, enchanters, sorcerers, spirits, demons, animals, rings and books (Ruggiero, 2001, p. 149). In Canto VII one of the central characters, Ruggiero, falls in love, like many to their misfortune already have before him, with the haggard old witch Alcina who, through her knowledge of magic, makes herself appear as young, beautiful and desirable (Mac Carthy, 2004) – a magical object. The steel and petroleum iron cage that is the automobile is not dissimilar. It emits noise to the point of deafening in cities and for those living or working next to motorways; it has led to massive road construction across much of the planet; it has turned public spaces into automobile thoroughfares (McShane, 1994); the exhaust fumes it releases stink and pollute, contributing not only to the physical and aesthetic destruction and degradation of local environments (Taylor, 2003) but, through CO_2 emissions, of the entire planet; through pollution (Burnett *et al.*, 2018; Zivin and Neidell, 2018) it contributes to nine million early deaths worldwide (38,000 annually in the European Union) and significant monetary health costs (€70 bn annually in the European Union) (Carrington, 2018); each year one and a quarter million people are killed in car crashes (approximately one person every three seconds) and fifty million are seriously injured. "Car-travel," as Urry (2004, p. 29) has put it, "cut[s] *mercilessly* through [the] slower-moving pathways and dwellings ... inhabited by pedestrians, children going to school, postmen, garbage collectors, farmers, animals" [my emphasis]. Yet the automobile is appropriated as a beautiful and desirable object. It has been so rendered and transformed not through magic of the sort employed by Alcina, but through the rational application of the magic that is peculiar to our own age, that of Hollywood, popular culture, of advertising agencies, the mass media, and the technical and aesthetic engineering design skills of automobile manufacturers. The magical properties of the automobile are no more vividly on display than at a motor show, but they inhere within each and every automobile.

That Detroit, Paris, Frankfurt, and Tokyo are sites of the world's major motor shows is not surprising. Detroit was the centre of automobile production in the United States for much of the twentieth century; Paris, Frankfurt and Tokyo are located in countries with significant automobile industries. That Geneva, a city in a country without any significant automobile manufacturing, should have become and remain the site of one of the world's five most important motor shows appears an anomaly. Yet if we think of Geneva as standing, as Weber (2001, p. 117) put it, at "the cradle of ... modern economic man", it is entirely appropriate that Geneva, the city of Calvin, the birthplace of the protestant ethic, later to be transmuted into the spirit of modern capitalism, has become the location of one of the planet's five most important motor shows. And just as contemporary capitalism no longer requires the support of the religious beliefs that brought modern economic man into existence (Ibid., p. 124) so it is no longer to Gothic cathedrals that the public makes regular pilgrimage, but to the magnificent cathedral that is a motor show. It is here where the automobile public pays homage, as Barthes put it, to the supreme creation of our era.

Acknowledgements

An early version of this text was presented in November 2016 at the Material Mobilities Conference at the Centre for Mobilities and Urban Studies (C-MUS) at Aalborg University. Financial assistance to attend that conference was provided by Webster University Geneva. I would like to thank Robert Braun for his invaluable suggestions and input.

References

Barthes, R., 1972. *Mythologies*. New York: Hill and Wang.
Böhm, S., Jones, C., Land, C. and Paterson, M., 2006. Introduction: impossibilities of automobility. In: S. Böhm, C. Jones, C. Land and M. Paterson, eds., *Against automobility*. Malden, MA: Blackwell, pp. 3–16.
Bourdieu, P., 1979. *La distinction: critique sociale du jugement*. Paris: Éditions de Minuit.

Burnett, R., Chen, H., Szyszkowicz, M., Fann, N., Hubbell, B., Pope, C.A., Apte, J.S., Brauer, M., Cohen, A., Weichenthal, S., Coggins, J., Di, Q., Brunekreef, B., Frostad, J., Lim, S.S., Kan, H., Walker, K.D., Thurston, G.D., Hayes, R.B., Lim, C.C., Turner, M.C., Jerrett, M., Krewski, D., Gapstur, S.M., Diver, W.R., Ostro, B., Goldberg, D., Crouse, D.L., Martin, R.V., Peters, P., Pinault, L., Tjepkema, M., van Donkelaar, A., Villeneuve, P.J., Miller, A.B., Yin, P., Zhou, M., Wang, L., Janssen, N.A.H., Marra, M., Atkinson, R.W., Tsang, H., Quoc Thach, T., Cannon, J.B., Allen, R.T., Hart, J.E., Laden, F., Cesaroni, G., Forastiere, F., Weinmayr, G., Jaensch, A., Nagel, G., Concin, H. and Spadaro, J.V., 2018. Global estimates of mortality associated with long-term exposure to outdoor fine particulate matter. *Proceedings of the National Academy of Sciences*, [online] 115(38), p. 9592 LP-9597. Available at: www.pnas.org/content/115/38/9592.abstract.

Carrington, D., 2018. Health effects of diesel "cost European taxpayers billions". *The Guardian*. [online] 27 November. Available at: www.theguardian.com/environment/2018/nov/27/health-effects-of-diesel-cost-european-taxpayers-billions.

Connell, R. and Pearse, R., 2015. *Gender: in world perspective*. Cambridge: Polity Press.

Cresswell, T., 2010. Towards a politics of mobility. *Environment and Planning D: Society and Space*, 28(1), pp. 17–31.

Curts, K., 2015. Temples and turnpikes in "The World of Tomorrow": religious assemblage and automobility at the 1939 New York World's Fair. *Journal of the American Academy of Religion*, 83(3), pp. 722–749.

Derrida, J., 1978. *Writing and difference*. Chicago: University of Chicago Press.

Fish, S., 1989. *Doing what comes naturally: change, rhetoric, and the practice of theory in literary and legal studies*. Durham, NC: Duke University Press.

Foucault, M., 1994. *The birth of the clinic: an archaeology of medical perception*. New York: Vintage Books.

Goffman, E., 1951. Symbols of class status. *The British Journal of Sociology*, 2(4), p. 294.

Goffman, E., 1956. The nature of deference and demeanor. *American Anthropologist*, 58(3), pp. 473–502.

Goffman, E., 1963. *Behavior in public places*. New York: Free Press.

Goffman, E., 1982. *Interaction ritual: essays on face-to-face behavior*. New York: Pantheon Books.

Gundler, B., 2013. Promoting German automobile technology and the automobile industry: the Motor Hall at the Deutsches Museum, 1933–1945. *Journal of Transport History*, 34(2), pp. 117–139.

Harvey, D., 2007. Neoliberalism as creative destruction. *Annals of the American Academy of Political and Social Science*, 610(1), pp. 21–44.

Heidegger, M., 1962. *Being and Time*. New York: Harper & Row.

Iser, W., 1979. *The act of reading: a theory of aesthetic response*. Baltimore: Johns Hopkins University Press.

Jasanoff, S. and Kim, S.-H., 2015. *Dreamscapes of modernity: sociotechnical imaginaries and the fabrication of power*. Chicago: University of Chicago Press.

Katz, J., 1999. Pissed Off in L.A. In: *How emotions work*. Chicago: University of Chicago Press, pp. 18–86.

Lamont, M., 2012. Accidents have no cure! Road death as industrial catastrophe in eastern Africa. *African Studies*, 71(2), pp. 174–194.

Le salon de l'automobile. 1955. France: Institut national de l'audiovisuel. Available at: www.https//www.ina.fr/video/AFE85006400ina.fr/video/AFE85006400.

Lindegaard, L.B., 2016. The discursive accomplishment of rationalities in the automobility regime. In: M. Endres, K. Manderscheid and C. Mincke, eds., *The mobilities paradigm: discourses and ideologies*. London: Routledge, pp. 68–88.
Mac Carthy, I., 2004. Alcina's Island: From imitation to innovation in the "Orlando furioso". *Italica* 81(3), pp. 325–350.
McShane, C., 1994. *Down the asphalt path: the automobile and the American city*. New York: Columbia University Press.
Möser, K., 2003. The dark side of "automobilism", 1900–1930. *Journal of Transport History*, 24(2), pp. 238–258.
Organisation Internationale des Constructeurs d'Automobiles, 2019a. *About Us*. [online] Available at: www.oica.net/category/about-us/ [Accessed 28 February 2019].
Organisation Internationale des Constructeurs d'Automobiles, 2019b. *Home Page*. [online] Available at: www.oica.net/ [Accessed 28 February 2019].
Organisation Internationale des Constructeurs D'Automobiles, 2014. *Tableau Salons 2013-2014*. [online] Paris. Available at: www.oica.net/wp-content/uploads//tableau-salons-2013-20141.pdf.
Palexpo SA, 2019. *Espace vivant*. [online] Geneva. Available at: www.palexpo.ch/sites/default/files/palexpo_fiches-techniques_fr_08-12.pdf.
Paterson, M., 2007. *Automobile politics: ecology and cultural political economy*. Cambridge: Cambridge University Press.
Phillips, P. and Robinson, W.I., 2018. *Giants the global power elite*. New York: Seven Stories Press.
Randell, R., 2017. The microsociology of automobility: the production of the automobile self. *Mobilities*, 12(5), pp. 663–676.
Ritzer, G., 2010. *Enchanting a disenchanted world: continuity and change in the cathedrals of consumption*. 3rd ed. London: SAGE Publications.
Rorty, R., 1982. "Philosophy as a kind of writing: an essay on Derrida". In: *Consequences of pragmatism*. Minneapolis: University of Minnesota Press, pp. 90–109.
Rose, N., 1993. Government, authority and expertise in advanced liberalism. *Economy & Society*, 22(3), p. 283.
Ruggiero, L.G., 2001. L'incanto delle parole e la magia del discorso nell' "Orlando furioso". *Italica*, 78(2), pp. 149–175.
Sheller, M., 2007. Bodies, cybercars and the mundane incorporation of automated mobilities. *Social & Cultural Geography*, 8(2), pp. 175–197.
Sheller, M. and Urry, J., 2006. The new mobilities paradigm. *Environment & Planning A*, 38(2), pp. 207–226.
Shelton, A., 2013. Critical museology. *Museum Worlds*, 1(1), pp. 7–23.
Taylor, N., 2003. The aesthetic experience of traffic in the modern city. *Urban Studies*, 40(8), pp. 1609–1625.
Urry, J., 2004. The "system" of automobility. *Theory, Culture & Society*, 21(4), pp. 25–39.
Urry, J., 2006. Inhabiting the car. *Sociological Review*, 54(s 1), pp. 17–31.
Weber, M., 2001. *The Protestant ethic and the spirit of capitalism*. London: Routledge.
West, C. and Zimmerman, D.H., 1987. Doing gender. *Gender and Society*, 1(2), pp. 125–151.
Wikipedia, 2019. Dave McCurdy. In: *Wikipedia Online*. [online] Available at: https://en.wikipedia.org/w/index.php?title=Dave_McCurdy&oldid=875471330.
Zimmerman, P., 1995. Boys and their indestructible toys. In: S. Zielinski and G. Laird, eds., *Beyond the car: essays on the auto culture*. Toronto: Steel Rail Publishing, pp. 32–39.
Zivin, J.G. and Neidell, M., 2018. Air pollution's hidden impacts. *Science*, [online] 359(6371), p. 39 LP-40. Available at: http://science.sciencemag.org/content/359/6371/39.abstract.

Interlude 1:
Immaterial immobilities and the infrastructuring of mobile utopia

Interview with Monika Büscher

Field(s) of enquiry

How do you define and see the field of research relevant to the material mobilities theme? Which disciplines are relevant and how do they interact? Are there any important disciplinary histories we need to know and remember?

Material mobilities need post-disciplinary analysis, because they generate many of today's 'wicked problems'. The 2008 BBC programme *Britain From Above* provides a glimpse of this: a 24-hour bird's-eye, time-lapse view of air traffic over Britain's busy airports, 75 million Britons and visitors criss-crossing the country in cars and trains, ships traversing the channel, taxis coursing through London's arteries. The series illuminates not only the cumulative performative materiality and rhythms of everyday life, but also how meanings literally materialise as a work day is translated into a pulsating stop-and-go of taxi drivers escaping congestion through rat runs to drop off their passengers. The chatter from millions of mobile phone conversations cuts like static over the visualisation of a country aglow with a uniquely human will to connect (Simmel 1907; Urry 2000). These lived mobilities materialise in other – even harder to perceive – ways, too: CO_2 and particulate matter are released into the atmosphere, soils are lost to wind and water, microplastics are deposited on the tops of the Swiss Alps and in the organs of animals and humans.

Such cumulative (im)material (im)mobilities spell tremendous troubles. Ecology and climate sciences show that humanity is 'burning the library of life' (Legagneux *et al.*, 2018). Current efforts under the 2015 Paris Climate Accord are 'bottom up', defined by individual nations according to their capacities. While the nations most affected (mostly in the Global South) are committing to reduce greenhouse gas emissions to allow the planet to stay below a threshold of 2 °C warming, the commitments by India, the EU, the USA and China are set to lead to 2.6°, 3.2°, 4° and 5.1 °C warming by 2100 (Robiou du Pont and Meinshausen 2018). While some bacteria and plants might survive such warming until the sun will burn Earth in billions of years, humanity might not survive the current sixth mass extinction (Ceballos *et al.*, 2017). As natural scientists turn to drastic language, speaking of 'biological annihilation' and a 'frightening assault on the foundations of human civilisation', a post-disciplinary approach is becoming literally vital (ibid.).

Theories and concepts

Some would argue that the new material turn and mobilities research problematises modern binary distinctions between humans and non-humans, subjects and objects, culture and nature. Do you agree? If so, how does this manifest itself in the theories and concepts? How should we develop theories and concepts of relevance to the future of material mobilities research?

The mobilities paradigm is, alongside many adjacent paradigms from actor network theory (Latour 1993) to feminist technoscience (Barad 2007), underpinned by a realisation that 'humans are nothing' without their entanglements with other beings, objects, and materialities (Urry 2007: 45). Agency, objectivity, subjectivity are emergent. There is no *inter*-action between pre-existing independent human or non-human monads, there is only relational co-constitution in *intra*-action (Adey 2006; Barad 2007). As Urry observes, relations may be temporarily stationary (garage, data centres), portable (passport, umbrella), corporeally interwoven (clothes, smartphone, food), prosthetic (hearing aid, location services), constitutive of mobility systems (car, space shuttle) or code space (earth observations) (2007: 45). With such considerations, the mobilities paradigm 'mobilises' critiques of humanism (Haraway 1990; Latour 1993; Hayles 1999), exhibiting just how 'reality is movement' (Bergson 1960: 328) at all scales.

A concern with materiality is not new in this endeavour. Bergson's insight that form is only a snapshot of an ever-emergent mobile reality has made materiality a central concern (Adey 2006). Mobilities are always 'located and materialised, ... occur[ring] through mobilisations of locality and rearrangements of the materiality of places' (Sheller and Urry 2006). 'Wicked' problems like climate change, the erosion of privacy and civil liberties through datafication, and antimicrobial resistance arise from mobile reality as problems without solutions (Rittel and Webber 1973; Morozov 2013; Urry 2016), and can be addressed afresh with a mobilities perspective. Theories and concepts like motility (Kaufmann *et al.* 2004); mobilities, immobilities, and moorings (Sheller and Urry 2006); comobility (Southern 2012); and mobility justice (Sheller 2018) allow us to discern (some of) the complexities arising from the ways in which the human will to connect is enacted today.

Do we need new theories and concepts in a twenty-first century of disasters (eScience 2012), as the maelstrom of mobilities connects the minute material mobilities of antimicrobial resistance with human mobilities that cause climate change, and up to one billion environmental migrants by 2050 (MacFadden *et al.* 2018, UNCCD 2016)? As our house is burning, acting on what we know seems a more pressing task.

Methods and approaches

What set of methods and approaches for investigating material mobilities are in your opinion the most fruitful? Are there any new methods or combinations of existing methods that you find particular promising?

The mobilities paradigm has helped drive a methodological paradigm shift that provides powerful resources. At the heart of this is a recognition that complex emergent systems cannot be known or controlled. 'Mode 2' post-disciplinary science acknowledges that science and society have become transgressive arenas, co-evolving not in benign leaps and bounds, but disruptive jolts (Nowotny *et al.* 2001), where 'collective experimentation' must critically involve public engagement (Felt *et al.* 2007). Mobile methods take this and concepts of responsible research and innovation (von Schomberg 2013), science with and for society (van Oost *et al.* 2016), as well as citizen science and citizen social science (Albert 2018) to build new approaches for making and acting upon knowledge of a world in motion.

Moving away from 'solutionism' (Morozov 2013) requires that research provides more than insight and critique. Addressing the complexity of societal change not only demands new scientific subjectivities and respons-abilities (Haraway 2010); it also entangles everyday life in 'experiment earth' (Stilgoe 2015), demanding new ways of understanding and conducting social-material-political everyday life. Here, mobilities research helps draw together a range of contemporary approaches and methods. Rosi Braidotti's call for 'affirmative critique' (2010), Donna Haraway's insistence to 'stay with the trouble' (2016), and Ruth Levitas' utopia as method (2013) are particularly potent, because when 'mobilised' with the analytical sensitivities of a mobilities perspective, they can inform a practical epistemology of changing mobilities across these interconnected scales, from the everyday to the international, the geopolitical and planetary.

When Bergson explained that to grasp how reality is movement, 'you must replace yourself within it[, i]nstall yourself within change' (Bergson 1960: 334), there was no methodological apparatus to do so. Mobilities research helps researchers to:

- 'Move with' the actors to understand their phenomenological experiences, practices, systemic connections. In my case that has meant physically moving along with people involved in disaster risk management, tracing (im)mobilities of collaborative work, and more metaphorically and creatively following the information, finding out where, when, how, and why sharing information with digital technologies may produce frictions.
- 'Move in' with research subjects, into the contexts where socio-material orders are made, where change may be needed and where it could be achieved. In my case, this produced an action research concern with post-disaster analyses that relentlessly criticise emergency response for 'a lack of interoperability' and call for technological fixes.
- Be 'moved by' phenomena and their effects, to listen, watch, feel carefully, and to unfold critique to consider who/what is affected and how. Where are inequalities, injustices, inefficiencies, unsustainable practices? But mobile 'affirmative' critique does not stop there. It inevitably gives rise to two questions. First, as Ole Jensen describes in this book, allowing oneself to be moved prompts us to speculate: 'What if?' How might things be otherwise? How should they be? Secondly,…
- … 'to move' others, to enthuse, persuade, convince people, to assemble a different reality, to not just discursively but practically, actually, materially articulate the changes that seem necessary to make a 'better' reality soon raises questions of 'What now?'. Creative, normative modes of research come with extraordinary complexities, and responsibilities. As one forgets or underestimates or is plain ignorant of connected stakeholders, publics,

dynamics, unanticipated effects when one starts changing mobilities, troubles arise. In my case, informing the design of digital systems for multi-agency disaster risk management has positively boosted the quality of disaster response, as well as enabling unprecedented datafication of human actions that undermines professional expertise and human values, and heightens capacity for surveillance and social sorting.

As these examples show, installing oneself in an emergent, moving reality does not produce superior knowledge. On the contrary, it shows that ignorance is inevitable. No one can know how socio-technical transformations will evolve. Faced with this problematic in a different context, Matthias Gross (2010) recommends methodologies that strategically produce surprises as an antidote to ignorance, that 'disclose' troubles and allow 'reversibility' (Introna 2007), that allow us to 'stay with the trouble' and ask 'What now?' repeatedly, in ways that mobilise the creativity of 'What if?' questions, but persistently, iteratively accompany change. This is a deeply social creative practice with much cause for contestation, and Pelle Ehn (2008), and Christopher A. Le Dantec and Carl DiSalvo (2013) show us ways of 'infrastructuring' for 'design in use', inclusion of diverse stakeholders, and contestation of different perspectives and interests.

Design and creation

How do you see concrete artefacts, systems and technologies facilitating and affording mobilities? What is the role of design? How are the construction, making and institution of artefacts and material critical to a new mobilities agenda? Are there specific 'designerly ways of thinking' that may influence and form future mobilities research? If so, in what ways? How do you see a role for (design) experiments and 'speculative approaches' in future mobilities research?

Ehn's notion of 'design in use' highlights that design does not only happen at design time, driven by professional Designers. People appropriate, assemble, repair, use, misuse designed artefacts, systems and technologies. In practice, the boundaries between research, practice, design and innovation are blurry; the agencies of knowledge production, everyday life, and creativity are multiple. Design and creation thus emerge as a second major territory for methodological innovation. Design research has proposed dematerialisation (Manzini and Cullars 1992) as a major move. Dematerialising our economies and everyday practices involves a shift from ownership of products (such as cars) to using services, placing greater emphasis on repair, renting, upgrading, reuse and recycling, reduction of the negative impact of products across an extended lifespan (Kiem 2012). Another major turn focuses on 'rematerialising' mobility systems and 'mobile situations', for example by retro-fitting parking lots for multiple uses. With their work on mobilities design, Jensen (2014) and Jensen and Lanng (2017) have brought mobilities research and design into conversation, observing how mobile situations are staged from above and below, providing ample opportunities for design to stage mobilities differently.

Speculative design (Galloway 2014; Michael *et al.* 2015) suggests that whether it's dematerialising or rematerialising that is the focus of design, a radically provocative approach to materialising futures can make critique concrete. It often focuses on undesirable aspects, highlighting troubles by trying to literally make elements of futures 'matereal'. This resonates deeply with the speculative, normative mobile methods outlined above. However, where speculative design often seeks to 'only' provoke, my practical speculative post-disciplinary epistemology-ethics-politics of making (co-designing) mobility systems seeks to make change happen concretely, in the messy, contradictory, changing, worldly mobility systems it has moved into, accepting the respons-abilities and responsibilities that come with this (see also Kimbell 2013; Tyfield and Blok 2016; Popan 2018). Whilst highlighting troubles, it is normative, affirmative, creative, seeking to find ways of making futures 'better', deliberately generating surprises, and creative friction around what might constitute 'better', about who should be able to say, and about unanticipated consequences.

Matters of concern and societal responsibilities

What are the critical issues of a public debate on material mobilities? What are the 'matters of concern'? How do you see mobilities research contributing to these agendas? How are the ethical responsibilities of a material mobilities research emerging? Are there any inherent political dimensions of the research into material mobilities that we need to be observing? Are there any particular societal claims on the research? How do you see the interaction space between research and the public(s)?

Myriad systemically unequal, productive and harmful (im)mobilities of everyday life are changing the planet. A collapse of humanity is not some far-away potential. We are living it, in the ruins of capitalism and modernity (Tsing 2015). When Ceballos *et al.* (2017) talk about biological annihilation, it is not just the habitats of invertebrates and animals that are shrinking. At the time of publication, 'we are witnessing the highest levels of [human] displacement on record. An unprecedented 68.5 million people around the world have been forced from home' (UNHCR 2018). An 'estimated 10 million stateless people have been denied a nationality and access to basic rights such as education, healthcare, employment and freedom of movement (ibid.), and between 2015 and 2018 19,293 migrants have died in the process of migration (Missing Migrants Project 2018). The newspapers are full of stories documenting inhumane treatment. Indeed, it seems that values of humanity may go extinct before we do as a species.

Reformist agendas such as the New Urban Agenda seek to ameliorate these troubles with 'solutions'. Efforts to decarbonise transport, for example, are turning to data for smart city sustainability, and digital technologies are an integral part of migration control. Maria Kaika (2017) calls this solutionist turn to technological fixes a form of neoliberal therapy or 'immunology' and she asks, 'What happens when communities refuse to be vaccinated with "smart cities" and indicators?' She highlights the activities of Grassroots Organisations (GROs), who, unlike Non-governmental Organisations (NGOs) do not necessarily have a commitment to collaborate with reformist agendas or government agencies. Initiatives include, for example, the Spanish Platform for Mortgage Affected People (PAH) formed in 2009 to support the more than 300,000 families in Spain who were evicted by banks when they could not repay their mortgage debts. The PAH 'does not accept the role of the state or banks as powerful authorities that can evict and subsequently "include" evicted citizens in discussions about housing. Instead, the PAH establishes housing as an indisputable and undeniable right for all. It contends that when this right is not granted, it is not to be negotiated through consensus-building frameworks. It is to be taken' (Kaika 2017: 96).

A core matter of concern for mobilities research, should, in my view, be the question of how research and design can engage with people who are, like PAH, materialising or 'prefiguring' alternatives. They are populous, perhaps (I hope) more in numbers than the populists. They are needed to bring about what is necessary to hold on to the idea of a good life, and that is nothing less than a great mobilities transformation. The great mobilities transformation is a transformation that is ideological, ethical, as well as societal and economic, a way of articulating alternatives to the great neoliberal transformation that allowed 'the market mechanism to be the sole director of the fate of human beings and their natural environment' which has resulted, as Polanyi foresaw, 'in the demolition of society' (Polanyi 1944: 73). How to achieve a great mobilities transformation? How to GROw it? The mobilities paradigm and the material mobilities focus uniquely position such an 'ethics of mattering' (Barad 2007) as a simultaneously epistemological, ontological, political, ethical, creative endeavour. Somewhat strangely, the concepts that are emerging at this juncture are 'human security' (Kaldor 2011), human internet (EuroDIG 2014), human mobilities. While such concepts have to be treated with caution (Lopes de Souza 2010), not least because 'we have never been human' (Latour 1993), humanity is a powerful value and capacity that may allow development of mobile methodologies to translate knowledge of systemic multiscalar fragilities into actions that might sustain life on Earth.

References

Adey, P. (2006). If mobility is everything then it is nothing: towards a relational politics of (im)mobilities. *Mobilities*, 1(1), 75–94.
Albert, A. (2018). Citizen Social Science: A Critical Investigation. PhD Thesis, submitted Manchester University and Lancaster University.
Barad, K. (2007). *Meeting the Universe Halfway*. Durham, NC: Duke University Press.
Bergson, H. (1960 [1911]). *Creative Evolution*. London: Macmillan.
Braidotti, R. (2010). on putting the active back into activism. *New Formations*, 68(1), 42–57.

Ceballos, G., Ehrlich, P. R., and Dirzo, R. (2017). Biological annihilation via the ongoing sixth mass extinction signaled by vertebrate population losses and declines. *Proceedings of the National Academy of Sciences of the United States of America, 114*(30), E6089-E6096.

Ehn, P. (2008). Participation in design things. In *PDC '08 Proceedings of the Tenth Anniversary Conference on Participatory Design 2008, Indiana University* (pp. 92–101). Indianapolis.

eScience (2012). Earth faces a century of disasters, report warns. http://esciencenews.com/sources/the.guardian.science/2012/04/26/earth.faces.a.century.disasters.report.warns [Accessed 5 July 2013].

EuroDIG (2014). Towards a human Internet? Rules, rights, and responsibilities for our online future | Internet Rights and Principles Coalition. http://internetrightsandprinciples.org/site/eurodig-lisbon-workshop-4/ [Accessed 1 January 2019].

Felt, U., Wynne, B., Stirling, A., Callon, M., and Goncalves, M.E. (2007). *Science and governance: taking European knowledge society seriously.* Working Paper. School of Business, Management and Economics. Brighton: University of Sussex.

Galloway, A. (2014). Three uncertain thoughts, or, everything I know I learned from Ursula Le Guin | Design Culture Lab. http://designculturelab.org/2014/10/23/three-uncertain-thoughts-or-everything-i-know-i-learned-from-ursula-le-guin/ [Accessed 9 November 2014].

Gross, M. (2010). *Ignorance and Surprise.* Cambridge, MA: MIT Press.

Haraway, D. J. (1990). A Cyborg Manifesto. In *Simians, Cyborgs, and Women: The Reinvention of Nature* (p. 312). New York: Routledge.

Haraway, D. (2010). Sowing Worlds: A Seed Bag for Terraforming with Earth Others. In *Beyond the Cyborg: Adventures with Donna Haraway* (pp. 137–146). New York: Columbia University Press.

Haraway, D. J. (2016). *Staying with the Trouble: Making Kin in the Chthulucene.* Durham, NC: Duke University Press.

Hayles, N. K. (1999). *How We Became Posthuman: Virtual Bodies in Cybernetics, Literature, and Informatics.* Chicago: University Of Chicago Press.

Introna, L. D. (2007). Maintaining the reversibility of foldings: making the ethics (politics) of information technology visible. *Ethics and Information Technology, 9*(1), 11–25.

Jensen, O. B. (2014). *Designing Mobilities.* Aalborg: Aalborg University Press.

Jensen, O. B. and Lanng, D. B. (2017). *Mobilities Design: Urban Designs for Mobile Situations.* London: Routledge.

Kaika, M. (2017). 'Don't call me resilient again!': the New Urban Agenda as immunology ... or ... what happens when communities refuse to be vaccinated with 'smart cities' and indicators. *Environment and Urbanization, 29*(1), 89–102.

Kaldor, M. (2011). Human Security. *Society and Economy, 33*(3), 441–448.

Kaufmann, V., Bergman, M. M., and Joye, D. (2004). Motility: mobility as capital. *International Journal of Urban and Regional Research, 28*(4), 745–756.

Kimbell, L. (2013). An Inventive Practice Perspective on Designing. PhD Thesis. Lancaster University. Available at: http://libweb.lancs.ac.uk [Accessed 22 December 2018].

Kiem, Matthew. (2012). Theorising a transformative agenda for craft. craft + design enquiry. doi: 10.22459/CDE.03.2011.04.

Latour, B. (1993). *We Have Never Been Modern.* Cambridge, MA: Harvard University Press.

Le Dantec, C. A. and DiSalvo, C. (2013). Infrastructuring and the formation of publics in participatory design. *Social Studies of Science, 43*(2), 241–264.

Legagneux, P., Casajus, N., Cazelles, K., Chevallier, C., Chevrinais, M., Guéry, L., Jacquet, C., Jaffré, M., Naud, M., Noisette, F., Ropars, P., Vissault,, Archambault, P., Bêty, J., Berteaux, D., Gravel, D. (2018). Our house is burning: discrepancy in climate change vs. biodiversity coverage in the media as compared to scientific literature. *Frontiers in Ecology and Evolution*, 5, 175.

Levitas, R. (2013). *Utopia as Method: The Imaginary Reconstitution of Society*. Basingstoke: Palgrave Macmillan.

Lopes de Souza, M. (2010). Which right to which city? In defence of political-strategic clarity. *Interface*, 2(1), 315–333.

MacFadden, D. R., McGough, S. F., Fisman, D., Santillana, M., and Brownstein, J. S. (2018). Antibiotic resistance increases with local temperature. *Nature Climate Change*, 8(6), 510–514.

Manzini, E. and Cullars, J. (1992). Prometheus of the everyday: the ecology of the artificial and the designer's responsibility. *Design Issues*, 9(1), 5.

Michael, M., Costello, B., Mooney-Somers, J., and Kerridge, I. (2015). Manifesto on art, design and social science – method as speculative event. *Leonardo*, 48(2), 190–191. http://doi.org/10.1162/LEON_a_00983.

Missing Migrants Project (2018) https://missingmigrants.iom.int [Accessed 30 December 2018].

Morozov, E. (2013). *To Save Everything, Click Here: The Folly of Technological Solutionism*. New York: PublicAffairs.

Nowotny, H., Scott, P., and Gibbons, M. (2001). *Rethinking Science: Knowledge and the Public*. Cambridge: Polity Press.

Polanyi, K. (1944). *The Great Transformation* (1957 edition). Boston: Beacon.

Popan, C. (2018). *Bicycle Utopias: Imagining Fast and Slow Cycling Futures*. London: Routledge.

Rittel, H. W. J. and Webber, M. M. (1973). Dilemmas in a general theory of planning. *Policy Sciences*. 4(2), 155–169.

Robiou du Pont, Y. and Meinshausen, M. (2018). Warming assessment of the bottom-up Paris Agreement emissions pledges. *Nature Communications*, 9(1), 4810. http://doi.org/10.1038/s41467-018-07223-9.

Sheller, M. (2018). *Mobility Justice: The Politics of Movement in an Age of Extremes*. London: Verso.

Sheller, M. and Urry, J. (2006). The new mobilities paradigm. *Environment and Planning A*, 38(2), 207–226.

Simmel, G. (1990[1907]). *The Philosophy of Money*. London: Routledge.

Southern, J. (2012). Comobility: how proximity and distance travel together in locative media. *Canadian Journal of Communication*, 37(1), 75–91.

Stilgoe, J. (2015). *Experiment Earth: Responsible Innovation in Geoengineering*. London: Routledge.

Tsing, A. L. (2015). *The Mushroom at the End of the World: On the Possibility of Life in Capitalist Ruins*. Princeton, NJ: Princeton University Press.

Tyfield, D. and Blok, A. (2016). Doing methodological cosmopolitanism in a mobile world. *Mobilities*, 11(4), 629–641.

United Nations Convention to Combat Desertification (UNCCD) (2016). Sustainability. Stability. Security. www.unccd.int/sustainability-stability-security [Accessed 23 December 2018].

United Nations High Commissioner for Refugees (UNHCR) (2018). Statistical Yearbooks www.unhcr.org/figures-at-a-glance.html [Accessed 30 December 2018].

Urry, J. (2000). *Sociology Beyond Societies: Mobilities for the Twenty-First Century*. London: Routledge.

Urry, J. (2007). *Mobilities*. Cambridge: Polity Press.
Urry, J. (2016). *What Is the Future?* London: Routledge.
van Oost, E., Kuhlmann, S., Ordóñez-Matamoros, G., and Stegmaier, P. (2016). Futures of science with and for society: towards transformative policy orientations. *Foresight*, *18*(3), 276–296.
von Schomberg, R. (2013). A Vision of Responsible Research and Innovation. In *Responsible Innovation* (pp. 51–74). Chichester, UK: John Wiley & Sons, Ltd.

4 Relating movement to information in consumer mobilities, using Space Syntax

Zofia Bednarowska and Jamie O'Brien

Introduction

The journeys that consumers make towards their desired destination stem from a process of *en route* information-gathering. Consumers gather information at different rates of interaction with their mobile environments and at multiple scales of metric distance. Their speed and modality of travel together make a difference to the kinds of information that are gathered, processed, and formed into knowledge. The mobile environment of the consumer journey generates a set of affordances for information-gathering, whether shaped through representational (deliberative) design, or through non-representational (evolutionary) actions (Jensen, 2016). Affordances for information-gathering might also comprise hybrids of representational and non-representational designs; for example, a consumer journey may follow a formal road network, and include occasions for ad hoc search activities, reflected in adjustments in travel speed, exploratory turn-offs, perhaps even risks taken in terms of traffic regulation. In a similar capacity, the well-known phenomena of 'desire paths' serve to materialise ad hoc affordances for information morphogenesis (Hillier, 2016), disrupting representational space in the built environment, and laying down a path of least effort towards a desired destination.

Within the urban landscape, different modalities of movement relate to modalities of information-gathering. Urban settlements are arranged around generic structural relationships of low-movement pathways connecting to medium- and high-movement pathways. They also comprise regular differences in the clustering of streets, from high-density to low-density formations. Moving and clustering within the urban network generates information by way of inhabitants' social interactions. Yet inhabitants move and cluster for different purposes, which involve different rates of movement and levels of clustering. Groupings of inhabitants are arranged around their informational demands. We invite you to consider these through a thought experiment.

Imagine a commuter by private car and a pedestrian searching a local area, passing through an urban space at the same time. The commuter by car seeks to make a path from her domicile to her place of work, in a journey lasting around 50 minutes. As such she takes a path of least effort along the longest stretch of road available, involving the lowest number of turnings available. At that same time in the morning, a pedestrian is walking from his domicile, also for 50 minutes. The morning traffic is very busy along the main road close to where he leaves, so he keeps away from its edge. This walk involves a series of short streets and pathways across a nearby park. The busy road hampers his movements, and his walk is shaped also by factors of visibility and intelligibility in the built urban environment.

Both the private-car commuter and the pedestrian are engaged in information-gathering, yet their modalities of movement engage them in different kinds of knowledge. The commuter is engaged with knowledge of the city at a 'motorised-transportation' scale along paths of least effort. The pedestrian is engaged with knowledge of the city at a 'journey-by-foot' scale along heuristic combinations of pathways. The commuter is generally less interested in searching within local community spaces. The pedestrian has little interest in encountering people who work in the city centre and reside in outlying villages. Commuter traffic moves past him, and its impact on his movement relates more to the boundary lines that it generates or represents. These boundaries compel him to move within a dense cluster of short streets that underpin some nearby places. In this period both walker and commuter have persisted in normal travel over a 50-minute period. Yet compare their experiences: the walker has moved along two miles of streets and pathways, while the commuter has moved along 40 miles of roads and streets. The pedestrian has gathered information relating to everyday movements – to suitable stopping-places, to others' search behaviours, to structures and conditions that affect everyday movements.

In order to explore the impact of movement on information-gathering and the generation of affordances, we focused our enquiry on rhythms and patterns of movement of mobile consumption. We used the new mobilities paradigm (Sheller and Urry, 2006) and followed the advisory to focus more attention on materialities in mobilities (Adey, 2014; Jensen, 2016). We researched how everyday-life mobilities, i.e. consumer travels, are affected by materialities of urban network infrastructure, i.e. roads, pavements, cycle paths. This essentially material infrastructure affects how consumer mobilities are produced, by designating transportation infrastructure and potential movement of consumers to shop.

We introduce a prototype method developed for mapping urban movements as they relate to consumer journeys, also considering consumers' mental modelling and information-gathering. The prototype uses spatial analysis and mobilities by combining methods of mapping workshops and Space Syntax to analyse road networks in terms of urban flows. Space Syntax includes a set of methods for analysing 'syntactical' forms and patterns of potential movements that are common to all urban networks. We have generated a Space Syntax road-network model of the Lancaster region, by which we visualised the urban network affordances for movement at different scales. Working with cartographic Ordnance Survey maps and Depthmap models, we aimed to observe how pathways at different scales overlay each other, so that functions of the network across a range of scale converge along the same road segments. We also sought to observe how affordances for consumer behaviours are based on these 'affordances' for movement, which are generative within urban environments as socio-technical domains.

The method was developed during the workshop 'Mobilizing the Urban Model: A Workshop on Spatial Analysis and Mobile Utopias of Consumption', organised by the Centre for Mobilities Research (CeMoRe) and the Institute for Social Futures (ISF) at Lancaster University in April 2016. The workshop was led by Zofia Bednarowska, Monika Büscher, and Jamie O'Brien, and was part of the project 'Mobile Utopia 1851–2016', comprising a large variety of workshops and activities that concerned utopian thinking and designing futures.

This chapter outlines the methodology used and its theoretical basis. The first section defines consumer journeys and positions them within consumer mobilities. The following two sections seek to understand how environmental affordances for consumer information, such as generative affordances for consumer behaviours, e.g. searching, discovering, and gathering, are related to urban movements. The subsequent sections present an introduction to the theory of Space Syntax and an urban model of Lancashire created using this method. We present an overview of the mapping workshops and data results, before discussing the potential for a mixed method of this kind in observing consumer journeys.

Consumer journeys as a part of consumer mobility

Mobilities are constitutive of consumption in different ways and for that reason they need recognition. The new mobilities paradigm (Sheller and Urry, 2006) was applied in order to introduce consumer mobilities (Bednarowska, 2016). As a paradigm it engages many distinct theories, broader than just transportation, movement, communication, as it reveals manifold aspects of mobility in everyday practices (Urry, 2007:18–19). To date, consumer mobilities have not constituted a separate topic, as is the case with many other types of mobilities, e.g. in *The Routledge Handbook of Mobilities* (Adey, 2006) but were analysed along with other types of mobilities.

Consumer mobilities constitute a phenomenon frequently reflected in social practices, as they are everyday-life mobilities. Consumers move at their own speed and rhythm between the points of purchase, such as stores, shopping malls, cafés and service points.

A significant part of consumer mobilities is constituted by consumer rhythms, which we propose to call 'consumer journeys' (not to be confused with marketing analysis of the consumers' decision journeys). Such journeys involve not only the purchasing of a product or service but also doing this at any kind of stopover in order to consume it (e.g. drink a coffee during a shopping day, eat lunch on the way to a shopping centre), as a part of the habitual consumer journey. These stopovers, as well as destinations, are 'third places'. They are distinct from home or workplace, but just as important, since spatial practices appear in these three social dimensions (Oldenburg, 1999). Oldenburg focused on coffee shops, bars, pubs and general stores. I consider shopping malls and retail chain stores to be third places, as a great deal of consumption takes place therein (Bednarowska, 2018b); they host coffee shops and other venues, but also offer a place of rest in consumer journeys.

Consumer journeys are mostly based on brick-and-mortar (non-Internet) shopping, even with the expansion of e-commerce. Online consumer journeys are a distinct type of shopping, as they are not mobile in terms of physical movement. They are, however, mobile in terms of online moving between stores (websites, portals), the delivery process, or the transferance of ideas. Therefore, we will not discuss this aspect here. However, online searching prior to shopping may complement brick-and-mortar shopping. Looking for stores online may help to plan the new consumer journey – map the consumption spots, discover new shopping places or supplement the process of shopping when looking for information. Nowadays, consumption space infrastructure is to a great extent mapped on the Internet and the whole journey can be planned in a detailed way prior to leaving one's house, including directions, updated traffic information, opening hours and current stock to choose from (e.g. clothes and footwear).

Movement during consumer journeys

Consumer journeys in terms of spatial behaviour involve not only purchasing, but also movement while travelling between stores or any other places of consumption (bars, cafés, etc.). A consumer journey path is shaped within the rhythm of the consumer's need or the consumer's decision-making process. There are a number of variables corresponding to consumer behaviour models, such as cultural environment, social norms, knowledge, attitudes, consumer behaviour habits, cycle of consumption and the level of satisfaction and loyalty (Antonides and van Raaij, 2003:23).

Choosing a commercial centre to shop in is a component part of everyday or weekly consumer choices. Consumer decisions in terms of spatial behaviour have been investigated by analysing travel modes for multiple purchasing purposes, which change over time (Clifton *et al.*, 2016). Mental accounting of travel distance is an important part of the consumer journey. During a single trip when consumers carry out several purchases, they usually combine different destinations and distances – they do not necessarily choose the nearest arrival point at which to buy all their goods (Clark, 1968). Travel distance minimisation (Dellaert *et al.*, 1998) is a factor impacting consumer travel choices. However, travel mode is not a significant predictor of consumer spending (Clifton *et al.*, 2016).

The consumer decision-making process is a key concept in consumer behaviour theory, based on the rational approach (Solomon *et al.*, 2006) where consumers are treated as rational individuals, making precise and rational decisions. It is particularly valuable since we live in information-rich environments (Lurie, 2004). It is widely recognised that consumers do not always follow a rational decision-making process (Solomon *et al.*, 2006:259).

Consumers often make choices of utility contrary to what would be expected (Brooks *et al.*, 2004) – such choices conform with transaction utility theory that a consumer's behaviour depends not only on the value of product in relation to the price, but also on the consumer's perception of the quality of the financial terms of the deal (Thaler, 1983). A similar process may happen during consumer journeys – even if the distance to store A is shorter than to store B, the consumer may still choose store B. It was proved that consumers recalculate, and perform mental accounting, which is a type of decision-framing that happens not only in decisions which involve money: 'A general conclusion […] is that decisions are not necessarily "irrational" if they fail to coincide with mental accounting-based expectations. Rather, individuals process information in a relatively consistent fashion' (Henderson and Peterson, 1992). Mental accounting includes spatial decisions during consumer journeys – where to shop, how to travel there, and what travel modes to choose. Consumer travelling also fits in with the topic of sustainable transportation and potential to use different modes of travel between different consumption spots. Therefore, another factor impacting their spatial behaviour is urban infrastructure and urban movement potential.

Information and affordance when shopping

Store location is arguably among the most crucial of factors in affecting consumption location choice, and can lead to equidistant trip chains and clustered destinations while shopping (Brooks *et al.*, 2004). During equidistant trip chains consumers minimise the distance they travel and, thus, the subjective costs in travel distance, similarly to the case in reference-dependent theory where they minimise psychological loss and maximise the perceived savings in travel distance as they refer to the neutral reference point (as in reference-dependent and transaction utility theories) (ibid.). In the case of total trip-chain length they refer to the sum of distance to make when visiting each destination via multiple single-stop trips – therefore they will choose destinations that are more clustered even if it takes more time to reach the cluster rather than closer but less-clustered destinations (ibid.). Furthermore, consumers (in an example from the USA), usually process and recall trip time knowledge rather than trip distance knowledge – they find it more accessible and they search for time rather than distance information, relying on that source of information, even when making map-based judgements (Kang *et al.*, 2003). This is an important factor impacting consumer journeys, crucial in analysing movement potential. Consumers perceive their journeys within urban space in terms of time, not distance.

Some of the examples of the already performed and analysed journeys, including participation in patterns of movement, highlighted different rhythms and patterns of mobilities. Maps are particularly supportive in order to investigate mobilities, including consumer mobilities, even if they only grasp some projection (de Certeau, 1988:97). It is easy to follow subjects, people and even ideas – thanks to using GPS software, via geotagged social media. Using geolocation and video ethnography in a research study enabled the investigation of negotiation during journeys of pairs (Voilmy *et al.*, 2008). Another method that involved map application was exploring side-by-side rearrangements in leader-follower setups (Laurier *et al.*, 2016). Both studies show how using geolocation-related technology may enrich mobility research from the technical aspect.

However, research proves that even if respondents had access to map information, they still relied on memory-based time information rather than reading distance from the map and that they may have better time knowledge because they differentially search for time rather than distance information (Kang *et al.*, 2003). How does this apply to the growing interest in mapping applications that are aimed to help consumers within consumption locations? Do consumers really not refer to maps? We tried to answer these questions during the workshop.

Space Syntax: core principles

A model of potential urban movement

In order to model the impact of movement on information-gathering, we employed a network-mapping method based on the Space Syntax approach. This theory supposes that urban network patterning is based on a self-similar, syntactical set of spatial forms (Hillier and Hanson, 1984; Hillier, 2007). The method also includes proxies for modelling urban way-finding based on affordances of sight-lines and turning-angles (Hillier and Iida, 2005). In this section, we outline some general aspects of Space Syntax methodology.

The methods of Space Syntax are based on the field's core technology, the Depthmap software application.[1] The application recalculates an axial map of the road network based on two network centrality measures of closeness and betweenness, which are termed in the field Integration and Choice, respectively. Integration is the measurement of origin-to-destination distances, representing the likelihood that any structures underpin movements from/to a location in the network. Choice is the measurement of flows along those certain structures, representing the likelihood that they underpin movements through the network. It is perhaps easier to remember that Integration represents affordances for *to*-movements, and Choice represents affordances for *through*-movements.

Urban movements and social meanings

Cities can be thought of as highly complex artefacts resulting from their inhabitants' functional configurations of network forms. As such they are exceptionally intricate and wide-ranging products of their inhabitants' connective activities within urban spaces. Their forms are based on street layouts, and the inter-relationships of specific street and road structures. Cities have a global form, involving the structural inter-connections of every street and junction on the entire network. They also have local forms, which bear similar street and junction patterns to those of the global level, albeit involving far fewer structures. The functions that result from these urban forms relate to patterns of movement throughout the urban network. Movement is the basic function of the city. Its inhabitants must move from home to work, from places of repose to places of activity, from places of consumption to places of production. The forms of the urban network, whether local or global, serve to underpin a range of urban movements. A combination of forms involved in a journey brings about a variegated functionality, possibly also including a diverse set of transport options – for example, bus and foot, or car and train, or bike and foot.

Space Syntax may serve as a background model, useful to analyse the potential movement of consumers. Different scales of urban network enable the comparison of consumer mobilities of pedestrians, public transport users and drivers. Hence, a centrality may bear a certain characteristic form at a local level (comprising the intersections of various streets); however, it may additionally bear various kinds of movement with respect to the different network scales at which it functions. Hence, observing that same 'local' centrality at a city-wide scale may reveal how regional flows also pass along its edges. In real terms, this means that a local centrality may carry local movements as well as regional movements – for example, short journeys from domicile to market as well as rush-hour or commercial traffic passing through the centrality en route to an economic centre elsewhere in the city. Here we can observe multiple strands of urban movements co-flowing along single conduits, very often coming into friction or collision. For this reason, it is essential to model any specific urban network structure at different scales.

Core methods in Space Syntax

How does Space Syntax work?

The observer of an urban configuration begins with a drawing of the urban network based on patterns comprising the least number of, and straightest, lines. The guiding principle for drawing this preliminary 'axial map' is that the urban inhabitant achieves way-finding through lines of sight along streets and roads. This also relates to an informational approach to way-finding based on the movement economy model of the 'path of least effort': pathways are created where a minimal number of turns need to be made to get from origin to destination. Of course, there are reasons not to configure a journey based on paths of least effort, not least where additional information needs to be gathered from the environment, which we find commonly in foraging models. For this reason, the axial maps require additional dynamics processing.

Mapping urban configurations

Depthmap also allows the analyst to calculate integration and choice at different network scales, which are each set to metric radius. Urban modellers seek proxies for movements based on the pedestrian scale of walkability, which by standard is 400 m (although this may vary based on ability, age, health, and so on). A scale of non-motorised transport (e.g. by bicycle) may be 1500 m, while motorised transport may be set at a scale of 2000 m and above.

Once the network centralities have been calculated, the road segments are colour-coded from warm to cool colours representing the relative range of high- to low-distance values. We may see a high-value integration structure (representing the high likelihood of its being an origin or destination) as coloured red, and a low-value integration structure as coloured blue. It is important to note that the colour-coded values are also relative to the scale of analysis. For example, an urban network structure such as a motorway may underpin high movement at the global scale, but low movement at a local scale.

Depthmap can also be used to recalculate the urban network as a segment map. Segments are formed along straight lines, where a line intersects with another at or close to the perpendicular. In other words, where a street intersects another street at right angles, or thereabouts, that street is divided into segments along the intersections. Segment maps are generated in Depthmap through angular segment analysis based on metric distances. This method provides a model of route-making through the urban network based intuitively on the ease by which the way-finder makes use of shallow angles and short paths to get from origin to destination. It is perhaps worth reflecting on our everyday methods for way-finding, as we are likely to avoid sharp turnings or long pathways when shallow turnings and short pathways are available.

By extension, syntactical segment analysis views the urban network as a combinatorial configuration. This allows us to consider how people make use of different sets of segments along their journey from origin to destination, sometimes making use of shallow angles in combination with short paths, and sometimes taking the lowest number of turns along longer paths. Segment analysis provides a powerful tool for evaluating the spatial accessibility of locations within the urban network.

Notes on the North Lancashire Depthmap models

We generated models of Lancaster (where the workshop took place) and the surrounding north Lancashire and south Cumbria region at four scales: 500 m, 2000 m, 5000 m and the global (entire network) scale. Figure 4.1 shows one example of these models. We looked at the network model at each scale in turn, and attempted to show how pathways at different scales overlay each other, so that different functions of the network converge along the same linear structures. We focused only on patterns based on betweenness centralities, using the Space Syntax 'choice' measurement. You will recall that betweenness or 'choice' represents the rate of potential movement *through* the network structures. We took a cursory overview of the model, and attempted to observe what each scale reveals about patterns of movement within the urban network.

Consumer mobilities and Space Syntax 67

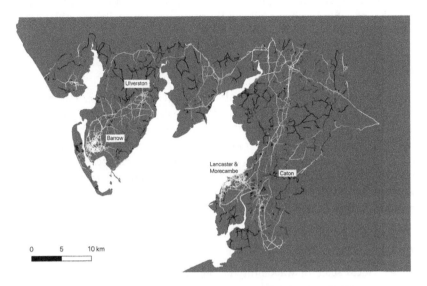

Figure 4.1 Example Space Syntax map of sampled area rendered in greyscale for normalised integration values at 5 km radial scale. Road segments have been rendered in light-to-dark gradation to represent high-to-low integration values respectively. The area sampled represents the extent of consumer journeys described by the workshop participants.

Global scale

The Depthmap model at the global scale reveals the structural convergences of the network as a whole, reflecting where regional traffic is most likely to flow. The computational process has revealed pathways formed by high-movement A-roads and motorways that connect the urban centres of Lancaster, Morecambe and Barrow. Within Lancaster and Morecambe it shows how the major routes underpin moderate movement in relation to the region as a whole. In effect, this is a scale of motorised transport, of private cars or logistics vehicles flowing between regional urban centres.

In terms of consumer mobilities this global scale of infrastructure mainly serves for consumer infrastructure, e.g. consumer goods supply to stores and merchandisers but also as a means of delivery of online shopping.

5000 m scale

Looking at the network model at the scale of 5 km, we see how B-roads underpin movement at the scale of shorter car journeys, and bus or cycling journeys, and at the scale of the typical daily commute, weekend consumer journeys or school drop-off. High-movement structures are concentrated within the urban centres of Lancaster, Morecambe, Barrow and Ulverston. Motorways come to share prominence with minor roads, reflecting their lesser likelihood of conveying the traffic of everyday life. High-movement conveyances are also seen within Morecambe, possibly serving to disrupt the movements of daily life at the urban scale of walkability.

2000 m scale

The model at a radius of 2 km reveals structural conveyances of movement within the urban centres, including Lancaster's outlying villages of Halton and Caton. Within Lancaster, the high through-movement centralities connect to medium-movement structures as traffic is diverted into the city's economic centre. Everyday movement within Lancaster and Morecambe seems to converge with higher-scale movements, especially as they meet at the natural boundary of the coastline. This possibly intensifies segmentation within the local urban network, which may affect flows between local community spaces.

500 m scale

At the very local scale of walkability among clusters of streets, we find prominent conveyances of movement within Morecambe close to the coastline, as well as leading towards Heysham, and within Lancaster close to the market square and one-way system, and along the A6. We can also compare the two Lune bridges, where the structure conveying traffic out of Lancaster has greater through-movement than that conveying traffic into Lancaster. This relationship is more-or-less reversed at the 5 km scale. This possibly suggests that one bridge bears greater 'walkability' or 'velomobility' into the local network than does the other. A high through-movement structure also poses a hard boundary to Lancaster, around the Ridge area. This possibly relates to a pattern of enclosed movements within, but not beyond, that local area. Another prominent pattern of enclosed movements is found within Morecambe's grid-pattern streets, recalling also how regional traffic forms high-movement structures within this grid. This possibly reflects overall medium pedestrian movements within this grid, which is possibly bounded by the flow of urban traffic. Hence, higher pedestrian through-movement structures may also form segmented boundaries to very local street networks.

Overall, the Space Syntax analysis of the network structure and potential movement helps to analyse shops locations (consumer infrastructure), and to visualise consumer mobilities. It is particularly straightforward when the network is determined by natural resources, such as coastline or rivers, as in this example. As we take a closer look at Lancaster's shop distribution, the majority of large stores can be seen to be located on one side of the river. One may say it is a result of the population density, yet mobility, especially consumer mobility, shows it does not need to be necessarily this way anymore. Due to generating a Depthmap model we can see what kind of movement may be potentially generated at different scales, and thus see what the potential consumer mobilities are.

Mapping workshop method overview

We asked workshop participants to visualise their consumer journeys on the maps provided. By collating their perspectives – an additional 'layer' on a map of urban potential movement structure – we could arrive at a better understanding of consumer mobilities and materialities.

Participants used printed-out maps of Lancaster and Lancashire in A3 format with a scale of 1:10,000 from Digimap (Digimap, 2016). The scale enabled the administrative boundaries of Lancaster to be rendered visible, and the Street View allowed the recognition of streets and paths even without all the names of the streets on the map being present. A few participants decided to sketch their consumption map on blank paper. The visual outputs of their mobile consumption were enriched with participants' comments, which enabled in-depth analysis (Figure 4.2).

Participants completed a short questionnaire, which measured their general attitude towards shopping, using a marketing seven-item scale. Respondents were then asked to think of their most typical consumer journeys. As a reference they were given three general types of journeys (Bednarowska, 2018a):

1. a spontaneous consumer journey – usually random routes and random stores, low degree of predictability, e.g. due to an urgent need
2. a regular consumer habitual journey – usually involves the same, well-known stores, the same route and even timing, a high degree of predictability, e.g. grocery shopping every week
3. a planned special-occasion-driven consumer journey. It includes a medium degree of predictability, e.g. looking for a gift, home furnishing or shopping for gifts.

A habitual journey is related to Lefebvre's rhythm analysis, who also refers to rituals (Lefebvre *et al.*, 1996). For many consumers, shopping may be called a ritual as it is a matter of repeated practice. Participants marked every type of journey with a different colour and a legend, marking starting-point, end-point and stopovers. When summarising their consumer journeys, they were asked about the goal of the journey/type of shopping, number of stopovers, types of shopping venues (stopovers), products they bought and modes of transport. Respondents were given a list of shopping categories.

Mapping consumer journeys showed that their consumer mobilities are embedded in everyday life practices and often constitute an element of planning ahead, among running errands. The novelty of our approach lies in combining respondents' routes, chosen stores and destination with mode of travel using the new mobilities paradigm (Sheller and Urry, 2006) in conjunction with materialities, i.e. urban movement potential in relation to a given urban space. Furthermore, instead of using stimulus-based map contexts as Brooks did (Brooks *et al.*, 2004), we used actual maps, as we believe it makes activity more realistic and closer to everyday experience.

Figure 4.2 Participants working on their consumer maps at the workshops. Lancaster, UK, April 2016.

Source: Photograph taken by Zofia Bednarowska.

Patterns of consumer mobilities – participant mapping results

The analysis of workshops outcomes verified the hypothetical types of consumer journeys that were assumed: spontaneous consumer journeys, routine journeys and planned special-occasion-driven consumer journeys. First, the participants showed a high level of discernment in relation to movement when shopping and using space to achieve their goal. It is possible that it was only the workshops that enabled some of the participants to fully appreciate how many types of consumer journeys they make, what kind of transport they use, and the difference in terms of their mobility capital (motility). Motility is understood as the ability to be mobile in social and geographical understanding of movement, and the notion links spatial and social mobility (Kaufmann *et al.*, 2004:750). Secondly, the participants were able to describe their consumer journeys in terms of different urban movement scales. They presented details of how their journeys combined regional, 'town', and local movement structures along their journeys.

The workshops helped to identify 'on the way' consumer journeys (suggested by professor Monika Büscher, who was in attendance) when the main goal of the journey is not consumption itself, but rather, when travelling for business or personal reasons (e.g. dropping children off at school, running errands), a consumer decides to take every effort to take advantage of the travelling time and nearby shopping infrastructure and purchase necessary products. Consumer journeys can occur when commuting, which is a part of everyday-life mobilities, or during mobile working, e.g. when a freelancer changes places of work and in the meantime is consuming. It is reminiscent of the analysis of the practices of nomads and the care of place in a computer-supported cooperative work environment (Liegl, 2014).

The participants had a moderately positive attitude towards shopping in general, moving within Lancaster, Lancashire, or Manchester. Regardless of their permanent place of residence, or the distance from the town centre, they frequently visited the same centrally located shopping places, using well-known shopping trajectories. This confirms the centrality of the town centre as being the main place to shop. The significance of central locations in shopping has been recognised many times in locational research (Brown, 1992). Centrality plays a crucial role in consumer habits in such mid-sized towns as Lancaster.

Regular, habitual journeys were mentioned by all participants, usually for the purpose of buying groceries. They involved all types of transport and at least one stopover. Planned special-occasion-type journeys were usually associated with recreation or buying products on the everyday shopping list, such as flowers or household items. They more often than not involved walking, in comparison to other types of travel. Spontaneous shopping journeys took place for different reasons and with different products bought, and involved the smallest number of stopovers. Other types of journeys were usually associated with leisure, often not only concerning shopping but consuming in general – theatre- or cinema-visits, eating out, or any kind of social event, and often included walking.

General knowledge of and discernment in the use of central streets, alleys and shops aids in the process of navigation and presumably prompts potential shoppers to make their purchases there, even if other stores are available.

Maps supported the analysis of consumer mobilities, being reflected in everyday consumer practices in relation to information (Figure 4.3). Exactly the same tools were given to all workshop participants, and it was interesting to analyse and discern patterns of consumer mobilities:

1 Cluster type. A scattered consumer space that – when looked at more closely – shows a cluster of places strongly related to the goal of the journey. For example, one of them involved taking care of a child, including locations close to each other related to child-feeding, walks with a child, etc. Other clusters were associated with sports activities, which enabled 'on the way' journeys.
2 A town centre as a large intersection between the lines of route of several different journeys that cross exactly in the town centre: this constitutes a connection between different journeys – a beginning of some and a termination point of others.
3 'Drive through': a town centre which is on the way from home to work or school.
4 The main road of the town or district being the central point, around which all the journeys take place. It is reminiscent of the significance of shopping streets which used to be the most visited places for shopping.

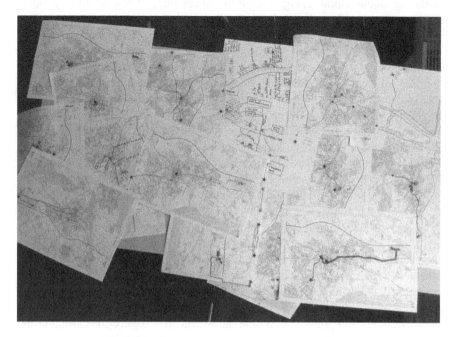

Figure 4.3 Some of the participants' maps showing their consumer journeys in Lancashire. They used colours to mark different types of journeys as well as dots or stars for marking stops or destinations. Lancaster, UK, April 2016.

Source: Photograph taken by Zofia Bednarowska.

5   Shopping centre-centred – shopping is around the stores at the shopping centre and the buildings themselves. It includes small, independent stores around the mall. Their closure, together with pedestrianised streets, enables walking for every type of journey.
6   A gate. The town centre of Lancaster serves as a 'gate': a different type and feel of town is experienced here after entering, where the heaviest shopping activity of different consumer journeys is observed.
7   A loop. The town centre and work place (mostly campus) serve as a loop – all the journeys take place in between them, which reflects everyday life mobilities.
8   'On the way'. The town centre is characterised by the highest density of consumer journeys, venues and stopovers, but it also works as a big 'on the way' between work and home. Here the town centre is a key area of any kind of shopping journey.

Comments made regarding the maps provided some good narratives, including a few detailed descriptions of the consumer journeys. They revealed the great potential of mobility inherent therein – mobility within a store and within shopping centres but also between different types of venues or stopovers.

Discussion

This chapter presents a prototype of the method that permits the research of consumer mobilities and their material dimension in the form of urban network infrastructure. By combining urban network and socio-spatial analysis, we investigated material infrastructure and everyday-life mobilities. We developed a model for affordances for information-gathering in the built environment based on Space Syntax road-network mapping. Space Syntax provides a theory and method for observing normalised affordances for movement across spatial structures such as road network segments, at various scales of metric distance, which we describe in great detail. We explore the possibility that bringing together the sociology of consumer journeys with design research based on Space Syntax offers a novel methodology for observing mobile affordances for informal gathering.

We have outlined key themes in urban movement modelling, and surveyed core theories and methods of Space Syntax. In conclusion, by modelling 'mobile utopias' we could possibly test whether these main points are relevant or useful to the modelling process.

Movement is a means of both consumption and production, and the struggle for control of movement systems is a focus of historical observation. Historical observation is a kind of participation, which depends on movement. 'Utopian' urban modelling requires semantically rich taxonomies of scale, from which we can recombine contrasting utopian scenarios. Urban scales are usually rendered as metric or functional distances, but we can also configure these semantically based on modulations of movements and their affordances for observation.

The Depthmap model provided a compelling example of various through-movement structures, relating to local and regional urban scales. When using this model to understand the urban network, it is important to look at specific configurations through their various scales, which can vary from a few metres to hundreds of kilometres. Network scales have significance for social-spatial connectivities that embed exchanges of information. Hence, spatial structures bear different connective functionalities relative to their various scales; and these functionalities underpin contrasting modularities in terms of informational flow, which in turn modulate affordances for perception. For this reason, we can, for example, think of the 500 m radius as a 'walkability scale', and 5000 m as a 'vehicular traversability scale'; each scale has implications for people's information-gathering and for their knowledge of the built environment.

Mapping consumer journeys shows that spatial behaviour of consumers is embedded in everyday practices, in particular everyday-life mobilities. A journey depends on the information regarding and awareness of the shopping venues, former experience, and mobility potential. All the stops in frequent journeys seem to be very considered and planned.

The Depthmap model of global scale visualised potential movement for consumer infrastructure, of 5000 m scale that for shorter car-based consumer journeys, and of 500 m that for walkable shopping. The models showed the potential of consumer mobilities, while the maps created by participants revealed the patterns of consumer mobilities that happen on different scales.

Working on maps and Depthmap, we configured a notion of urban scales based on movement, and how these relate to affordances for consumer behaviours (searching, discovering, etc.). We argue that 'affordances' for consumer journeys are generative within urban environments as movement infrastructure domains. Our approach is based on the fact that we combine consumers' routes and chosen stores with travelling mode using the new mobilities paradigm (Sheller and Urry, 2006) in association with the urban movement potential of a given urban space.

The mode of our method worked well. It proved participants' engagement, and provided us with insights on consumer mobilities, and how movement is related to information in consumer journeys. Analysing the results in terms of the method prototype shows that in order to explore better consumer journeys themselves, one needs to add some more in-depth methods, such as IDIs (in-depth interviews) or FGIs (focus-group interviews).

The types of the journeys that were verified via the participants' maps, together with Space Syntax, were able to be further investigated, including a higher usage of rhythm analysis. Knowledge of such types can greatly contribute to the further understanding of consumer mobilities. Our method of using the participant maps, together with Space Syntax, can also make a significant contribution to research on consumer mobilities. They might supplement two key mobile methods that could be applied in this case: observing the movement of objects, and 'participating' in patterns of movement (Buscher *et al.*, 2011:8). Furthermore, our approach helps to understand how everyday-life mobilities are produced (by using participants' maps) and recognises the critical role of materialities of consumer mobilities (by applying the Space Syntax method).

Note

1 https://varoudis.github.io/depthmapX/.

References

Adey, P. (2006) 'If mobility is everything then it is nothing: towards a relational politics of (im)mobilities', *Mobilities*, 1(1), pp. 75–94. doi: 10.1080/17450100500489080.

Adey, P. (2014) *The Routledge Handbook of Mobilities*. Abingdon: Routledge.

Antonides, G. and van Raaij, F. (2003) *Consumer Behaviour [Zachowanie konsumenta]*. Warszawa.

Bednarowska, Z. (2016) 'Consumer mobilities', in *Social Science Intellectual/Party Summer Conference*. Lancaster: Lancaster University.

Bednarowska, Z. (2018a) *Spatiality and mobility as a framework for understanding the Consumption Space Paradox. Doctoral thesis.* Jagiellonian University.

Bednarowska, Z. (2018b) 'The consumption space paradox: over–retailed areas next to dead malls', *Acta Universitatis Lodziensis. Folia Oeconomica*, 5(338), pp. 21–40. doi: 10.18778/0208-6018.338.02.

Brooks, C. M., Kaufmann, P. J. and Lichtenstein, D. R. (2004) 'Travel configuration on consumer trip-chained store choice', *Journal of Consumer Research*, 31(September), pp. 241–248. doi: 10.1086/422104.

Brown, S. (1992) *Retail Location: A micro-scale perspective*. Aldershot, Brookfield: Avebury.

Buscher, M., Urry, J. and Witchger, K. (2011) *Mobile Methods*. Abingdon, Oxon; New York, NY: Routledge.

Clark, W. A. V. (1968) 'Consumer travel patterns and the concept of range', 58(2), pp. 386–396.

Clifton, K. et al. (2016) 'Consumer behavior and travel mode: an exploration of restaurant, drinking establishment, and convenience store patrons', *International Journal of Sustainable Transportation*, 10(3), pp. 260–270. doi: 10.1080/15568318.2014.897404.

de Certeau, M. (1988) *The Practice of Everyday Life*. Berkeley, CA; London: University of Carolina Press.

Dellaert, B. G. C. et al. (1998) 'Investigating consumers' tendency to combine multiple shopping purposes and destinations', *Journal of Marketing Research*, 35(2), pp. 177–188.

Digimap (2016) *The Ordnance Survey Collection*. Available at: https://digimap.edina.ac.uk/ (Accessed: 31 March 2016).

Henderson, P. W. and Peterson, R. A. (1992) 'Mental accounting and categorization', *Elsevier Organizational Behavior and Human Decision Processes*, 51(1), pp. 92–117.

Hillier, B. (2007) *Space is the machine. A configurational theory of architecture, Space Syntax*. Available at: discovery.ucl.ac.uk/3881/1/SITM.pdf.

Hillier, B. (2016) 'What are cities for? And how does this relate to their spatial form?', *Journal of Space Syntax*, 6(2), pp. 198–212.

Hillier, B. and Hanson, J. (1984) *The Social Logic of Space*. Cambridge: Cambridge University Press.

Hillier, B. and Iida, S. (2005) 'Network and psychological effects in urban movement', in *Proceedings of Spatial Information Theory: International Conference*. Ellicottsville, NY: COSIT 2005, pp. 475–490.

Jensen, O. B. (2016) 'Of "other" materialities: why (mobilities) design is central to the future of mobilities research', *Mobilities*, 11(4), pp. 587–597. doi: 10.1080/17450101.2016.1211826.

Kang, Y.-S., Herr, P. M. and Page, C. M. (2003) 'Time and distance : asymmetries in consumer trip knowledge and judgments', *Journal of Consumer Research*, 30(3), pp. 420–429. doi: 10.1086/378618.

Kaufmann, V., Joye, D. and Bergman, M. M. (2004) 'Motility: mobility as capital', *International Journal of Urban and Regional Research*, 28(4), pp. 745–756.

Laurier, E., Brown, B. and McGregor, M. (2016) 'Mediated pedestrian mobility: walking and the map app', *Mobilities*, 0101(March), pp. 1–18. doi: 10.1080/17450101.2015.1099900.

Lefebvre, H., Kofman, E. and Lebas, E. (1996) *Writings on Cities*. Cambridge, MA: Blackwell.

Liegl, M. (2014) 'Nomadicity and the care of place – On the aesthetic and affective organization of space in freelance creative work', *Computer Supported Cooperative Work*, 23(2), pp. 163–183. doi: 10.1007/s10606-014-9198-x.

Lurie, N. (2004) 'Decision making in information rich environments: the role of information structure', *Journal of Consumer Research*, 30(4), pp. 473–486.

Oldenburg, R. (1999) *The Great Good Place: Cafés, Coffee Shops, Bookstores, Bars, Hair Salons, and Other Hangouts at the Heart of a Community*. New York, [Berkeley, CA]: Marlowe: Distributed by Group West.

Sheller, M. and Urry, J. (2006) 'The new mobilities paradigm', *Environment and Planning – Part A*. PION LTD, 38(2), pp. 207–226.

Solomon, M. *et al.* (2006) *Consumer Behaviour: A European perspective* (3rd ed.),. Harlow, UK; New York: Financial Times/Prentice Hall. doi: 10.1007/s11096-005-3797-z.

Thaler, R. (1983) 'Transaction utility theory', *Advances in Consumer Research*, 10(1), pp. 229–232.

Urry, J. (2007) *Mobilities*. Cambridge: Polity Press.

Voilmy, D., Smoreda, Z. and Ziemlicki, C. (2008) 'Geolocation and video ethnography: capturing mobile internet used by a commuter', *Mobilities*, 3(2), pp. 201–222. doi: 10.1080/17450100802095304.

5 "It's going to be very slippery"
Snow, space and mobility while learning cross-country skiing

Paul McIlvenny

Introduction

This chapter investigates the ways in which a child learns to sense and move through a transient environment while recreational cross-country skiing within the context of familial social interaction. A mobile video ethnography was undertaken of family skiing sessions while on a seasonal holiday, in which a parent instructs and guides a novice child on how to ski. Using an interactional mobility analytical approach, the chapter examines how snow – a complex, dynamic materiality that can afford spatial movement on its surface – is sensed, felt and made salient in spatio-interactional practices.

In order to analyse the skiers' feeling for snow in this case study, it is important to understand how we sense and experience space and mobility. Spinney (2006) explores the idea that our movements in and through a place define our engagement with it and help to constitute it as a place. In particular, he focuses on the embodied rhythms and kinaesthetic sensations that accompany the movement of cycling. In their study, van Duppen and Spierings (2013) ride along with urban commuter cyclists to discover their everyday, embodied experiences that constitute their diverse personal sensescapes, particularly as manifested in their passage through the city on complete journeys between home and work. Using in-depth interviews with, and photo diaries kept by, ordinary people in inner London, Middleton (2010) explores the sensory, sensual and embodied experiences manifested in urban walking. Others who have examined how we sense space socially and culturally include Hockey (2006), Turner and Turner (2006), Pink (2007), Imai (2008), Olwig (2008), Saerberg (2010), Dickinson and Aiello (2016), and Ness (2016).

How we sense space and matter has also been studied by researchers interested in the discursive and interactional practices and ethnomethods in which they come to have meaning and salience. For example, Goodwin (1999) has analysed scientists at work to uncover how archaeologists perceive and categorise soil matter within the social, cultural and spatial practices at an archaeological dig. Büscher (2006) has followed landscape architects as they use powerful IT design tools to visualise the land. And Markus and Cameron (2002) have combined their respective research perspectives on architecture and on language/discourse to understand how architects visualise and textualise space and buildings. These studies demonstrate the insights that discursive and interactional analyses of empirical materials can bring to our understanding of the mundane practices of scientists and professionals in which space and matter become meaningful.

However, there are not many studies as yet of how H_2O in its liquid or solid state is sensed and felt in mundane everyday mobility practices. Particular types of snow and ice are the building blocks of transient natural and human-made structures, such as glaciers, igloos and ski tracks. Fallen snow affords movement along its fragile surface. Forsyth et al. (2013) make the case that human geographers need to re-examine the notion of surface. They contend that surfaces matter, for example in their function as limits of matter and as spaces for material exchange. Drawing on Deleuze, Day (2005, p. 149) argues that we need "to characterize the nature of bodies – structures and identities – in terms of powers, expressions, and the material surfaces that allow those powers to express themselves as personal and collective bodies". He uses the example of rain falling on surfaces to highlight the different dispositional and affective powers manifested by the surface of macadam or sand, for example. Surfaces have texture, durability and extension due to repetition and foldability. For Day, the term 'infrastructure' must be thought of in terms of expressive events through which both bodies and notions of space are arrived at. Moreover, surfaces provide material infrastructures for mobility, but they are not static or causal (Latham and Wood, 2015). Waitt et al. (2008) have studied the experiential knowledge displayed by a heterogeneous group of people who regularly walk through a maze of criss-crossing paths in a suburban Australian reserve. They argue that routine walking is best conceptualised as a territory-making process. Within the social context and bodily experiences, walking offers possibilities of making points of connection with 'nature'.

Despite sharpened attention to phenomena such as surface, trails and the sensing of the landscape, studies of the mundane geography of snow from a social and cultural perspective are scant. Moving through snow often leaves an inference-rich visible trace. Walking and skiing in newly fallen snow means that tracks and trails emerge, though they are transient, that can shape future actions and practices. In their study of the traditional knowledge and local perceptions of the environment in Northern Finland, Ingold and Kurttilla (2000) note their informants' childhood memories of skating on the ice in winter and of being able to ride a bicycle on the hard snow-crust in spring, and yet how new technologies, such as snow scooters, require a different appreciation of the depth and consistency of snow than required for skiing. This chapter reports on a study of how it is, in the first place, that one comes to appreciate snow – its depth, consistency, surface and affordances – in order to ski recreationally.

Skiing as a sociocultural spatial practice

Nordic or cross-country skiing is a common and popular recreational and sports pursuit wherever there is adequate snow cover in the world. To become a cross-country skier one needs a pair of cambered skis with bindings, a pair of ski poles, and a pair of ski boots which can attach at the toe to a binding on each ski. As a technology, skis are designed to take the weight of the skier and afford gliding over the surface of prepared snow. Some skis have a grooved pattern embossed onto the centre zone to enable the skier to press down by a transfer of weight and to grip the snow; however, most skis require a temporary wax appropriate for the snow conditions to be applied to the central 'kick zone' in order to facilitate the leg movement required to propel the ski over the surface of the snow. Ski tracks – equidistant embedded grooves in the snow – are very useful for the cross-country skier. Without them, one must exert more effort to step slowly through thick snow or hold a straight line over compressed snow and ice.

Most research on skiing focuses on the sports science perspective – for example, research on biometrics and the technical side of the sport – or sociocultural studies of the cultural capital and symbolism of skiing, as well as quantitative studies of the incidence of such leisure pursuits across a population. Studies of similar leisure and sport pursuits – for example on snow, ice or water – are common, and include snowboarding, (wind)surfing, ice climbing and ice skating (Stranger, 1999; Edensor and Richards, 2007; Karlsson, 2011; Barratt, 2012). Only a few studies, however, attend to the actual practices of practitioners as they engage skilfully with water and interact with other practitioners or learners (Dant and Wheaton, 2007; Anderson, 2012; Geenen, 2013a, 2013b).

Interactional mobility analysis

Until recently, the automobile has been the primary mode of transport in many studies concerned with social interaction and members' methods of sense-making while mobile (Watson, 1999; Laurier *et al.*, 2008; Noy, 2009; Haddington *et al.*, 2012). Many of the methods developed to study the car as affording a social and interactional space can be used to investigate other modes of transport or leisure mobility, such as walking (Broth and Lundström, 2013), cycling (McIlvenny, 2014, 2015) or skiing. My approach in this chapter is to treat skimobility as a social and interactional, embodied practice.

There are several key elements of a multimodal interactional approach to mobility. First, there is a focus on situated mobile practices. It can be argued that by focusing on practices, rather than categorising different types of mobilities, it becomes possible to view individuals not as mere mobile subjects, but as actors who are engaged in shaping and (re)producing mobilities and mobile formations-in-action. Second, one can study mobile ethnomethods (Watson, 1999; Ryave and Schenkein, 1974; Hester and Francis, 2003; Allen Collinson, 2006) – that is, the emic methods that people use to assemble and account for the sensefulness of their mobile formations, practices and actions. Third, there is the power of an inductive methodology to examine sequences of mobile action (for recent work see McIlvenny *et al.*, 2009; Haddington *et al.*, 2012; Haddington *et al.*, 2013; McIlvenny, 2013). Such an approach is therefore an antidote to 'just so' accounts of micro-mobility practices that assume mobility is a social and cultural practice but without ever elaborating or investigating just how.

Data collection

The data collected for this study includes video recordings made during a seasonal winter holiday in the north of Finland. The author and his eight-year-old daughter (with other family members and relatives present in some recordings) are the principal participants in the mobile video 'active participant' ethnography. The spoken language used in the data is predominantly English, though on occasion Finnish is spoken.

The main site of the study is a municipal public playground near a relative's house on the outskirts of a small town in north central Finland. The child and parent practised at this site on five separate days over a period of seven days (two intermediary days were cancelled because of miserable skiing weather), which are named Days 1 to 5 in this chapter. One of the goals of practising at the playground was to enable the family at some point to go to a local recreational cross-country skiing area with groomed tracks on the outskirts of the town. When they reach the playground covered in snow (see Figure 5.1), some parts of the snowscape had already been adulterated. The ground is sloped gently down from the top of the map to the bottom. On Day 1 a temporary track was made in a loop.

Two body-mounted 'sports' video cameras were used to record the participants in a reasonably unobtrusive way that did not hinder their ability to ski. The use of head- and body-mounted video cameras has been tried and recommended for a variety of analytical reasons (Brown *et al.*, 2008; Brown and Spinney, 2010; Spinney, 2011; Laurier, 2013; McIlvenny, 2014, 2015). For most of the recordings, one camera is mounted on the adult's or child's head, and the other is mounted on a chest harness that the adult is wearing. This configuration did not impede the arms or the legs, and despite reproducing two similar scenes most of the time, the headcam indicates changes of attention on the part of the wearer (it cannot be assumed to give a subjective, point-of-view perspective), and most of the time it captured aspects of the scene that the other camera missed.

The video recordings were transcribed in order to further the investigation using ethnomethodological conversation analysis as a methodology (Hester and Francis, 2004; Have, 2007; McIlvenny *et al.*, 2009; Haddington *et al.*, 2013). The analysis focuses on embodied interaction and the sequential organisation of the participants' actions. In the transcripts, the child is referred to as Anabel, and the parent, Peter. Transcript conventions are given in the appendix and are described more fully in Jefferson (2004). A comic transcript is also used to present the data in a novel form that is more readable for short excerpts (Laurier, 2014).

Analysis

Snow can provide a surface for embodied movement – for example, for skiing – and with it one can build a temporary spatial infrastructure for mobility in the

Learning cross-country skiing – mobility aspects 81

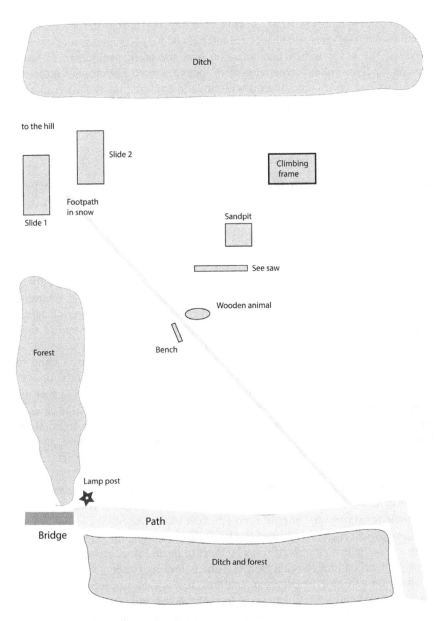

Figure 5.1 Virgin site on Day 1.

wild, for instance by constructing tracks. Much as for Micronesian navigators in small sailing craft on the high seas (Hutchins, 1994), the playground site was *wild* in that the senseful activity of skiing had to be constructed in an unpredictable space without the benefit of abstract representations, instruments and laboratories – it was the result of an embodied cultural and spatial practice (Hutchins, 2008, p. 2013). In the practice of skiing, surfaces, materialities, infrastructures, technologies and spaces are interleaved by participants to afford ski-mobility. The analysis will first focus on how the participants learn to sense snow as a polymorphous material surface for movement that changes moment-to-moment and day-to-day. Then it will move to explore how the material geography of snow is territorialised by the participants in the form of tracks that afford ski-ability.

Sensing snow as a polymorphous surface for movement

A landscape covered with fresh snow is not quite a *tabula rasa* – a two-dimensional blank slate – that scrubs clean the landscape to afford mobile action across its surface. The snow undulates with the geography of the natural and anthropogenic landscape it covers. Thus, particular routes and cadences of movement are possible that are to some extent visible to the trained eye, but that also need to be discovered in and through movement. In good conditions, snow is an almost frictionless surface for spatial movement. Yet, if it is too slippery or icy, then it is difficult to generate momentum or is painful if one falls. Learning to ski means learning to discriminate and feel the dynamic and ever-changing snow conditions and to adjust accordingly in order to generate movement, flow and rhythm to successfully traverse the surface.

There are some basic properties of snow that are important for a child to learn. In order to use the skis to grip, kick and glide (and more subtly, how to use the poles to gain purchase, pivot/push and release), it is crucial to feel the slipperiness or stickiness of the snow since this affects the ability of the skier to grip the snow (with a waxed or a waxless ski). Other qualities that are vital for ski-ability are the friction or drag of the snow that affects speed/glide, and the age and compression of the snow over time that can also affect the ice crystal structure.

When conditions are poor, the slippery condition of the snow becomes an abiding concern. On Day 1, the temporary tracks are made in relatively good conditions for skiing, and after finishing the first loop, Peter even comments that "the snow is just right". However, on Day 2 the conditions for skiing get worse, and this is noted in a number of ways by Peter as he and Anabel warily approach the playground on foot carrying their skis and poles (see Excerpt 5.1).

After rain and near-freezing temperatures, the surface has refrozen into ice. The parent and child tentatively walk from the house to the site, carrying their skis and poles. Thus, before they even start on the track proper, Peter and Anabel are orienting in different ways to the current snow conditions in anticipation of their skiing:

1   As they approach the site and it comes into view, Peter first notes the slippery conditions – "y'see there's still snow there it'll just be a bit more slippery today" (lines 10–12).

Learning cross-country skiing – mobility aspects 83

```
1   P:   and then we shall have to go over the bri:dge
2        (1.2)
3   P:   might be a bit icy: on the bri:dge
4        ((P slips))
5   A:   i think you should co:me on the sno:w
6        ((P moves off the path onto the snow))
7        (4.5)
8        ((P glances at A who looks at P))
9        (4.5)
10  P:   y'see there's still sno:w the:re
11       (1.0)
12  P:   it'll just be a bit more slippery: (.) toda:y.
13       (5.5)
14       ((P glances at A trailing behind))
15       (10.0)
16       ((P crosses the bridge carefully))
17  P:   okay, ((P turns to A behind, yet to cross the bridge))
18       the track's still the:re.
19  A:   is it slippery:?
20  P:   no it's not too: slippery the:re.
21  A:   pardon
22  P:   it's not too slippery on the bridge
23       but there's a bit of ice:
24       ((A comes over the bridge and arrives at the site))
25       ((P turns to look up the site))
26  P:   see there's=
27  A:   =there there is a tra:ck
28  P:   yeah (0.5) just abou:t
29       ((P puts A's skis down on the old track))
30  P:   it's going to be very slippery:
31       (1.5) ((P puts his own skis down next to the track))
32  P:   the ice: °on: the tra:ck°
33       (2.5) ((A steps out of ski binding))
34  P:   so let me- ((P bends down next to A))
35       (25.0) ((P fits A's left boot to binding))
36  A:   is it gonna be slippery:
37  P:   yeah (.) it'll be so- more slippery than yesterda:y.
38       ((P fits right boot into binding on first go))
39  P:   °there°
40       (6.0) ((A moves forward on the old track))
41  P:   you see, (.) can you feel it being slippy=
42       =it'll be fa:st coming dow:n.
43  A:   ↓huh: [↑ya:    ]
44  P:         [it'll be]
45       (1.0)
46  P:   well luckily we made a tra:ck
47       (1.5)
48  P:   'coz no:w we have a tra:ck.
49       ((P adjusts binding))
50       ((A steps forward on the old track)
```

Excerpt 5.1

2 As Anabel approaches the bridge that crosses a small drainage creek, she asks about the slipperiness – "is it slippery?" (line 19), to which Peter replies "no it's not too slippery there" [on the bridge] (line 20).

3 After Peter puts down Anabel's skis on the old track, he says "it's going to be very slippery" (line 30).

4   While Peter helps Anabel with fixing her boots to the bindings, Anabel asks "is it gonna be slippery" (line 36) again, to which Peter responds "yeah it'll be so – more slippery than yesterday" (line 37).
5   As they start on the track, Peter asks Anabel about the track condition in terms of a quality that one can feel, e.g. "you see can you feel it being slippy" (line 41).

First, Peter orients Anabel to the observable and inspectable features of the site as they approach it. This is done in the form of an observation and an assessment, both in relation to a gloss on what was experienced yesterday, e.g. "there's *still* snow" (line 10) and "a bit *more* slippery" (line 12) [my emphasis]. Second, Anabel requests a confirmation from Peter of his situated assessment of the snow conditions in the context of crossing a bridge (lines 19–23). Third, as they prepare for skiing by putting on their skis, Peter makes relevant again a reformulated (re)assessment of the conditions (lines 30–32), constituting this as an ongoing process of assessment and attentiveness to the conditions as they move through and over the snowscape. Fourth, as they complete the preparatory stage, with Peter fixing the last boot to the binding on Anabel's ski, Anabel asks again about the slippery conditions (line 36). Some of the questions and statements have been about the quality of slipperiness in relation to a future action (*is going to be* or *will be*) – namely, to ski. The assessment of this quality is repeatedly bound to the activity and in anticipation of it. Fifth, as they begin to traverse the old track, Peter asks Anabel to assess the feeling of the snow as a practical, embodied, tactile experience as a skier (line 41): it can be felt as well as known in advance by visual inspection. The caregiver frames the experience as a touch/response-feel (Norris, 2012), e.g. a property ("being slippy") of the snow that expresses itself (a response that is felt) when one pushes against it (a touch) with the skis. Over this excerpt, we can see that Peter and Anabel are collaboratively rendering the snowscape sense-able and readable, both to gain access to the site and to anticipate the activity of skiing.

Much time is spent on Day 2 with learning about and calibrating the new snow conditions. What we can hear on many occasions is that Peter (and Anabel) repeatedly orient to both:

1   the conditions now, which are dynamically changing (in contrast to the steady state in the past).
2   the latent track (e.g. the trace of the track from previous days), which is always skied for another-first-time.

Thus, the practical issue of the quality of the snow in relation to human movement is replayed by both Peter and Anabel in their preparation for skiing on the second day. Moreover, it is returned to repeatedly over the course of the five days, as Peter and Anabel render the amorphous snowscape and the ambivalent space of the playground into a knowable environment with teachable objects in which skiing can take place. For example, the parent invokes categories and qualities that are rendered visible or can be felt in the embodied practice of moving the ski over the surface of the snow.

Learning cross-country skiing – mobility aspects 85

On Day 4, the track is again in poor condition after a stormy, wet night. Peter is adjusting Anabel's ski bindings ready for the first loop. As Anabel sets off on the icy track, Peter, who is not yet on the track, asks "is it slippery" (see the comic transcript in Figure 5.2).

Anabel reports that it is not (at least not very) slippery, and then she initiates, in an experimental mode, her own practical 'procedure' to 'test' the snow and thus

Figure 5.2 Testing the snow's slipperiness.

determine its slipperiness. She steps forward at the loop joint and brings her skis together side-by-side on the track and moves them quickly back and forth while standing still, using her poles to support her (see Figure 5.3). The skis slip and slide underneath her. In surprise, she quickly acknowledges in response to Peter's original question that the track is indeed slippery, "okay: ye::s", and Peter confirms. A short while later (not in the comic transcript), as Anabel makes progress on the track, she stops and comments "it's slippery", which Peter acknowledges. Peter then motivates further progress to make the track more ski-able.

As the days progress, we see a shift from explicit calls to sense the snow, especially what is visible and inspectable, to feeling the snow as an embodied experience in the action of skiing itself. Nevertheless, talk about the weather and snow surface conditions at the site is a motivated resource for instructed mobile action. We see many instances of the interdependencies of the feeling for snow with the track, technology/technique and instruction. For example, on Day 5, when Anabel is slipping on the up slope of the track, Peter initiates talk about maintaining grip in these present conditions (see Excerpt 5.2).

Peter orients to the conditions as noticeably different from the day before (line 6). When Anabel slips while ascending the incline, he instructs her to feel the grip as an embodied experience, a touch/response-feel, and reformulates this as a 'gripping point' one has to find (line 13). He demonstrates rhythmically the definite stepping movement of the ski on the snow, with each affirmative step timed with a stress on key words (e.g. "down", "foot", "feeling", "grip", "pushing" and

```
 1          ((A slips again))
 2    P:    op
 3          y'see,
 4          (you're totally ou:t)
 5    P:    you gotta get use:d t'it=
 6          =it's different from ye:sterday.
 7          (1.0)
 8    P:    you have to walk u:p
 9          ((A continues up the slope))
10          (2.0)
11          ((A slips))
12    A:    argh
13    P:    (thin-) fi:nd the gri:p
14          ((A stops to watch P pass))
15          ((P demonstrates))
16    P:    so when you press DO:WN with your foot,
17          ((A continues))
18          you're feeling it gri:p
19          and you're pushing forward
20          (1.5)
21    P:    i don't have any grip on the:se
22          so i have to use sti:cks
23          (1.5)
24    P:    if i put wa:x on i'd be able to do: it.
25          (1.0)
26    P:    but you have little ma:rks
27          (2.0)
28    P:    if you find the gri:pping point (.)
29          then you can run (1.5) °forward°.
```

Excerpt 5.2

Learning cross-country skiing – mobility aspects 87

"forward") in the instructed action (lines 16–19). Additionally, the type of ski one uses becomes salient, in that a ski without wax or grooves has no traction.

Making tracks: a practical infrastructure for mobility in the wild

In the setting of the snow-covered playground, the malleable snowscape is (re)territorialised by the skiers, who lay down tracks on the virgin snow, which can be reused by themselves (and other skiers), both in the same session and across sessions. As we have seen, each subsequent day is different – e.g. with new snow, rain and/or fluctuating temperatures – and the tracks have to be recolonised or started afresh. In an official ski resort or site, the tracks are made and refreshed using specially designed equipment that flattens the snow surface on a prepared path and inscribes a pair of parallel tracks for two-way traffic. One can ski on virgin snow (the skis really need to be longer and wider), but it is hard work if the snow is soft and deep since every step/stride is tentative and progress is slow.

As they set off to ski to the playground on the first day, Peter orients Anabel to what they are to do when they get there: "and we go down here to the playground alright and we'll make a track there". As they arrive at the playground, in Excerpt 5.3, Peter suggests they make a track immediately, but Anabel wants to play on a nearby hill with her friends. Anabel has two local girl friends with her, Suzie and Rita, one of whom is also on skis.

```
1    P:    so we'll make a tra:ck no:w
2          alri:ght?
3          ((A edges onto the rough track left by S))
4          ((P follows behind A))
5    P:    well you're not going to go do:wn the hill
6          in the ski:s alri:ght
7          ((A stops and looks up))
8          it's [too dang-]
9    A:         [(pardon) ]
10   P:    you're not going to go down the hill in the ski:s
11         ((S stops and looks round to A))
12   P:    it's too dangerou:s °for [you°]
13   A:                             [how ] about su:zie
14   P:    she can (0.5) but you can't
15         (0.8)
16   P:    ((P points with right hand))
17         we're gonna go round here:=anabel ↑look
18         ((A twists left and looks at P))
19         ((P repoints and pans to right))
20   P:    we're gonna go round, (.) and here, (.)
21         and back down, (.) and rou:nd again=
22         ((P draws a loop in the air))
23         =make a loo:p
24         ((A turns to look forward))
25         ((P and A discuss the hill that's too steep))
26   P:    ((P points with right hand))
27         they'll be a hill ↑the:re
28         ((A twists to look right))
29         when you come do:wn
```

```
30              (1.0)
31              you'll find that quite fa:st
32              (0.5)
33              that's what i did when i was learni:ng
34       A:     °oka:y° ((A looks back at hill))
35       P:     so let me make a track fi:rst ((A twists right))
36              if you step out the wa:y
37              ((A steps to the left))
38              ((P moves forward to start a track))
39       P:     it's fine to go there on a sli:de but not
40              on uh skis [yet   ]
41       A:                [ha::]
42       P:     so w'jus' going t'make a tra:ck
43              (2.0)
44       P:     you follow me:
```

Excerpt 5.3

When they cross the bridge, Suzie heads straight towards the hill at the top left from position [H]. In Figure 5.3, the photo taken from Peter's position shows Anabel by the lamp post about to follow Suzie (and Rita) on the tracks she has just made.

As they set off from point [A] into virgin snow after their arrival at the site on Day 1, Peter informs Anabel about the track (lines 1–2). There is some negotiation between Peter and Anabel concerning just what Anabel is to do at the site. In fact, Anabel is warned away from playing on the steep hill with skis. Instead, a plan is presented for making a loop track, which is sketched out with gestures punctuating features onto the snowscape of the playground (lines 16–31). In order to sketch his plan (and justify why Anabel must concentrate on practising on the track), he calls on Anabel to look (line 17) while he talks and points out the circular route of the track. He justifies that there will be a downhill stretch that will be "quite fast" (line 31). Anabel finally agrees. When Anabel agrees, Peter moves to begin the track: "so let me make a track first" (line 35) and "so w'jus' going t'make a track" (line 42). He asks Anabel to step aside while he makes a track, and then he begins to blaze an initial track into the virgin snow, with a request that Anabel follow behind.

In Figure 5.4, photos from different points on the initial track give an indication of the geography of the snowscape. The photos are frame grabs from one of the wide-angle-lens cameras that Peter is wearing. The direction of view is indicated by the camera icon, though there is some distortion of straight lines caused by the lens. In images 1 and 4 in Figure 5.4, there is no track for the simple reason that Peter is making the track for the first time and when looking forward there is no track yet to be seen.

As the track is being made in the snow, a loop (with stations for relevant activity) has to be established (see Figure 5.3). Points [D] and [E] come to be important rest points where talk and instruction take place before the downslope is navigated or they embark on another loop. After the first loop is complete, at point [A], Peter continues quickly around the loop for the second time to catch Anabel at [E]. During Loop 1, Peter asks Anabel to tell her friend Suzie that she

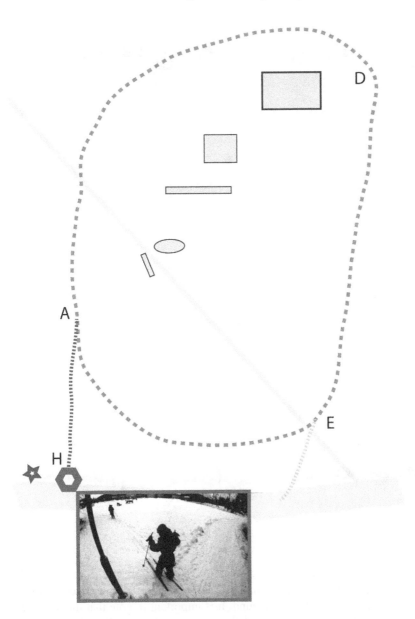

Figure 5.3 Arrival at the site on Day 1.

is going to practise the loop track first and he makes a circular gesture. Thus, it has been established that the space will be structured as a repeatable 'loop' and it will therefore have a recurrent familiarity.

As they gradually inhabit the amorphous geography of the snowscape, a practical infrastructure for mobility and learning is developed and maintained *in situ*

90 P. McIlvenny

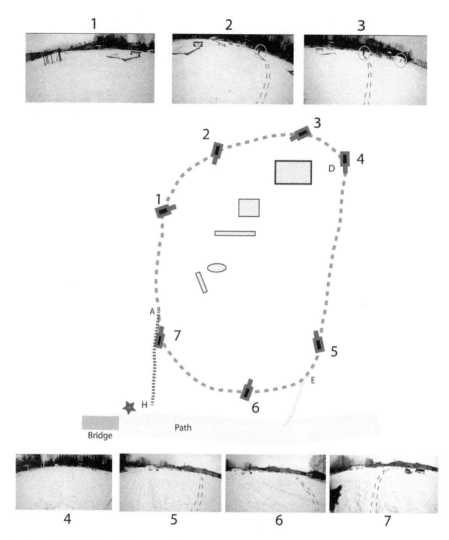

Figure 5.4 Building the loop track.

(see Figure 5.5). The core of the transient infrastructure is a loop track [MT] that circumscribes most of the playground. It is important to note that the temporary track at this site is revisited each day and it needs to be rediscovered, repaired and stabilised to constitute its apparent continuity over time and to extend its transient existence. For example, a parallel track [PT] is opened up by the parent on the downslope stretch to enable the two skiers to ski side-by-side (and therefore also to race each other), which is later appropriated by the child (see Excerpt 5.5). Also, the track can be traversed in both directions. In total the loop is traversed 46 times, 13 of which are anticlockwise.

Learning cross-country skiing – mobility aspects 91

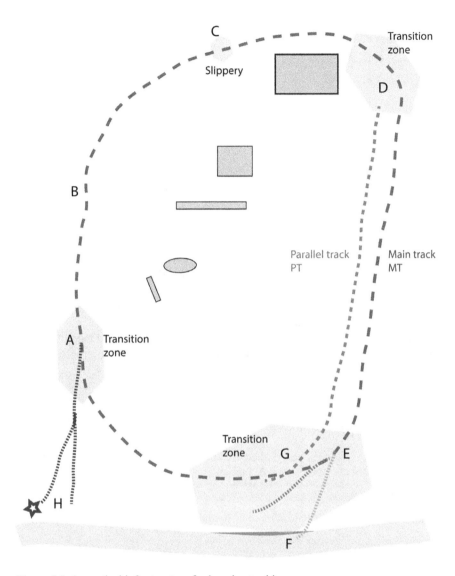

Figure 5.5 A practical infrastructure for learning to ski.

Over the course of five days, as the track is re-territorialised so that it becomes a practical material infrastructure for mobility, specifically for learning to cross-country ski, the parent attends to and attunes the child to a number of features of the track, including its authenticity. On Day 1, after Peter rejoins Anabel at the bottom of the slope, they head off from location [A] on what is now the second loop with Anabel in front this time (see Excerpt 5.4).

```
1   P:   y'see i made a track no:w
2        ((A stops and looks to the side))
3   P:   now this is like a [proper t-]
4   A:                     [(wait in ] the track now)
5        ((A reaches down to pick up snow))
6   P:   it's like a proper tra:ck.
7        (1.5)
8   P:   the snow is just ri:ght.
9        (3.0)
10       ((A stands up holding a ball of snow))
11  A:   yeah it is:
12       ((A twists towards P and throws a snowball))
13  A:   for snowba:lls
14  P:   ARGH [heheh]
15  A:        [heheh] ha
```

Excerpt 5.4

Peter draws attention to the integrity and authenticity of the track that he has made as well as the quality of the snow. He observes that "it's like a proper track" (lines 3–6) and that "the snow is just right" (for skiing) (line 8). Anabel stops and responds playfully to Peter's call to attend to the qualities of the track and the snow. Instead of commenting on the snow's ski-ability, Anabel throws a snowball at P (requiring the snow to have sufficient moisture to retain its shape when compressed in the hand).

At a particular stage on Day 2 (see Excerpt 5.5), on the second loop of the day, Peter began a parallel track [PT] from [D] to [G] in order to be closer to Anabel.

```
1        ((A and P reach the top of the slope))
2        ((P moves off the track beside A))
3   P:   come we'll go down toge:ther
4   A:   NAH::
5   P:   i'll go here,
6        (1.5)
7   P:   and you go the:re
8   A:   alright (.) >one two three GO:<
9        ((A starts down the track))
10  P:   ready::
11  A:   go:
12       ((A and P start down the slope))
13       (3.0)
14  A:   can you go: without [a tra]:ck
15  P:                       [yeah ]
16  P:   we:ll because it's so icy: (.) then my skis
17       ride over the to:p so it's oka:y.
18       (1.0)
19  P:   otherwise they would fa:ll right
20       ((A loses balance))
21  P:   in [the sno:w=woa::::]
22  A:      [((A screams))    ]
23       (2.5)
24  A:   i won't go so fa:st toda:y,
25  P:   nah not [i-]
26  A:          [be]cause there:'s i::ce.
27  P:   yeah
```

Excerpt 5.5

While at the transition zone [D], Peter steps to the right side of Anabel, who is lined up first on the downslope track. Anabel initially refuses the offer to "go down together" (lines 3–4), but when Peter elaborates that he will descend in a parallel fashion, she agrees. Immediately, she starts off in competitive mode with her fast countdown "one two three go" (line 8). Peter takes charge and redoes the start using an alternative form "ready", which Anabel quickly completes as "go". As they descend together, Anabel asks "can you go [down] without a track" (line 14), revealing an assumption she now has that skiing happens in tracks, which Peter answers by accounting for the quality of the snow that makes it possible (and not possible). Anabel almost falls and then announces she will moderate her speed today because of the presence of ice that Peter has noted (lines 24–26). Peter agrees.

On Loop 3, as they descend the slope side-by-side, Anabel slows down and asks if she can try the new parallel track. A short while later, while Peter and Anabel are at the transition zone [E], Anabel asks again if she can try the parallel track. Peter denies the request on the grounds that the fresh track is not yet deep enough. On Loop 5, while Peter and Anabel are at the transition zone [D], Anabel asks yet again if she can try the parallel track now. This time she gets a go.

It is clear that as Peter and Anabel return to the site to practice skiing each day, there is a strong orientation to the old track, and thus to account for the site in terms of recurrent features that are revisited. The track serves as a delicate material archive – a trace of past actions, activities and events – in terms of its brief history of use. In their study, Waitt *et al.* (2008, p. 47) note that "the regular, repetitive weaving through the familiar crisscrossing paths, and the ability to view the land from a variety of perspectives, enables the walker to move through, and to territorialise the reserve as 'their' place". In this case, great effort is spent at the site in order for it to be (re)territorialised despite the vagaries of the weather. On Day 2, for example, Peter notes the significance and prescience of making the track on Day 1 in good conditions: "well luckily we made a track 'coz now we have a track" (Excerpt 5.1: lines 46–48). It would not have been possible to make a new track on Day 2 in such icy conditions.

On occasion, Anabel takes part in the search for signs demonstrating the legibility of the geography of the site, and thus demonstrating her competence in reading the snowscape. In Excerpt 5.1 given earlier, Peter crosses the bridge, quickly surveys the site, and draws attention to the visibility of the track – it is inspectable from their current location – that they made for the first time the day before: "the track's still there" (line 18). After Anabel has crossed the bridge, Peter turns to look up the site again, and begins: "see there's..." (line 26), upon which Anabel says "there there is a track" (line 27), attempting to demonstrate a competence that Peter displayed just a minute ago. One might say that Anabel is doing 'being' a good apprentice. Peter acknowledges the visible trace of the track, though it is only just noticeable, and in this case just about skiable, to which he adds that "it's going to be very slippery" (line 30). Therefore, Peter and Anabel mutually construct a practice of 'reading' the snowscape in terms of its history and its ski-ability, to which they return each day.

Although the track is accumulating a history for them, it has the potential to be ruptured at a future date when "the track" will disappear because of the vagaries of the weather. On some days, the old track was very clear to the naked eye. On other days, they struggle to make the track visible. On Day 4, in Excerpt 5.6, after the previous day's storm resulting in debris over the ground, Peter and Anabel walk to the playground carrying their skis and they arrive by the lamp post [H].

```
 1   P:   uh: let's see:
 2        ((P and A walk to the track))
 3        so it's been in a sto:rm (  )
 4        (1.0)
 5   P:   there's a lot of twi:gs
 6        (2.0)
 7   P:   but there is a bit of a tra:ck,
 8        (.) still, (.) just a little bit,
 9        ((A walks up to track and prods it with pole))
10        (1.5)
11   P:   not mu:ch.
12        (2.0)
13   P:   so: let's jus' try a bit
14        ((P sorts out the skis and poles))
15   P:   it's good to practise
16        as much as we ca:n before we go to the big slo:pe
17        ((P helps A with ski bindings))
18   A:   at the bi:g slo:pe
19   P:   yea:h (.) °well° (the proper ski place)
20   P:   °yes°
21        (2.0)
22   P:   hopefully with some new sno:w
23        they make some new tra:cks
```

Excerpt 5.6

Initially, Peter orients to the necessary assessment work to be done: "uh let's see" (line 1). They walk towards the track and Peter brings out features of the environment that are noticeable in this respect. For example, there is the visible evidence of the effects of a recent storm and the presence of twigs, showing that the snowscape is not just shaped by the landscape underneath but also the vertical dimension of natural elements, such as trees. As they reach the track, Peter determines that there is "a bit of a track" (line 7), "just a little bit" (line 8), and Anabel moves her pole to jab at the track near her: another 'experimental technique' she has learnt to assess the snow conditions. Thus, Anabel displays her recognition of the presence of a track, but she does not yet give her verbal assessment. Peter pursues extracting an assessment from her by modifying his assessment "not much" (line 11). He adds that it is skiable, and anyway they need to practise (despite the poor conditions) before the big event on Day 6.

After four days of skiing on this track there is a routine, which once again is made manifest as they arrive at the lamp post on Day 5 (see Excerpt 5.7).

Peter suggests that they find the track, "our track" (line 2), and as they inspect the track, Peter claims he "can see a little bit" (line 3). Anabel gives her mitigated assessment that constitutes agreement (line 6). The track has to be remade given its very poor condition and Anabel requests that Peter go first (line 8). As Peter

Learning cross-country skiing – mobility aspects   95

```
1   P:    oka:y (1.0) shall we find the tra:ck,
2         (2.0)
3   P:    is our track here:=i can see a li:ttle bit
4         can you see it,
5         (1.5)
6   A:    a tee:ny wee:ny
7         (0.5)
8   A:    =[but] can you just go fi:rst this ti:me
9   P:    =[so:]
10  P:    yeah well i'll make the tra:ck ((P looks behind))
11        (1.5)
12  P:    =[f- ]
13  A:    =[sha]ll i wai:t
14  P:    no no you follow behi:nd me
15        (1.0)
16  P:    we'll just try and ma:ke it agai:n
17        (18.0) ((P moves forward on track))
18  P:    i can just about see: it ((P stops))
19        can you see it,
20        (1.5)
21  P:    just abou:t
```

Excerpt 5.7

heads off, he comments repeatedly on the visibility of the track: "[I] can just about see it" (line 18). In places, the track is not traceable and so bridging tracks are made to repair the loop and thus rediscover "our track" (line 3), the same track since Day 1.

In fact, on each day the track is stabilised by the first traversals. Peter orients Anabel to the need to condition the track, e.g. to make it more stable and faster. For example, on Day 1 (Excerpt 5.8), Peter is already orienting to the need to condition the track, e.g. to make it more compressed so a skier can stay in the track and go faster.

```
1   P:    y'see when we go round the track mo:re and mo:re (.)
2         it gets harder and harder (.) the grou:nd,
3         and it gets easier to stay in the tra:ck.
4         (0.5)
5   P:    then you could focus on going fa:ster.
```

Excerpt 5.8

On Day 3 (Excerpt 5.9), as they finish the first loop with Anabel rejoining the track to start the next loop, she asks if they can "do a lot today" (line 3). Peter responds affirmatively.

```
1   P:    alright. (.) on the tra:ck.
2         ((A gets on the track and stops))
3   A:    can we do a lo:t today (pappa)?
4         ((A returns to moving on the track))
5   P:    yeah. (.) let's get the track nice and fa:st again.
6         (1.0)
7   P:    if we go over the track, (1.0) it will get
8         fa:ster and fa:ster.
```

Excerpt 5.9

Building on her request, Peter suggests that it is a priority that they "get the track nice and fast again" (line 5) by going "over the track" (line 7). He orients to the need to recondition the track for speed, which is to be valued, and this can be heard as a prerequisite to doing a lot that day.

On Day 5 (Excerpt 5.10), after some new snow has fallen overnight, Anabel has completed a loop on her own and returns to where Peter is standing.

```
 1   A:   but pete:r
 2   P:   hmm
 3   A:   it's just because (.) >all of a sudden
 4        i go here< then i start out to sli:de
 5   P:   i know 'coz the track is not dee:p enough
 6        ye:t
 7        ((P prods the track with the ski pole))
 8   P:   i'm trying to make it (.) deep
 9   A:   can i try and go first
10   P:   you go first then
11        ((A passes P and then stops and turns))
12   A:   but but you have to wai:t for me
13   P:   no i'm going rou:nd, (.) so we're making
14        the track better and better
15        every time [we go rou:nd]
16   A:              [you have to ] wait for me
17   A:   when i go down that hill
18   P:   aha
```

Excerpt 5.10

Anabel complains that she slipped on the turn (lines 1–4). Peter accounts for this in terms of the depth of the track that he is trying to improve, and he prods the track to demonstrate (lines 5–8). They negotiate who should go first on the next loop and whether or not Peter should wait again. Peter insists that he will follow her so that together they can make the track, thus orienting her to the combined effort of two skiers to compress the snow and condition the track (lines 13–15).

From these examples, we clearly see that the track does not remain in prime condition without their labour. It is only through its use and calibration *in situ* that it reaches peak performance for all practical purposes. For the parent, and for the child learning, their temporary loop track is hand-made in and through their repeated attempts at sensing and feeling the snow – in the skier-binding-ski-pole-snow assemblage – as they revisit the track as it evolves over time with use.

Conclusion

This chapter has demonstrated an analytical concern with actual, mundane practices that negotiate and maintain the geography of tracks through snow as traces of past action and as conditions for future action. The calculation of the snow's affordance for low-friction sliding on its material surface is a complex science, but for these skiers their feeling for the snowscape is calibrated to their concerns. Sometimes the participants focus on sensing the snow; on other occasions, it is the track that must be established and maintained; and at other times it is specific ski actions that must be practised as necessary components of skiing. We have seen how snow can be talked about, how it can be handled and how it can be felt in motion. Indeed, the participants make use of practical 'tests' for sensing the snow and the track. For example, they can stand on the track and slide their skis back and forth (see Figure 5.2) or prod the snow in the track with a pole (see Excerpt 5.6). These feelings for snow are action-directed, in the sense that they only make sense in their practice of cross-country skiing in this environment. The track itself is transient and ephemeral, but the participants work hard to re-territorialise the ever changing snowscape for their purposes and to recondition the track for speed and ski-ability.

We have seen also how the track becomes a temporary infrastructure for skiing and learning. Much as the sensing of snow conditions is crucial for rendering the site ski-able and instructable, so is the track a dynamic resource for instructing and practising skiing. It is clear that it is not possible to ski well unless one integrates an embodied awareness of the affordances of snow, the track and the skier-pole-binding-ski assemblage. For example, repeated slipping on the kick brings to the fore the conditions of the packed snow on the track (and possibly the status of the wax on the ski) or it might expose the tiredness of the skier who is failing to transfer weight for the kick; or it might point to the poor state of the track, which means the skier is often sliding out of the track. In this way, the cultural practices of cross-country skiing are inculcated *in situ* in and through an embodied geography of snow.

Nevertheless, it may seem rather flippant to say that the participants constructed a spatial 'infrastructure' for mobility and that it was 'in the wild'. Yet analysis shows that key aspects of the site were infrastructural – for example, there was repeated attention to maintaining an appropriate and robust structural surface for supporting movement. Inevitably, a few days after the site was used by the family, with some new snow, new users and changing weather patterns, the practical infrastructure they had carefully built in the wild had disappeared. All that remains are the memories, the trace of the experience and the activities in historical bodies, and the video ethnography.

This study is based on a mobile 'active participant' ethnography that enables particular insights into the cultural meanings and social interactional practices of this family at this, for them, historic site. Although it is a single case study, following a practitioner and a learner in instructional moments provided access to salient practices. The study informs our understanding of transient and ephemeral geographies in which participants generate mobility and a situated material-spatial awareness in unpredictable terrain within a nexus of social and cultural practices. It is noteworthy that the interactional mobility analysis was not undertaken simply by reference to the social and cultural background of the skiers involved.

The study contributes, as well, to the need to investigate children's and not just adult (or extreme) mobility practices, both in the context of learning to be mobile in an adult world and understanding what mobility means in a child's everyday life (Horton *et al.*, 2013) and how children are made mobile

(Kullman, 2010). More research is required to determine whether the findings are generalisable beyond this case study – for example, with investigations of how families and caregivers in other social situations or cultures teach their children to appreciate the materialities that afford mobility, or of how snow-covered or other 'wild' landscapes are sensed, traversed and transiently territorialised in practice, for example by free skiers or users of snow scooters.

Appendix: transcription conventions

push	stress
STOp	high volume
°glide°	low volume
> <	fast talk
< >	slow talk
:	stretching of prior syllable
par-	cut-off
.h	inbreath
h	outbreath
↑ ↓	high or low pitch at the start of the following segment
(1.5)	timed pause in seconds and tenths of seconds
[ ]	beginning and end of overlapping speech
=	latching (no break)
()	dubious hearing/unsure transcription
(())	transcriber's comment

References

Allen Collinson, J., 2006. Running together: Some ethnomethodological considerations. *Ethnographic Studies*, 8, pp. 17–29.

Anderson, J., 2012. Relational places: The surfed wave as assemblage and convergence. *Environment and Planning D: Society and Space*, 30(4), pp. 570–87.

Barratt, P., 2012. 'My magic cam': A more-than-representational account of the climbing assemblage. *Area*, 44(1), pp. 46–53.

Broth, M. and Lundström, F., 2013. A walk on the pier. Establishing relevant places in a guided tour. In: P. Haddington, L. Mondada and M. Nevile, eds. *Interaction and mobility: Language and the body in motion*. Berlin: de Gruyter. pp. 91–122.

Brown, K.M. and Spinney, J., 2010. Catching a glimpse: The value of video in evoking, understanding and representing the practice of cycling. In: B. Fincham, M. McGuinness and L. Murray, eds. *Mobile methodologies*. Basingstoke: Palgrave Macmillan. pp. 130–51.

Brown, K.M., Dilley, R. and Marshall, K., 2008. Using a head-mounted video camera to understand social worlds and experiences. *Sociological Research Online*, 13(6). doi: 10.5153/sro.1818.

Büscher, M., 2006. Vision in motion. *Environment and Planning A*, 38(2), pp. 281–99.

Dant, T.I.M. and Wheaton, B., 2007. Windsurfing: An extreme form of material and embodied interaction? *Anthropology Today*, 23(6), pp. 8–12.

Day, R.E., 2005. 'Surface': Material infrastructure for space. In: P. Turner and E. Davenport, eds. *Spaces, spatiality and technology*. Dordrecht: Springer. pp. 139–50.

Dickinson, G. and Aiello, G., 2016. Being through there matters: Materiality, bodies, and movement in urban communication research. *International Journal of Communication*, 10, pp. 1294–308.
Edensor, T. and Richards, S., 2007. Snowboarders vs skiers: Contested choreographies of the slopes. *Leisure Studies*, 26(1), pp. 97–114.
Forsyth, I., Lorimer, H., Merriman, P. and Robinson, J., 2013. What are surfaces? *Environment and Planning A*, 45(5), pp. 1013–20.
Geenen, J., 2013a. Actionary pertinence: Space to place in kitesurfing. *Multimodal Communication*, 2(2), pp. 123–54.
Geenen, J., 2013b. *Kitesurfing: Action, (inter)action and mediation*. Doctoral dissertation. Auckland: Auckland University of Technology.
Goodwin, C., 1999. Practices of color classification. *Mind, Culture & Activity*, 7(1–2), pp. 19–36.
Haddington, P., Keisanen, T. and Nevile, M., 2012. Meaning in motion: Sharing the car, sharing the drive. *Semiotica*, 191(1/4), pp. 101–16.
Haddington, P., Mondada, L. and Nevile, M., eds, 2013. *Interaction and mobility: Language and the body in motion*. Berlin: de Gruyter.
Have, P.t., 2007. *Doing conversation analysis: A practical guide*. London: Sage.
Hester, S. and Francis, D., 2003. Analysing visually available mundane order: A walk to the supermarket. *Visual Studies*, 18(1), pp. 36–46.
Hester, S. and Francis, D., 2004. *An invitation to ethnomethodology: Language, society and interaction*. London: Sage.
Hockey, J., 2006. Sensing the run: The senses and distance running. *The Senses and Society*, 1(2), pp. 183–201.
Horton, J., Christensen, P., Kraftl, P. and Hadfield-Hill, S., 2013. 'Walking ... just walking': How children and young people's everyday pedestrian practices matter. *Social & Cultural Geography*, 15(1), pp. 94–115.
Hutchins, E., 1994. *Cognition in the wild*. Cambridge, MA: MIT Press.
Hutchins, E., 2008. The role of cultural practices in the emergence of modern human intelligence. *Philosophical Transactions of the Royal Society B: Biological Sciences*, 363(1499), pp. 2011–19.
Imai, H., 2008. Senses on the move: Multisensory encounters with street vendors in the Japanese urban alleyway Roji. *The Senses and Society*, 3(3), pp. 329–38.
Ingold, T. and Kurttilla, T., 2000. Perceiving the environment in Finnish Lapland. *Body & Society*, 6(3–4), pp. 183–96.
Jefferson, G., 2004. Glossary of transcript symbols with an introduction. In: G. Lerner, ed. *Conversation analysis. Studies from the first generation*. Amsterdam: John Benjamins. pp. 13–31.
Karlsson, A.-M., 2011. Online outdoor: Technological, discursive and textual transformations of the activity of skating. *HUMAN IT*, 11(1), pp. 103–38.
Kullman, K., 2010. Transitional geographies: Making mobile children. *Social & Cultural Geography*, 11(8), pp. 829–46.
Latham, A. and Wood, P.R.H., 2015. Inhabiting infrastructure: Exploring the interactional spaces of urban cycling. *Environment and Planning A*, 47(2), pp. 300–19.
Laurier, E., 2013. Capturing motion: Video set-ups for driving, cycling and walking. In: P. Adey, D. Bissell, K. Hannam, P. Merriman and M. Sheller, eds. *The Routledge handbook of mobilities*. Abingdon: Routledge. pp. 493–502.
Laurier, E., 2014. The graphic transcript: Poaching comic book grammar for inscribing the visual, spatial and temporal aspects of action. *Geography Compass*, 9(4), pp. 235–48.

Laurier, E., Lorimer, H., Brown, B., Jones, O., Juhlin, O., Noble, A., Perry, M., Pica, D., Sormani, P., Strebel, I., Swan, L., Taylor, A.S., Watts, L. and Weilenmann, A., 2008. Driving and 'passengering': Notes on the ordinary organization of car travel. *Mobilities*, 3(1), pp. 1–23.

Markus, T.A. and Cameron, D., 2002. *The words between the spaces: Buildings and language*. London: Routledge.

McIlvenny, P., 2013. Interacting outside the box: Between social interaction and mobilities. In: P. Haddington, L. Mondada and M. Nevile, eds. *Interaction and mobility: Language and the body in motion*. Berlin: de Gruyter. pp. 409–17.

McIlvenny, P., 2014. Vélomobile formations-in-action: Biking and talking together. *Space & Culture*, 17(2), pp. 137–56.

McIlvenny, P., 2015. The joy of biking together: Sharing everyday experiences of vélomobility. *Mobilities*, 10(1), pp. 55–82.

McIlvenny, P., Broth, M. and Haddington, P., 2009. Communicating place, space and mobility. *Journal of Pragmatics*, 41(10), pp. 1879–86.

Middleton, J., 2010. Sense and the city: Exploring the embodied geographies of urban walking. *Social & Cultural Geography*, 11(6), pp. 575–96.

Ness, S.A., 2016. *Choreographies of landscape: Signs of performance in Yosemite National Park*. Oxford: Berghahn Books.

Norris, S., 2012. Teaching touch/response-feel: A first step to an analysis of touch from an (inter)active perspective. In: S. Norris, ed. *Multimodality in practice: Investigating theory-in-practice-through-methodology*. Abingdon: Routledge. pp. 7–19.

Noy, C., 2009. On driving a car and being a family: An autoethnography. In: P. Vannini, ed. *Material culture and technology in everyday life: Ethnographic approaches*. Berlin: Peter Lang. pp. 101–13.

Olwig, K.R., 2008. Performing on the landscape versus doing landscape: Perambulatory practice, sight and the sense of belonging. In: T. Ingold and J.L. Vergunst, eds. *Ways of walking: Ethnography and practice on foot*. Farnham: Ashgate. pp. 81–91.

Pink, S., 2007. Sensing Cittaslow: Slow living and the constitution of the sensory city. *The Senses and Society*, 2(1), pp. 59–77.

Ryave, L. and Schenkein, J.N., 1974. Notes on the art of walking. In: R. Turner, ed. *Ethnomethodology*. Harmondsworth: Penguin. pp. 265–74.

Saerberg, S., 2010. Just go straight ahead: How blind and sighted pedestrians negotiate space. *The Senses and Society*, 5(3), pp. 364–81.

Spinney, J., 2006. A place of sense: A kinaesthetic ethnography of cyclists on Mont Ventoux. *Environment and Planning D: Society and Space*, 24(5), pp. 709–32.

Spinney, J., 2011. A chance to catch a breath: Using mobile video ethnography in cycling research. *Mobilities*, 6(2), pp. 161–82.

Stranger, M., 1999. The aesthetics of risk: A study of surfing. *International Review for the Sociology of Sport*, 34(3), pp. 265–76.

Turner, P. and Turner, S., 2006. Place, sense of place and presence. *Presence: The Journal of Teleoperators and Virtual Environments*, 15(2), pp. 204–17.

van Duppen, J. and Spierings, B., 2013. Retracing trajectories: The embodied experience of cycling, urban sensescapes and the commute between 'neighbourhood' and 'city' in Utrecht, NL. *Journal of Transport Geography*, 30, pp. 234–43.

Waitt, G., Gill, N. and Head, L., 2008. Walking practice and suburban nature-talk. *Social & Cultural Geography*, 10(1), pp. 41–60.

Watson, R., 1999. Driving in forests and mountains: A pure and applied ethnography. *Ethnographic Studies*, 3, pp. 50–60.

6 Moving forward – left behind: asynchrone experiences

The use of mobile media technologies when young people leave

Ida Wentzel Winther and Rune Bundgaard

Introduction

Education plays an absolutely key role in the lives of children and youth. Getting an education is regarded as future-proofing and is closely tied to the idea and belief that education is the path to development and progress. Education is often considered the route to change; as the way in which children are given the opportunity to think for themselves, to make good choices, and to form their own opinions. Furthermore, education is a prerequisite for sustainable development and the establishment of a democratic society. Concepts such as magic, gift, and hope have been used in anthropological analyses of education, but also the understanding of education as a trap which dazzles/seduces/attracts young people; at the same time, school has created new oppositions and broken dreams because not everyone manages to complete various educations. In Denmark, our country of origin and residence, there are schools spread throughout the country and the vast majority of children complete primary and secondary education whilst living at home. However, the same is not the case in a global context where, in a historical perspective, travelling in order to get an education has gone from being a phenomenon largely confined to the children of the upper classes to a common occurrence. According to Olwig and Valentin (2015), across the globe, people migrate for the sake of education, resulting simultaneously in a geographical movement, a forwards and upwards educational process, and a change in social status. Geographical mobility is often necessary in order to achieve personal and social mobility (Anderson-Levitt, 2003; Salazar and Smart, 2011; Olwig and Valentin, 2015; Valentin and Olwig, 2015). But even if they do not need to actually migrate, a large number of children and young people have to move, whether geographically, culturally, linguistically, or socially, in order to get an education.

This is particularly the case in Greenland – the world's largest island, 80 per cent of which is covered by ice. A total of 56,000 inhabitants are spread across 16 towns and 60 smaller settlements. None of these are linked by roads, but are located like small islands surrounded by ocean, mountains, or ice. Most settlements have their own primary school, but in many places the children have to travel to the nearest town in order to attend the final years of lower secondary education (e.g. see Elixhauser, 2015). There are four upper secondary schools in Greenland: one in the capital Nuuk, one on the southern tip in Qaqortoq, and two north of the polar circle in Aasiaat and Sisimiut. Young people from many parts of Greenland therefore have to travel cross-country (approx. 1000 km from the east coast or south halfway down the west coast) where they live in student accommodation.

An upper secondary education requires not only that students travel geographically and often also linguistically (East Greenlandic and West Greenlandic are, to all intents and purposes, two separate languages), but also to an upper secondary school where the principal language of instruction is Danish, whereas primary and lower secondary education is in Greenlandic. Far from all students are from educated families; nevertheless, the dominant metanarrative at both the national and the individual level concerns a desire for and belief in education as the way forward. Getting an education requires hard work: students must be able to cope not only with the schoolwork (the intellectual/academic), but also with moving away from home – from the social forms and systems of the family – to the world of education and an everyday life where they have to fend for themselves, both emotionally and in terms of practical tasks, far from home. Some succeed while others fail and drop out. Dropouts fall between two stools: a home which they have left behind and an outside world (the educated) where they fail to establish themselves (e.g. see KUFK 2001; Johnson-Hanks, 2006; Meinert, 2009; Meinert and Kølner, 2010). In Greenland, upper secondary dropout rates in 2009 were approximately 24 per cent (Kjær, 2010). Furthermore, it is not unusual for students to spend – not three years as normal period of study in Denmark – but five or six years gaining an upper secondary qualification (starting, stopping, spending time in Denmark at a lower secondary boarding school [*efterskole*] to improve their Danish language skills, starting again, becoming pregnant, stopping, starting). This disjointed chain of events may have little to do with what takes place during school hours and more to do with what takes place outside school. Some of the young people enjoy their lives far away from their parents; others suffer severe homesickness. They are heading out into the world and taking an educational step forward. Their parents are left with a feeling of having to let their children go, while at the same time offering help and support from afar (e.g. money, phone calls, and (virtual) support). This is an example of what the German philosopher Ernst Bloch terms asynchrony or non-contemporaneity (Ungleichzeitigkeit), where experiences and interpretations are not aligned and where we often live in a multiplicity of times. The individual can, so to speak, be in the time without being one with the time, and we can have radically different experiences despite being in exactly the same time. One might say that they flow through us (Bloch, 1985).

In this article our focus is on some of the challenges faced by young people (aged 16–18) when they, on every level, have to learn to live with and in the conditions of mobility within Greenland (from settlement to small town to larger town offering upper secondary education), as well as on the challenges facing their parents when sending their children far away. We will not be examining transnational migration (e.g. see Schiller and Salazar, 2013; Olwig and Valentin, 2015), or mobility as a frictionless postmodern form of movement (Augé, 1992; Bauman, 1998), or student mobility between Greenland and Denmark

(Sørensen, 1993; Flora, 2007, 2015). Our chapter is a contribution to the new mobility 'turn' examining the microprocesses of everyday life, whereby we 'do', feel, and practise mobility (Cresswell and Merriman, 2011; Ingold, 2011; Löfgren, 2015; Werner, 2015; Winther, 2015a), which have emerged over the last 15 years within the broader field of mobilities turn (Urry, 2002, 2007; Cresswell, 2006; Vannini, 2010; Jensen, 2013). We want to include the material dimension and a sensibility to mobile and educational research.

Our research questions are: What experiences, reactions, and interpretations occur among, respectively, the young students and their parents across time and place? How are asynchrone experiences manifested? How are these experiences materialized though mobile media technologies? The chapter is structured in the following way: First, we introduce the empirical study and the theoretical inspirations lying behind. Secondly, we do multiple analyses starting with our methodological framework, where we describe how we have worked actively with asynchronicity in the creation process; and then we present an (asynchrone) 'more-than-representational'. In this part, we present scenes from our documentary film *Matup Tunuani*; and offer a more classic analysis where we interweave scenes and reflections. Finally, we present a summing-up/conclusion.

Theoretical inspirations and the empirical study

Our approach to researching how mobility is practised and done on a small scale is inspired by de Certeau (1984), who focuses on the routines and movement patterns of everyday life. De Certeau was interested in how we use, do, walk – how everyday practices, tactile activities, and bodily movements can be understood as tactics that are often practised through normal (perhaps banal) activities and routines. Practising is a way of conquering a space and making the as-yet-unknown, the as-yet-unpractised geographical place 'one's own place'. According to Ingold (2011), our sense of belonging is closely linked to our ways of being rooted in the landscape, the place, and the concrete space, and this has an impact on how we, both alone and with others, leave footprints wherever we tread. In our research, this connection to the landscape (*topos*) is interwoven with an interest in how materialities interacts with memories, senses, and emotions. Löfgren (2015) describes how objects are moved around, reorganized, and recycled; how relationships with objects are pregnant with emotions and narratives; and how objects help organize habits and routines and become the order of rules, rhythms, and morale. Winther (2017) describes how objects are weaved into a socio-material practice and are created, recreated, and transformed in various ways. The material space can 'tune' us and become planted in our bodies as a sounding board. Objects can serve as an echo from the past, primarily audible to the owner of the object, or be evocative, sending us on a trip down memory lane. 'Evocative objects' (Turkel, 2007), 'ordinary affects' (Stewart, 2007), and 'sensitive objects' (Frykman and Frykman, 2016) represent different ways of endeavouring to exceed the dualistic contrast between subject-object, nature-culture, human-nonhuman, and structure-actor. With different theoretical approaches,

Actor Network Theory (ANT) and Science and Technology Studies (STS) also operate with not only fixed and demarcated actors, but also nodes that constantly shift and are re-created in the effects of relationships between both human and non-human actors. Shifts from the human experience of things to the things themselves is also in focus in the kind of ecological and 'more-than-human' perspective (Lorimer, 2005; Brennet, 2010).

We are interested in how the young people discussed here move away from home to a new and, for them, undefined geographical location, which they have to transform into a place of their own.

A complex web of different forms of movement and socio-material practices is involved and thereby how the young people form and are formed by the material surroundings in, with, and through which they live, and in our fieldwork mobile media technologies had a central position as an actor.

These theoretical and analytical perspectives are included in the study, as well as the research team's experience from some years spent among young Greenlanders (Bundgaard and Ottesen, 2013, 2015; Svinkløv, 2016). During four months of filmed ethnographic fieldwork in spring 2015, the primary fieldworkers lived in a hall of residence. The researchers closely monitored seven young key informants inside and outside their rooms: while they cooked, ate, played music, and played computer games; on their way to school, football, the shops, and parties; and while visiting support families and friends. In this way, we sought to observe how they 'do' everyday life (cf. de Certeau's 'ways of operating'). We were likewise interested in the lines and links between the hall of residence and the home: for example, material objects (photographs, telephones), face-to-face encounters (physical visits), as well as via mobile media technologies (e.g. Skype and FaceTime), or stories told about the young people by their families. We travelled around Greenland visiting the families, witnessing how the absent young people were materially manifested within the home. In interviews and conversations, parents and grandparents told us about their hopes and dreams for their children, their thoughts on education and why they consider it important, and how they provide everyday support from afar. We listened to the ways in which the families' stories and memories help construct and maintain understandings. Through a combination of participation, observation, and interviews, we gained insight into how the parents let go of their children and how the young people let go of their parents – and how both the young people and their parents live in and with absence and homesickness. All in all the research team spent the months filming and have subsequently striven to show (in film) how the young people and their parents undertake and deal with these transitions.

Multiple analyses

Multiple analyses as methodology: asynchronicity in the creation process

In film, coherence is established through the joining together of images: clips are positioned one after another and shifts, montages, and transitions are made.

Using a camera lens, and with the resultant 'fieldbody' constituted by the camera (Winther, 2013), the research team, Rune Bundgaard (R1) and Martin Svinkløv (R2), produced a 'thick description' and let the visual and the sensual take centre stage in terms of how to experience and create insight, also taking the approach that visual material is formative in and for analysis (Møhl, 2004; MacDougall, 2006).

The film constitutes an analysis (through camera angles, edits, and dramaturgy), and the analyses are created during the process of filming and experiencing and during the editing of footage. We worked with different kinds of asynchronicity in the creation process.

During the filmed fieldwork we worked with layers of analysis. R1 and R2 did the visual fieldwork. Ida Wentzel Winther (R3) was affiliated with the project in the role of academic consultant from Aarhus University, and was involved in the project's design and part of the fieldwork (for one month of the total of four months). She both visited the young people's parents and, in particular, spent time on the video footage and the initial analyses, which R1 and R2 had already conducted. On this basis, she performed a form of 'secondary analysis' (Kofoed and Thomson, 2018). When working with 'secondary analysis', the material is revisited. This can either be done by another person (i.e. someone not involved in the production of data) or by applying previously alien analytical or theoretical perspectives, thereby twisting the material in a way other than originally envisaged. In this way, material can travel and other, sometimes unconventional, interpretations can emerge. For us this meant that R3 reviewed the material while physically spending a month in the field; R3 met the young people, was at their halls of residence, met some of their parents, was at their school, in the town, followed the same routes, visited the same shops, froze in temperatures 35 degrees below freezing, heard the snow crunching under her boots, and squinted in the February sun. In other words, R3 had first-person access to the field, which tuned in her sensory apparatus to the topographical universe in which the study took place without her being the primary ethnographer, who had these embodied experiences for several months. She was able to sit and look through the material (to visit the material) and begin to see connections and common characteristics, allowing different ideas to weave in and out of the material. For example, it was striking how often homesickness was referenced; R3 therefore began to search the footage for passages where homesickness is thematized and where the young people deal with it in various ways. In Greenland, homesickness is often described as the major challenge and as part of a master narrative (Kjær, 2010; Bundgaard and Ottesen, 2013), which R1 and R2 encountered again during their first months of working on the project. R3 did not have the 'same-frame' story about Greenlandic young people and homesickness, but drawing on years spent working with notions of home, domesticity, 'Heimat' and 'homing oneself' (Winther, 2006, 2009), concepts related to homesickness kept cropping up: separation pangs, yearning for home, homesickness, nausea, and 'containing'. New concepts grew out of her visits within the material, and R1 and R2 continued to work with these concepts at the back of their minds in the ensuing months while the cameras whirred and they followed the everyday lives of the young people. In the project's final stages, Erik Mortensen (R4), who had operated as a creative consultant, arrived. R4 took pains *not* to meet the young people, *not* to occupy the hall of residence, and *not* to participate in the production of material. He watched the clips on a computer and listened to the analyses of material as a whole by the rest of the team, observing how it was gradually beginning to take shape as a story. Both R3 and R4 then questioned the many implicit assumptions by the 'primary analysts' (R1 and R2). R3 tried, at times, to extend the analyses beyond what the material could support and R1 and R2 brought things back down to earth if the analysis became too speculative. R4 tried to visually accentuate the sentiments that R1 and R2 had uncovered through their analyses and filming, but which they had to make sure they could illustrate visually using the available footage. R4 was able to contribute to this process with an outsider perspective. He then sparred with R1 and R2 regarding the use of new and different sound recordings and montages and a freer approach to production than the 'primary analysts' had felt they could allow themselves due to their obligations to the material; when R4's ideas became too visually speculative and unreal, they once again brought things back down to earth so the film did not become a mere construction. R1 and R2 brought all these inputs – R3's and R4's outsider perspectives and analyses and the material which emerges among multiple analysts – with them as they began the editing phase (the third analysis). Here, based on the primary and secondary analyses and on R4's visual input, R1 and R2 edited approximately 100 hours of footage into a 90-minute ethnographic documentary film. We are dealing with a form of asynchronicity in the creation process; and finally, the fourth analysis – written one year later – where there is some distance to the material, and for which R3 is the first author. Here, both the temporal factor and the secondary analyst's detachment have an impact. And once again, R1 had to pull back if R3's analyses became too speculative.

As mentioned above we follow two tracks – the film scenes and the written analysis. Graphically the film scenes are presented in *italics*. In this track, we have also included a number of screenshots from the footage, which visually present stills from the scenes we describe. With this track – the film scenes and photographs – we hope to draw the reader into the young people's world as we have seen and experienced it. However, we also try to depict the ways we have filmed and used the camera, allowing ourselves to take our time and take long shots, resulting in extremely long and intense scenes where both physical and emotional movements are apparent. It may seem as though we are the ultimate authority in interpreting the scenes in the film. We are not, but by switching back and forth between these two tracks (the film scenes and the written analysis) we want to communicate an atmosphere, but also to show and describe the material and spatial universe in which the young people are situated. Our ambition is that this will allow us to describe some of the microprocesses of everyday life, where the focus is on doing, feeling, and practising mobility, and thereby conduct mobility studies including 'blood, sweat, and tears', as called for by

Cresswell and Merriman (2011; Vannini, 2012), Ideally, the reader of this chapter will also watch the film: http://matup.gl/filmen.

An (asynchrone) "more-than-representational" text moving between film and analyze

Virtual containing – scene 1 (36:57–47:03)

Najaaraq has travelled 800 km across the ice cap to attend upper secondary school. She comes from a town on Greenland's east coast and now finds herself on the west coast in one of Greenland's largest towns. She is in the second year and is one of the only East Greenlanders at this upper secondary school. During the 18 months she has spent here, Najaaraq has suffered extreme homesickness. She has a clear plan: To complete upper secondary education she will have to live in here for three years, after which she will move to Denmark to study medicine. This will allow her to return to East Greenland – as a doctor – where she can start her proper life again. Her hometown in East Greenland is home to her parents, three younger brothers (one of whom is to join her at the upper secondary school this summer), and the rest of their family.

Najaaraq walks holding her iPhone while using FaceTime (see Figure 6.1). She shows the hall where she lives to her family at home. Via her phone, she shows them the noticeboard, including a cleaning rota. Her mother asks whether the building is taller than where her grandmother lives. Najaaraq replies that it is a lot taller – there are lots of floors with a family area on the ground floor (this is where the students who have children of their own live). *Holding the phone in front of her, she enters her room.*

In this way, Najaaraq and her family gain insight into each other's worlds and the material settings in which they are currently located. At home in East Greenland, the family is gathered for Easter lunch, Najaaraq's grandmother is visiting, and her youngest brother is mucking about while eating an ice cream. According to Najaaraq it is nice to participate a bit from a distance. This can be viewed as a way in which she tries to maintain her role in the family even though she is not physically present. Those at home get to see the halls of residence for the first time (domestic flights are very expensive in Greenland). They are not familiar with her location but are curious to see it.

Najaaraq stands with her back to the camera, which has been watching over her shoulder while she presented her world and spoke with those at home. She says that she does not want to hang up, but both her father and mother can be heard saying goodbye and they hang up. The camera continues to film Najaaraq diagonally from behind. After 15 seconds, she pulls her hands up in front of her face and we can see her shoulders shake and her begin to cry (the whole sequence is unedited and lasts 10 minutes).

For 45 seconds we watch her cry (filmed from the back), she dries her eyes and tries to get herself together. Precisely one minute after her mother had hung up, her mother calls again. Najaaraq says that she had been upset. Her mother

Figure 6.1 Najaaraq shows where she lives to her family at home (to the left) and virtual containing (to the right).

says that she had too and they both cry, all the while with Najaaraq caressing her mother's face. "I wish I could touch you", she says, and tells that she is really tired and sad and her mother replies that Najaaraq is not tired, she just misses them. That she is proud of her, that she's smart, that they are there for her and look forward to Najaaraq coming home, that she's got much further than her mother (who dropped out of school and never got an education). *We hear Najaaraq sniffle, see her caress her mother's face, and see the mother's face, which is also dissolved in tears.* For six minutes she is virtually contained (enveloped, embraced, and comforted). It is our interpretation that the mother expresses her hope that Najaaraq can do social mobility, but she knows there is a price to pay. The mother's way of dealing with the situation makes Najaaraq feel safe. She cries and allows herself to be enveloped and comforted like a small child. As viewers, we can see how Najaaraq and her parents share their feelings and sense of yearning. And we see how these feelings develop between them and are even strengthened when the conversation is initially ended. They disconnect and the void becomes clear. Cinematically, the clip shows the material universe in which both Najaaraq and her family are situated. The mobile phone is Najaaraq's anchor and, as viewers, we watch Najaaraq use the phone's webcam function to show and to observe. Najaaraq shows her world. She goes in and out of the spaces which she is in the process of making her own place. *We see how the room is decorated: the campaign poster of her father (who is a politician), photographs of her brothers on the fridge. As viewers we watch them watch each other. Najaaraq asks her little brother about some details and he does not reply but sticks out his tongue. We can hear Najaaraq's grandmother ask her what she's had to eat and Najaaraq's response of meatballs and chips – the grandmother does not look up;* perhaps she does not fully understand how mobile media technologies works. In this way, we as viewers of the film sequence see for ourselves the interaction and seem to feel the emptiness when we hear Najaaraq's tears – which creep into our stomachs during the long minute for which the camera just dwells on her shoulder. And when they reconnect, we sit there with tears in our eyes at the mother's knowing embrace while simultaneously revealing her own sadness. They cry together and we sense how they generate intimacy from afar. When Najaaraq tells her mother that she is tired, her mother could support this feeling, but instead she gently corrects the assertion and says: "No, you're not tired. You just miss us." In this way, the mother sets out what is at stake and reinterprets in a form which Najaaraq may find it easier to cope with. Both mother and daughter attempt to create some pockets of intimacy amidst the absence and it appears as though the mother builds a bridge between them and helps Najaaraq to tie her worlds together. The strong emotional movement in which they both find themselves can be sensed through the clip. It appears as though Najaaraq is split and holds onto the home and the people at home. She does not want to let go. She talks about how this town is not her home, but her place of study. For Najaaraq, home is still back home, where things appear stable and immobile. She says that she is scared of losing the closeness to the people and things at home if she lets herself become fully integrated with and embraces the new place. She is in a gap – an interzone – where she has physically moved away but is now in one long emotional movement, stretched between what is at home and the new place. She seems to be fighting to not let go and thereby lose her hometown, which has hitherto functioned as her spacious, meaning-saturated topos, to which she has been attached and where both family and landscape have accommodated her (Ingold 2000; also see Elixhauser 2015 for a description of the importance of place for East Greenlanders). She repeatedly talks about homesickness and how she is battling with these feelings, which almost seem to take the form of contraction-like cramps. The homesickness seems to empty and exhaust her; all the while she slowly moves further and further into the physical place in which she must be and make her own in order to become what she wants. She is the incarnation of the classic home-away-home theme. She was home, had to move away in order to gain an education, and wants to return home (as a qualified doctor). We encounter her while she is learning to live in the 'away position' and hear and see how she yearns for home 1 and starts to fear that home 2 will never happen: because she imagines that the transformation while away means that home 1 can no longer be inhabited.

Now there is a change of scene, from Najaaraq and her virtual containing, to a scene with a mother and father who are slowly realizing that their son has moved away, while they are left behind.

Asynchrone experiences – scene 2 (53:00–59:00)

We see the façade of a white housing block. We then cut to a view from a window with half the screen showing an embroidery of an individual dressed in an anorak and smoking a pipe and the other half showing the airport terminal they live next to. The camera tours the apartment.

"He's logged on. I've just asked him what he's up to." We cut to Piitaq, who is lying on his bed with the computer, before cutting back again. "He's just lazing around. What about us?" The father reads his message while looking at his wife, who is sitting at the other end of the corner sofa. She says that it's become so empty since Piitaq left. Continuing, she says that she had not realized it would take so many years when he first talked about GUX (upper secondary school). The father looks at her lovingly and smiles. "All of a sudden, someone or other said it would take three years. Three years!! Oh no" (she then repeats the relationship between one and three years several times). "Then I cried a lot." For the next five minutes, the mother talks about how she is slowly beginning to understand that he has left. As viewers, we sit there watching and listening to a middle-aged woman who is without education herself, to whom it was a great surprise that upper secondary qualification takes three years for her son.

She is similarly unaccustomed to the fact that her little boy is becoming an adult and thus moving away. At first, we as viewers are surprised that she did not know, but, at the same time, a knot begins to form in our stomachs. She is puzzled by seeing her son move away – away from home, from her cooking (see also Figure 6.2 with photographs of the child who is no longer there). She did not know that an upper secondary qualification takes three years; nor did she know that this mobility would mean that their only child would become so busy with friends and his new life that he would be incapable of sitting still and spending time with her – the radical nature of absence and his movement away becomes apparent to her – and we as viewers watch and feel the pain she experiences. She presents to us without the filter of self-preservation, and it floors us. *While the mother talks to the camera in close-up, we cut to the father, who smiles the whole time. He says, "Maybe he wasn't quite ready. There are things he hadn't come to terms with but, as far as we can tell, he's figured it out now. It's real now." The camera takes another trip around the apartment, into Piitaq's room, and we crosscut to life in the halls of residence.*

"Right now, I'm sitting here and thinking about how now he's actually starting to move away from home. We only get to borrow him during the holidays."

Figure 6.2 Family photographs back home.

Mobile media use by young people leaving 111

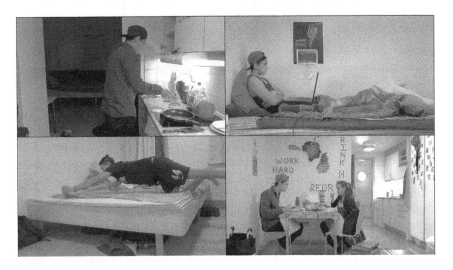

Figure 6.3 Everyday life at the halls of residence.

We cut to the mother, who nods. They talk together about how they are only just beginning to realize how much he has to struggle with all the practicalities (cooking, cleaning, shopping, paying for things himself; see Figure 6.3). They had not anticipated that at all. They search for the right words; not only because they seem to struggle to find the right words in Danish, but especially because it seems painful for them to express what they are thinking. *We watch Piitaq lying in bed, playing music, eating, and playing Ludo. The mother says: "I can sense that he's really growing up. He doesn't need me anymore."*

This sequence shows how, 100 kilometres away, Piitaq's parents are slowly beginning to discover and realize that a new era has already begun. They have decided to support him in his decision to move to move away: they have chosen strategy of only calling him once a week in order to set him free; they support him financially. They experience their son moving away (physically, socially, and mentally). As viewers, during the film's 90-minute duration, we can watch Piitaq gradually getting better and better at cooking, dealing with all the practicalities (see Figure 6.3), and thereby being en route – at the same time, we witness his parents' sense of being left behind physically (immobile), but in the process of making an intense mental movement (emotional mobility). The experiences of the son and his parents are staggered and are temporally and emotionally out of sync.

A change of scene to Aqqaluk, who is currently unable to deal with his mother and her interference.

'Living the life' – scene 3 (47:05–49:27, 50:31–53:00)

The crunch of snow underfoot on an icy morning. We watch Aqqaluk walking towards his school as he talks about how much his mother's constant phone calls irritate him. He is fed up with her interfering and her fear that he will oversleep, arrive late for class, have a poor attendance record, and end up having to drop out. "I just say ... shut up mum, I'm fine." She calls every day, asking the same questions, and he "hasn't got the strength". "Most of the time, I just say that I've been at school, even though I haven't. She's ridiculously overprotective." We cut back and forth between his trudge through the snow and his bed, where he sits with a friend Piitaq from home. Piitaq sits there, poker-faced, and drily comments: "He's always lying." Aqqaluk laughs. Earlier in the film, we have watched the two boys get out of bed, get dressed, grab a bag of crisps as they leave for school, and discuss what should be added to fried rice other than soy sauce. The whole time, we see and hear Aqqaluk playing guitar (see Figure 6.4). He practises for hours on end and his melodies soundtrack the film.

We follow the two childhood friends throughout the film as they take charge of their new life in the halls of residence, one day at a time. They have moved and receive financial support from home to attend upend secondary school. Aqqaluk talks with great certainty about his parents' belief in and love for him. Not for one second do we see the friends doing homework or anything school-related. In other words, at first glance, they do not seem particularly dedicated to establishing the educational mobility for which their parents have offered them support, but rather are preoccupied with living and being young far away from home. One might perhaps say that they are 'Living the life'. Unlike in Najaaraq's case, it is not a question of 'home-away-home' but of a 'home-away-further away' movement (Winther 2009).

We watch as Aqqaluk catches a plane home. He is in the process of being thrown out of school due to absenteeism and missing coursework. His mother meets him at the airport (see Figure 6.5). They embrace; later they sit together on the sofa. She is visibly disappointed. He responds evasively to questions and constantly fiddles with his mobile phone. She is irritated, both by his phone and, even more so, by his inability to complete the first year of upper secondary school. Disappointed and irritated, she stands up. He seems to be caught, emotionally, between his parents' shattered belief in and hopes for his education and his own desire to play music and just be young and lazy. At the same time, he is aware of the trap he risks falling into. His movement is not compatible with his parents' hopes. The mobile phone seems to

Figure 6.4 Everyday life at the halls of residence.

Mobile media use by young people leaving 113

Figure 6.5 Home to serious conversation.

be used to keep a distance from the mother who is, in the current situation, maybe too present.

Conclusion

In the chapter, we have tried to show how some young people and their parents perform and deal with the different movements discussed and how they deploy different strategies to move and adapt – both emotionally and practically. In a way, the young people and their families are trying to cope with the circumstance of having a physical distance wedged between them. Via mobile media technologies, the parents attempt to connect; maybe this can be understood as an attempt to create pockets of intimacy amidst the absence, or to stick to the parent-child relation – which can be difficult to free oneself from. Some of the young people share a need to keep abreast of their family's comings and goings and thereby be a part of each other's everyday lives – Najaaraq and her mother, for example, who move one another emotionally, with the mother able from afar to use her phone to connect and gently contain her unhappy daughter. Najaaraq walks around and presents her material universe before silently weeping, allowing herself to be embraced by her mother's solace until the crying subsides and, via their mutual emotional efforts, she regains her composure. They are moved together. Others, like Aqqaluk, are 'fed up with' their mothers' constant interference. He wants to 'Living the life', be free, stand on his own two feet, and create his own place. He wants to conquer the world and move it with his music. The material object of a phone has a double meaning; it helps in creating an intimacy, and at the same time it can establish and keep a distance from the parents when they 'mother' (Winther, 2015b) too much, and become too present.

All the family homes contain lots of photographs and other material traces and echoes of the children who are no longer there. There are also photographs and mementoes from home in the young people's rooms, but, nevertheless, they no longer directly share their everyday lives with their families. The parents have different strategies for supporting, containing, and setting free their offspring. The young people move out into the world on their own and have correspondingly different dreams of getting away from home, standing on their own two feet, making new tracks, overcoming and living with the longing and homesickness, or clinging to the feeling of homesickness to ensure the movement away from home does not become too great. There is clearly a common hope and dream concerning education and a better future. For most of the parents, this has to do with ensuring a better and easier life than they themselves have led. From this point onwards, the young people are treading new ground in relation to the older generation. Piitaq and Aqqaluk are moving forwards. Their parents are left behind. Some young people use mobile media technology as a kind of virtual mobility to maintain and participate in the 'back home' family life while others use the physical separation to achieve accelerated release from the parents and, as part of that, try to limit virtually contact with their parents.

This chapter is, as such, also a methodological attempt to intertwine the sensory impressions and atmospheres that arise, which can be captured in film with the reflections of written language. Our ambition was to include the material dimension and a sensibility to mobile and educational research. We want to communicate an atmosphere, but also to show and describe the material and spatial universe in which the young people are situated. Our ambition is that this will allow us to describe some of the microprocesses of everyday life, where the focus is on doing, feeling, and practising mobility. We do this despite being well aware that what we present will always be but a poor reproduction and that it is not really possible to describe in words what film can present sensually and materially.

The ambition to work along two tracks and with staggered analyses is not a question of genre, but a desire to explicitly and transparently demonstrate that, by interweaving a written text analysis (with the challenges in terms of representation analysis always involves) with written film scenes referencing the filmed sequences (which have similar challenges regarding representation), it is perhaps possible to create a text which is entirely dependent on the empirical material (*realis*) while at the same time being the researchers' construction (*irrealis*) – a transparent text, as required in scientific contexts, that is simultaneously interwoven with sensual fragments which all stem from *realis*, but which, through our analysis – both cinematic and textual – conveys 'blood, sweat, and tears'. When we discuss, do, and write this kind of multiple research we show – instead of tell – what happens when analytical material is processed, considered, and revisited.

References

Anderson-Levitt, K., 2003. A World Culture of Schooling? In: K. Anderson-Levitt, ed. *Local Meanings, Global Schooling: Anthropology and World Culture Theory*. New York: Palgrave Macmillian. pp. 1–16.

Augé, M., 1992. *Non-Places: An Introduction to Anthropology of Supermodernity*. Le Seuil: Verso.

Bauman, Z., 1998. *Globalization: The Human Consequences*. New York: Columbia University Press.

Bloch, E. 1985 (1935). *Erbschaft Dieser Zeit.* Frankfurt am Main: Suhrkamp Verlag.
Brennet, J., 2010. *Vibrant Matter: A Policital Ecology of Things.* Durham, NC: Duke University Press.
Bundgaard, R., 2015. *At navigere på et grønlandsk gymnasium – en analyse på film og skrift af generthed, skolerum og qallunajaqqat* [Navigating a Greenlandic upper secondary school – an analysis in film and writing of shyness, school spaces and *qallunajaqqat*]. Master Thesis. København: Aarhus University.
Bundgaard, R. and Ottesen, H., 2013. *Et bidrag til en grønlandsk efterskolepædagogik* [A contribution to a Greenlandic pedagogy for lower secondary boarding schools.] Odense: Nationalt videnscenter for frie skoler.
Cresswell, T., 2006. *On the Move: Mobility in the Modern Western World.* New York: Taylor & Francis.
Cresswell, T. and Merriman, P., 2011. *Geographies of Mobilities: Practices, Spaces, Subjects.* Burlington: Ashgate.
de Certeau, M., 1984. *The Practice of Everyday Life.* Berkeley: University of California Press.
Elixhauser, S.C., 2015. Traveling the East Greenlandic Sea- and Landscape: Encounters, Place and Stories. *Mobilities,* 10(4), pp. 531–551.
Flora, J., 2007. Tilknytning og selvstændighed – unges fravalg af uddannelse [Attachment and independence – young people opting out of education]. In: W. Kahlig and N. Banerjee, eds. *Børn og unge i Grønland – en antologi* [Children and young people in Greenland – an anthology]. Nuuk: Milik Publishing. pp. 148–163.
Flora, J., 2015. Ikke som alle de 'andre' – mobilitet og selvstændighed blandt grønlandske studerende i Danmark [Not like all the 'others' – mobility and independence among Greenlandic students in Denmark] In: K. Valentin and K.F. Olwig, eds. *Mobilitet og tilknytning – migrantliv i et globaliseret Danmark* [Mobility and attachment – migrant lives in a globalized Denmark]. Aarhus: Aarhus Universitetsforlag. pp. 201–220.
Frykman, J. and Frykman, M.P., 2016. Affects and Material Culture. In: J. Frykman and M. P. Frykman, eds. *Sensitive Objects.* Lund: Nordic Academiv Press. pp. 9–30.
Ingold, T., 2000. *The Perception of the Environment – Essays on Livelihood, Dwelling and Skill.* London, New York: Routledge.
Ingold, T., 2011. *Being Alive: Essays on Movement, Knowledge and Description.* London, New York: Routledge.
Jensen, O.B., 2013. *Staging Mobilities.* London: Routledge.
Johnson-Hanks, J., 2006. *Uncertain Honour. Modern Motherhood in an African Crisis.* Chicago: University of Chicago Press.
Kjær, L., 2010. *Frafaldsundersøgelsen 2010 – En undersøgelse af frafaldet på de gymnasiale uddannelser.* [The dropout study 2010 – A study of dropout in upper secondary education]. Nuuk: Departementet for Kultur, Uddannelse, Forskning og Kirke.
Kofoed, J. and Thomson, R., 2018. A Fellow Traveller: The Opening of an Archive. An Essay. In: R. Thomson., L. Berriman., S. Bragg, eds. *Researching Everyday Childhood in a Digital Age: Time, Technology and Documentation Time.* London: Bloomsbury Press. pp. 163–172.
KUFK, 2001. Hvem får en uddannelse? – en undersøgelse af de forhold, der er bestemmende for unges påbegyndelse og gennemførsel af Uddannelse [Who gets an education? – a study of the conditions determining young people's enrolment in and completion of education]. Nuuk: Direktoratet for kultur, uddannelse, kirke og forskning.
Löfgren, O., 2015. Recycling the Home: On the Constant Flow of Domestic Stuff, Emotions and Routines. In: K.M. Ekström, ed. *Waste Management and Sustainable*

Consumption: Reflections on Consumer Waste. London, New York: Routledge. pp. 13–28.

Lorimer, H., 2005. Cultural Geography: The Busyness of Being 'More-Than-Representational'. *Progress in Human Geography*, 29(1), pp. 83–94.

MacDougall, D., 2006. *The Corporeal Image – Film, Ethnography, and the Senses*. Princeton, Oxford: Princeton University Press.

Meinert, L. 2009. *Hopes in Friction. Schooling, Health and Everyday Life in Uganda*. Charlotte, NC: Information Age Publishing.

Meinert, L. and Kølner, M., 2010. Håbets fælde? Fortryllelse og universel skolegang i Uganda og Tanzania [The hope trap? Enchantment and universal schooling in Uganda and Tanzania]. *Tidsskriftet Antropologi*. 62. København: Københavns Universitet. pp. 103–125.

Møhl, P., 2004. Synliggørelsen – med kameraet i felten. In: K. Hastrup, ed. *Ind i verden* [Into the World]. København: Hans Reitzels Forlag. pp. 163–183.

Olwig, K.F. and Valentin, K., 2015. Mobility, Education and Life Trajectories: New and Old Migratory Pathways. *Identiities: Global Studies in Culture and Power*, 22(3), pp. 247–257.

Salazar N. and Smart, A., 2011. Introduction: Anthropological Takes on (Im)Mobility. *Identities: Global Studies in Culture and Power*, 18(6). pp. i–ix.

Schiller, N.G. and Salazar N.B., 2013. Regimes of Mobility Across the Globe. *Journal of Ethnic and Migration Studies*, 39(2), pp. 183–200.

Sørensen, Bo Wagner. 1993. Bevægelser mellem Grønland og Danmark: Etnicitet, følelser og rationalitet i migration [Movements between Greenland and Denmark: Ethnicity, emotions, and rationality in migration]. *Tidsskriftet Antropologi*, 28. Københanvs Universitet. pp. 31–46.

Stewart, Kathleen. 2007. *Ordinary Affects*. Duke University Press.

Svinkløv, Martin. 2016. *Acting Bodies in Whole Acts – En ny narrativ poetik til etnografiske dokumentarfilm og en undersøgelse af den sociale energi mellem dramaturgi, antropologi, æstetik og sandhed*. [A new narrative poetic for ethnographic film, and an exploration of social energy between dramaturgy, anthropology, aesthetics and truth]. Master Thesis. Aarhus University.

Turkel, Sherry. 2007. *Evocative Objects – Things We Think With*. Cambridge, MA: MIT Press.

Valentin, K. and Olwig, K.F., 2015. Nye horisonter i dansk migrantionsforskning" [New horizons in Danish migration research]. In: K. Valentin and K.F. Olwig, eds. *Mobilitet og tilknytning – migrantliv i et globaliseret Danmark* [Mobility and attachment – migrant lives in a globalized Denmark]. Aarhus: Aarhus University Press. pp. 201–220.

Vannini, P., 2010. Mobile Cultures: From the Sociology of Transportation to the Study of Mobilities. *Sociology Compass*, 4(2), pp. 111–121.

Vannini, P., 2012. *Ferry Tales: Mobility, Place, and Time on Canada's West Coast*. New York: Routledge. See also: http://ferrytales.innovativeethnographies.net.

Vannini, P., ed. 2015. Enlivening Ethnography Through the Irrealis Mood – In Seach of a More-Than-Reprensentational Style. In: *Non-Representational Methodologies – Re-Envisioning Research*. London, New York: Routledge. pp. 112–129.

Werner, A., 2015. Introduction: Studying Junctures of Motion and Emotion. In: *Culture Unbound*, 7(2), pp. 169–173.

Winther, I.W., 2009. Homing Oneself: Home as a Practice. In: B. Penner and Pavlovits, D., eds. *Harceity Papers*, 4(2), pp. 49–84.

Winther, I.W., 2013. Children's Everyday Lives (re)constructed as variable sets of 'Field bodies': Revisiting the 'Exotic' remote Island – a case Study. *Nordic Studies in Education*, 2, pp. 112–123.

Winther, I.W., 2015a. To Practice Mobility – On a Small Scale. I: *Culture Unbound*, 7(2), pp. 215–231. Linköping University Electronic Press: www.cultureunbound.ep.liu.se.

Winther, I.W., 2015b. *Siblings – Practical and Sensitive Relations*. København: http://edu.au.dk/fileadmin/edu/Forskning/E-book_-_Siblings.pdf.

Winther, I.W., 2017. Materialitet – sansning og erfaring" [materiality – sense perception and experience]. In: E. Gulløv, G.B. Nielsen, I.W. Winther, eds. *Pædagogisk Antropologi – Tilgange Og Begreber* (Educational Anthropology – Approaches and Concepts). København: Hans Reitzels Forlag. pp. 245–257.

Urry, J., 2002. Mobility and Proximity. *Sociology*, 36(2), pp. 255–274.

Urry, J., 2007. *Mobilities*. Cambridge: Polity Press.

7 Mapping unknown knowns of transit infrastructures

Elisa Diogo Silva, Ditte Bendix Lanng and Simon Wind

Introduction: mapping transit infrastructures

This chapter considers material urban transit infrastructures as possible design sites: these can be road networks, train stations, bike parking facilities, and other nodes and corridors of urban transit (see Figure 7.1). Our task here is to foreground and analyse the operational process through which designers may work analytically and creatively at existing infrastructural sites to "secure and convey spatial knowledge graphically" (Cosgrove, 1999, p. 9). This is the process of mapping.

Some elements of spatial knowledge, or 'site conditions', of infrastructures, such as quantitative flows and material structures, offer themselves as relatively easy to be recognized and conveyed graphically (though we do recognize that

Figure 7.1 Berlin public transport infrastructures.
Source: © Elisa Diogo Silva, Ditte B. Lanng and Simon Wind.

large numbers of professional and academic competencies, methodological reflections, tools and technologies, issues of colonization and uneven power distribution, and disciplinary, political and societal controversies are embedded in such mapping operations). Yet, our argument here is that mapping should not only be a process that secures and conveys such solid things and quantifiable conditions, as if that is all that is involved in infrastructures. This, we find, contributes to the neutralization and objectification of infrastructures as technical utility lines for transport flows.

Rather, we argue, mapping should be a process that engages with infrastructures as multifaceted socio-material environments for the many and diverse lives on the move.

Here, we follow Denis Cosgrove's recapture of acts of mapping as "moments in coming to knowledge about the world" in which "the map is both the spatial embodiment of knowledge and a stimulus to further cognitive engagements" (1999, p. 2). This further engagement is crucially important in design, since mapping is not without effect; it may have significant potency in not only knowing the world, but also shaping it for the future (see Corner, 1999). And so, the urgency of our undertaking is underlined: designers, who often act with influence in scripting and re-scripting the material world, need to reflectively engage with mapping, so as to question reductionist neutralizations of infrastructure and, instead, cultivate insights into other, perhaps less representative, site conditions.

In urban design, 'site mapping' is known as the entangled methodological attempt to recognize, represent and examine the solid, material conditions of a design site as well as a wide a host of other and less representative conditions (see Corner, 1999). These other conditions include social, ecological and cultural embeddedness of a design site, its history, and constraints and possibilities of alternative futures, the needs, aspirations, activities and experiences of inhabitants, the political and economic formations of which the site is part, and more (see also Lippard, 1997; Cresswell, 2004; Burns and Kahn, 2005; Massey, 2005). In this inclusive and networked sense, mapping is a convoluted activity, as well as being an important and evocative requirement to urban designers' commitment to designing material environments that can be places of relevance and resonance for a wide host of conditions.

It is characteristic for infrastructural nodes and corridors that they are sites for travellers' continuing and diverse everyday journeys. These infrastructures, often made of durable, static materials such as granite, concrete, steel and metal, are sites where humans move and gather, temporarily and across distances. Though they are often mundane and may often be unnoticed, multiple, heterogeneous, embodied, social and cultural practices and encounters are performed along routes and in nodes. Emotions, atmospheres, approximations and resistances constantly materialize and dissolve, merge and separate, when infrastructures are inhabited as lived environments (e.g. see Urry, 2007; Bissell, 2010; Cresswell and Merriman, 2011; Vannini, 2012;).

The acknowledgement of such a richness of mobile lives infers that transit infrastructures should not be known only as utility lines for 'shuffling' neutral, disembodied, generic, particle-like "transported travellers" (Ingold, 2007, p. 78) across the city (Lanng, 2014). Rather, designers must understand these sites as 'lived' environments, where lives are lived on-the-move. Hence, designers' site knowledge should include insight into less-representative *unknown knowns* of transit infrastructures. These include, but are not limited to, travellers' multisensorial embodied 'dwelling-in-motion' (Urry, 2007), which is our focus here. With the term *unknown knowns*, we point to the existence and significance of tacit, embodied knowledge that we may have of everyday embodied journeys in infrastructures, while acknowledging the difficulties encountered when seeking to capture, describe and represent their occurrence, significance and particularities by site mapping.

In this chapter, we aim to contribute to a reflective expanse and customization of mapping methodology and designerly insight. We focus on mapping operations to sensitize mobilities designers to transit infrastructures as lived environments composed by relational configurations of material features and embodied mobilities. Structured by James Corner's (1999) mapping operations of 'extracts' and 'plotting', the chapter thus illustrates and discusses how site mapping operations might be analytically enhanced to identify, demonstrate and amplify unknown knowns of urban transit infrastructures.

The chapter is structured as follows: below, we first clarify the wider research agenda of the chapter's aim, as well as introduce the mapping operations of 'extracts' and 'plotting'. Second, we outline a fieldwork experiment with autoethnographic 'mapping-in-motion' in Berlin, the methodology of this experiment and an analysis and discussion of one example of mapping a journey through Berlin, extracting sensorial impressions, travellers' behaviours and atmospheres from the networked, temporal imbrications of Berlin's transit infrastructural sites. Third, we analyse and discuss four other mapping examples that also seek to extract sensorial impressions and atmospheres of urban material sites and to plot new or latent relationships from these extracts. In conclusion, the overall task recaptures how these collected examples demonstrate varieties of the way in which mapping operations are performed, and how map-makers are attuned to lived environments as well as to mapping practices in two ways: attunement to the field – to being in, sensing and knowing infrastructural sites as lived environments; and attunement to the act of mapping – to the intricacies of practising mapping operations.

Mobilities design

This chapter is part of an emerging research agenda that concerns the analysis and design of transport infrastructures, mobilities design (Jensen *et al.*, 2016a; Jensen and Lanng, 2017; Lanng *et al.*, 2017; Lanng, 2018; see also Mossop, 2006; Stoll and Lloyd, 2010; Ruby and Ruby, 2017). Mobilities design combines hybrid perspectives from mobilities research (e.g. Urry, 2007; Sheller, 2011; Vannini, 2012; Jensen, 2013), with Science and Technology Studies (STS)-related streams of work on architecture and design (e.g., Fallan, 2008;

Latour and Yaneva, 2008; Yaneva, 2009), and with the professional and disciplinary complex of knowledge, methods and commitments of urban design (e.g. Venturi et al., 1977; Whyte, 1980; Jacobs and Appleyard, 1987; Moudon, 1992; Arefi, 1999; Burns and Kahn, 2005; Krieger and Saunders, 2009; Mumford, 2009).

With mobilities design we seek to identify and examine critical issues in relation to the design of infrastructure. Motivations for this research include the need to move beyond technical-only transport considerations and explicitly work to open up a space for discussing (and including in future designs) the wider host of social, cultural, political, ecological and affective agencies of which these infrastructures are part. Hence, with mobilities design we bring forth a critique and concern for a lack of consideration of the wider agencies of material infrastructures. These include a lack of a meaningful and responsible ecological agency of infrastructures, which tend to be inconsiderately imposed upon ecosystems, drain resources, and co-produce unsustainable practices, and a lack of social agency, seen for example in the apparent deficit of design consideration for individuals as well as collective populations of citizens who actually traverse these infrastructures, and the inequalities that infrastructures tend to co-produce or sustain. Working with an outlook for these serious deficits, mobilities design is a research programme that aims to ask questions, produce knowledge and shape a conversational space around futures of mobilities spaces and structures.

Our work on mobilities design has its set-out, and hence its scope, based on urban design. The design of spaces, structures and systems of urban mobilities has been the collective physical territory of primary interest. This chapter follows this stream of work on mobilities design in its layout and scope, focusing on 'site mapping' as one key method for the designer of material transit infrastructures.

The agency of mapping

In our analysis and discussion of the mapping method, we find our point of departure in architectural scholar James Corner's essay, *The Agency of Mapping* (1999). Corner's notion of mapping describes the entangled processes that designers engage in of identifying, representing and analysing existing conditions of a physical site, and of generating design potentials from those conditions. To Corner, knowing a site and designing for it, are not two phases of a design process, but intricately connected in and through the practice of mapping: a "map is already a [design] project in the making" (ibid., p. 216). Mapping is a precondition to the designer's work with imagining and developing alternative futures through design proposals, actualizing potentials, herein sometimes underexposed conditions.

In his essay, Corner distinguishes between 'tracing' and 'mapping'. Tracing, to Corner, is a representational practice of extracting elements and conditions, which are already known, from the site. Corner finds that tracings "propagate redundancies" (ibid., p. 214): they produce closure and finality. Instead of tracing, Corner pleads for designers to avoid the failure of "universalist approaches towards master-planning and the imposition of state-controlled schemes" (ibid.), leave claims of representational accuracy, formal clarity and ease of use, and instead embrace mapping as an open and inclusive process of disclosure and enablement. Corner unfolds this powerful agency of mapping as an active and more-than-representational experimentation with and 'actualization' of site complexities and contradictions, occurrences, processes, interrelations and potentials for the future.

Like James Corner, other authors, in relation to design, recognize the power of mapping to perform tasks other than representation of the strictly material realm. Julie Nichols, for instance, advocates that in order to achieve a kind of representation of a space, various dimensions from physical to imaginal, spiritual and ideological must be selected, interpreted and assembled in the process of mapping (Nichols, 2014). Nadia Amoroso, in accordance with these understandings, argues that maps as artefacts have the power to show "the 'invisible' forces that shape our urban environment" (Amoroso, 2010, p. xi). She brings forth several examples of non-traditional, creative mapping, for instance, the architectural studio MVRDV's mapping projects built on data and on utopian 'what-if' designerly speculations aimed at creating environmental awareness. Likewise, Les Roberts reports on several examples of mapping using less conventional methods (Roberts, 2012). Roberts refers for instance to Sohei Nishino's *London Map Diorama* that consists of an immense collage of pictures that represents his personal pedestrian perspective and his memoir of the city. These works suggest that mapping as a method is up for debate, challenge and ingenious re-imaginations in both academia and artistic and designerly practices. Like the mapping examples that we will discuss in this chapter, these resources question and experiment with how we can learn about site conditions and possible futures through mapping.

In a previous experimental research study on 'more-than-representational mapping', we also deliberated on mapping mobilities (Lanng, 2018). In that study, we coupled Corner's arguments of the agency of mapping with non-representational research, so as to contribute to a denaturalization of transit spaces. In this work, we examined one instance of a 'mobilization' and customization of the method of mapping to use it for cultivating insight into actual sites of mobilities, and discussed how it could help us to learn about the 'eventfulness' of these mundane spaces, about the 'relationality' of material sites and lived mobilities, and about invoking the 'yet-to-be', i.e. engaging in possible futures of these sites. To these ends, we experimented with and reflected upon an empirical mapping experiment in mundane suburban transit spaces. The experiment drew on film-elicitations of local travellers' everyday-life journeys in and across these sites, showing us glimpses of traveller's sensorial impressions, their practices, and how they 'share agency' (Yaneva, 2009) with artefacts, surfaces, structures and spaces of material infrastructures as they move. The mapping study demonstrated that, while transit spaces may be assumed to be neutral, technical, utility infrastructures, they may indeed, through mapping, be known as relational and networked collective spaces enacted and co-produced by lived mobilities, though extracts of these tend to be less representational and difficult to capture on a map. Through this examination of mapping as a more-than-representational tool, we found mapping to be capable of contributing to the animation of some of the intangible, fleeting qualities of mobile lives on infrastructural sites; to not only represent what was there already but to also present these eventful and relational mobilities anew, in visualizing and juxtaposing them as disparate site conditions.

In this chapter, we build upon that prior work, and seek to add to the reflection and cross-verbalization of urban design, mobilities and mapping. Unlike the study on more-than-representational mapping, which mapped suburban spaces through film-elicitation of local travellers' journeys, this chapter looks at a student experiment with auto-ethnographic mapping of metropolitan transit infrastructures. It considers in particular the analytical and representational operations of mapping that designers, or students, may employ when mapping infrastructures, and discusses how an attunement to these operations helps to facilitate the designers' attunement to relational sites of mobilities.

Mapping operations

We will now introduce one way of structuring the operational process of mapping transit infrastructures – that which guides our investigation in this chapter. Again, we follow Corner's essay, in which he structures the mapping method through a three-step process, with three mapping operations: *'field'*, *'extracts'* and *'plotting'*.

The creation of a *'field'* is the first mapping operation. To Corner, this is the setting up of the system of organization that conditions the two other operations. This system includes the representational choices that must be made: scale, frame, orientation, etc. that make up the schematical equivalent to the actual ground. The way in which the system is set up, significantly affects what is seen and known, and how knowledge is organized.

The second mapping operation is *'extraction'*. Corner states:

> Extracts are the things that are often observed within a given milieu and drawn onto the graphic field. We call them extracts because they are always selected, isolated and pulled-out from their original seamlessness with other things; they are effectively 'de-territorialized'.
>
> (Corner, 1999, p. 230)

That is, extracts are "things" – moments, conditions, artefacts or specific categorized 'layers', such as topographical features, building typologies, or materials of the site. In Corner's operational terminology extracts are 'taken' from the territory, they are *de*-territorialized, through selection and capture.

The third mapping operation is *'plotting'*. Corner describes it as follows:

> Plotting entails an active and creative interpretation of the map to reveal [...]. Plotting is not simply the indiscriminate listing and inventorying of conditions, [...] but rather a strategic and imaginative drawing-out of relational structures [...] plotting produces a 're-territorialization' of sites.
>
> (ibid.)

Plotting is thus the *re*-territorialization of the previously captured *'extracts'*, in other words, the compilation and transferral of the 'taken' *'extracts'* into a new territory, which is not only the *representation* on a map, but also the evocative *presentation* of the site and the extracts anew, in plotting new interrelationships and narratives.

In this chapter the latter two operations are foregrounded in our examination of the acts of mapping infrastructures. Following our consideration of the lived environments, we focus on extracts and plottings that attempt to secure and convey spatial knowledge about sensorial and atmospheric engagements with infrastructural sites. In our examination we will bring in a fieldwork experiment with mapping Berlin infrastructures, and, after that, four other examples of mapping that contribute to widening our understanding of the great variety with which one can engage in mapping such less-representational site conditions.

A fieldwork experiment: mapping-in-motion in Berlin

In this section we retell a fieldwork experiment with mapping from 2016. The experiment was initiated as a study trip assignment and carried through by Master's students in Urban Design from Aalborg University. In the first part of the section we introduce the methodology of the experiment, and in the latter part we describe and analyse one example of mapping Berlin's transit infrastructures.

Methodology: auto-ethnographic mapping-in-motion

In the spring of 2016, a class of students went on a study tour to Berlin. In that city, a sophisticated public transportation infrastructure network providing diverse modes of urban mobility to inhabitants and visitors has been developed over the course of the city's historical development and transformations. The transit network includes the S-Bahn, the U-Bahn, the tramway, and a regional railway system combined with a system of buses. The aim of the study tour was to explore and map these complex mobilities systems of Berlin, in an experiment with students primed to map sites of lived mobilities, herein to experiment with mapping operations.

In groups of five, students tested auto-ethnographic 'mapping-in-motion', capturing and analysing urban mobilities sites of Berlin's public infrastructure network from their own perspectives as travellers. With given points of departure (point A) and arrival (point B), each mapping assignment included the mapping of a journey by pre-selected modes of transport. The assignment included experimentation with mapping operations, herein selection of 'extracts' to capture as well as paying careful attention to (re-)presentational techniques on a two-dimensional map, drawing on Corner's reflections of the significance of setting the 'field' and of plotting new and latent relationships.

At the outset, students were asked to consider which extracts they would seek to capture and map. A list of inspiration was provided beforehand. It included as diverse extracts as 'sounds' and 'smells', 'environmental affordances' (see Gibson, 1986; Jensen et al., 2016b), 'spatial dimensions', 'activities', 'speeds', 'colours', and 'boundaries'. Likewise, an inspirational list of notation techniques was provided. It included, for example, 'field notes', 'photos', 'drawings', 'sound clips', 'stories', 'samples', and 'measurements'. The lists were intended to inspire students to go beyond visual modes of doing ethnography and to invoke their creative minds as to experimenting with how to capture what is going on in the field and how it feels to travel through Berlin infrastructures, and if and how particularities of infrastructural transit sites could be invoked as lived environments through mapping. After the field work students were asked to graphically convey their spatial knowledge on a map.

The mapping experiment took its point of departure in Jensen's theoretical framework '*Staging Mobilities*' (2013, p. 6). The Staging Mobilities model considers mobile situations in three dimensions: the materiality and design of the physical settings, such as signage and architecture, people's embodied performances, and the social interactions among users. The model centres its attention on the intricate relationship between what is fixed and what moves in situations, and, consequently, relational effects between them.

Students used their own embodied experience, their bodies, and sensorial perceptions as auto-ethnographic instruments for capturing extracts while being in mobile situations. Hence, they engaged in capturing their observations made on others, as well as their own involvement with the physical settings and other travellers. As such, it became an immersed, situated mapping experiment to extract and represent spatial-material particularities for doing mobility in Berlin.

The aim of analysing in some detail one of the five student mapping experiments, as we will do below, is to examine analytical and representational modes through which designers might become emphatically attuned to mobile situations in infrastructures as lived environments. We will consider how students combine different techniques to *'plot'* relationships of many diverse de-territorialized *'extracts'* from the infrastructural sites, and how these operations and combinations support the generation of an understanding of the infrastructural sites.

Analysis and discussion of one example: mapping a journey through Berlin

The experiment reported upon here, and depicted in Figure 7.2, is based upon an S-Bahn journey, including both underground and ground-level stations. Throughout their journey, students stopped at a series of stations, identified with

126 E.D. Silva et al.

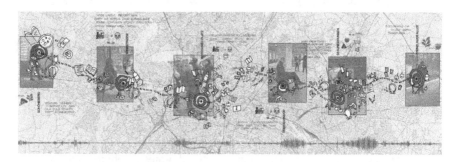

Figure 7.2 The journey through the city centre of Berlin: A story told through embodied experiences – and emojis.

Source: © Aalborg University (AAU).

red rings, to map their experience. Students chose to focus on capturing the following 'extracts': sounds, smells, travellers' behaviours and atmospheres. Every 'extract' is added on the map through a combination of representation techniques. The combination of words and several graphic elements provides the map-reader with a composite understanding of extracts, and is the students' attempt to engage in the third mapping operation of 'plotting'. Such assemblage of techniques can be seen in more detail in the four mapping moments selected from the Berlin map and represented in Figure 7.3. Below we will briefly describe the four extracts of this example, and reflect upon how they 're-territorialize' the infrastructural site through the maps.

Sounds were mapped mainly through words, drawings and sound waves. Combined, the aim was to represent the existing sounds and their amplitude, as they were perceived by the autoethnographic mappers. Words identify the origin of the sound, which in combination with a colour – green, red or black – illustrates the sensation attached to it by the students, pleasant, disturbing or neutral, respectively. For example, the *'creaking from the rolling stairs'* at Potsdamer Platz Station was mapped in red, thus, as a constant and annoying sound. As for the drawings, these focus on sounds originating from people's presence, such as people chatting, children running or even silence illustrated by people enclosed in their own personal spheres occupied with a phone or reading a book. The sound line, which can be seen in Figure 7.2, represents the volume of the sounds.

Smells were mapped through emojis illustrating both the origin of the smell and the emotion they provoked on the persons mapping them. For instance, smells coming from the green surroundings or from food were plotted through the use of smileys illustrating in a straightforward manner sensations of joy and well-being, for example at Prenzlauer Allee Station. The same applies to less-pleasant smells. For instance, at Nordbahnhof Station the ones coming from cigarettes or trains were represented as toxic and repulsive. As for words, although not widely used, the same logic applies. When the scent of perfume was detected, words were used to define its origin, and its association with the colour black illustrates it as a pleasant

Unknown knowns of transport infrastructures 127

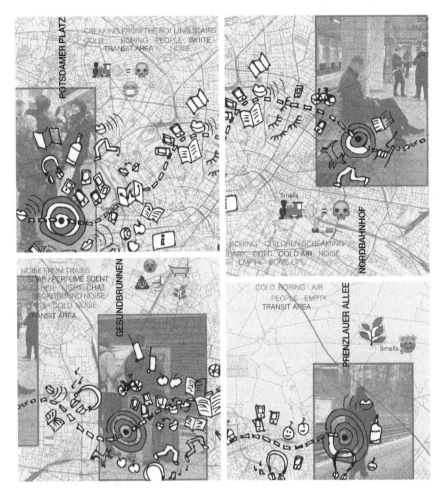

Figure 7.3 Four stations, four mapping moments taken from: The journey through the city centre of Berlin: A story told through embodied experiences – and emojis.

Source: © Aalborg University (AAU).

smell, although not dominant, since emojis reveal any prevailing smells, as depicted at Gesundbrunnen Station (see Figure 7.2).

Travellers' behaviours were mapped through drawings of various kinds of performances. For instance, the actions of people running and people chatting were mapped in and from Potsdamer Platz station until Gesundbrunnen station. The dense clustering of drawings shows these as the most crowded stations on the journey. Likewise, the human–artefact relation of, for instance, people interacting with their phones was also represented in drawings through small sketches of artefacts that travellers were carrying en route.

128 E.D. Silva et al.

As regards the stations' *atmospheres*, the students approached these by mixing all the captured *extracts* and representation techniques. Potsdamer Platz station, for instance, is described using words such as '*creaking from the rolling stairs*', '*cold*', '*boring*' and '*noise*', emojis showing the toxic and unappealing smell from the trains, which, all taken together, suggest the presence of an unpleasant spatial atmosphere. Consequently, it is described as 'just a transit area'. The picture presents its main users, children, while drawings illustrate the activities and interactions among travellers, such as running, chatting, reading and so on. Those who are not interacting with others are often searching for some kind of interaction through their phones.

Through these extracts, and through representation of them on the map, this experiment explored sites in Berlin's transit infrastructures, from 'within' mobile situations. Students experimented with 'de-territorializing' non-tangible 'extracts', in particular sensorial impressions and atmospheres. The selected, captured and represented '*extracts*' are all accounts of fugitive and less-representational moments that came with several methodological challenges. These included considerations of, for example, how silence can be captured and represented on a map, and how a dark and uninviting situation can be mapped. Though the experiment did not produce particularly imaginative or evocative (re-)presentations of the sites, it remains an attempt to secure and convey spatial knowledge about these sites as lived environments. In particular, the final extract of atmosphere is interesting for this purpose, since it is already a creative and mixed interpretation of other extracts. Atmosphere, as perhaps the least-representational phenomenon at stake here, is a relational between-phenomenon, according to Böhme (1993); it stands between the physicality of the place and the subject's mobile perception, and it implies the presence and sensitivity of the subject immersed in the 'wholeness' of the lived environment. With the mapping of atmospheres, the students attempt to attune themselves and their mapping practise to relationships between human activity, sensorial impressions, and solid materialities. Through plotting these relationships they get to know and present the sites as processual and hybrid places. This is a site knowledge of infrastructures that opposes any objectification of these infrastructures as neutral transport sites. Both the selected 'extracts' and 'plotting' differ in each group and therefore the results are dissimilar, as Figure 7.4 illustrates. Nonetheless, our effort was to analyse one of the auto-ethnographic 'mapping-in-motion' outcomes in more detail and to bring forth other and distinct mapping experiments.

Below, we will expand our discussion of such a mapping practice through bringing in four other resources that show some of the variety with which mapping operations can be performed, thus aiding our reflections on the process.

Analysis and discussion of variations on mapping sensorial impressions and atmospheres

The following mapping examples share common ground with the mapping experiment described above in scope, and address the topics of lived urban

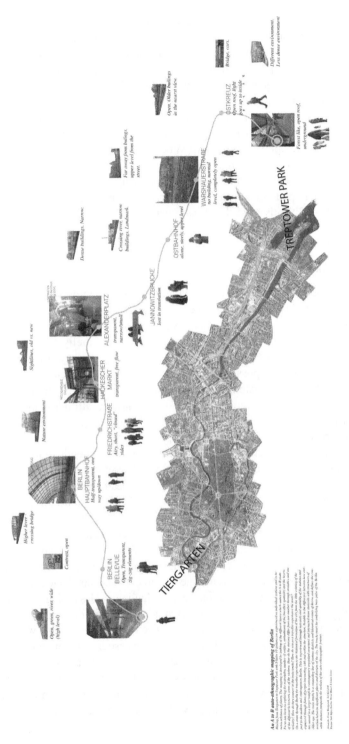

Figure 7.4 An A to B auto-ethnographic mapping of Berlin.

Source: © Aalborg University (AAU).

environments, movement, and the selection of 'extracts'. We will use these examples to widen our understanding of the great many ways in which one can engage in mapping sensorial impressions and atmospheres of sites, so as to employ mapping as a process that reaches beyond physical and quantifiable attributes of sites and engages in learning about lived environments.

The first two maps we refer to, stem from the Good City Life project: the 'Smelly Maps' and 'Chatty Maps' systematically attempt to extract knowledge on sensorial experiences of places (the maps can be found at www.goodcitylife.org/smellymaps/index.php and www.goodcitylife.org/chattymaps/index.php respectively). The two above-mentioned mapping examples we refer to stand out for their artistic-creative procedures of capturing extracts and representing them in ways that plot unexpectedly evocative urban relationships. The third example, 'Naked City', is from the situationist Guy Debord and the fourth, from Frank Dresmé, is entitled 'Project 360 degrees'.

Smelly Maps and Chatty Maps

The project Good City Life seeks to capture sensorial impressions of urban environments – smells, sounds and even emotions. Focusing on these aspects, examples such as 'Smelly Maps', 'Chatty Maps' and 'Happy Maps' demonstrate ways of de-territorializing sensorial impressions. The 'Smelly Maps' explore urban smells and their impact, thereby challenging the primacy often given to vision. Focusing on the possibility of urban scents influencing urban life, Quercia et al. (2015), advocate that smells contribute significantly to the perception and use of places: "Smells impact our behavior, attitudes and health. Street food markets, for example, have dramatically changed the way we perceive entire streets of global cities" (ibid., p. 1).

In their study, the researchers found that smells are often identified using words describing their origin, like 'floral' or 'earthy'. Therefore, they developed an 'Urban Smell Dictionary'. Using those words, the researchers created the 'Urban smellscape taxonomy' that categorizes urban smells in the form of an 'aroma wheel'. Afterwards, 'smellwalks' were conducted involving locals to identify the smells of particular urban environments. Through social media, researchers were able to match the 'smell words' with users' locations, and create an interactive, navigational city map that identifies dominant smells in five main categories: emissions, nature, food, animals, and waste. The researchers also conducted studies that associate smells with certain emotions and behaviours classifying words into positive and negative emotions through systematic tools, and developing a correlation between the smell categories and the presence of positive-emotion words. For instance, nature or food smells were found to have an association with positive sentiments. Their next step was to integrate those results into the same interactive map so that the existing relation between urban smells and emotions could be illustrated. A Smelly Map shows for example that in a street in Barcelona the dominant smell comes from food, as well as showing prevailing sensations of joy and trust in an association with that smell.

The same group of researchers extended their studies to explore urban sounds, creating 'Chatty Maps'. In a similar procedure to the 'Smelly Maps', researchers classified urban sounds. Resorting to social media in order to geo-reference and match the collected data, they created the first 'urban sound dictionary' and an 'urban sound taxonomy'. On this basis an interactive city map was developed that illustrates the dominant sounds of each street, in the categories of humans, nature, transport, music and building. Through further work, researchers associated words with typical emotional responses: anger, fear, anticipation, trust, surprise, sadness, joy and disgust. A Chatty Map shows, for example, that in a randomly selected street of Barcelona, the dominant sound emanates from transports. Emotions associated with this sound is shown to be primarily fear, sadness and anticipation, while there is also the presence of trust due to other sounds deriving from nature and humans.

These two types of maps exemplify a systematic, scientific approach to mapping sensorial impressions of urban environments. They seek first to de-territorialize smells and sounds from the sensorial ecologies of streets, by isolating them and breaking the process of extraction down into systematic steps. Thereafter, they re-territorialized smells and sounds by reinserting the dominant ones in the street maps and plotting relationships with emotions, thus interrelating sensorial impressions, emotions and places. As such, these mappings do convey some of the less-representational relational realms of the streets that we were also analysing in the Berlin experiment. In comparison with this experiment however, these maps demonstrate a far different level of facticity in their documentation of conditions, striving for a high degree of representational accuracy and ease of use. Though facticity should not be denied in mapping, since much of the power of maps resides therein (Corner, 1999, p. 251), these maps tend to orchestrate a distance to, reduction of, and closure of the environment being mapped. Through this, they assume a scientific neutralizing stance that stands in contrast to Corner's argument of the opaque, imaginative and evocative agency of mapping.

We will now turn to the last two examples mentioned, which significantly contrast Smelly and Chatty Maps in their situated openness and artistic abstraction. No rational overview is purported in these examples; rather, the immersed, nomadic and contingent character of the city is asserted (see also Corner, 1999, p. 233).

Naked City and Project 360 degrees

The Situationists International movement used *drifting*, or *derive*, as a technique of moving freely and spontaneously through the city's different settings and ambiences. The starting premise was that cities and their environments have a psycho-geographical effect on people's behaviours, perceptions and emotions, creating attractions or repulsions towards some environments. 'Naked City' is constituted by Guy Debord's maps from 1957 extracting atmospheres of Paris' city blocks and the psycho-geographic influences the materiality of the city poses on the drifter, i.e. areas perceived to have had a particular or unique atmosphere (a sample can be found in Simon Sadler's (1998) book *The Situationist City*, page 60 or online on Yale University Library at https://brbl-zoom.library.yale.edu/viewer/1044447). The representation techniques of plotting the extracts on a two-dimensional map are aimed at reflecting these actions and engagements. Each unity of ambience is represented separately and is re-linked afterwards through red arrows, illustrating different city forces acting on the drifter. The psycho-geographic slopes and their intensity are represented through the arrows' patterning, thickness and shape. This experimental mapping of Paris demonstrates the influence that the physical environments and their atmospheres can have on people's movements through the city, contrasting any dominant image of the city as a rational, readable entity, and foregrounding it instead as an ephemeral, embodied, contingent, and fragmented concentration of spaces and links.

The mapping project 'Project 360 degrees' (available at Frank Dresmé's website at www.frankdresme.com/project360) is influenced by the situationists and the concept of psycho-geography (for commentaries see Sichi, 2011 and Manaugh, 2015). It is a response to a frustration towards conventional city maps that represent the world as a flattened surface. Through the perspective of a commuter, Frank Dresmé assembled collages of photos and drawings illustrating the physical realm of Amsterdam. Instead of representing the exact route, despite there being routes between his personal destinations, he mapped how it felt to move through the city, representing physical resistances and openings. Dresmé's maps focus on present and dominant elements of the urban space, such as infrastructures and signage, but juxtapose these in unexpected ways. Similarly to the Berlin experiment, both 'Naked City' and 'Project 360°' are two-dimensional maps that rely on more than one technique to re-territorialize extracts. Guy Debord's 'psycho-geographic guides', through small three-dimensional excerpts (de-territorialized not from the embodied immersion into the field, but) from a conventional Paris city map, and re-territorialized afterwards through more or less intense arrows, represent the street-level perception and different acting forces between the various selections. The result is less of a pursued exact description of the lived environment and more of a perceptual mapping of the turns and detours of the mapmaker (Corner, 1999). As for Frank Dresmé's maps, collages of photographs and drawings give more hints about each moment than photos by themselves may illustrate. The results of Dresme's hybrid plotting technique are intense collages that present anew a particular relational and multiple character of the prevailing urban moments. As a patchwork of crude and independent elements of Amsterdam, they are evidently not aiming at providing navigational information, or at depiction as such. Rather, and like the Naked City maps, they present abstractions of the relational impacts of routes, sites, and embodied mobility. The raw, yet graphically seductive, representations of these moments are also presentations of new evocative narratives of characters and atmospheres of the networked and disparate elements and concentrations of cities. This, in comparison to the Smelly and Chatty Maps above, resonates clearly with Corner's agency of mapping:

[T]he unfolding agency of mapping is most effective when its capacity for description also sets the conditions for new eidetic and physical worlds to emerge. [...] The capacity to reformulate is the important step. [...] Through rendering visible multiple and sometimes disparate field conditions, mapping allows for an understanding of terrain as only the surface expression of a complex and dynamic imbroglio of social and natural processes. In visualizing the interrelationships and interactions, mapping itself participates in any future unfoldings.

(Corner, 1999, p. 214)

Conclusion

This chapter took at its outset 'mobilities design' (Jensen and Lanng, 2017), an emerging interdisciplinary research agenda, that seeks to denaturalize and de-objectify transport infrastructures and to open up a space for knowing, and including in future design practices a wider range of social, cultural, political and affective agencies of the lived environments of infrastructures. In accordance with this research agenda, the chapter has reported, analysed and discussed a site mapping experiment in Berlin's public transportation system, as well as discussing mapping operations from this experiment against those of four other mapping models.

Taking as a point of departure architectural scholar James Corner's reflections on the agency of mapping, we have argued that designers should engage in mapping infrastructures as more-than-technical facilities, i.e. as multifaceted socio-material environments for bountiful and diverse lives on the move. Mapping is not without effect; it may have significant potency in knowing the world and shaping it for the future. Hence, it matters how designers engage with infrastructures through mapping: mapping practices should not neutralize infrastructures as technical utilities. Instead, mapping should aid to question reductionist neutralizations of these sites and support the cultivation of insights into nuanced site conditions.

With that as the imperative of our analysis of the Berlin experiment as well as four other mapping examples, we have demonstrated some of the variety with which one can engage in mapping operations that target multisensorial impressions and atmospheres of infrastructures. Our analysis and discussion show diverse procedural attitudes that significantly affect the agency of mapping, from the systematic representational procedure with structured breakdown of the process of mapping sensorial impressions from sites, as we saw in the Smelly and Chatty Maps of the Good City Life Project, to the artistic, critical and intuitive practices of mapping in the Situationist project, Naked City, and Frank Dresmé Project 360 degrees. These latter examples *present*, rather than *represent*, relational abstractions of the situated imbrications of physical attributes of routes, sites, and embodied mobility. As such, the latter examples resonate with Corner's consideration of the potential for design and planning in the agency of mapping. They evoke the sites as lived environments, configured by much more than solid, concrete and quantifiable flows. As with Corner, these examples do not pursue mapping as an accurate representational practice, with a built-in striving for rationalization, universalization, and closure in the design process and of sites. Instead, they are examples that embrace mapping as an open and inclusive process of disclosure and enablement.

Through carrying out our own experiment in Berlin, we sought to attune students to this powerful agency of mapping as an active and more-than-representational experimentation with and 'actualization' of infrastructural site complexities and contradictions, occurrences, processes, interrelations and potentials for the future. In our reflection upon this experiment we find this process of attunement to be twofold.

One process of attunement regards being in, sensing and knowing infrastructural sites beyond quantifiable aspects of everyday mobilities and the assumed triviality of the sites. To aid the facilitation of this, we customized the auto-ethnographic method of mapping-in-motion for this experiment, situating students *in* the sites, allowing them to engage in "coming to knowledge" (Cosgrove, 1999, p. 2) about infrastructural sites from immersed positions along journey trajectories. The objective is the attunement of the designer to infrastructural sites and to embodied mobilities, akin to what mobilities scholar Justin Spinney suggests for the auto-ethnographic researcher of cycling: "The researchers need to attune themselves to the practice in question in as many registers of meaning as possible to minimise the dangers of misinterpretation" (Spinney, 2011, p. 173).

The other process of attunement, intertwined with attunement to the field, regards the practice of mapping. Through attunement to the sites and to embodied mobilities, students familiarized themselves with the lived environments of infrastructures. But attuning to the mapping operations required another attitude, a sort of abstraction or de-familiarization of the field, in order to extract moments and plot relationships. Attunement to the multiplicity of opportunity in how one chooses to practise mapping, is key here. Mappings will unavoidably be partial and provisional, omitting much more of the complexity and contradiction, process and life of sites, than they can possibly include. Choosing, prioritizing, omitting, excluding and obscuring is as much part of practising mapping as foregrounding, including, juxtaposing and interrelating. Acknowledging this entails that little rational overview is purported; rather, the immersed, nomadic and contingent character of the city is asserted through such agency of mapping. Paraphrasing landscape architectural scholar James Corner (1999), the chapter has, through attunement to this agency and to the mapping operations of extracting and plotting, examined creative site-mapping techniques as a means of enablement and emancipation of infrastructures from their "encasements of convention and habit" (ibid., p. 252).

References

Amoroso, N., 2010. *The Exposed City – Mapping the Urban Invisibles*. New York: Routledge.
Arefi, M., 1999. Non-place and placelessness as narratives of loss: rethinking the notion of place. *Journal of Urban Design*, [e-journal] 4(2), pp. 179–193. 10.1080/13574809908724445.

Bissell, D., 2010. Passenger mobilities: affective atmospheres and the sociality of public transport. *Environment and Planning D – Society & Space*, [e-journal] 28(2), pp. 270–289. 10.1068/d3909.

Böhme, G., 1993. Atmosphere as the fundamental concept of a new aesthetics. *Thesis Eleven*, [e-journal] 36(1), pp. 113–126. 10.1177/072551369303600107.

Burns, C. and Kahn, A., eds., 2005. *Site Matters*. New York: Routledge.

Corner, J., 1999. The Agency of Mapping: Speculation, Critique and Invention. In: D. Cosgrove, ed., 1999. *Mappings*. London: Reaktion Books Ltd. pp. 213–252.

Cosgrove, D., 1999. Introduction: Mapping Meaning. In: D. Cosgrove, ed., 1999. *Mappings*. London: Reaktion Books Ltd. pp. 1–23.

Cresswell, T., 2004. *Place. A Short Introduction*. Oxford: Blackwell.

Cresswell, T. and Merriman, P., 2011. Introduction. In: T. Cresswell, and P. Merriman, eds., 2011. *Geographies of Mobilities – Practices, Spaces, Subjects*. Farnham: Ashgate. pp. 1–18.

Fallan, K., 2008. Architecture in action: traveling with actor-network theory in the land of architectural research. *Architectural Theory Review*, 13(1), pp. 80–96. 10.1080/13264820801918306.

Gibson, J., 1986. *The Ecological Approach to Visual Perception*. Reprint 2015. New York: Psychology Press.

Good City Life, 2016. *Good City Life*. [online] Available at: http://goodcitylife.org/index.html [Accessed 26 October 2016].

Ingold, T., 2007. *Lines: A Brief History*. London: Routledge.

Jacobs, A. and Appleyard, D., 1987. Toward an urban design manifesto. *Journal of the American Planning Association*, [e-journal] 53(1), pp. 112–120. 10.1080/01944368708976642.

Jensen, O. B., 2013. *Staging Mobilities*. London: Routledge.

Jensen, O. B. and Lanng, D., 2017. *Mobilities Design – Urban designs for mobile situations*. London: Routledge.

Jensen, O. B., Lanng, D. and Wind, S., 2016a. Mobilities design – towards a research agenda for applied mobilities research. *Applied Mobilities*, [e-journal] 1(1), pp. 26–42. 10.1080/23800127.2016.1147782.

Jensen, O. B., Lanng, D. and Wind, S., 2016b. Artefacts, Affordances and the Design for Mobilities. In: J. Spinney, S. Reimer, and P. Pinch, P eds., 2016. *Mobilising Design, Designing Mobilities: Intersections, Affordances, Relations*. London: Routledge. pp. 143–154.

Krieger, A. and Saunders, W., eds., 2009. *Urban Design*. Minneapolis: University of Minnesota Press.

Lanng, D., 2014. How Does It Feel to Travel Through a Tunnel? Designing a mundane transit space in Denmark. *Ambiances, Experimentation – Conception – Participation*. 10.4000/ambiances.454.

Lanng, D., 2018. A 'more-than-representational' mapping study: lived mobilities + mundane architectures. *Nordic Journal of Architectural Research*, 30(1), pp. 153–174.

Lanng, D., Wind, S. and Jensen, O. B., 2017. Mobilities design: on the way through unheeded mobilities spaces. *Urban Mobility – Architectures, Geographies And Social Space*, 2017(1), pp. 69–84.

Latour, B. and Yaneva, A., 2008. Give Me a Gun and I Will Make All Buildings Move: An ANT's view of architecture. In: R. Geiser, ed., 2008. *Explorations in Architecture: Teaching Design, Research*, Basel: Birkhäuser. pp. 80–89.

Lippard, L., 1997. *The Lure of the Local. Senses of Place in a Multicentered Society*. New York: The New Press.

Manaugh, G., 2015. Transecting Amsterdam. *BLDGBLOG*, [blog] 29 June. Available at: www.bldgblog.com/2015/06/transecting-amsterdam/ [Accessed 9 November 2016].

Massey, D., 2005. *For Space*. London: Sage.

Mossop, E., 2006. Landscapes of Infrastructure. In: Waldheim, C., ed., 2006. *The Landscape Urbanism Reader*. New York: Princeton Architectural Press. pp. 163–177.

Moudon, A. V., 1992. A Catholic Approach to Organizing What Urban Designers Should Know. In: M. Larice, and E. MacDonald, eds., 1992. *The Urban Design Reader*. New York: Routledge. pp. 438–460.

Mumford, E., 2009. *Defining Urban Design. CIAM Architects and the Formation of a Discipline, 1937–69*. New Haven, London: Yale University Press.

Nichols, J., 2014. *Maps and Meaning: Urban Cartography and Urban Design*. Palo Alto: Academica Press.

Quercia, D., Schifanella, R., Aiello, L. and McLean, K., 2015. Smelly Maps: The Digital Life of Urban Smellscapes. In: ICWSM (International AAAI Conference on Web and Social Media), *The 9th International AAAI Conference On Web And Social Media*. Oxford, United Kingdom, 26–29 May 2015. Palo Alto: AAAI Press.

Roberts, L., 2012. Mapping Cultures: A Spatial Anthropology. In: L. Roberts, ed., 2012. *Mapping Cultures – Place, Practice, Performance*. New York: Palgrave Macmillan. pp. 1–28.

Ruby, I., and Ruby, A., eds., 2017. *Infrastructure Space*. Berlin: Ruby Press.

Sheller, M., 2011. Mobility. *Sociopedia.isa*, [e-journal] pp. 1–12. 10.1177/205684601163.

Sichi, F., 2011. Situationists Dérive. *Fiona's Blog*, [blog] 4 April. Available at: https://fionasichi.wordpress.com/2011/02/06/situationists-derive/ [Accessed 27 October 2016].

Spinney, J., 2011. A chance to catch a breath: using mobile video ethnography in cycling research. *Mobilities*, [e-journal] 6(2), pp. 161–182. 10.1080/17450101.2011.552771.

Stoll, K. and Lloyd, S., eds., 2010. *Infrastructure as Architecture. Designing Composite Networks*. Berlin: Jovis Verlag.

Urry, J., 2007. *Mobilities*. Cambridge: Polity Press.

Vannini, P., 2012. *Ferry Tales*. New York: Routledge.

Venturi, R., Scott Brown, D. and Izenour, S., 1977. *Learning from Las Vegas*. Cambridge, MA: MIT Press.

Whyte, W., 1980. *The Social Life of Small Urban Spaces*. New York: Project for Public Spaces.

Yaneva, A., 2009. Border crossings. Making the social hold: towards an actor-network theory of design. *Design and Culture*, 1(3), pp. 273–288.

Interlude 2:
Five ways to make design and mobility political

Interview with Albena Yaneva

Field(s) of enquiry

How do you define and see the field of research relevant to the material mobilities theme? Which disciplines are relevant and how do they interact? Are there any important disciplinary histories we need to know and remember?

I will tackle the theme of 'material mobilities' at the everyday level of mundane relational sociality, or relational politics. We have witnessed the 'material turn' in a number of disciplines and mobilities studies, too, gaining the attribute 'material' as a result. Instead of focusing on 'material' in mobilities, let us rather shift our attention to the mobile aspect of mobilities, to those things and material arrangements that make us move. How do things become mobile? How can a building, a bridge, a master plan, a key or a chair be mobile and generate effects, social, political and cultural? What does an atrium do? How do material arrangements matter socially? How can the design of a lecture theatre stimulate thinking? How can mundane activities as simple as climbing stairs or taking the elevator have social effects? These ordinary artefacts and environments are commonly discussed in the process of design and planning and widely used in daily practice. To understand their social valence, we need to embrace a dynamic view, a mobile view. The Science Studies tradition with the writings of Bruno Latour, Madeleine Akrich and Michel Callon, John Law, Anne-Marie Mol, among others, provides a conceptual framework to look at the mobile nature of things. These theories 'flourished' in the 1980s in the aftermath of the structuralism wave and generated new concepts and methodologies for the understanding of the social.

Embracing a Science and Technology Studies (STS)-inspired view to things and material arrangements that are commonly considered neutral, passive, immutable, we do not assume that there is a society *behind* a key, a building, an auditorium or elevator – we rather trace how social relations emerge as we interact with, stroll, inhabit and let ourselves being guided by these mundane artefacts and material arrangements; we trace how they are shaped to become mobile and how they are actively explored as mobile in the process of use or dwelling. That is, we form a dynamic view that can make all buildings, all design artefacts reminiscent of the gull in the work of Etienne Jules Marey, not static projective surfaces of societies, but 'birds in a flight', flights that can become 'social', or 'political' (Latour, B. and Yaneva, A. (2008). 'Give Me a Gun and I Will Make All Buildings Move: An ANT's View of Architecture'. In: R. Geiser (ed.), *Explorations in Architecture: Teaching, Design, Research*, 80–89. Basel: Birkhäuser).

Theories and concepts

Some would argue that the new material turn and mobilities research problematises modern binary distinctions between humans and non-humans, subjects and objects, culture and nature. Do you agree? If so, how does this manifest itself in the theories and concepts? How should we develop theories and concepts of relevance to the future of material mobilities research?

To illustrate how dominant binary distinctions are in current social science scholarship, let us stick to the theme of design and politics. Existing attempts to connect architecture and politics typically strive to reveal the politics behind design or the design techniques disguised as politics. In the existing scholarship, architecture is considered as important factor in the construction of nationalist imaginaries. Buildings can act as 'socially classifying devices' and can become powerful metaphors for social relations. Architecture's relation to politics is commonly understood in the light of traditional foundational theories of politics related to ideology, state, nation, government, policies and activism. These realities are foundational in the sense that we tend to start with them before proceeding to justify and explain everything in architecture within their terms. Politics is a separate domain of action with its own logics, institutions and practices; it is *outside* of architecture's remit and far from the architectural objects and processes. We trace linear causal relations between politics and architecture.

In the literature we always find an asymmetrical equation: politics is used as a specific type of causality to account for aspects of architecture. Some of the most common asymmetric projections and ontologies read: 'Architecture reflects politics and can produce political effects'; 'Architects are agents of power'; 'Architectural styles mirror political shifts'; 'Politics is imprinted on cities'; 'Architecture helps the construction of identities'; 'Building types embody politics'.

The architectural literature has preciously preserved the modernist roots of official architectural scholarship and, in particular, the dualist split between people and things, between the free-standing material world of architecture and infrastructure, created, fabricated, built, governed, mastered and controlled by powerful humans. The overall ontological vision here is an asymmetric dualism between the world as knowable, buildable and controllable, and humans as genuine agents of creativity. The key questions remain 'Who acts?', 'Who decides?' and how this is reflected in built form and urban fabrics.

However, in practice architects fail to exemplify this asymmetrical ontology. The ethnographies of architectural design developed in the past ten years have demonstrated that architects at work are far from 'deciding', far from mastering materials or controlling the world. Designers engage in a rather symmetrical open-ended and performative creative process. If we follow design in the making, people in the process of strolling in buildings, interacting with material arrangements and infrastructures, we suddenly start to think about the world in non-dualist terms and, more importantly, we see that there is an indefinite number of ways to stage a non-dualist ontology. When we follow design and urban processes and we trace mobile things, objects appear less as reflections of power. The need to explain architecture becomes less significant; this dynamic view allows a symmetrical treatment of the shaping of the architectural and the political.

Thus, if we question the relations, the groupings and associations, and the agency, the question is no longer 'Who acts?', 'Who participates?'; it is rather *how* specific capacities to act are performed through design and urban practise. How does design 'engage' people and transform human experiences? Or, in other words, it is important to ask, 'What acts?' and to turn our attention to the practices that shift the trajectories of things and persons. It is important to tackle the mobile nature of things. This means to study the settings and objects which allow humans to grow endowed with specific qualities, to get transformed. These settings are sites of political action.

Methods and approaches

What set of methods and approaches for investigating material mobilities is in your opinion the most fruitful? Are there any new methods or combinations of existing methods that you find particularly promising?

On a methodological level, architectural theory embraces an understanding of buildings as having an objective reality 'out there' while a number of subjective perspectives *to* the building are being expressed, compared, weighed and reconciled. This interpretation is termed as 'perspectival flexibility': design has *a meaning* for many actors (users, planners, citizen groups). Designers have *a perspective*; they acknowledge also *the perspectives of others*, their points of view in relation to the objective reality of built forms. The only methods that have a future are those that take a step away from this dominant perspectivalism in architectural theory, and to rather foreground the practicalities, materialities and events of buildings and mobile material arrangements; that is, to trace the complex processes of transformation, inhabitation, and renovation of buildings. If we foreground the practices of making, dwelling, urban planning, renovation, construction, buildings will cease to be passive objects that can be understood and interpreted from various perspectives. The analysis would escape perspective. The buildings will not be seen any longer as political symbols or embodiments of big political forces; they will rather become a part of what is done in design, renovation and dwelling. This will place the analysis within the 'aperspectival objectivity' of things, of built form; the variability will be placed within the things.

To better explore the political dimension of things, a pragmatist Actor-Network Theory (ANT)-methodology can equip us with the tools to trace this variability, and to examine how politics *transpires* in design and planning offices, on construction and renovation locales, in public presentations. These are sites (often) unrelated to the traditional *loci* of political action, sites where both the architectural and the political are performed in a mobile way. ANT can provide the methodological toolkit to scrutinise these sites, to trace discursive and non-discursive formations, and generate empirical accounts of various sets of practices and design techniques which can have political effects. At the level of the practice, at the level of making, both the political and the architectural get decomposed to myriad of small elements – fluid and unstable, fragile and composite. The political emerges as an underlying dimension of practices that can only be grasped by following *how* they unfold.

Design and creation

How do you see concrete artefacts, systems and technologies facilitating and affording mobilities? What is the role of design? How are the construction, making and institution of artefacts and material critical to a new mobilities agenda? Are there specific 'designerly ways of thinking' that may influence and form future mobilities research? If so, in what ways? How do you see a role for (design) experiments and 'speculative approaches' in future mobilities research?

In the past fifteen years STS, and ANT in particular, has gained popularity among researchers in the field of design and architecture studies. Embracing an ANT-inspired view of things and material arrangements that are commonly considered mute, neutral, passive, immutable, as well as of the practices of their makers (designers, engineers and architects, planners) a new field of scholarly research emerged. We witnessed a new wave of ethnographic studies that focused on practising architecture (Jacobs and Merriman, 2011). Inspired by pragmatism and following in the steps of Dana Cuff's and Donald Schön's ethnographies, this body of research aimed at grasping the socio-material dimension of architectural practice (Callon, 1996). Some of the researchers involved trained as architects, others were just anthropologists, but they all engaged in studies of the unfamiliar cultures of design-making in contemporary societies. Their studies demonstrated architecture as a collective process of negotiation, and one that is also shared with a variety of nonhumans (materials, models, software, renderings). Design appeared in these accounts not just as a social construction, as per Cuff's account, but rather as a composition of many heterogeneous elements, an assemblage. These 'assemblage ethnographies' followed the principles of 'no hierarchy', attention to the details, and symmetry: attention to what happens between humans and nonhumans; and undivided attention to the words and the gestural and non-verbal language of the designers themselves. Scrutinising the texture of the ordinary life of designers, they generated 'thick descriptions' of the knowledge practices of different participants in design; their studies resulted in long ethnographic accounts that made sense of the world of architects, computation models, sounds labs, and city maps, design knowledge, professional beliefs and work rituals (Houdart and Minato, 2009; Yaneva, 2009a, 2009b; Loukisass, 2012). Termed as the 'ethnographic turn in architecture' (Yaneva, 2017), this recent trend is the outcome of several related processes: the emergence of a reflexivity trend among architectural professionals as a key epistemological feature of architectural studies, the growing realisation of architecture as a social practice, the social nature of the outcomes of architectural production, and the tendency to acknowledge the collective nature of design. This development holds significant potential to dislodge the certainty of traditional architectural knowledge, the belief placed in the absolute authority of the historical archive, and the simplifications of its practitioners who reduce, even naturalise architectural research, to the production of critical discourse about practices.

Matters of concern and societal responsibilities

What are the critical issues of a public debate on material mobilities? What are the 'matters of concern'? How do you see mobilities research contributing to these agendas? How are the ethical responsibilities of a material mobilities research emerging? **Are there any inherent political dimensions of the research into material mobilities that we need to be observing?** *Are there any particular societal claims on the research? How do you see the interaction space between research and the public(s)?*

Political philosophy has witnessed a rapid development in the last twenty years. In the 1990s Beck argued that there is a displacement of politics (Beck, 1992, 1999). That is, political scientists look for politics in the wrong places as political action now often takes place *next to* or *across* institutionalised political orders. He suggested that in order to regain a handle on political dynamics, political scientists should engage in studying the 'subpolitical' processes that take place outside the domain of formal politics. A number of STS authors, including Andrew Barry and Gerard de Vries, also argued that politics is no longer to be found in the big concepts of 'domination', 'inequalities', 'power struggles', 'elections', and 'revolutions' and cannot be limited to citizens, elections, votes, petitions, ideologies and institutionalised conflicts. At a time marked by the displacement of politics, the crisis of legitimation of party-based and national politics, to accept that buildings and architectural projects can miraculously legitimise or embody power is a form of anachronism; to assume that the simple participation of users in design is sufficient for democratic design is to indulge in facile politicisation. Politics is foundational, irreductivist; this means that there is no prepared and defined ground on which it rests; nor can it become a ground for explaining the cultural realities of architecture or urban design.

Design can help us to reimagine the forms of political representation and reinvent the sites of political action. The *locus* of political action has shifted, indeed. The 'political' is understood as the ontological condition of politics and of being-together in general; it is performed on many sites related to design, construction and renovation practices; it is enacted in a mobile way by visuals, experiments, material arrangements and urban artefacts. The political can be explored and generated at the level of practice; it *emerges* and can be witnessed as we trace the transformation of objects, sites, urban publics, and the multiple realities of a city (see Yaneva, 2017).

A good mobile design is not one which is neutral but one which deforms, constrains and enables in thought-provoking ways. Architecture and urban design transform and fabricate new capacities. *There* lies their political dimension. This urges us to develop another definition of politics by asking: What does architecture and urban design (artefacts, technologies, sites, material arrangements, built forms) *do* to those who are engaged in them? Architecture plays an active role in 'doing politics' as the political emerges on many different sites, often unrelated to the traditional loci of political action: design firms, planning offices, construction sites. Doing politics is no longer a procedural attempt to reach a good decision or to achieve the perfect 'consensus'. Doing politics is rather a substantive move to 'materially refigure' the practices, reshape the connections, and redistribute the agency in a slow, mobile, and relationally efficient way.

Let us return to the classic example of politics and design: the bridges of Robert Moses designed in the 1920s are political. Winner's interpretation presents a very anaemic version of technology, as only the height of the bridge is discussed. Yet, there is no mention of materiality, shape, construction, technological innovations, users and so on; nor is there a mention of natural forces and how they happen to be channelled in a specifically shaped artefact – the "low bridge". On the other side, only one type of politics is discussed – racial discrimination. Winner reduces politics to racial politics. He puts the bridge's height and racism into a kind of equation of causal explanation. In this way he reproduces the divide between politics and technology.

If we rather focus on the mobility of the bridge, we will see that the bridge is neither simply material, nor is it merely political; it can only be understood as the intersection and the balance of a range of forces, from the political to the natural, from the real to the metaphorical. If we explore its various dimensions, if we witness the bridge technology in action, if we observe the bridge being used, failing and being repaired, we gain a more dynamic, more mobile understanding of its nature. A bridge never exists without builders, construction and maintenance workers, planners, policemen, senators, engineers and traffic controllers. We need a much larger crowd of actors around the bridge. Thus, embracing a mobile view, following how a bridge works, how it is being repaired and how it acts, we ask: "What does the bridge do?" "Where and how?" "What are its modalities of actions?" "How, when, to what extent, and under what circumstances can design become political or generate political effects?" In other words, the questions are not any longer the ones traditionally asked by political theories, the old and exhausted questions of Winner: "Do artefacts have politics?" and "What is an artefact?" as these types of questions trap all interpretations of buildings and infrastructure in metaphysics of essence. The bridge is political not because it *embodies* racial politics. A bridge, an infrastructure, a building, a key, a seatbelt, a staircase can become political to the degree to which they can engage people, group and regroup, and gradually transform; they can act in a mobile way to enact political relations.

References

Beck, U. 1992. *Risk Society: Towards a New Modernity*. New Delhi: Sage.
Callon, M. 1996. Some Elements of a Sociology of Translation: Domestication of the Scallops and the Fishermen of St. Brieuc Bay. In: *Power, Action and Belief: A New Sociology of Knowledge*, Law, J., ed. London: Routledge, pp. 196–223.
Houdart, S. and Minato, C. 2009. *Kuma Kengo. An Unconventional Monograph*. Paris: Editions Donner Lieu.

Jacobs, J. M. and Merriman, P. 2011. Practising architectures. *Social and Cultural Geography*, 12(3): 211–222.

Loukisass, Y., 2012. *Co-Designers: Cultures of Computer Simulation in Architecture*. London and New York: Routledge.

Yaneva, A. 2009a. The Making of a Building: a Pragmatist Approach to Architecture. Oxford: Peter Lang.

Yaneva, A. 2009b. *Made by the Office for Metropolitian Architecture: an Ethnography of Design*. Rotterdam: 010 Publishers.

Yaneva, A., 2017. *Five Ways to Make Architecture Political. An Introduction to the Politics of Design Practice*. London: Bloomsbury Publishing.

8 Designing places for experiences
A study of architectural practices

Jørgen Ole Bærenholdt and Anita Schou Kjølbæk

Introduction

Creating attractive places is imperative in the experience economy. Experiences are drivers not only for attracting foreign visitors, but also for the quality of everyday life and for attracting residents. Therefore it is vital in regional and local development that places are designed well and can offer unique experiences, making them a destination, or landmark, both for tourists and for locals. To better understand how such places are designed, this chapter presents findings from field work in a young architectural office in Copenhagen, which has specialised in destination development. Inspired by the work of Yaneva, the investigation seeks to understand architectural designs through the design practices that go on inside and outside the office.

Therefore this is a chapter about a least two different kinds of material mobilities. First, the frame is the material mobility involved in people's experiences of places. Second, the investigation is about the materials and material mobilities involved in architectural practices aiming to create attractive places of the first kind. In fact, the chapter is about practices of material mobility connecting architectural sites and an architectural office: on one side, peripheral places developing into tourist destinations; on the other side, the architectural firm NORRØN located in a loft in an old back-building in central Copenhagen, next to the Royal Castle, committed to destination development under the slogan 'Territory for Dreaming' (NORRØN, 2016a). Places for experiences – far from the office – are designed in the white and light space of the NORRØN office. But how does this take place? How are the places designed-for taken into the office, how do design processes take place there, and how are designs taken back to become destinations? Through a complex pattern of mobile and material translations, it seems.

Architecture is a profession with a long-standing tradition and reputation, enacting forms and functions, which in one way or another become parts of society's material fabric. Architectural designs are first made, second built and third, work in practice in an 'on-going process' (Yaneva, 2016b, p. 238) of *uncertainty* (Till, 2013; Yaneva, 2016a). Till critically scrutinises architecture for not always being aware of its characteristics. Importantly, architecture has two meanings – it is both about the discipline/profession of the architect and about the resulting architecture/buildings – and both are *contingent*. Till (2013, p. 50) builds his argument around this double contingency. Both the design practices and the products of designs are highly contingent, dependent on so many other factors which cannot be controlled.

The investigation was carried out in April and May 2016, cooperation with NORRØN architects having been established gradually in the course of the year before this. Each author spent around one week in the office, and observed and took part in activities. In addition to this, we conducted interviews with the three partners and most of the staff, some of whom are interns with a bachelor's degree in architecture. We took part in design meetings with sound recording and photo-documented how working life, and especially design meetings and models, went on. Very many projects were on the move at different stages, but there were mainly four projects going on in the design practices we followed and interviewed about. These projects are about those 'out there' places in Denmark: first, on the island Møn, the Camøno hiking trail (NORRØN, 2016b; Camønoen, 2016), where design processes were long finished and the firm had leading responsibilities for the implementation process. Apart from signs, maps and web-pages hosted by Møn Museum and the municipality of Vordingborg, NORRØN designed and directed the production of nine iconic benches for the Camøno rest places. Second, on Blåvand at the westernmost tip of Jutland, NORRØN submitted their Blue Plateau Centre bid in winter 2016 and later won the competition for this first exception from Danish planning regulations in coastal areas (NORRØN, 2016c). The second author followed the subsequent work and design meetings, leading to NORRØN's local planning act preparation for this project, which had not yet been realised by the end of 2018. Third, on a hilly peninsula at the fjords outside of Kolding, eastern Jutland, the Houens Odde project for a new combined international scout and experience/conference centre to take over from existing facilities. In the end, NORRØN did not get this project. Finally, on the island of Lolland, in the small town of Rødby, a double project for making the historical warehouse into a cultural centre and for revitalising the main street of Rødby (NORRØN, 2018). These latter two projects were followed at their initial stages by the first author, including attending two design meetings about each project.

These four projects are all about the making of attractive places in peripheral areas, and they were at different stages and thus give an insight into how design processes go on at different stages. The field work was open-ended, and our data pushed the research question to become *how architectural practices emerge in intersections with the places designed for and the anticipated designs*, when the experience (economy) of place is the core issue. The main focus is on design practices in the studio, but the aim is to understand how these practices have implications for spatial designs for experiential places produced in the future. There are obvious methodological limitations in studying this with the main data deriving from only the studio itself, since the ideal would be longitudinal studies from studio practices to built design in use. But we do have two types of sources about NORRØN's intersection with places and designs 'out there'. First, we and especially the first author have worked with them for a while, including following and taking part in meetings and evaluations on design, especially in the early *Camøno* case that forms the background for the present chapter (but see Bærenholdt, 2018) and in the later Rødby diffuse market town hotel project (Bærenholdt and Grindsted, forthcoming). Second, our field work in the architectural office includes data on how design processes involved communication with and about places and designs 'out there' at destinations.

Following the review and the introduction to the case of NORRØN, the analysis investigates first how narratives and cultural history are used in designing. Second, the chapter focuses on how design processes take place in the office, with models, storyboards, references and meetings, mobilising materials. The conclusion highlights three central findings: (1) The role of narratives in designing places; (2) Multiplicity as an important principle and business model with which to govern and hold open design scenarios, managing the absent-present; and (3) Fellowship as central in terms of assembling collectives, especially in the office, in order to cope with multiplicity and uncertainty.

Review of research in design practices in architecture and experiential places

Design practice in making places for experiences is not really an existing research field, but there is multiple relevant literature to build on.

First, architecture has been researched *as* experienced places from the perspective of architecture and built heritage as attractions, experienced and performed by tourists (Lasansky and McLaren, 2004); heritage research is also part of this (Waterton and Watson, 2015). Here for example are studies of mundane and incremental changes in architecture taking place with the inflow of tourists, registering how this changes local architecture (Palmer, 2014); and there has also been research into the experience of holiday homes and the possibilities for architectural intervention therein (Larsen and Laursen, 2012). However, these approaches show little interest in design processes or in what architects do. Architecture is approached in the second sense (see Till, 2013, referred to above) of the constructed building.

Second, there have been some more programmatic publications arguing for an interest in how tourist places are designed, including contributions from architects. Some contributions are mainly conceptual, outlining design procedures for how to animate the world and for ecological sensibility in designing, slowing down the processes of design (Ren *et al.*, 2015, Huijbens *et al.*, 2016). Other programmatic contributions are based on case studies in tourism and museums, outlining how research into tourist experience and performance could lead to a better understanding of how and what tourist places can afford and how this can be integrated into design processes (Haldrup and Bærenholdt, 2010). The latter draws on Schön's (1983, 1987) pragmatic approach to 'the reflexive practitioner', first highlighting how architects traditionally are trained in practice and second, arguing for designers/architects and researchers to learn from each other through taking part in the same processes.

Finally, looking deeper into architectural practices, inspiration has to be drawn from architectural writing (Avermaete, 2010; Berre and Lysholm, 2010; Nagbøl, 2014). Looking in more depth into how architects work, while not focusing on tourist places, Yaneva's work (2005, 2009, 2016a, 2016b) develops the tradition from Cuff (1992) by taking the step of introducing Science and Technology Studies (STS) and, more precisely, Actor–Network Theory (ANT) into the architectural firm, doing ethnographic field work in the design studio. Thereby a crucial empirical focus on the actual processes of design-making is established, enabling research into 'how architecture happens' (Yaneva, 2016a, p. 44). In this way, research manages to come behind and beyond all the conceptual principles often used in architectural branding. Architecture thereby appears not as autonomous as it might otherwise look; Yaneva (2016a, p. xiv) agrees with Till (2013).

Yaneva's approach resonates well with Ingold's (2013) phenomenological approach, observing the role of, again, uncertainty in the design process. Ingold pushes our attention to the fact that designs (drawings) are never full representations of what is actually constructed and, furthermore how buildings are used and thereby (re)designed after their initial design. Ingold's interest is away from original drawings and turns to how small and incremental creative practices continuously change buildings and place through use, residence, etc. Ingold's way of thinking thus also resonates with Till's critical approach to understand architectural practices as messy, contingent and dependent. So while architecture and design are always about *anticipation* in search of the unknown (Ingold, 2013, pp. 69, 71), designers know well that the future will always develop in unexpected ways. It is characteristic for designing (1) that it intends to find a solution to a problem, (2) that it produces an outcome, but (3) that the actual outcome often does not correspond to what was intended (Simonsen *et al.*, 2010, p. 202). Therefore iteration is at the heart of design processes, not only before finishing the design (the blueprint), but also in taking what has been constructed into use. Redesign is the rule. In Yaneva's words: 'design means to redesign. Imitation and reiteration constitute the matrix of invention' (Yaneva, 2009, p. 96). Design is itself an experience with 'vertiginous hesitation, tentative moves, mistakes, miscalculated gestures, fundamental meandering, dancing' (Yaneva, 2009, p. 62).

In addition to the inspiration deriving from Yaneva's field research, there are parallel approaches inspired by STS, pragmatism, phenomenology and the tradition of design thinking. Moore and Karvonen (2008) suggest the potential of STS perspectives working more with the built environment and, in doing so, also engaging in design studies. Their aim is 'to examine not what designers say, but what they do through interaction with the communities they serve' (Ibid., p. 31). Their examples are given with the three types of design thinking, i.e. context-bound, context-free, and context-rich, where, especially the latter, more complex example is interesting. Context-rich design thinking tries to build a middle ground between inspiration from local communities and from research/education, blurring distinctions and widening perspectives. However, Moore and Karvonen found that this kind of approach also suffers from problems such as the risk of domination by charismatic leaders, of lowest-common-denominator design, and of universities involved failing to deliver enough support to projects – but also the lack of incentives to do so in research/education (Ibid., p. 40).

Binder *et al.* (2011) give ethnographical accounts of design processes they have been involved in themselves. Drawing on Schön (1983, 1987) and the wider tradition of phenomenology and pragmatism, they develop an approach more oriented to the collective processes of design than was the case with Schön's attention to master–apprentice relations. Through many smaller cases, they show how a diverse multiplicity of actors interact ' "through" a collection of artefacts of various kinds' (Binder *et al.*, 2011, p. 13), stressing the materiality and the openness of design processes. Contrary to parts of the design thinking tradition, they insist on not modelling design processes into particular listings,

> but rather to focus on particular 'qualities' of the environment of space and artifacts in which design takes place that are supportive of a highly creative, mediated, and distributed process. It leads from *prescribing* particular patterns of workflows to *describing* and *enabling*. It allows moving from a rather general 'theory' of design to concept-based accounts of observed practices.
>
> (Ibid., p. 26, italics in original)

It is thus, first of all, the work of Yaneva and of Binder and colleagues that inspires the present chapter in terms of methodology. However, from our field work comes another focus towards the intersection with experiential places. This focus has emerged with the rise of the so-called experience economy (Pine and Gilmore, 1999), which is part of mainly American, but also Danish (Bærenholdt and Sundbo, 2007), discourse on commodified and performed places such as theme parks (Bryman, 2004; Ritzer, 2005; Lonsway, 2009). Lonsway (2009) takes the experience economy inspiration from Pine and Gilmore into architecture, working his way through an array of American experiential places that are run as businesses, including theme parks. While Lonsway, coming from architecture, does in fact address both designs and design processes, he does not go into any particular details of design processes, but is more into how architecture can be constructed in order to optimise the economy of designed experienced places. The design processes in the architectural office are something taken for granted in most studies on tourism and the experience economy, and are therefore not studied in detail. However, this chapter tries to engage with the issue, focusing on an architectural firm that has placed itself in the field of the experience economy, including tourism.

The case of NORRØN architects

NORRØN was founded in spring 2014 by two young architects, Marco Berentz and Poul Høiland de la Cruise, first based on funding for rural development from the Ministry of Cities, Housing and Rural Areas (*Ministeriet for By, Bolig og Landdistrikter*) that was part of the 2011–2015 government. In autumn 2015, one more partner with long-standing experience in architecture, Anna Maria Indrio, joined. By the end of 2016, NORRØN was employing around 14 people, including many interns and trainees. There were three partners, two (more) architects, one project developer (human geographer), two architect trainees from Italy, and a growing number of interns, having finished their bachelor's degree in architecture.

NORRØN present themselves as driven by the desire to create authentic and solid architecture in the realm of the experience economy. This is a goal in each project, but it also serves as a mind-set in the development of new projects and as a strategy for the whole company. They always strive to develop their projects by focusing on the inherent stories and potential that they uncover through research and discussion. When redesigning for a place, it is important to take into consideration what makes this place unique, and how this place (and its history and characteristics) is connected with the area it is part of. The stories that a place holds are a key to understanding the site, and NORRØN's idea is to let these stories impact their way of designing for a place. Stories thus influence and are reflected in the materials, shapes and colours used.

NORRØN develops destinations under the slogan: 'territory for dreaming'. They want to create places that people wants to travel to and that generate economic spin-offs for investors, local people, municipalities, or others. Their strategy is about destination development (NORRØN, 2016a). This strategy also implies choosing to engage themselves in the debates about how we construct our future society. One of their key concerns is the future of the rural areas/outskirts of Denmark, where many of their projects are also located. According to NORRØN, they not only make architecture, but also help communities to further develop, and prevent them from becoming ghost towns. Therefore, much of the development of the ideas and the projects happen in close collaboration with different local partners (e.g. municipality, property owners, volunteers). This is important for NORRØN, as a close connection with local entrepreneurs enhances their ownership and makes it possible to test the recognisability of the stories.

In sum, NORRØN describes their own competences with three ways of working:

1 The Library; the cultural heritage and inherent stories in a place should be developed and used today as an asset (the unique and site-specific)
2 The Forum; participate in debates in society (and attract funds related to the subjects discussed)
3 The Lab; use their artistic and creative space that is related to their design of a project/place.

Designing with narratives of place

The history and cultural heritage of a place have a very important role in the design practices of NORRØN. One of the interns stated: 'When we begin a new project we collect as much knowledge and information that we can get. From there we narrow our focus until we know which story we want this place and its buildings to tell.'

In the 'Blue Plateau' project in Blåvand, research into history inspired choices in a whole range of areas. Probably inspired by the blue colour (*blå*) in the place name, it led to the use of a certain blue colour on the tiles, to try to get more nature back into the area (as it used to be), to design the building with links to the old dune farm and a closed courtyard, and to provide a portal view from inside the construction (NORRØN, 2016c).

Also, research into the history and heritage of places is played out in the use of pictures from other places. These pictures have an important role as references in the design processes. Combined with desk research about the history of a place, such pictures are used on the storyboards and in design meetings to create the same images in the minds of all the participants (see next section). At Blåvand, a vacation resort project was added, and the design of this was inspired by the traditional bathhouses on the beach. The idea is that the word 'bathhouse' and pictures of one example enable our imagination of iconic landmarks, colours and so on. Such images are used to kick-start discussions, making sure that everybody talks about the same typology, thus inspiring the design. Pictures and other references sometimes also play important roles in the first presentations and sales meetings with clients, to ensure exactly the same kind of alignment.

Throughout the process of design meetings, conceptual designs/illustrations/models, meetings with the entrepreneur and going back and revising the projects, we see and experience that the reference pictures (and pictures of their own models and other internal projects) are used and inspire redesigns. This way, researching and using landscape history and cultural heritage is a way to design and tell the story of a place in each project.

One of the partners explained that NORRØN's view of good architecture is based on two parameters: beauty/aesthetics, which everybody can comprehend and feel good about, and a strong story that you understand. One of the other partners added that this way of designing can create a completely new life for cultural heritage by strengthening and showing inherent stories in architecture. Heritage, which is otherwise absent, this way comes to play a role today. But of course this is also a matter of selection. Architects select specific absent and present elements of a place and relate them to different realities (Yaneva, 2016b, pp. 248–250). The experience from participant observation of two design meetings about the Rødby project illustrates this well.

In the second meeting, 18 days had gone by since the first meeting on the Rødby project, and between the two meetings the partner, intern and trainee working with the project had visited Rødby for the first time. The intern started her presentation with the help of a developed storyboard of several pages on the end wall of the studio (Figure 8.1). But another partner had grown up in the area and was eager to add more dimensions in making this an ambitious project – highlighting things not visible in the current landscape: from the past, there was the history of draining Rødby Fiord, in order to gain more agricultural land and

Figure 8.1 Second Rødby design meeting (27.05.2016, 14:07).
Source: Photograph taken by Jørgen Ole Bærenholdt.

to protect against flooding. Therefore the warehouse could be reached by ship in the past, and archaeologists know about the remains of a wharf hidden in the ground next to the warehouse. Also looking into the future, the Fehmarn Belt tunnel will affect the place, since traffic from Germany might well appear from the tunnel near to Rødby and the old half-timbered warehouse at the entrance to Rødby (see model in Figure 8.1). The partner therefore pushed for making contact with and mobilising both the local archive and the Fehmarn Belt Company, in order to make these absent, past and future, elements active in the project.

However, having visited the place, the three were more eager at developing a commercial attraction in the woods north of Rødby. Based on the visit to Rødby, this partner made it clear that 'the feeling out there is that there is nothing'. And much of the meeting was about what the main narrative to build on was. The other partner took up the theme:

> there is the question of what is the narrative. If we look at Houens Odde [see next section of this chapter!] as we do, we have this analysis about the narrative of the moræne landscape, the valley–hill–valley–hill thing. Here I think the big narrative is about the border (the 'grænseland') between water and land – and therefore the harbour construction – the old Bolværk [the wharf] is the big story – I think this is the big story. What is then the off – what is the seductive narrative?

Much discussion was about what was realistic, and about whether there needed to be water again. But the interesting thing was that much of the detail of this absent narrative had already been presented by the same intern in the first meeting 18 days before. Also, the partner who knew the place well stressed the role that drainage of agricultural lands had played in both local and national Danish narratives from the nineteenth century. But this narrative was not present and even not figuratively absent when visiting the place. This way the question of what narrative to select became central and there were multiple sources available for this. Visiting and registering a place might not mobilise absent narratives, which might have been forgotten. However, enacting absence-presence can be central in destination development (Bærenholdt, 2012).

How materials are mobilised in design meetings

Design processes are forever on-going in the studio of NORRØN. Everybody sits in the same open space, and models are co-actors, placed as they are at adjacent tables. The dominant colour is white. There is only one extra room, used for some of the more organised meetings and for taking longer phone calls. Interaction is spontaneous and builds on the open access to co-workers. In general, the two non-partner architects, interns and trainees are the ones working with designs on their computers. They ask for advice among themselves and, if possible, from one of the three partners, who are almost never working with design details on computers. However, sometimes one of the young partners does take a leading role in design, also having the 'master version' of the on-going project on his computer. The relaxed atmosphere of the design studio is crucial.

> Music vibrates in the background – French press coffee is available – models are all over the place – people move around and look at models – sit with their computers – talking with the person besides them – having meetings standing or at the computer.
> (Field notes Thursday 31.03.2016)

Working with the Blåvand project, much is about detail, not only about the overall design or concept. Small things matter, such as where to secure access for emergency vehicles, how materials are to be maintained, what are the choices to be made about lighting and where lights are allowed, how parking places should be submerged (Field notes 31.03.2016).

> Often somebody calls one of the others asking them to come to the person's computer just to talk over a project. For example one of the partners calls one of the interns to discuss something she e-mailed him, then gives her feedback and explains to her the changes he wants. Very quickly he has made up his mind what he wants and communicates this in a clear way.
> (Field notes 01.04.2016)

The same afternoon, a design meeting on the Blåvand project is held, focusing on phase two and following up on a meeting with municipal planners the day before. Two of the partners play a clearly coordinating role, summing discussions up in work packages and the like, while the third partner is the one posing critical questions. Overall, the three partners are the ones doing most of the talking, while the interns are mostly taking notes about their tasks.

Moving from impressions of atmosphere and working style to the more detailed processes, we will now discuss the example of how designs for the Houens Odde scout and experience centre developed during the following month. We particularly look into how models, storyboards and references are used in design meetings. Overall, the project developed from an intentionally very open first design meeting that ended in a total mess, with things placed on the model and intense discussions, to the second meeting having more participants and suddenly leading to a new concept, where design facilities were spread over several locations on the Houens Odde peninsula. Two weeks later the model was redeveloped and improved, constructed in sections, and then, together with four people (including the interviewed intern), driven in a packed car to a meeting in the middle of the week with the client at the Houens Odde location, with matters then being concluded in the days following. Obviously mobile models are a core element in the design process, which we will now discuss in more detail.

The first design meeting (see Figure 8.2) took place in the architectural office's main room, with everybody present taking part, standing around the

Figure 8.2 First Houens Odde design meeting, overview (04.05.2016, 17:06).

Source: Photograph taken by Jørgen Ole Bærenholdt.

model of the landscape of Houens Odde. The intern responsible started by presenting research into the narratives around the name of the place, leading to the idea of the 'Hall of the Gods', since 'Houen' comes from the word 'Hov' for 'Hall' in old Norse tradition. Throughout the meeting, one of the partners kept this reference alive, triggering discussions on various religious spaces. It was combined with the intern's research into architectural references to Viking Hall buildings. These references as well as photos and maps from the area were also present on storyboards on the wall (the chimney in the room, Figure 8.2). Meanwhile there was also intense discussion of the topography, orientation, views, existing buildings, vegetation, clearings, etc. in the area, where the two founding partners explained what they saw when they visited and had a workshop with the client (see Figure 8.3). The participants were enthusiastic about the different locations possible in the hilly landscape. Building bricks equivalent to the 600 m^2 to be built were available and moved around on the model. The two dominant elements in the discussions were narratives and landscape topography (both also represented in storyboards on the wall and in papers on the table/model) and how they could be combined.

The two partners brainstormed ideas for a design, and at some point one of the trainees was asked for design ideas. They are nevertheless always hesitant to enter design discussions too early, given their concerns about narratives and landscape. Therefore, the design interest was framed this way: 'It is always good

Figure 8.3 First Houens Odde design meeting, discussion on topography (04.05.2016, 17:19).

Source: Photograph taken by Jørgen Ole Bærenholdt.

to do this at an early stage, even though we may not use it, since it makes you think about what works and what does not work.' The trainee suggested three different design scenarios with a lot of models invading the landscape model. The partners focused on the advantages and disadvantages of the different alternative locations in the landscape. They also referred to the client's wishes for flexibility in the design, and this led into other participants suggesting references from both Muslim and Japanese architectural tradition. Towards the end, the meeting got rather messy. The model at the centre of the discussions was holding things together, but the mess produced by the number of building models in the landscape (see Figure 8.4) was also illustrative of the partners' constant appeal to keep several scenarios open, among those 'that we like'.

The second design meeting on Houens Odde was held five days later in the adjacent meeting room, this time with people sitting around the table. More research into landscape formation and cultural history had been done, but since one partner had not taken part in the first meeting, much had to be repeated. Lots of references, including precise maps and a number of architectural references with flexible walls, Japanese style, were circulating around the table and model (Figure 8.5). Furthermore, earlier models were sitting in the background on shelves along the wall. One trainee was asked to explain a proposal for a construction crossing the valley, which was a much-discussed location possibility in the first meeting, inspired by NORRØN's previous 2nd-prize project for the

Figure 8.4 First Houens Odde design meeting, model in mess (04.05.2016, 18:01).

Source: Photograph taken by Jørgen Ole Bærenholdt.

A study of architectural practices 159

Figure 8.5 Second Houens Odde design meeting, references being handled (09.05.2016, 16:34).

Source: Photograph taken by Jørgen Ole Bærenholdt.

Hammershus Visitor Centre. The discussion of this proposal got into design details, while one of the partners put a lot of effort into the main location question. Suddenly, agreement emerged on the advantages of having the centre decentred into several locations around the peninsula, thus affording movement and landscape experience on paths between parts. A smaller group summed up the conclusions to inform further work. There was still mess around the model, but neither narratives nor location in landscape could be discussed without the landscape model. 'Stories' and 'landscape analysis' were the key words in the summing up.

The two founding partners insisted on the broader perspective, zooming out – scaling down – discussions at this stage. This was clearly explained by one of them in the middle of discussions in his attempt to reset the agenda:

> I think actually, we should zoom a little bit out, not the shape of it, I think it is very important that we don't discuss the shape, the spatial quality, so far; this is very important since last time we found out that there is a story about the landscape, which we can articulate, a story which I think they do not know at all. We found more about the name of the place, that we can work with; so I think it is very important that next time we use the story from the landscape as a diagrammatic story – what is happening. The other thing that

is very important to discuss is how we place this building in the landscape in different ways. And how we benefit from doing so and what problems does that present. And the discussion is a little too much into the detail...

There are two central points from these arguments: first of all, the scale issue is a central concern (see Yaneva, 2005), and for the open-ended kinds of processes and concepts at NORRØN, it is important to scale down, in order to give space to 'the story from the landscape'. There are also stories not so present but in need of respect in tandem with humility. The second thing learned is the importance of this being stated clearly in discussions with the (mainly Italian) more design-oriented perspective present in NORRØN. The on-going debate, where things are made precise, serves to sharpen the embedded profile and common understanding among all employees at NORRØN. It is part of a learning process where interns and trainees via their 'legitimate peripheral participation' (Binder et al., 2011, p. 25) learn from taking part, 'by doing'. In other words, NORRØN has specific modes of communicating their philosophy, 'selling points', both internally and externally, and communication is a central component of the design process itself. The interviewed interns confirm this as a special feature of NORRØN – to use lots of words.

This is also clear in interviews with two of the participants 17 days after the second design meeting on Houens Odde (referred to above): the emphasis is on landscape and cultural history, but also on the needs of the scouts using the place. To understand the specifics of a place, including for its users, is central. Therefore, as much knowledge and information about the place as possible needs to be collected, thereafter sharpening the focus on specific elements, forming storyboards and building up relevant references. Model building in several phases is then the central tool in the design process, since it is much easier to stand around a model and talk, thereby leading to fewer misunderstandings. In the words of Binder et al. (2011, p. 13), the model also produces the collective 'thing' of people taking decisions (decision-taking assembly). Project presentation papers also include photos taken of the model.

Furthermore, the model is built in sections from the very beginning, thereby making it easier to move. On Wednesday 25 May 2016 the refined model took a longer journey to the 'real' Houens Odde location, packed into NORRØN's small car together with four people with sections of the model on their laps, and other sections and parts in the boot. The project at this point suggested the building of three halls at three different locations (hilltop, boat-house on the sea and in the woods at the wetland) on Houens Odde. Having arrived there, the model was first presented and explained to the local working group of 15 people from Kolding Municipality, the scout centre and the conference centre. Here the updated printed project presentation was handed out. One of the partners, standing at the model, presented the project as unfinished and in need of their input. Although some participants also liked the existing (all hilltop) facilities that the project was meant to replace, they engaged in the process and were keen on the idea of having facilities spread out in different locations in the landscape.

The whole group took a joint walk on the peninsula to the two other locations, and after discussions on-site, one of the locations was changed. The suggested location was in the woods to too great an extent, and everybody agreed on an elevated site in the wetland as a better location. This conclusion might have been possible to arrive at based on maps in the office, but came much easier this way, the intern explained. Thereafter the group was divided into three smaller groups, each working on brainstorming potential activities to take place in each of the three halls; notes were taken, especially by the intern. And further discussions took place in a positive atmosphere among the four on the long car-journey back to Copenhagen, the model arriving back in-office. While this was only a sketch project that was never realised in full, the conveyance of the model (and the architects' trip) to the place, and the meeting of local people, walking around and specifying activities, gave the project new energy. It was crucial to 'face-the-place' (Urry, 2002) to qualify the project, to bring the model there, but also travelling together and working on the move brought the team working on the project more proximate to each other and into each other's focus.

NORRØN always keep several scenarios open, and things are held together by strong procedural structures for how processes are run – thus allowing for the more open and non-structured outcomes. It is thus the strong governance of the process structure that keeps the outcome open, since it allows several scenarios to stabilise – and the process does not depend on too-quick conclusions about following only one track. In our later meeting with partners, presenting the findings of this chapter, they explained that they always, and increasingly, challenge several design scenarios through a process of three (Disney-inspired!) stages: dreams, realism, and attempts at spoiling. Design processes are thus stabilised in order to test design ideas against the contingencies and dependencies they might meet if realised. The basis of this procedure is the use of models and material things, which can be moved but also produce a 'thing' (assembly) of committed people.

Conclusion: narrative, multiplicity and fellowship

While focusing on practices taking place *in* the office, this chapter has investigated how practices in the office intersect with places designed for, and anticipated designs. This is a course of practice full of detours and unpredictable events, taking place in the competitive environment architects find themselves coping with. Like Binder and colleagues and Yaneva we have tried to describe and give an account of on-going design processes with the material mobilities involved in the interesting case of the NORRØN architectural firm. There were three particularly interesting findings.

First and foremost, architectural practices are governed by how places can tell stories. Experiential places are staged as a question of what the embedded narratives are, thus relating to narratives that cut across past, present and future in spatial practices around a place (see Simonsen, 2004, 2008). Narratives are thus inherently also about people – whether they are users, visitors or customers. In many ways, NORRØN talks about narratives rather than about users, since experiential places have to offer the user/visitors unexpected and new experiences. There is an implicit understanding that place designs communicate specific narratives, at the centre of the experience of the place. The *narrative* principle involves a respect for heritage, which on the other hand is also open to be performed in multiple ways. There is not just one heritage; there are several, and project ideas have to consider which of them to build on.

Second, *multiplicity* is another important principle. The studied design practices were led by concern for not closing design scenarios too early. There was a willingness to keep as many tracks as possible open, so that various layers of narratives, materials and so on could unfold. This is a business model required to meet clients' unforeseeable needs. But multiplicity is governed by and restricted to only working with design scenarios and their associated narratives among 'those we like'. Multiplicity is also about detailed landscape analysis and the mobilisation of a diversity of stories from the past, present and future – about making the absent present. Managing the absent-present is a central part of staging and designing experiences in place – and place, especially the tourist destination, is itself a concept about assembling the multiple (see Bærenholdt, 2012, 2016).

Third comes *fellowship*. This is the principle of building and assembling collectives or societies of people through shared practices (see Jóhannisson, 2007; Duim et al., 2012). In architectural practices this is widely secured via the use of the model, and also the sharing of storyboards, references and the open office space of the studio, making it easier to attune people to one another. But fellowship also has a broader and larger-scale societal meaning, since it refers to the institutions of society, and therefore the relevance and meaning of architectural projects stabilising and revitalising heritage and designs as something shared – and in between, at meso-scale, the collectives made in networking and working with clients. But it is first and foremost about the fellowship in office, coping with multiplicity and the uncertainty of future surprises. The 'we' that interviewees referred to, signifies the fellowship in the office, as enacted around the table and the model at design meetings.

Narratives, multiplicity and fellowship act in concert: there are indeed multiple narratives, absent-present and the like, but there is also a need that the fellowship decides what 'we want' places to tell. Stories are thought of as inherent in a place (the NORRØN 'Library' element, see above) but can also be developed. Furthermore, NORRØN places itself in the 'forum' of societal debates on the peripheries, destinations and possible clients – their societal and business engagements are two sides of the same coin. Multiplicity is also in place when it comes to involve many actors, since 'more knows more', while at the same time following the traditional Nordic (*Norrøn* = Norse, mostly West Nordic) utilitarian saying 'getting more from less' (*'få mere ud af mindre'*).

Such conceptualised ideas are brands but they do, as shown, in fact also structure practices in design meetings, stabilising procedures for keeping designs open, etc. 'Narratives' are popular and used in all kinds of contemporary managerial and branding exercises – everybody is told to perform stories about what they do. But narratives in architectural practices are in fact more precise. Here, we are not talking about the branding of NORRØN, their self-promotion. Narratives and stories relate directly, and explicitly, to places and their multiple absent, present and absent-present elements (Bærenholdt, 2012, 2016). In the case of the Camøno project, the Camøno benches are not so much benches to sit on, but, much more, material symbols communicating the narrative. This hints at how narratives, multiplicity, and fellowship are held together through the devices of models in designing and through designs with inherent narratives more than through practical functions. There is a certain kind of *material semiotic* at play. If this were to be a 'hidden symbolic meaning *behind* the building' (Yaneva, 2016a, p. 1), she would argue that we have been trapped in one of several modernist oppositions and would be better off engaging in studying 'the architectural' as processes of making. But narratives are absent-present actants at play, beyond the hidden symbolics of architectural tradition, and part of wider societal traces of heritage.

The idea of the experience economy was developed from retail psychology and marketing of commercial products (Pine and Gilmore, 1999), but it is also about 'creating a narrative construct out of our everyday spatial environments. ... A story is told ... not merely through its symbolic representation, but through its manifestation as a spatial environment' (Lonsway, 2009, p. 51). The specific kind of architectural practices studied in NORRØN is an example of how design processes can be organised, when the aim is to design places for experiences, in markets organised along experience economy principles.

Acknowledgements

This research was funded by the INVIO network and the INNOCOAST project, both supported by the Danish Innovation Fund. Thanks to the partners and employees of NORRØN for their openness and cooperation, and for questions, comments and remarks at four different oral presentations of this text in November–December 2016 as well as from the editors in January 2019.

References

Avermaete, T., 2010. 'Vers une aarchitecture des loisirs': Reconsidering the norms and forms of French mass tourism. In: J.C.L. Pasgaard and J. Kvorning, eds., 2010. *Tourism and Strategic Planning: Report from conference at Center for Urbanism.* Copenhagen: The Royal Danish Academy of Fine Arts, School of Architecture. pp. 27–52.

Bærenholdt, J.O., 2012. Enacting destinations: the politics of absence and presence. In: R.van der Duim, C. Ren and G.T. Jóhannesson, eds., 2012. *Actor–Network Theory and Tourism: Ordering, Materiality and Multiplicity.* London: Routledge. pp. 111–27.

Bærenholdt, J.O., 2016. The disconnected experience of some designed places. In: M. Bille and T.F. Sørensen, eds., 2016. *Elements of Architecture: Assembling Archaeology, Atmosphere and the Performance of Building Spaces.* London: Routledge. pp. 406–23.

Bærenholdt, J.O., 2018. Decentred practices of innovation in the experience economy. In: A. Scupola and L. Fuglsang, eds., 2018. *Services, Experiences and Innovation: Integrating and Extending Research*. Cheltenham: Edward Elgar. pp. 129–46.

Bærenholdt, J.O. and Sundbo, J., eds., 2007. *Oplevelsesøkonomi: Produktion, Forbrug, Kultur* [*Experience Economy: Production, Consumption, Culture*]. Frederiksberg: Samfundslitteratur.

Bærenholdt, J.O. and Grindsted, T.S. Forthcoming. Mobilising for the diffuse market town hotel: A touristic place management project to reuse empty shops. In: C. Lassen, L.L.H. Laursen and G.R. Larsen, eds. Forthcoming. *Mobilities and Place Management*. Routledge.

Berre, N. and Lysholm, H., eds., 2010. *Detour: Architecture and Design along 18 National Tourist Routes in Norway*. Norway: Statens vegvesen/Norsk Form.

Binder, T. et al. (the author collective Telier, A.), 2011. *Design Things*, Cambridge, MA: MIT Press.

Bryman, A., 2004. *The Disneyization of Society*. London: Sage.

Camønoen, 2016. Camønoen: kongerigets venligste vandrerute. [online] Available at: http://camoenoen.dk [Accessed 13 February 2019].

Cuff, D., 1992. *Architecture: The Story of Practice*. Cambridge, MA: MIT Press.

Haldrup, M. and Bærenholdt, J.O. 2010. Tourist experience design. In: J. Simonsen et al., eds., 2010. *Design Research: Synergies from Interdisciplinary Perspectives*. London: Routledge. pp. 187–200.

Huijbens, E.H., Costa, B.M. and Gugger, H., 2016. Undoing Iceland: The pervasive nature of the urban. In: M. Gren and E.H. Huijbens, eds., 2016. *Tourism and the Anthropocene*. Abingdon: Routledge. pp. 34–51.

Ingold, T., 2013. *Making: Anthropology, Archaeology, Art and Architecture*. London: Routledge.

Jóhannisson, G.T., 2007. *Emergent tourism: An actor-network approach to tourism economies*. Ph.D. Roskilde University.

Larsen, J.R.K. and Laursen, L.H., 2012. Family place experience and the making of places in holiday home destinations. In: R. Sharpley and P.R. Stone, eds., 2012. *Contemporary Tourist Experience: Concepts and Consequences*. London: Routledge. pp. 181–200.

Lasansky, D.M. and McLaren, B., eds., 2004. *Architecture and Tourism: Perception, Performance and Place*. Oxford: Berg.

Lonsway, B., 2009. *Making Leisure Work: Architecture and the Experience Economy*. London: Routledge.

Moore, S.A. and Karvonen, A., 2008. Sustainable architecture in context: STS and design thinking. *Science Studies*, 21(1), pp. 29–46.

Nagbøl, S., 2014. *Oplevelsesanalyse og arkitektur* [*Experience Analysis and Architecture*]. Denmark: Bogværket.

NORRØN, 2016a. NORRØN – Territory for Dreaming. [online] Available at: http://norroen.dk [Accessed 13 February 2019].

NORRØN, 2016b. Camønoen: Danmarks venligste vandrerute. [online] Available at: http://norroen.dk/project/camonoen/ [Accessed 13 Feburary 2019].

NORRØN, 2016c. Det blå plateau: en scene i Blåvands klitter. [online] Available at: http://norroen.dk/project/det-bla-plateau/ [Accessed 13 February 2019].

NORRØN, 2018. Købstadshotellet: Ekkoer fra det inddæmmede land. [online] Available at: www.livogland.dk/sites/livogland.dk/files/dokumenter/publikationer/koebstadshotellet_norroen_2018.pdf [Accessed 13 February 2019].

Palmer, C.T., 2014. Tourism, changing architectural styles, and the production of place in Itacaré, Bahia, Brazil. *Journal of Tourism and Cultural Change*, 12(4), pp. 349–63.

Pine, B.J. and Gilmore, J.H., 1999. *The Experience Economy*. Boston, MA: Harvard Business School Press.

Ren, C., van der Duim, R. and Jóhannesson, G.T., 2015. Postscript: Making headways, expanding the field and slowing down. In: G.T. Jóhannesson, C. Ren and R.van der Duim, eds., 2015. *Tourism Encounters and Controversies: Ontological Politics of Tourism Development*. Farnham: Ashgate. pp. 239–44.

Ritzer, G., 2005. *Enchanting a Disenchanted World*. Thousand Oaks: Pine Forge Press.

Schön, D.A., 1983. *The Reflexive Practitioner*. New York: Basic Books.

Schön, D.A., 1987. *Educating the Reflexive Practitioner*. San Francisco: Jossey-Bass Publishers.

Simonsen, J., Bærenholdt, J.O., Scheuer, J.D. and Büscher, M., 2010. Synergies. In: J. Simonsen *et al.*, eds., 2010. *Design Research: Synergies from Interdisciplinary Perspectives*. London: Routledge. pp. 201–12.

Simonsen, K., 2004. Spatiality, temporality and the construction of the city. In: J.O. Bærenholdt and K. Simonsen, eds., 2004. *Space Odyseeys: Spatiality and Social Relations in the 21st Century*. Aldershot: Ashgate. pp. 43–61.

Simonsen, K., 2008. Place as encounters: Practice, conjunction and co-existence. In: J.O. Bærenholdt and B. Granås, eds., 2008. *Mobility and Place: Enacting Northern European Peripheries*. Aldershot: Ashgate. pp. 13–25.

Till, J., 2013. *Architecture Depends*. Cambridge, MA: MIT Press.

Urry, J., 2002. Mobility and proximity. *Sociology*, 36(2), pp. 255–74.

van der Duim, R., Ren, C. and Jóhannisson, G.T., 2012. Tourismscapes, entrepreneurs and sustainability. In: R. van der Duim, C. Ren and G.T. Jóhannesson, eds., 2012. *Actor–Network Theory and Tourism: Ordering, Materiality and Multiplicity*. London: Routledge. pp. 26–42.

Waterton, E. and Watson, S., eds., 2015. *The Palgrave Handbook of Contemporary Heritage Research*. Houndmills: Palgrave.

Yaneva, A., 2005. Scaling up and down: Extraction trials in architectural design. *Social Studies of Science*, 35(6), pp. 867–94.

Yaneva, A., 2009. *Made by the Office for Metropolitan Architecture: An Ethnography of Design*. Rotterdam: 010 Publishers.

Yaneva, A., 2016a. *Mapping Controversies in Architecture*. London: Routledge.

Yaneva, A. 2016b. Politics of architectural imaging: Four ways of assembling a city. In: M. Bille and T.F. Sørensen, eds., 2016. *Elements of Architecture: Assembling Archaeology, Atmosphere and the Performance of Building Spaces*. London: Routledge. pp. 238–55.

9 A material review of Costa Rica's attempt at carbon neutrality

Assembling heterogeneous actor-networks of emissions, mobilities and calculations

Yamil Hasbun

Introduction

As of today, 'green' trends have erupted in wide variety of markets, sporting an equal variety of consumer goods, spaces and experiences. Perhaps to the uncritical eye it may seem as if 'greening up' markets is the embodiment of a pinnacle-momentum of human self-awareness as it finally understands that 'evil' capitalism's tendencies to exploit nature, pollute indiscriminately and eat chemically infested food are not only 'old fashioned', but also 'morally wrong'. More precisely, these tendencies are nowadays gradually becoming condensed as 'unsustainable' practices belonging to (self-)destructive lifestyles.

This general picture describes the shift taking place in easily identifiable 'modern industries' that ultimately create solid trading goods through the extraction of materials from so-called nature, but also depicts a broader shift of *sociotechnical landscapes* (Temenos et al., 2017) taking place in contemporary 'postmodern post-industrial' networks that exploit 'nature' *in situ* (Fletcher, 2010). Therefore, the issues discussed here concern all networks embedded in global capital exchange markets where different actors compete among each other to employ a wider range of entities regardless of whether the products are 'detached' (i.e. bio-certified carrots in a supermarket) or 'non-detached' (i.e. an eco-certified hotel at an eco-tourism destination).

The tendency to use 'green' tags as market differentiators is precisely what relates these issues directly to the fields of urban design and planning, to environmental governance and to the new mobilities paradigm. Accordingly, 'cleaner' transportation networks, pristine 'sustainable' tourism destinations and 'greener' cities or nations are now all highly desirable commodities not only favoured by 'eco-conscious' consumers, but by large-scale actor-networks seeking to 'green up' their own image.

Grounded on the conceptual devices of Actor-Network theory and the mobilities 'turn',[1] the present chapter in turn coins these 'green' spatial assemblages as ensembles of heterogeneous, eco-socio-technical materials and non-materials oriented towards the redesign of urban relations between 'human' and 'non-human' entities in 'greener' directions (Blok, 2013). It will be also discussed how the process of assembling those heterogeneous *actor-networks*, in turn enacted as emergent *sociotechnical regimes* (Temenos *et al.*, 2017), is neither an unproblematic exercise, nor performed in a political vacuum.

These issues will be examined in the case of Costa Rica, a nation historically and internationally recognized as a 'green' country which in recent years has stood out thanks to its 'green' actor-networks, and namely as a consolidated hub for eco-tourism, for allegedly producing 98.95 per cent of its electric energy in 2015 solely by renewable sources[2]; and finally, for its ambitious self-imposed claim to become one of the world's first carbon-neutral nations by 2021. However, as will be argued, despite the appearance of robustness that any given 'green' assemblage may achieve to project over time, such an assemblage is always held together *precariously* (Law, 2007) through a constant performative negotiation both within its own heterogeneity internally, and among other contending 'green' actor-networks externally.

In that particular examination of the Costa Rican case, three different arguments are drawn. First, that 'green' spatial assemblages must performatively negotiate a continuous balance between 'concrete' material implementations and 'abstract' discursive rhetoric in order to avoid a network breakdown.

Secondly, that the performative process of calculations designed to determine what constitutes a 'green' product, not only (re)constructs 'nature' as a politically embedded entity under the discursive umbrella of 'sustainable development', but also includes (and hierarchizes) certain entities while others are deliberately left out.

Thirdly, that these pseudo-scientific calculations – designed and performed by technocrat 'experts' to ultimately render 'nature' governable – are often mobilized as allegedly 'unbendable objective' discursive devices in order to silence any uncooperative or unaligned 'non-expert' actors and entities.

This chapter will show how the 'de-carbonizing' calculations and techno-scientific claims emerging from the contingent practices of Costa Rica's 'green technocracy' on the one hand reduce 'nature' to a *commodity* waiting to be *ordered*, while on the other, re-construct nature as a politically embedded entity in which certain entities are included and measured while others are deliberately left out.

Thus, in spite of the modest but promising evidence of a current tendency towards rendering low *carbon innovations*, actions and experiences (such as low carbon mobility systems, or less energy-intensive tourism) more 'fashionable' for the *consumer communities* of – at least – the rich north (Urry, 2013), attention needs to be invested in following the contingent practices of calculations performed by carbon 'experts', particularly as "systems persist through routinized actions of actors throughout the system, as they perform the practices which reproduce the institutions and relations comprising that system" (Temenos *et al.*, 2017, p. 122).

The second section of this chapter provides its theoretical foundation. After a brief review of the emergence of standards and certification schemes in response to the widespread practices of 'greenwashing', and thus to the need to validate and legitimize 'green claims' through techno-science, the ontological conditions and repercussions of the emergent enactments of 'nature', and of the socio-technical calculations, inscriptions and displacements, which allow the materiality of 'nature' to be governable, will be discussed.

The third section introduces two controversies surrounding two key mobility systems in Costa Rica which are deeply rooted within the country's carbon neutrality network. A third controversy will discuss how techno-scientific calculative devices allow the political construction of 'nature' through a patterned order of deliberate inclusion and exclusion of certain material entities.

How 'nature' is made governable

According to LePree (2009), the term 'greenwashing' was coined as early as the 1970's when consumers first started to care about the environmental impacts of their consumption choices.

This concept made reference to products being launched into various markets and labelled with environmentally friendly-type market differentiators, regardless of the actual 'environmental' impacts of their manufacturing or their material constituencies in general.

In order to avoid such exaggerated or false claims increasingly swaying markets which gradually favoured 'environmentally friendly' products, and to determine what actually constitutes a 'green' product, practice or business – and thus, what does not – a system of 'standards' became apparent.

These systems of 'standards' or *calculations* (Lansing, 2010) are intended to become the *obligatory passage point* (Callon, 1986) through which any claim is validated and legitimized; with which consumers are assured that the 'green' qualities of the products they consume are guaranteed; and finally as an opportunity for companies to possess a competitive advantage anytime their products are favoured by those *calculations*.

Commonly, these *calculations* take the form of certification schemes that usually mark their certified products with a logo, allowing the buyer to take an informed purchase decision.

Over the course of time, a milieu of certification schemes has emerged worldwide in a wide variety of industries including produce, processed foods, paper manufacturing, timber, tourism and greenhouse gas (GHG)[3] emission standards, just to name a few. Although some effort has been made in the transnational accreditation of certification schemes,[4] these largely remain rooted within national or regional borders. The case study on which this paper is based is precisely Costa Rica's own carbon emission certification or 'C-Neutral', which is intrinsically linked to certain controversies regarding the nation's urban mobilities.

However, before visiting the specific case study, it may be important to revise what generally constitutes a certification scheme, what is actually being calculated, what is being constructed and ultimately, what the taken-for-granted assumptions 'resulting from' and 'resulting in' these *calculations* are.

Constructing 'nature(s)'

Firstly, material-semiotic stances, such as Actor-Network Theory (Callon, 1986; Latour, 1999, 2005; Law, 2004, 2007), contend that there is no such thing as a 'nature' *out there* that may 'objectively' be approached through techno-scientific knowledge (Escobar, 1996; Cook and Swyngedouw, 2012); and at the same time, that 'nature' is not simply 'socially' constructed either (Castree, 2003). These post-structuralistic stands hold that instead of a single monolithic 'nature', there are multiple 'nature(s)' and each one is constructed through the assemblage of heterogeneous entities ranging through discourses, concrete materials, abstract non-materials and technologies which are all performatively arranged 'socially' (Law, 1992). In other words, the 'social' is an emerging effect of patterned ordering, and not a pre-given *uncoded category* that modernists oppose to a distinct other named 'nature' (Latour, 1998). Additionally, much like Latour pointed towards a fundamental contradiction found in modernist political ecology, our understanding of 'nature' is not even about 'nature', but about endless imbroglios in which human involvement is always present (Ibid.). In other words, instead of condensing 'nature' as a whole, it is about particular places, species, situations and events. Thus 'nature' is constructed not as a stable monolithic entity with which expert-scientists reductively isolate its constituent parts in order to elaborate calculations, but on the contrary, 'nature' is the emerging effect of practices of *calculation* (Lansing, 2010). In more concrete terms, 'nature' surfaces as an abstract 'generalization' from the negotiation between conflicting heterogeneous entities caught up in the middle of a controversy over 'this river', 'that tree species', 'those carbon emissions', etc. Moreover, 'nature' often becomes a relevant topic only after 'its' materiality is caught up in some controversy relating to a productive activity. In that light, Asdal (2008) shows how 'nature' embodied as Norwegian surface waters becomes a relevant socio-political topic as it is involved in a controversy concerning fish-stocks, and not for its own sake.

Altogether, this also explains why 'nature' is in fact a *multiple* (Law, 2007) to the extent that it can simultaneously *afford* (Harré, 2002) several – and often competing – constructions over the very same materiality. For instance, 300 hectares of trees in Costa Rica can *afford* to be a Quetzal bird 'research site' for ornithology biologists, a 'sanctuary' for bird-watching tours, a stock of 'timber' for logging industries or a 'carbon sink' for offsetting markets.

Regardless of how each of these actor-networks will construct 'nature' for its own purposes, they all perform a set of fundamental *calculations* to render it governable. First, they all *simplify* (Callon and Latour, 1981) the materiality of 'nature' by reducing the thousands of units of trees, the entire mass of soil, organic material, water, minerals and so forth to '300 hectares of trees', and even more so, to simply 'forest area'. Secondly, they all depart from the inductive assumption that 'what is true for a few is true for the whole' of the population; namely, any given *calculation* can be applied to a reduced number of trees, or soil samples that any given expert-scientist – not 'nature' itself – designates as the *spokesman* (Callon, 1986) for the entire forest.

Since *nature(s)* – in plural – are biased performative constructions that depend on the specific sets of *calculations* enacted by any given eco-socio-technical network, they are always *fluid* and necessarily *imagined*. Likewise, there will continuously exist a gap between the materialities of 'nature(s)' and their *inscriptions*, as any given material form will always inadequately embody a symbolically charged construction that necessarily remains *fluid* (Cook and Swyngedouw, 2012).

Returning to the example used above, 300 hectares of trees in Costa Rica can be scripted in a variety of ways such as digital maps, aerial photographs, or an article in a tourism magazine. Thus, the materialization of that piece of forest becomes inseparable from its *displaced* 'representations', and these in return become 'useful' *inscriptions* or *calculations* (Lansing, 2011) that allow each actor-network that enacts them to render 'nature' governable for a specific purpose. Or as Whatmore (2006) argued:

> [L]ivingness of the world shifts the register of materiality from the indifferent stuff of a world 'out there', articulated through notions of 'land', 'nature' or 'environment', to the intimate fabric of corporeality that includes and redistributes the 'in here' of human being.
>
> (p. 602)

At the end of the day, 'nature' seems to emerge as a stable entity 'out-there' that quite unproblematically appears to be real to everybody.

The *value* of these constructions of 'nature' is never found in their materiality or inscriptions, but rather in a reductively understood notion of their *usefulness* (Lansing, 2010). They emerge as *valuable* to the extent that they are reduced as a 'standing reserve' or 'stock' made ready to produce or generate something else – carbon offsets, tourism, etc. Hence, the final purpose of these heterogeneous assemblages is to (re)construct 'nature(s)' as *governable* and *improvable* objects, spaces and entities (Li, 2007) ready to be *commodified*.

Enacting carbon-neutrality calculations

In 2007, Costa Rica announced its intention to become one of the world's first carbon-neutral nations by 2021. The choice of that particular date corresponds to the decision of the government of that time to match this self-proclaimed goal with the bicentennial celebration of independence from the Spanish Empire.

Four years after that bold announcement, the nation's next government in office published the 'National Voluntary Standard for Demonstrating Carbon Neutrality', which allowed private businesses in Costa Rica to voluntarily become certified as carbon neutral (or 'C-Neutral') anytime they successfully satisfied the somewhat basic equation: $E-R-C=0$.

In order to be enrolled in the C-Neutral certification network, applicant actors must calculate their net emissions for a specific period (E), minus their reductions or internal emission removals (R), minus their compensated emissions (C), which should equal zero (0).[5] Put differently, carbon-neutrality is not only accomplished by the materiality of emissions and their *displaced* representations made *useful*; but by also the utilization of trees, software, water, GPS systems, computers, soil, 'human' entities, micro-organisms, discourses and knowledge, just to name a few.

In regard to the general policy to achieve carbon-neutrality by 2021, it was established that the nation's GHG emissions of that future date are to match those of the year 2005, as the data for that earlier year are the first emissions inventory available from the National Meteorological Institute.

Shortly after the self-proclaimed goal was announced, this ambitious project found much criticism in the national and international press (see Rogers' press release from 10 October 2009), as well as in various academic fields (Baltodano, 2008; Fletcher, 2013; Kowollik, 2014), pointing out doubts about the ability of Costa Rica's actual implementation methods to reach *carbon neutrality* at all, and their 'socio-economic' and 'environmental' impacts on the ground.

From those criticisms, two particular issues stand out which are shared by those authors in one way or another. First, the belief that the Costa Rican state lacks any sound policies to actually pursue the reduction of its GHG emissions at all; and secondly, that if there are any such policies, they consist of a dubious strategy in which the country simply seeks to "plant its way out of the carbon-emissions problem" (Rogers, 2009).

While both criticisms are essential to fully grasp the overall controversy, and while both represent interesting case studies to dissect the performative heterogeneous processes of construction of nature, this chapter will focus on the first issue as it directly pertains to issues of urban design and planning, as well as mobilities.

The growing material/non-material gap

As was discussed earlier, any given material form will always inadequately embody the symbolically charged construction – in our case, 'nature' – it is meant to enact and vice versa. This inherent incompatibility also means that there will continuously exist an irremediable gap between the *materiality* (Law, 2007) and the *inscription* (Cook and Swyngedouw, 2012) of any given 'nature', place, body, or object since these constructions are always held together *precariously* through the constant negotiation between 'concrete' and 'abstract' entities.

The selection of the specific 2021 deadline for reaching 'carbon neutrality' in Costa Rica is evidence alone of not only this inherent gap, but also of the actual heterogeneity behind the constituencies of the 'nature' constructed in the carbon neutralization network; and of the agency that an 'abstract' entity can hold in a network regardless of how 'technical' it may appear. What appears to 'only' be an abstract symbolic entity (a commemorative date), in reality plays an unquestionable role within this network to the point that it replaces any other technoscientific entity in the selection of 'the' deadline by which Costa Rica will neutralize its carbon emissions. The following extract from an interview made by the author with a high-ranking representative of one of the two auditing agencies authorized in the 'C-Neutral' project illustrates this tension:

INTERVIEWEE: The original idea – hmmm – in 2008 was … "Let's make Costa Rica carbon neutral".
INTERVIEWER: Hmmm.
INTERVIEWEE: Ok … by when? … 2021. Why? They never asked themselves.
INTERVIEWER: Hmmm.
INTERVIEWEE: And why in such short time? They also never asked themselves.
INTERVIEWER: Hmmm.
INTERVIEWEE: Additionally, the answer is very political … "Because we celebrate our bicentenary" [of independence from the Spanish Empire].
INTERVIEWER: Right.
INTERVIEWEE: There is nothing technical about it [-giggles-].
(Member of the Environmental Department of INTECO, personal communication, 7 April 2016)

This extract shows how, despite the common assumption that 'scientific controversies' are the 'stuff' of scientific control, non-scientific entities (a political one in this case) can become the *obligatory passage point* for a network, overriding any techno-scientific calculations and 'expert' knowledge.

So far it has been held that constructions of 'nature(s)' in general are essentially heterogeneous assemblages of material and non-material *inscriptions* that finally reduce 'nature' to a *commodity* or 'stock' made ready to be used. And particularly, as Lansing (2012) argues, that Costa Rica's carbon-offsetting network is a clear-cut example of such processes of (re)construction of nature through essentially market-driven calculations.

Yet, Fletcher (2013) argues that the carbon-neutrality goal for 2021 is little more than a branding mechanism to boost Costa Rica's 'green' credentials while creating a competitive edge by promoting the supply of 'C-Neutral' products in specific markets of interest.

Both Fletcher (2013) and Kowollik (2014) suggest that the carbon neutral campaign is assembled almost exclusively by *non-material* 'rhetoric' or 'abstract discourses' with hardly any actual on-the-ground *material* 'practices', or 'concrete implementation'. This also means that the network's enduring abilities are put at risk precisely because of the failure to utilize a wider range of *durable* (Callon and Latour, 1981) heterogeneous materials embodied as concrete implementation strategies and practices.

Following up on this second contradiction between 'abstract' and 'concrete' entities, the last report published by the programme State of the Nation, or PEN,[6] showed that while the national population had grown only 23.4 per cent during the period 2000–2015, the fleet of motor vehicles had doubled in size (Programa Estado de la Nación [PEN], 2015, p. 173).[7] Even though the increase of that fleet did not correspond with the growth in GHG emissions by itself, it does seem to be the case in Costa Rica that 66 per cent of the total gross emissions are produced by motor vehicles (Ibid., p. 178). The same report reveals that by far the largest number of those vehicles (62.7%) are private transport vehicles, i.e. automobiles, SUVs, motorcycles, etc., followed by freight-line trucks (21.1%), and finally – and very revealingly – public transport (15.2%). As a side note, the latter includes taxi-cabs as well.[8]

Additionally, the Costa Rican Ministry of Environment and Energy (MINAE) states that the vehicles forming that fleet are 15 years old on average. This is the result of inexistent state controls regarding the importation of new and used vehicles, as well as the prevalence of weak policies to incentivize the incorporation of new – and thus more 'environmentally efficient' – technologies for both private and public transport sectors (MINAE, 2015, p. 99).

In a nutshell, not only does the Costa Rican state not mobilize its own carbon-neutrality regulatory frameworks to engage in efforts to either restrict the indiscriminate consumption of fossil fuels in this sector (PEN, 2015, p. 210), or to directly reduce the amount of combustion engine vehicles; but much to the contrary, the country has allowed the amount of polluting agents to grow and even to duplicate precisely during the years following the nation's self-imposed challenge to reach carbon neutrality in 2021.

Moreover, despite the comparatively few emissions produced by public transportation systems in Costa Rica, the elevated growth of private vehicles in conjunction with a significantly slower growth in population seems to indicate a tendency to favour private rather than public transportation. To add evidence to this claim, the graph from the PEN report (see Figure 9.1) shows that within the last three decades the public transportation subsector has not shown any signs of growth, while there has been a rapid growth of privately owned vehicles at the same time (PEN, 2015, p. 306). This trend is perhaps neither surprising nor exceptional, but can nevertheless be interpreted as being fairly paradoxical. As Urry (2010) argued, "The apparently 'rational' decision of millions of individual people to exercise their right to drive has resulted in carbon gas discharges that threaten the long-term survival of the planet (even where most motorists are aware of such consequences)" (p. 361).

Finally, the PEN report (2015) also concludes that "the intensive use of hydrocarbons is associated with a scarce use of renewable sources based on technologies and investments that would allow resolving, above all, consumption in the transport sector" (p. 177, author's translation). This means that despite Costa Rica's installed capacity to generate power from 'renewable sources'[9] and its potential to further develop such energy-producing networks, 72.1 per cent of all energies consumed are imported hydrocarbons (Ibid.), and 66 per cent of those fossil fuels are consumed in the transport sector (MINAE, 2015, p. 93).

Thus, it is argued that Costa Rica's Carbon-Neutral campaign exemplifies a scenario in which the constituent *discourses* and *practices* of the actor-network are incompatible with one another to such an extent that the gap between its conflicting *materialities* and *inscriptions* poses the threat for a network breakdown;

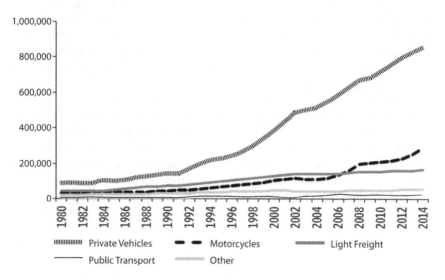

Figure 9.1 Evolution of Costa Rica's motorized fleet, according to vehicle type.
Source: Programa Estado de la Nación (PEN), 2015, p. 306.

and this in return is the result of the failure to perceive both *discourses* and *practices* as fundamental *actants* of the same actor-network.

Gössling (2009) introduces another controversy embedded in carbon-neutralization networks. Instead of incongruities between constituent entities of the same network, the conflict confronts three deeply interrelated *macro* actor-networks: carbon-neutralization, air travel industries and sustainable tourism.

He holds that a contradiction between these two networks emerges, as the increasing demand for 'sustainable tourism' and particularly for 'carbon-neutral' destinations also equals a growing demand for international flights to and from these destinations. Consequently, as air travel grows, so do the GHG emissions associated with this type of mobility. In other words, this shows how a development strategy that sells 'carbon-free products' – in this case spaces – paradoxically relies heavily on a carbon-intensive product – air travel. In the end, these co-constituted networks may well be producing the very contrary effect on 'climate change' mitigation that they both are supposedly concerned about.

Gössling argues that regardless of these effects, the countries included in this trend mobilize 'carbon-neutral' tags as mere 'product differentiators' to compete in the highly profitable market of 'eco-products' and in this case in particular, to attract a fast-growing number of 'eco-concerned' tourists. Therefore he argues, 'carbon neutral' themes in their present form are neither believable nor rigorous, and are better understood as discourses merely assembled to "…justify business-as-usual tourism development with a view towards self-regulation, and might in practice even prevent the implementation of serious climate policy measures" (Ibid., p. 33).

However, the reason for reviewing the two controversies discussed above is not to say that 'discourses' and 'practices' are irremediably confronted within and/or among every actor-network; and nor is it to argue that 'discourses' are never anything more than *non-material*, abstract or even empty rhetoric. On the contrary, the boundaries between 'discourses' and 'practices' are always permeable, mutable and in a constant process of transformation and co-construction (Haraway, 1991).

And even if it were possible to establish a boundary between the two, Deleuzian and Foucauldian post-structuralist perspectives often argue that materialist analysis can simply not be separated from discursive analysis in the first place, since language is in fact a constitutive actor in the construction of reality, and not just a reflection of it (see Escobar, 1996).

Assembling the calculating device

Aside from the emergent mismatching between the 'abstract' and 'concrete' constituents of particular actor-networks, the question of which entities are included in the assembling of such networks in the first place also presents a relevant discussion to consider – particularly when these networks are embodied as obligatory passage points (Callon, 1986) designed in relation to the materiality of 'nature' as calculable and thus governable through regulatory frameworks and standards.

In that light, Asdal (2008) asks: "Which numbers to feed into the calculating machine?" (p. 129). This question directly relates to the fact that 'nature(s)', places, bodies, or any other object are constructions that depend on the specific sets of *calculations* that their enacting heterogeneous actor-networks perform, and in doing so negotiate which entities are included and thus, which entities are excluded from the object's *symbolically charged inscription* (Akrich, 1997) anytime that these correspond – or not – with the specific purpose of the enacting network.

Accordingly, Gössling (2009) argues that the growing GHG emissions produced by the equally growing air travel industry remain in a virtual 'no man's land' as these emissions have so far escaped international regulation in spite of the not-so-binding 'Davos Declaration' in 2007 by the United Nations World Tourism Organization (UNWTO). This declaration does not conclusively hold any actor responsible for these emissions and, what is more, some actors such as airlines and aircraft manufacturers are not even mentioned in the Declaration (see UNWTO, 2007).

Of course, 'carbon-neutral' destinations are not the exception either to this tendency or to this lack of regulations. And much like Fletcher (2013) found in the way GHG emissions are produced in national hydroelectric power production, air travel emissions are not taken into account in calculating Costa Rica's carbon balance.

Finally, Gössling (2009) also argues that the entire 'carbon-neutrality' concept is in itself "... an oxymoron, as emissions of greenhouse gases from tourism are not 'neutralized', [instead] they are *compensated for*, usually through projects that save emissions in other, non-tourism sectors" (p. 19, original emphasis). He later proposes the use of more accurate concepts such as 'carbon compensated', which relates more explicitly to those offsetting activities outside of the tourism sector such as reforestation and avoided deforestation, among others, which have enjoyed central stage in Costa Rica as opposed to 'emission reductions' and other 'climate change adaptation' measures as have been discussed throughout this section.

The process in which this particular political construction of 'nature' is assembled, and the deliberate inclusion and omission of entities as constituents of the 'carbon-neutrality network' in Costa Rica and elsewhere, shows two things: First, that the limits of nature's materiality are always drawn and redrawn as nature is constructed through the heterogeneous assemblage of 'politically' prioritized materials and discourses reduced to *inscriptions* or *calculations*; and thus secondly, that these calculations are in fact both 'politically' and 'scientifically' biased.

Black-boxing 'expert talk'

With the global advent, rise, and consolidation of different and highly profitable markets of 'eco-products', the need to determine what exactly constitutes a 'green' product, space, or service – in order to avoid the practice of *greenwashing* – has become apparent. The general response to such a challenge was the elaboration of several systems of 'standards' mobilized to validate and legitimize the many 'sustainable', 'environmentally friendly' and 'carbon-neutral' claims.

There is no such thing as an omnipresent cross-network standard, but instead there are multiple standard-schemes, each one devised as the *obligatory passage point* of each specific actor-network. This relates to the earlier discussed condition in which the quantitative and qualitative *heterogeneous calculations* mobilized in each actor-network are constantly (re)negotiated within each specific network as nature's materiality is always drawn and redrawn. Henceforth, each 'green' network assembles its own standard-schemes and calculations according to the specific needs of its own 'market'. This at the same time explains why some 'calculations' and standards-schemes are embodied as eco-certifications,[10] while others are condensed checklists of minimum requirements for specific purposes.[11]

Lansing (2011) holds that the different mobilized claims resulting from these *black-boxed* (Callon and Latour, 1981) *calculations* can never exist in isolation; they are always assembled in relation to a framing field of other similar statements. In particular, and while looking into the specific carbon-offsetting network in Costa Rica, Lansing (2011) found that "...the ability of the carbon calculations to emerge as discursive statements that can be *evaluated as* true or false comes from their relation to a historically embedded set of discursive rules..." (p. 744, original emphasis).

Hence, the separation between particular 'green' claims and the standards-schemes that calculate them is essentially artificial. This is particularly important since calculations, standards and certification-schemes can never be made in a political vacuum, as has been discussed. If calculations are then perpetually embedded in political subjectivity, so are the 'claims' that these will mobilize.

However, these biases appear to remain outside of the public eye. It may even be argued that these seem to disappear to the extent that carbon-neutral calculations have so far been successfully *black-boxed* as unbendable scientific tools based on objective techno-scientific knowledge and the positively given facts of 'nature'.

In spite of that, it can be argued that academics and practitioners alike continue to almost carelessly mobilize these taken-for-granted notions as if they were dealing with, or more precisely assembling, controversy-free instruments and facts. Moreover, this process of *black-boxing* has been so thorough that these concepts and claims are now being systematically mobilized not only among 'experts' and 'detractors', but in day-to-day environmental jargon by 'non-experts' alike.

Arguably, these calculations remain unchallenged precisely because they have deliberately been assembled to tell the story of complicated calculations to deal with complicated issues, far too complicated to be understood by the 'untrained eye'. Or as Holden (2011) puts it "... work toward sustainable development generally, is widely accepted as demanding high levels of expertise, defining and achieving citizen participation that makes a difference to these efforts is difficult..." (p. 315).

Then, modernist technocratic 'expert' knowledge may ultimately be a mechanism mobilized to deliberately constrain non-expert participation in debates of 'techno-scientific complexities' such as reaching 'sustainable development' or mitigating 'climate change'. To add to this point, Latour (2008) argues that "... the whole language of science and engineering might be portrayed as anything other than the boring carriers of the indisputable necessities that modernism has rendered popular" (p. 10). This means that the mere vocabulary mobilized in technocratic 'expert' discourses has in itself been assembled to impose considerable constraints on public debate while at the same time rendering scientific knowledge and agency as irrefutable *matters of fact* (Ibid., p. 2).

These matters of fact are not limited to debates of environmental governance. In the urban planning field in particular, Leffers (2015) argues that "[t]he reliance on scientific, expert knowledge legitimates discourses by giving them authority and rules in which to operate, and dismisses competing discourses as uninformed and incapable of accessing the truth" (p. 133). With that, he argues that expert-planners likewise mobilize their own 'green' constructions and calculations – such as intensification, sustainable urbanism, resilience, green place branding, and so forth – to the extent that these are stabilized as a sort of synonym of 'good' for the urban space, while at the same time any opposition to these *black boxes* is rendered as a sign of unreason and ignorance which those knowledgeable 'experts' may correct through proper 'education' and 'discipline' (in a Foucauldian sense).

Similarly, in his discussion about the agency of landscapes and the production of infrastructures, Bélanger (2016) argues that the role performed by technocratic engineers in fact personifies the 'risk of reason' in the extent that she or he mobilizes "... the implementation of legal limits, and categories of accountability – institutionalized through standardization and systematization..." (p. 199). The author continues stating that "[r]emoved more and more from regional resources and dynamic biophysical processes, the neutralization and normalization of process is heightened by the security found in quantitative logic and numerical precision" (Ibid.). Therefore, the taken-for-granted 'neutrality' of these modernist *calculations* further reinforces the rule of expert-instrumentalism and at the same time the underlying understanding of limitless capital growth that is embedded in these particular discourses and inscriptions.

Thus, it can be argued that so-called objective techno-scientific expert knowledge largely remains as an unchallenged *black box* that transcends the agency of those *much-more-serious-professionals* (Latour, 2008) of fields condensed as science and technology. Additionally, Latour (1998) holds that the modernist smokescreen of unbendable scientific objectivity is not limited to the calculations performed by elite 'experts' or 'top-down' *macro actor-networks* but is equally found in 'bottom-up' discourses of contestatory political-ecology activists and in general. In his own words: "Scientific knowledge continues to remain, with extremely rare exceptions, a *black box* in the eco-movements, where the social sciences rarely serve as a point of reference for opening controversies between experts." (p. 10).

Conclusions

The overall objective of this chapter has been to shed new light on the mechanisms of *calculation*, *displacement* and *stabilization* of certain mobilized sociotechnical constructions of nature(s) found in regulatory frameworks of environmental governance – particularly those embodied in the process of 'de-carbonizing' economies as a new trend to consolidate greater competitiveness in increasingly globalized markets. In so doing, it has sought to reveal several taken-for-granted conceptions about the constituencies of so-called nature beyond the rather simplistic binary-dualisms of positivism and social-constructivism. This has been done by using some of the analytical and conceptual devices of *actor-network theory* and of the new *mobilities turn* as both of these particular material sensitive stands provide usable tools to understand a world in which the boundaries between nature, science, society and technology are eroding in controversies rooted in environmental governance, urban planning and complex mobility systems.

In the more theoretical sense, it is debated that instead of the modernist understanding of a monolithic, stable positively given 'nature' out there, there are multiple and simultaneous 'nature(s)' under constant negotiation, each one constructed through the assemblage of heterogeneous material and non-material entities performatively arranged 'socially'. Thus, 'nature' is precisely the emerging effect of those processes of 'social' ordering or performative practices of *calculation*.

Additionally, it is argued that our modernist understanding of 'nature' is not even about 'nature', but about endless imbroglios in which human involvement is always present. It is precisely here where 'nature' becomes a relevant topic only to the extent that 'its' materiality is employed in some controversy relating to a productive activity. Stated differently, 'nature' is deemed relevant to the extent that it is re-constructed as a commodity in and by a specific actor-network through its own performative practice of calculations intended to ultimately render 'nature' governable. Hence, *nature(s)* are biased performative constructions that depend on equally biased sets of *calculations* enacted by specific eco-socio-technical networks.

Moreover, it is held that because of the subjectivity and multiplicity behind these constructions and calculations of nature, they are always *fluid* and hold together *precariously*. With that, it is construed that there will continuously exist a gap between the materialities of 'nature(s)' and their *inscriptions*, as the former will always inadequately embody a symbolically charged construction that necessarily remains *fluid* and *imagined*.

In a more practical sense, I have shown this gap as it is currently unfolding in the specific case of Costa Rica's 'Carbon Neutralization Network'. This has been done by following two different controversies in which two contradictions continue to develop and thus far remain largely overlooked. The first controversy shows how the Costa Rican state has not only not mobilized its own carbon-neutrality regulatory frameworks to engage in efforts to reduce the GHG emissions from the transport sector – identified as the largest obstacles to reach the carbon neutrality in 2021, but instead has permitted the number of combustion-engine vehicles to double in the years following the proclamation of that ambitious self-appointed challenge.

The second controversy discusses how the increasing demand for 'sustainable tourism', and particularly for 'carbon-neutral' destinations, also equates to a growing demand for international flights to and from these destinations. Nevertheless, I have shown how in the contingent sociotechnical process of measuring, calculating and stabilizing carbon inventories, 'nature' is performatively (re)constructed as a fluid, abstract and politically embedded 'generalization' within which certain entities – e.g. trees, volcanoes, humming birds – are included and measured while others – such as the ever-growing emissions generated by air travel to this internationally renowned ecotourism hub – are deliberately 'removed from the equation'. Consequently, this translates to a new emergent paradox: While carbon-neutral' tourism destinations consolidate themselves as the new sites for 'sustainable tourism'– an alternative to energy-intensive mass tourism for example, the growing number of eco-concerned consumers identified by Urry (2013) who increasingly seek powered-down lifestyles and experiences – such as those reputedly offered in sustainable tourism, entails use of carbon-intensive mobility systems.

Both of these controversies suggest how the nation's Carbon-Neutral campaign has been assembled to a large extent as little more than a 'market differentiator' sustained by 'abstract' rhetoric – and much less so as involving serious climate-change mitigation policies based on concrete implementations. Additionally, it has been discussed how those few implementations that have in fact been mobilized so far have been dispersed at best – an oxymoron at worst.

Again in a more theoretical sense, it has been contended that the limits of nature's materiality are always drawn and redrawn as nature is constructed through the heterogeneous assemblage of 'politically' prioritized materials and discourses reduced to inscriptions or calculations. A general and a specific argument can be drawn from this inference. First, and in general, the 'de-carbonizing' calculations and discourses are in fact both invariably 'politically' and 'scientifically' biased; and secondly and specifically, Costa Rica's particular carbon-neutrality goal has not been pursued heterogeneously as its 'discourses' and 'practices' have not been conceived as integral actants of the same process of translation; hence the network's overall stability and durability are prone to break down. In this respect, I believe that a material mobilities approach provides a promising space for further research on the unpredictable and non-linear role that local knowledge and local action have at the emergent global level (Urry, 2000). More precisely, this particular approach is particularly well equipped to follow how individual action – whether the routinized practices of a local group of technocrat 'experts', or the choices for travel destinations of a local family – translates into the proliferation of global connections and implications that are captured, represented, marketed and generalized elsewhere (Urry, 2011, p. 361). A material mobilities approach simultaneously allows researchers to understand how a small perturbation in a system at a local level can result in unpredictable and chaotic branching of such a system at a global one.

In spite of all the above-mentioned contradictions, inconsistencies and biases, 'nature' seems to continue to emerge quite unproblematically as a stable and monolithic entity 'out there' that appears to be 'real' and even 'obvious' to everybody. It has been argued that this at least partly relates to the way in which techno-scientific discourses, knowledge, and *agency* have been black-boxed under the modernist smokescreen of scientific objectivity, which is mobilized not only by technocratic 'experts' or 'top-down' *macro actor-networks* through their own performative *calculations* and *discourses*, but is equally found in 'bottom-up' discourses of contestatory political-ecology activists and mobilizations as well as in the day-to-day environmental jargon of 'non-experts' on a far more general scale. Here, once again, I believe that the particular analytical sensibilities of the mobilities paradigm are distinctively fit to enable critical analysis of complex sociotechnical networks like that followed in this chapter precisely because this approach entails that *agency* is a transformative quality that is not exclusively reserved for human entities.

Instead, this perspective holds that humans are only capable of exerting agency "in circumstances which are not of their own making; and it is those circumstances – the enduring and increasingly intimate relations of subjects *and* objects – that are of paramount significance" (Urry, 2010, p. 357, original emphasis). The mobilities paradigm therefore entails that, rather than a uniquely human society, societies are complex hybrid networks. Hence, following technocrat 'experts' alone will never be enough to understand the emergence, transition and stabilization of complex *sociotechnical regimes* and *landscapes*.

Nevertheless, this chapter has shown that the modernist technocratic *calculations*, discourses, language and knowledge may all in fact be mobilized to deliberately constrain non-expert participation of any unaligned actors and entities in debates of 'techno-scientific complexities' such as achieving 'sustainable development' or mitigating 'climate change'. In this fashion, the proliferation of controversies in these topics is silenced-off for the sake of the so-called common good, which is at the same time based on the re-construction of 'nature' as a commodity ready to be *ordered* in 'green' industries and markets.

Notes

1 I.e., Bruno Latour, *Reassembling the social: An introduction to actor network theory* (Oxford: Oxford University Press, 2005) and John Urry, *Climate Change and Society* (Cambridge: Polity Press, 2011) respectively.
2 See Ecowatch, press release, 24 December 2015.
3 GHG: Greenhouse gases.
4 See Klooster (2010) on FSC trans-nationally-scaled, multi-stakeholder product certification systems.
5 Instituto de Normas Técnicas de Costa Rica (2016).
6 PEN is a research programme that belongs to the National Rectors Council (CONARE), which includes the country's four state universities and deals with 'sustainable human development' in Costa Rica.
7 This same source reveals that this tendency shows signs of a further increment of the motorized fleet of an additional 5 per cent between 2013 and 2014 alone (PEN, 2015, p. 171).
8 PEN (2015, p. 179).
9 See Fletcher (2013) for a critical discussion on how hydropower in particular has been *black-boxed* as a flagship example of 'clean' and 'renewable' energies in Costa Rica – and globally – despite being associated with several 'social' and even 'environmental' trade-offs.
10 See: Haaland and Ass (2010), LePree (2009) and Blackman *et al.* (2014) for certifications in ecotourism; and Klooster (2010) and Eden (2009) for certifications in forestry networks.
11 See Lansing (2010, 2012) on the quantification involved in carbon offsetting markets in Costa Rica; and Rice (2011) on minimum sustainable attributes as required in Building Regulations and Planning Laws in the UK.

References

Akrich, M., 1997. The De-scription of Technical Objects. In: W. Bijker and J. Law, eds., 1997. *Shaping Technology/Building Society: Studies in Sociotechnical Change.* Cambridge, MA: The MIT Press. pp. 205–224.
Asdal, K., 2008. Enacting things through numbers: Taking nature into account/ing. *Geoforum*, 39(1), pp. 123–132.
Baltodano, J., 2008. Los peligros del doble discurso. De lo Internacional a lo Local: El caso de la propuesta 'Costa Rica Carbono Neutral 2021'. *Economía y Sociedad*, 33/34, pp. 7–19.

Bélanger, P., 2016. Is Landscape Infrastructure? In: G. Doherty and C. Waldheim, eds., 2016. *Is Landscape...? Essays on the Identity of Landscape*. Oxon: Routledge. pp. 199–227.

Blackman, A., Naranjo M.A., Robalino, J., Alpizar, F., Rivera, J., 2014. Does tourism eco-certification pay? Costa Rica's Blue Flag Program. *World Development*, 58(C), pp. 41–52.

Blok, A., 2013. Pragmatic sociology as political ecology: On the many worths of nature(s). *European Journal of Social Theory*, 16(4), pp. 492–510.

Callon, M., 1986. Some Elements of a Sociology of Translation: Domestication of the Scallops and the Fishermen of St Brieuc Bay. In: J. Law, ed., 1986. *Power, Action and Belief: A New Sociology of Knowledge?* London: Routledge. pp. 196–223.

Callon, M. and Latour, B., 1981. Unscrewing the Big Leviathan; Or How Actors Macro-structure Reality, and How Sociologists Help Them to Do So? In: K. Knorr-Cetina and A. Cicourel, eds., 1981. *Advances in Social Theory and Methodology*. London: Routledge & Kegan Paul. pp. 277–303.

Castree, N., 2003. Environmental issues: Relational ontologies and hybrid politics. *Progress in Human Geography*, 27(2), pp. 203–211.

Cook, I.R. and Swyngedouw, E., 2012. Cities, social cohesion and the environment: Towards a future research agenda. *Urban Studies*, 49(9), pp. 1959–1979.

Ecowatch, 2015. *Costa Rica Powers 285 Days of 2015 With 100% Renewable Energy*. [press release] 24 December 2015. Available at: http://ecowatch.com/2015/12/24/costa-rica-renewables [Accessed 3 February 2016].

Eden, S., 2009. The work of environmental governance networks: Traceability, credibility and certification by the Forest Stewardship Council. *Geoforum*, 40, pp. 383–394.

Escobar, A., 1996. Construction nature: Elements for a post-structuralist ecology. *Futures*, 28(4), pp. 325–343.

Fletcher, R., 2010. When environmental issues collide: Climate change and the shifting political ecology of hydroelectric power. *Peace & Conflict Review*, 5(1), pp. 1–15.

Fletcher, R., 2013. Making 'Peace with Nature': Costa Rica's Campaign for Climate Neutrality. In: C. Roger, D. Held and E. Nag, eds., 2013. *Laggards to Leaders: Climate Change Governance in the Developing World*. London: Polity Press. pp. 155–173.

Gössling, S., 2009. Carbon neutral destinations: A conceptual analysis. *Journal of Sustainable Tourism*, 17(1), pp. 17–37.

Haaland, H. and Ass, Ø., 2010. Eco-tourism certification – does it make a difference? A comparison of systems from Australia, Costa Rica and Sweden. *Scandinavian Journal of Hospitality and Tourism*, 10(3), pp. 375–385.

Haraway, D., 1991. *Simians, Cyborgs, and Women: The Reinvention of Nature*. New York: Routledge.

Harré, R., 2002. Material objects in social worlds. *Theory, Culture & Society*, 19(5/6), pp. 23–33.

Holden, M., 2011. Public participation and local sustainability: Questioning a common agenda in urban governance. *International Journal of Urban and Regional Research*, 35(2), pp. 312–329.

Instituto de Normas Técnicas de Costa Rica, 2016. *Norma para demostrar la Carbono Neutralidad. Requisitos* (INTE B5:2016). San José, Costa Rica: INTECO.

Klooster, D., 2010. Standardizing sustainable development? The Forest Stewardship Council's plantation policy review process as neoliberal environmental governance. *Geoforum*, 41, pp. 117–129.

Kowollik, M., 2014. Costa Rica carbono neutral: un país pequeño con metas grandes. *Perspectivas. FES Costa Rica*, No 8/2014, pp. 1–6.

Lansing, D., 2010. Carbon's calculatory spaces: The emergence of carbon offsets in Costa Rica. *Environment and Planning, D: Society and Space*, 28(3), pp. 710–725.

Lansing, D., 2011. Realizing carbon's value: Discourse and calculation in the production of carbon forestry offsets in Costa Rica. *Antipode*, 43(3), pp. 731–753.

Lansing, D., 2012. Performing carbon's materiality: The production of carbon offsets and the framing of exchange. *Environment and Planning A*, 44(1), pp. 204–220.

Latour, B., 1998. To Modernize or to Ecologize? That's the Question. In: N. Castree and B. Willems-Braun, eds., 1998. *Remaking Reality. Nature at the Millenium*. London/ New York: Routledge. pp. 221–242.

Latour, B., 1999. *Politics of Nature: How to Bring the Sciences In to Democracy*. Cambridge, MA: Harvard University Press.

Latour, B., 2005. *Reassembling the Social: An Introduction to Actor Network Theory*. Oxford: Oxford University Press.

Latour, B., 2008. *A Cautious Prometheus? A Few Steps Toward a Philosophy of Design (with Special Attention to Peter Sloterdijk). Keynote lecture for the 'Networks of Design' meeting of the Design History Society*. [online] Available at www.bruno-latour.fr/sites/default/files/112-DESIGN-CORNWALL-GB.pdf [Accessed 17 May 2016].

Law, J., 1992. Notes on the theory of the actor-network ordering, strategy and heterogeneity. *Systems Practice*, 5(4), pp. 379–393.

Law, J. 2004. *After Method: Mess in Social Science Research*. London: Routledge.

Law, J., 2007. *Actor Network Theory and Material Semiotics*. [online]. Heterogeneities-DOTnet: John Law. Available at: www.heterogeneities.net/publications/Law2007ANTandMaterialSemiotics.pdf [Accessed 5 June 2016].

Leffers, D., 2015. Conflict in the Face of Planning? Power, Knowledge, and Hegemony in planning practice. In: E. Gualini, ed., 2015. *Planning and Conflict: Critical Perspectives on Contentious Urban Developments*. Oxford: Routledge. pp. 127–144.

LePree, J. G., 2009. Certifying sustainability: The efficacy of Costa Rica's certification for sustainable tourism. *Florida Atlantic Comparative Studies Journal*, 11(1), pp. 57–78.

Li, T. M., 2007. Practices of assemblage and community forest management. *Economy and Society*, 36(2), pp. 263–293.

MINAE, 2015. *VII Plan Nacional de Energía 2015–2030. Programa de las Naciones Unidas para el Desarrollo PNUD*. [online] San José, Costa Rica: MINAE. Available at: www.minae.go.cr/recursos/2015/pdf/VII-PNE.pdf [Accessed 23 June 2017].

Programa Estado de la Nación PEN, 2015. *Vigésimo primer Informe Estado de la Nación en desarrollo humano sostenible*. [online] San José, Costa Rica: CONARE. Retrieved from: www.estadonacion.or.cr/21/assets/pen-21-2015-baja.pdf [Accessed 10 April 2016].

Rice, L., 2011. Black-boxing sustainability. *Journal of Sustainable Development*, 4(4), pp. 32–37.

Rogers, T., 2009. *Costa Rica's President: It's Not Easy Staying Green*. [online] TIME USA, LLC. Available at: www.time.com/time/world/article/0,8599,1927452,00.html [Accessed 15 September 2016].

Temenos, C., Nikolaeva, A., Schwanen, T., Cresswell, T., Sengers, F., Watson, M. and Sheller, M., 2017. Ideas in motion: Theorizing mobility transitions an interdisciplinary conversation. *Transfers: Interdisciplinary Journal of Mobility Studies*, 7(1), pp. 113–129.

UNWTO, 2007. *Davos Declaration. Climate change and tourism. Responding to global challenges*. [online] Available at: http://sdt.unwto.org/sites/all/files/docpdf/decladavose.pdf [Accessed 2 August 2016].

Urry, J., 2000. *Sociology Beyond Societies*. London, New York: Routledge.
Urry, J., 2010. Mobile sociology. *The British Journal of Sociology*, 61(Suppl. 1), pp. 347–366.
Urry, J., 2011. *Climate Change and Society*. Cambridge: Polity Press.
Urry, J., 2013. A low carbon economy and society. *Philosophical Transactions of the Royal Society A*, [e-journal] 371(1986), pp. 1–12. http://dx.doi.org/10.1098/rsta.2011.0566.
Whatmore, S., 2006. Materialist returns: Practicing cultural geography in and for a more-than-human world. *Cultural Geographies*, 13(4), pp. 600–609.

10 Acupunctural mobilities design 'from below'

Reflecting on uneven material mobilities in the Global South, the Caracas a pie case

Andrea V. Hernandez Bueno and Ditte Bendix Lanng

Introduction

The emerging debate on mobility justice is enquiring into the power that influences (im)mobility and seeking a better understanding of the real meaning of the freedom of movement and how to emancipate subjects to become mobile, to the right to move and to the "right to the city". This overall concept addresses (in)equalities and uneven mobility from a mobilities perspective: in different realms and on multiple scales, from the human and experiential scale to global dimensions, looking at justice as fluid, and as a "process of emergent relationships in which the interplay of diverse (im)mobilities forms a foundational part" (Sheller, 2018, p. 20).

Uneven mobilities refer to the uneven distribution of mobility, herein social, political and economic capacities and different forms of capital such as financial, cultural, and social (Ibid., p. 15), and also to the lack of access to mobility in multiple dimensions:

> [T]he unevenness of mobility may take the form of uneven *qualities* of experience, uneven access to *infrastructure*, uneven *materialities*, uneven *subjects* of mobility, and uneven *events* of stopping, going, passing, pausing and waiting.
> (Adey *et al.*, 2014 in Sheller, 2016, p. 17, italics in original)

Uneven mobilities consider the politics of mobilities, equalities and mobility qualities (Adey, 2010; Cresswell, 2010). First, uneven mobilities are created by mobility regimes that organize, sort, shift and segregate different kinds of flows and activities producing (im)mobile subjects (Sheller, 2018). These mobility regimes are enacted by infrastructures, urban spaces, technical systems, regulatory norms, and social and cultural practices (Ibid.). Secondly, uneven mobilities in some cases catalyse the emergence of active participation of civic and social movements that claim equal ways of moving.

In the global south, practices of uneven mobilities and social movements of civic and urban activism are catalogued as 'informal'. The unevenness refers to individual appropriation of public spaces, marking territories with commercialization or traffic-related modes of transport that prevent pedestrian mobilities, increased private and individual modes of transport, lack of access to different modes of transport both economically and physically, lack of organization and alternatives to mass transportation to help achieve sustainable and human-friendly urban mobilities, the lack of public spaces that creates congestion and segregation, and dangerous alternatives/sometimes anarchic ways of moving in the city; while civic activism refers to DIY alternatives of dwelling and moving (Vasudevan, 2011). We want to move away from that connotation of 'informality' by recognizing the very actual, material dimension of those practices, as real, relational to other socio-politic-economic-material aspects and embedded in the mobilities culture and the human condition. We do not embrace the concept of 'informality' from the social-class perspective or legal approach, or from the 'exotic' commodification of human and urban realities, but as spontaneous, creative, organic and natural practices and human mobilities responses 'from below', that shift/expand 'legal' and urban boundaries into public domains: actions of urban acupunctural socio-material mobilities. We recognize those socio-material mobilities practices and actions of site emancipation as 'political infrastructures' and 'radical incrementalism' (Pieterse, 2008), and, therefore, as practices of empowerment from civic society and 'insurgent urbanism' that might inform future urban politics and urban mobilities design actions (Mcfarlane and Vasudevan, 2014).

This chapter discusses a contemporary example from Caracas, Venezuela, of the materialities that influence the complex problem of mobility justice, unpacking socio-material dimensions of uneven mobilities and acupunctural practices of activism in a city in crisis.

Venezuela's corruption, and political and economic crash, in an oil-dependent country, are continuously affecting its social, economic, political, urban and cultural dimensions and the development of the country. This situation is preventing and basic distribution of food and goods, money, industrial activity and productivity, urban mobilities, and more. Caracas is facing urgency in terms of improving its urban mobilities and city connectivity and continuity under such extreme circumstances. In this situation, it may seem like urban design and planning solutions for the complex problem of urban mobilities in Caracas have to be wide-ranging and overarching. Indeed, the more mundane practices of everyday-life urban mobilities are being increasingly degraded. For example, ordinary walking or crossing the street are often difficult practices in Caracas, as we will show below. To facilitate these practices, not only are overarching urban transformation plans needed, but also – or included in such plans – focalized 'acupunctural' interventions at particular places, that target, for example, 'legal' materialization of pedestrian crossings and incorporation of public spaces to help create continuity and an 'imaginary' of the city as a whole from the pedestrian citizen's viewpoint of practising embodied mobilities. The materialization of such 'solutions' or embodied mobilities have been carried out using citizens' initiatives, for example the one called *Caracas a pie* (walking Caracas). This initiative provides evidence that emerging ways of understanding and facing the mobility problems of the city are present and needed. We focus entirely on walking mobilities, by exploring the material and normative dimensions involved. The former entails unpacking the materialities embedded in practices of social mobilities, and the latter, drawing socio-material scenarios and alternatives of urban design mobilities culture. We address those two dimensions by contributing a discussion of one instance of how material mobilities in the global south are being transformed by citizens 'from below' and through acupunctural interventions, using *Caracas a pie* as a case study. Our aim is to contribute to a wider knowledge base and discussion relating to uneven materialities, intertwined as it is with the complex problem of unevenness of mobility.

The remainder of the chapter is structured as follows: the second part outlines the theoretical and methodological frameworks that help us to understand the materialities behind Caracas' uneven mobilities through the lenses of tactical urbanism (Lydon and Garcia, 2015), urban acupuncture (Lerner, 2014) and mobilities design (Jensen and Lanng, 2017). The third part discusses the situation prevailing in Caracas from the general understanding of its urban mobilities related to the specific case study, *Caracas a pie*. The fourth part gives three examples of acupunctural mobilities design based on the case study. Finally, the conclusions reflect on acknowledging practices of urban mobilities activisms as sources of locally produced knowledge (Rynning *et al.*, 2018) and also reflect upon alternative cultures of mobilities through the implementation of acupunctural mobilities design approaches.

Theoretical and methodological frameworks

Previously we addressed the concepts of mobility justice and uneven mobilities that explore mobility inequalities and lack of access to spatial mobilities as multi-scalar assemblages of materialities and cultural, social, economic and political aspects – i.e. practices and agencies. Moving from the focus on transport to the spatial imaginary on the city scale, people's experiences, and mobility qualities (Sheller, 2018), we put the focus on the aspect of spatial justice that emerges from social movements claiming the right to move and to the city (Ibid.). In order to do so, we analyse the case study *Caracas a pie* from the above-mentioned standpoints of tactical urbanism, urban acupuncture and mobilities design.

Tactical urbanism argues for an interdisciplinary collaboration of different actors, including governments, experts and communities in the process of city-making. It advocates that the direct participation of citizens and emergent social movements as political actions can improve the 'otherwise lifeless public spaces' through short-term actions that can bring long-term changes (Lydon and Garcia, 2015, p. 4). Tactical urbanism moves from imagination, social and spatial experience to actions, using the city as a lab. Urban acupuncture, as well as tactical urbanism, focuses on precise and rapid actions of urban transformation from the local level (Lerner, 2014). A few examples of this 'new type' of urbanism are present in South America in places where the equal right to urban mobilities is affected or even neglected by governmental actions and the influence of modernity in city planning, e.g. zoning or car-based planning schemes. In Brazil the construction of the Minhocão highway in 1971 caused congestion, pollution and liveability problems in the São Paulo neighbourhood, such as noise and vibration in buildings very close to the infrastructure, drug dealing in the underpass areas and insecurity. Concerns were raised by citizens' movements that encouraged political awareness over the contested infrastructure. Recent political actions provided, as one alternative, the temporary de-activation of the highway during weekday evenings, Saturday afternoon and all-day Sundays in order for it to be used as a public elevated park, while evaluating the total elimination of the highway (Millington, 2017). In Caracas, a similar political strategy is being applied in one part of the highway (La Cota 1000), near to one of the most emblematic natural monuments of the city (the Avila Mountain), which is open to public and leisure activities every Sunday. In Bogota the *Ciclovía* ("bike path") initiative is based upon the same idea of temporary road closure for leisure and cycling activities (Lydon and Garcia 2015). Those open street actions in Caracas, São Paolo and Bogota are just a few examples of social activism in the Global South supported by governmental actions, where the temporal de-activation of roads, and, in the case of São Paulo a highway, transformed car infrastructures into public spaces for pedestrian activities motivated by increasing traffic congestion and urban mobility problems (Pineda, 2009; Millington, 2017). Other governmental transport actions held in Curitiba and Bogota involving the implementation of Bus Rapid Transport systems –mass-transport systems with exclusive bus lanes – included the existing bus-transport operators' participation in and integration into the new system during the process of development (Pineda, 2009; Lerner, 2014). Those approaches background the mobilities and design perspectives that we are interested in here. Mobilities design embraces several aspects of tactical and acupunctural urbanism, from a material and mobile perspective. Developing from an understanding of situated mobilities (Jensen, 2013), mobilities design argues for a more nuanced understanding of the materialities of mobilities by using the term 'design' in broader terms, in seeking to examine, articulate and establish relationships between public spaces in the city and citizens' involvement and appropriation of such spaces (Lanng, 2014; Jensen, 2017; Jensen and Lanng, 2017). Mobilities design advocates and invites creative and critical ways of thinking about the design of mobilities, and the genesis of a 'spatial sensitivity' by the exploration of physical materials and design interventions (Jensen, 2017) in mundane spaces, such as paths, parking lots, train stations, bus stops, etc.

Caracas – the case

Caracas' urban mobility is characterized by being a complex mix of private and public, disrupted by a lack of public spaces, including green and grey areas (found in a city that combines natural and concrete landscapes as part of its urban scenography); it has a mix of different means of transport (spontaneous transport such as jeeps, a potpourri of buses, underground metro system), infrastructures and public spaces. No rules or schedules are followed for the functioning of urban mobility in Caracas, and, in this sense, it is organic, fragmented and always an act of negotiation or transgression. This affects everyday-life decisions, usual and necessary ways of engaging with the city, and the citizens' everyday lives. In this chapter, we seek to tackle the emergency of re-thinking practices of urban mobilities design by analysing acupunctural mobilities in the city of Caracas using as a methodology the *Caracas a pie* empirical case.

Caracas: city and urban mobilities

"Mobility is ubiquitous, it is something we do and experience almost all the time" (Adey, 2010). However, in Caracas city mobility is not accessible for everyone; moving is not a democratic practice. There is a lack of connectivity within different parts of the city, as well as a lack of possibilities and alternatives to move freely. This can be seen in the lack of public spaces and pedestrian and transport infrastructures and their coherent relation with, and organization of, the existing types of public transport, and the emergence of motorcycle-based private and public transport (moto-taxi) (see more about these studies in Finck, 2015; Behrens *et al.*, 2016,) as an alternative to circumvent the mobility problems that transgress pedestrian and motorized rights. The 'informal' (Cervero and Golub, 2007; Behrens *et al.*, 2016), 'spontaneous' (Salomón, 1997) and 'anarchic' functioning of the surface means of transport (buses are colloquially called 'camioneticas' or 'carritos') is managed by chauffeurs' associations – these aspects are seen and explored in depth as ways of dealing with the fast growth of mobility in developing countries and second economies but also as ways of affecting them (Cervero and Golub, 2007). Looking at the case of Caracas, we argue that even though there is a lot of potential in the mobility cultures and practices developed and ways of negotiating the urban spaces in the city that can shed light on helping to shape and improve future mobilities, there are also side effects of those 'informal' practices that create mobility for some and immobility for others (Graham and Marvin, 2001, in Jensen, 2013) and minimize or neglect the lack of regulations and the role of public authorities (Behrens *et al.*, 2016). For instance, in Caracas there exist an unbalanced organization of routes, lack of capacity and the creation of informal 'stops' and 'spontaneous open-air terminals' in some areas of the city (Salomón, 1997) as a necessity to mobilize the growing masses of the population – those mobility practices make evident the organic use of the urban spaces in the city but at the same time generate congestion and conflicts within the same transport systems and affect other mobilities such as walking. In the case of the underground transport system, Caracas Metro, managed by public authorities, there is a lack of efficiency and capacity; however, it is one of the most popular means of transport because it 'avoids' surface traffic (depending on the peak-hour direction; e.g. in the morning in the west to east direction, the city of Caracas presents a strong rush-hour, while in the afternoon this situation is reversed) and creates a sense of safety that is apparently better than that for surface-level walking. The lack of public spaces and their connectivity, and car-oriented city development (more road construction to improve urban mobility) are also factors that affect mobility in Caracas. Additionally, there is a lack of urban policies and attempts to improve demand in the existing means of transport, and most importantly a lack of willingness of government to understand the extant problems from the perspective of citizens' needs (Vallmitjana, 2007). Therefore, the act of moving from A to B in Caracas is an uncertain process and often a stressful procedure, because there is no control over arrival and departure times due to the organic and unpredictable traffic congestion, and it cannot be taken for granted that urban spaces in the city can be transited by walking, as is the case in many other parts of the world, supportive politics of mobilities around 'pedestrianism' (Lorimer, 2010) not being something that can be taken as a given (see Adey, 2010). In Figure 10.1 are shown examples of urban mobility situations in two very contrasting areas of Caracas (Chacao [centre-east] and Catia [west]) which were parts of areas of study in an earlier urban mobility project that demonstrates urban mobility situations in Caracas.

The photo collage shows examples of the problematic nature of urban mobilities in Caracas. From left to right/top to bottom. a. Street intersection without crossing path, not projected in the intersection, but used by citizens; b. Example of 'spontaneous open-air terminal', jeep transportation to informal settlements and buses; c. Traffic, appropriation of the street by informal economies and motorcycles parking, lack of capacity in public spaces to walk and public life; d. Street section, car-infrastructure domination over public and pedestrian spaces, a ray of hope from one informal merchant that uses the street parking area as a place to read a newspaper – under the shadow of a tree as an answer to tropical weather conditions; e. Street section, peak-hour-direction; f. Chaotic feeling, lack of public spaces, traffic and commercial economy, no boundaries between the different spaces, the street becoming a 'spontaneous' shared-space. g. Fences as urban elements to prevent pedestrians from crossing a main, wide, and long avenue; the legal crossing paths distance is very long between intersections, and sometimes crossings are not formalized; h. A pedestrian crossing and negotiating the street; i. A 'spontaneous' moto-taxi 'terminal' (Salomón, 1997), an example of the organic, fragmented and chaotic use and appropriation of public spaces in combination with everyday basic practices of urban mobilities; j. An example of ground transport led by 'private transport associations' and 'spontaneous open-air terminals' created in a line after a bus stop (extension of bus stops into open-air terminals); k. Intersection where just one pedestrian crossing is allowed to the north; however, pedestrians cross the street from different directions or between the vehicles; motorcycles show anarchical behaviour, parking on the sidewalk and crossing between vehicles on the move; l. Lack of public spaces and the irregular use of sidewalk as a parking area for motorcycles. These situations show one dimension of the lack of governmental awareness and understanding of pedestrian mobility.

The Caracas a pie case 191

Figure 10.1 Caracas urban mobilities from focalized places in the west (Catia) and east (Chacao). Libertador and Chacao Municipalities.

Source: © Andrea Victoria Hernandez Bueno.

How did Caracas urban mobility get to this point? In order to understand urban mobility problems and challenges in Caracas, it is necessary to understand its historical process of growth. During the 'oil boom' (since 1927) many of the important roads, public spaces and transport infrastructures were completed. Nowadays, the city is experiencing the consequences of its rapid development and of projects highly influenced by the philosophy of modern urbanism (the car as the centre for development) and lack of urban development to deal with the high demand for mobility. Recent attempts at metro service development (new lines to connect north and south) have been made, however the lack of capacity in the east-west direction affects the capacity and accessibility of the entire system. Other parallel initiatives like urban competitions promoting alternative ways of moving like walking and biking have been launched to create social and political awareness of the improving urban mobility in the city. Venezuelan cities are characterized as fragmented, heterogenic and disrupted; urban and economic growth has occurred by the addition of different typologies of urban configurations with their own centralities and ways of functioning in time (Napoleón, 2011). For example, in Caracas is found a colonial configuration (reticular) in its historical centres, 'garden city'-type urbanization areas, and urban zoning strategies during the period of city expansion (Ibid.). This way of growing has had repercussions for urban problems and inequalities as for example the lack of efficient and democratic mobility systems that in turn affects the continuity, unification and "readability" (Lynch, 1960) of Venezuelan cities. Caracas, the largest city of Venezuela, is not the exception; its morphology is compounded by different types of disarticulated urban fabric (Napoleón, 2011), developed in different periods and influenced by, to a large degree, the different economic, political and social circumstances. Caracas has grown from its historical centre to the east; therefore, its development took place on a west-east axis, where the biggest investments in infrastructure and public transport were made, during the modern era between 1936 and 1960, and due to the morphological and topographical conditions of the city (a valley) (Ibid.). This modern conception, together with other social, economic and political factors, has created a strong car dependency and a political agenda of improving urban mobility by focusing only on the construction of more roads, stimulating private and individual ways of moving over the public and collective. Not only are technical collective systems to facilitate mass transportation neglected; there is also a lack of accommodating mobilities in an embodied, experiential sense – the experience of moving and the urban configurations and public spaces understandings and implementations that facilitate social interactions and urban engagements.

These challenges of urban mobilities in Caracas have been the catalysts for emerging initiatives that are trying to create awareness of those urban problems and open a public debate to find solutions for recovering the right to move and the right to the city. *Caracas a pie* is one of those initiatives. It started as a weekly newspaper publication to provide information on the possibilities, ways and challenges of moving in Caracas by walking, and moved forward by the application of temporary interventions in public spaces that claimed the right to move, questioning authorities' and professionals' urban mobility decisions.

Caracas a pie: an example for the proclamation of urban mobilities change

Caracas a pie ('walking Caracas') was an initiative that aimed to open up the possibility for claiming, protesting and inviting citizens to recover the right to the city by moving through it. It was initiated by two journalists, José Carvajal and Juancho Pintó, who were concerned about the impossibility of moving freely in Caracas. Mobility problems had affected their everyday life experiences in the city since childhood, and motivated them to explore new routes by the act of walking (Carvajal, 2016). Carvajal and Pintó wanted to stimulate a debate around walking the city of Caracas, especially since they found that the general perception and feeling of citizens was that it was not possible, due to the lack of public spaces, the inefficient public transportation, and car dependency, all enhanced by the valley topographical situation of the city. Carvajal and Pintó found that experiencing the city by walking was crucial to discover the possibility of moving in a city characterized by disrupted spaces and routes and fragmentation. Therefore, they started to write a 'sightseeing' guide of Caracas called *Guía del Ocio* ('Leisure guide') in 1994. This evolved into weekly newspaper articles in *El Nacional* newspaper about those very specific journeys experienced in Caracas, called *Pero en Caracas* ... ('But in Caracas'...) in 2006, which then further evolved into an entire section in the same newspaper called *Caracas a pie* (from 2007 to 2012) (Carvajal, 2016). This newspaper section was published for five years, and the newspaper only stopped its publication due to economic crisis and the scarcity of material for paper production. Subsequently, the book *Caracas a pie (Walking Caracas)* was published as a compilation of all those publications (Ibid.). The publications in *Caracas a pie* made it possible to draw alternative identities and social and urban dynamics of different areas of the city, and – simply – invited people to walk through the city. In addition, the *Caracas a pie* articles and book publication allowed the authors to get involved in public debates of urban mobility and to influence urban initiatives for the future development of the city from a citizen's perspective (city forums, urban design competitions for the city of Caracas, plan for the city of Caracas (Carvajal, 2016)).

The Caracas a pie method: experiencing mobilities and anthropological mappings

In Caracas, it is a complex matter to understand the magnitude of the mobility problems extant, due to the city's extension and polycentrism (Napoleón, 2011). However, experiencing mobilities as a method acknowledges the urban and social dynamics and configurations. *Caracas a pie* publications experienced the city by creating what Carvajal called 'anthropological mappings' (Carvajal, 2016) that recognized the morphology and plurality, and polycentric and fragmented nature of the city, and focused on mapping what we would term 'mobile situations' (following Jensen, 2013; see also Jensen and Lanng, 2017, for this term used to facilitate a particular situational, embodied and social sensitivity in urban design practice) of specific places by suggesting, via photo registrations, diagrams, writing and sketching, simple acupunctural solutions to Caracas' particular mobility cultures. By experiencing the city through embodied practices of walking, Carvajal and Pintó could recognize the different parts, identities and practices performed in a particular location within the city, unfolding challenges and potentials that could help to inform design practices and mobility solutions. They re-drew the city morphology by the use of these anthropological mappings (Figure 10.2), in order to offer "a different glance towards the city, and invitation to explore the city walking" (Carvajal, 2016).

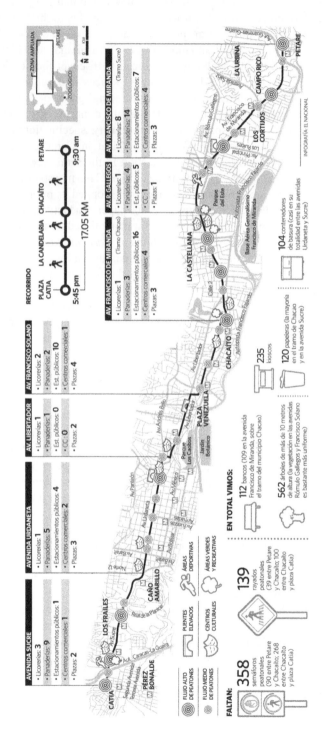

Figure 10.2 'Anthropological mappings' example (Carvajal, 2016), *Caracas a pie: Y sin embargo se mueve* ('Walking Caracas: But it moves' – our translation from Spanish). *Caracas a pie, 2012*. El Nacional publications.

Source: © El Nacional newspaper, used with permission.

Caracas a pie became a compilation of written and graphical material showcasing pedestrian paths, situations, problems, and commercial and recreational activities that put in evidence how the simple act of walking the city was perceived as a strange, even 'suspicious', practice among citizens (Carvajal and Pintó, 2012). However, Carvajal and Pintó found that not walking the city was part of the creation of feelings of insecurity and a transformation towards a more hermetic city with the fence as the main landscape – influenced even more by other social, economic, political and cultural issues. It also created a feeling of distrust among citizens, as identified by Carvajal and Pintó, and for that reason *Caracas a pie* became an example of a necessary and important political commitment for claiming urban spaces, urban transformation and change:

> [A] city like ours, so full of borders everywhere, unintegrated and bipolar, needs that its inhabitants practice it beyond the banal recognition of its more recognized urban landmarks [the authors refer here to the Avila mountain, a natural landmark that embraces the city and that is always recognized as the main identity of the city] ... [However] is looking towards the street how we [the authors] have encountered the real city ... walking through it, we have seen the mundane and the extraordinary, the patterns and the exceptional ... We have witnessed how, while the city has been growing, paradoxically it has reduced itself to a sum of territories. Instead of more city, instead of bigger cohesions of public spaces, Caracas is the result of a sum of fragments.
>
> (Ibid., 2012, p. 7; our translation from Spanish)

Caracas a pie publications unfold mobile ethnographies of the city that focus on understanding different urban situations related to pedestrian mobilities and touches on aspects as diverse as social interactions, activities, architectural landmarks and injustices present in the different fragmented urban territories of Caracas. As such, they narrate a particular, and otherwise inadequately told, story from the understanding of the place by favouring its social dynamics 'from below', like people's flows and mobile practices, and its relation with the urban configurations that are established 'from above', such as formal regulations, system features and design of public spaces, infrastructure, and transport systems (Jensen, 2013, suggests this double approach to how mobilities are being 'staged'). In our conception, those ethnographic understandings of the city make it possible to identify nodes of discontinuity and non-democratic urban configurations – areas without sidewalks or sidewalks that end nowhere, without crossings, too-small areas making it difficult to walk, and a lack of public spaces that connect different modes of flows and modes of transport. These are material configurations that limit access to mobility and the right to the city (and its transformation includes attention being paid to people's flows and mobile experiences). In most of the areas in the city where pedestrian mobilities are disrupted, people's flows and mobility practices trace 'non-official' or 'informal' pedestrian crossings which are part of the main landscape of urban pedestrians' practices.

From *Caracas a pie* to acupunctural mobilities design – examples of interventions

From the *Caracas a pie* publications we selected three distinct examples of urban areas that show the imaginary claiming of pedestrian mobility to the possible implementation of acupunctural mobilities as urban interventions. In Figure 10.3, case 1 shows a newspaper article emphasizing that people are crossing important avenues, streets and passageways where is not allowed, and claiming as an acupunctural mobilities solution the simple act of painting a zebra crossing path. The article pictures some mobile situations of chaos and disobedience of the transit rules by vehicles and pedestrians, which actually happen everywhere in Caracas, especially in important nodes of connection and activities – areas where different modes of transport and hence commercial activities meet, areas that bridge commercial and dwelling foci in the city, areas that are important green urban spaces that are fenced and hence work only within a limited time during the day. According to Carvajal, it is necessary to incorporate new, simple connections such as pedestrian crossings in some city areas to solve this problem; therefore, he started to realize that proposal by creating pedestrian crossings by painting them onto the street surface as an intervention for claiming their legal incorporation into the urban fabric.

Case 1. Top to bottom: *Caracas a pie: Caracas infinita* article (*'Walking Caracas: Caracas, infinite city'* – our translation from Spanish), *Caracas a pie, 2012*. Copyright: *El Nacional publications.* Used with permission. Acupunctural mobilities: Crossings as simple mobilities design solutions. Copyright: Andrea Hernandez Bueno. *'The Pedestrian week'* event picture: Marking 'disrupted/conflict' areas where people cross a street at a place not designed for that purpose; however, as a way of creating awareness and creating evidence for the urgency of a formalized pedestrian crossing, on the road surface is written 'A pedestrian crossing is missing here'. Copyright: Cheo Carvajal, used with permission. **Case 2**. Top to bottom: *Caracas a pie: Y sin embargo se mueve* article (*'Walking Caracas: But it moves'* – our translation from Spanish), *Caracas a pie, 2012*. Copyright: *El Nacional publications.* Used with permission. Acupunctural mobilities: Elevated crossings, Copyright: Andrea Hernandez Bueno. *'Pedestrian week'*: Cheo Carvajal painting a message concerning pedestrian mobility on the street surface, another example of a situation wherein the spatial dimension had become insufficient for the level of flow passing each day. Copyright: Cheo Carvajal. Used with permission. **Case 3**. Top to bottom: *Caracas a pie: Tendiendo puentes para conectar norte y sur* article (*'Walking Caracas: Drawing bridges to connect North and South'* – our translation from Spanish). *Caracas a pie, 05, El Nacional, September 2007.* Copyright: *El Nacional newspaper. Used with permission.* Acupunctural mobilities: Pedestrian-bridge spaces as connectors of city areas. Copyright: Andrea Hernandez Bueno.

The second case shows similar simple solutions in routes and areas where even though crossings exist, they are not respected by the existing, sometimes problematic, aspects of the 'mobility culture' (Jensen, 2013) of vehicular traffic

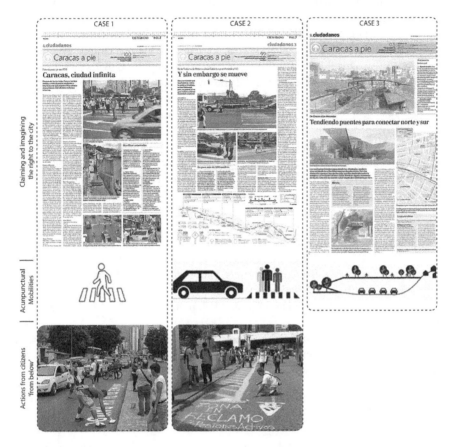

Figure 10.3 Three cases: From experiencing and imagining the city to urban action.
Source: © Editorial CEC SA/Andrea Victoria Hernandez Bueno/Jose Luis Carvajal.

(either public or private). Owing to this lack of responsibility and disrespect shown towards pedestrian areas, Carvajal proposed in the *Caracas a pie* article the elevation of the level of the crossing paths, in order to decrease vehicular speeds and to start creating awareness of pedestrians' mobilities.

The third case proposes the connection of a very dense residential area (El Valle) with another important symbolic public space, called Paseo Los Próceres, these locations being separated by a motorway. This connection, according to Carvajal, can be effected by building a pedestrian bridge that will be placed over the motorway but meeting the level of urbanization, recognizing the topography and solving mobility connections. Nowadays, people have to circumnavigate the area to get to their destination, probably involving a one-hour trip in a traffic jam that could otherwise be transformed into a pleasant pedestrian journey (Carvajal, 2016) and equal rights to mobilities.

Those mobile practices are examples of urban resistance to uneven socio-material mobilities, such practices being used for re-thinking and implementing design interventions in different areas of the city, as political actions for protest purposes. These include social activities, for example the one called 'The pedestrian week', where different journeys are taken in city areas with disruption of pedestrian mobility (Ibid.). As part of the overall action taken, urban interventions like painting messages depicting concerns over pedestrian mobility are carried out as a means of claiming the right to move and to materialize the 'weight' of pedestrians' flows. These actions caught the attention of a local municipality (Ibid.), which took on the idea and implemented new pedestrian crossings in the area. *Caracas a pie* was, then, a platform to catch the attention of authorities in a positive way and hence create pedestrian mobilities solutions for the city:

> The transformation of the city of Caracas starts from the fact of understanding and assuming the mobility in a radically different way than the one we are getting used to. ... Every day we attend a battle between pedestrians and vehicles ... a few city examples show that the street is still alive and it offers a huge transformative potential.
> (Carvajal and Pintó, 2012, p. 8; our translation from Spanish)

The mapping, narration and urban interventions based on the city experienced by walkers gave rise to insights both about what is lacking and what is working in terms of urban mobility from the pedestrian point of view.

Concluding remarks and perspectives: designing more even acupunctural mobilities?

Caracas a pie contests any assumed neutrality and singularity of the design of mobilities. It situates Caracas' material infrastructures in the midst of a complex political, economic, social, cultural and physical situation of controversy, power and unevenness.

In this chapter we have discussed this case as a pertinent example of, first, how uneven urban materialities create unevenness of mobility. And, second, how locally produced acupunctural interventions have sought to respond to this. Caracas is a city where the in-private moving of 'a few' seems to have gained primacy of consideration over the even distribution of mobility options, and where public spaces are designed with individual ways of moving in mind and not collective, plural and sustainable solutions. These are instances of a serious situation of crisis in which materialities increase the likelihood of citizens losing their right of moving and to the city.

We have demonstrated how, at focalized locations in Caracas, material design tends to produce disruptions and insecurity in relation to the mobile act of walking. *Caracas a pie* is an example of mapping 'mobile practices' 'from below' so as to draw reflections on the mobility regime's lack of proper, even urban mobility, and to make evident the lack of consideration of the authorities to citizens' pedestrian movements, and to the generation of a more connected, integrated and walkable city. In this case, mobile practices as exemplified by walking through the city became ways of protesting and claiming the right to the city. Enacting, inhabiting and experiencing the city by walking became a political tool to claim improvements in the uneven materialities of mobilities.

Further, we have discussed a series of tangible citizen-based design interventions that came about in the *Caracas a pie* initiative. Due to their focalized attention to particular places of discontinuity and unevenness of the pedestrian realm, we have conceptualized these as practices of acupunctural mobilities design. This concept targets how these small interventions carry a strategic outlook for the greater cohesion of the urban fabric and the more even distribution of mobility; they suggest a wider vision of joining-up the city as a whole by 're-connecting' the gaps between and in Caracas' territorial fragments through the reconstruction of pedestrian public spaces. Rather than technical, top-down design interventions, these examples grow from situated, contextualized and spatialized local understandings of place and embodied mobilities.

The case study analysis and discussion here then, demonstrate one instance of how material mobilities in the global south are being transformed, through acupunctural citizen-based designs, within the complex problem of rectifying uneven mobilities. In perspective, we will briefly draw out key points from this case discussion for the research agenda of designing mobilities.

Matters of concern for the future of designing materialities of mobilities include critical and nuanced attention to the relational impacts of material infrastructure on socio-political issues. Herein it includes consideration of how infrastructure enacts the organization, sorting, shifting and segregating of different kinds of flows and activities created by mobility regimes. Modernist programming of urban mobility, with its standardization, division and technical efficiency, has to a large extent sought to wrench infrastructure free of the networked socio-political and ecological formations and inevitable contingency of which it is part. As an assumed rational, neutral, technical endeavour, functionalist logics and technical design differentiations, as well as disciplinary specializations, have guided the extensive production of infrastructural systems, spaces and structures in the twentieth century. In this chapter, we have shown an example of how this 'civilizing march' of modernity into the territory of infrastructure actually co-produces uneven mobilities, and how it is being opposed and differentiated by activist, tactical, acupunctural mobilities design.

In our analysis, this oppositional design practice indicates several points that contribute to the examination and shaping of a responsible design agenda for the future of mobilities. These include epistemological and methodological considerations of the relationality and embeddedness of material design, in order to facilitate and build knowledge and action with much more insight into the multifarious, interdisciplinary issues that urban infrastructure intersects with and impacts on. This entails a critical reconsideration of how the powerful agency of design is distributed among the multiple stakeholders involved in the production, re-production and continuous inhabitation of infrastructure. Infrastructure, in this embedded sense, is no neutral technical territory, nor is it a territory of consensus, and, hence, in reconsidering processes of designing and re-designing material mobilities, the controversies, embodiment, 'informality', unevenness, and multiplicity must be addressed proactively. Acknowledging this embeddedness of infrastructures teaches us that these material utility lines are actually socio-material sites of politics, including resistances and unevenness, and we need to address them as such. This chapter has provided an example of doing so that localizes, contextualizes, and spatializes infrastructure.

References

Adey, P., 2010. *Mobility*. London, New York: Routledge.
Adey, P., Bissell, D., Hannam, K., Merriman, P., Sheller, M., eds. 2014. *The Routledge Handbook of Mobilities*. London: Routledge.
Behrens, R., McCormick, D., Mfinanga, D., eds., 2016. *Paratransit in African Cities*. London: Routledge.
Carvajal, A., 2016. On Caracas a Pie history. Interviewed by Andrea V. and Hernandez B. [video conference interview] Copenhagen/Caracas.
Carvajal, J. and Pintó, J. 2012. *Caracas a Pie*. Caracas: El Nacional publicaciones.
Cervero, R. and Golub, A., 2007. Informal transport: A global perspective. *Transport Policy*, 14(6), pp. 445–457.
Cresswell, T., 2010. Towards a politics of mobility. *Environment and Planning D: Society and Space*, 28(1), pp. 17–31.
Finck Carrales, J.C., 2015. *Transporte Emergente en colonias periféricas de la Ciudad de México: El caso de los Bici y Moto-Taxis en La Conchita Zapotitlán, Tláhuac*. Master thesis in urban development. Universidad Iberoamericana de Mexico City.
Graham, S. and Marvin, S., 2001. *Splintering Urbanism*. London: Routledge.
Jensen, O. B., 2013. *Staging Mobilities*. Routledge: London.
Jensen, O. B., 2017. Urban design for mobilities – towards material pragmatism. *Urban Development Issues*, 56, pp. 5–11.
Jensen, O. B. and Lanng, D. B., 2017. *Mobilities Design. Urban Design for Mobile Situations*. London: Routledge.
Lanng, D., 2014. How does it feel to travel through a tunnel? Designing a mundane transit space in Denmark. *Ambiances*, 07/01/2014. doi: 10.4000/ambiances.454.
Lerner, J., 2014. *Urban Acupuncture*. Washington, DC: Island Press/Center for Resource Economics.
Lorimer, H., 2010. Walking: New Forms and Spaces for Studies of Pedestrianism. In Cresswell, T. and Merriman, P., eds., *Geographies of Mobilities: Practices, Spaces, Subjects*. London: Routledge.
Lydon, M. and Garcia, A., 2015. *Tactical Urbanism: Short-term Action for Long-term Change*. Washington, DC: Island Press/Center for Resource Economics.
Lynch, K., 1960. *The Image of the City*. Massachusetts: MIT Press.
McFarlane, C. and Vasudevan, A., 2014. Informal infrastructures. In Adey, P., Bissell, D., Hannam, K., Merriman, P., Sheller, M., eds. *The Routledge Handbook of Mobilities*. London: Routledge. pp. 163–171.
Millington, N., 2017. Public Space and Terrain Vague on São Paulo's Minhocão: The High Line in Translation. In Lindner, C., and Rosa, B., eds., *Deconstructing the High*

Line: *Postindustrial Urbanism and the Rise of the Elevated Park*. New Brunswick; Camden; Newark, NJ; London: Rutgers University Press. Ch. 12, pp. 201–218.

Napoleón, C. H., 2011. Caracas, ciudad histórica diversa: Aproximación a la valoración espaciotemporal de los tejidos urbanos. *Bitacora*, 19(2), pp. 21–38.

Pieterse, E. 2008. *City Futures: Confronting the Crisis of Urban Development*. London: Zed Books.

Rynning, M. K., Uteng, T. P., Lucas, K., 2018. Epilogue: Creating Planning Knowledge Through Dialogues Between Research and Practice. In Uteng, T. P. and Lucas, K., eds., *Urban Mobilities in the Global South*. New York: Routledge. pp. 215–222.

Salomón, I., 1997. Modelos de configuración espacial para terminales urbanos de integración modal aplicable a zonas de alta densidad de construcción. *URBANA*, 20, pp. 65–84.

Sheller, M., 2016. Uneven mobility futures: A Foucauldian approach. *Mobilities*, 11(1), pp. 15–31.

Sheller, M., 2018. *Mobility Justice: The Politics of Movement in an Age of Extremes*. London: Verso.

Vallmitjana, M., 2007. Actuaciones Urbanísticas, y el caso de Caracas Metropolitana. *URBANA*, 12, pp. 11–19.

Vasudevan, A., 2011. Dramaturgies of dissent: the spatial politics of squatting in Berlin, 1968. *Social and Cultural Geography*, 12(3), pp. 283–303.

Interlude 3:
Material mobilities

Interview with Ole B. Jensen

Field(s) of enquiry

How do you define and see the field of research relevant to the material mobilities theme? Which disciplines are relevant and how do they interact? Are there any important disciplinary histories we need to know and remember?

The turn to materialities within the mobilities turn is not fully new. Rather, we have seen matters of material concern within the mobilities turn across areas such as geography, sociology, and planning for some time. There is, however, something different to the more recent attention to materiality and materialities. Thinkers such as Jane Bennett with her seminal book *Vibrant Matter* (2010, Duke University Press) and Tim Ingold with his *Being Alive* (2011, Routledge) are vivid examples of a change in the conceptualization and ontology of materialities. To put matters a bit bluntly we may say we have moved from an abstract notion of 'the material' onto a much more sensitive and detailed understanding of the material condition of human and non-human existence. The turn to 'new' materialities has taken important queues from disciplines with a more attuned eye to the ways in which we sense the world and engage with materials in multi-sensorial and embodied practices (see Jensen, O. B. (2016) Of 'other' materialities: why (mobilities) design is central to the future of mobilities research. *Mobilities*, vol. 11, no. 4, pp. 587–597). So fields of thoughts such as anthropology, ethnography, post-phenomenology and object-oriented ontologies are amongst the contributors to an emergent cross-disciplinary research horizon. In my own research I have been inspired by these but even more by architecture, urban design, and 'designerly ways of thinking'. We may for instance learn a more detailed sensitivity and language for the affordances made possible by choice of particular materials (e.g. in the difference between driving on asphalt and gravel stone). Or we may learn a new conceptual apparatus for dealing with three-dimensionality and the volumetric conditions of voids and spaces (e.g. between building volumes in urban spaces). So in my work on 'mobilities design' I am particularly interested in exploring the disciplinary histories and potential of fields such as architecture and design.

Theories and concepts

Some would argue that the new material turn and mobilities research problematizes modern binary distinctions between humans and non-humans, subjects and objects, culture and nature. Do you agree? If so, how does this manifest itself in the theories and concepts? How should we develop theories and concepts of relevance to the future of material mobilities research?

Yes, and here the mobilities turn towards materialities connects to wider agendas, as for example to one set by Bruno Latour and ANT (e.g. *Reassembling the Social*, 2005, Cambridge University Press). In particular, the so-called symmetry thesis according to which we should learn to see a much more 'modest' role for human agency in relation to nature, technology, and non-human organisms. And wider, we may think of philosophers such as Donna Haraway and her book *Staying with the Trouble* (2016, Duke University Press) or Arturo Escobar and his book *Designs for the Pluriverse* (2018, Duke University Press). These works offer fascinating inspiration into how we may open up our theoretical vocabulary and thus enable research agendas avoiding the bias of 'human exceptionalism'. However different these are in their backgrounds they share a concern for the place of common existence, Planet Earth and all its species and inhabitants. Rethinking the relationship to nature and non-humans is one important dimension of this profound critique of the modern binary (by the way a critique which has existed for much longer time than the mobilities turn). Another is then the task of exploring the social exclusionary practices and power. One might extend this list into the endless but I would stop by including also the key insights around design and affordance as ways in which we may sharpen our attention to the actual practices of concern. I have written a book chapter titled 'Dark Design' about how social exclusion is materializing through design interventions (Jensen, O. B. (2019) Dark Design. Mobility Injustice Materialized, in N. Cook and D. Butz (eds.) *Mobilities, Mobility Justice and Social Justice*, London: Routledge, pp. 116–128). In the chapter I discuss how artefacts such as leaning benches and spikes in doorways pushing homeless people to be on the move.

Methods and approaches

What set of methods and approaches for investigating material mobilities are in your opinion the most fruitful? Are there any new methods or combinations of existing methods that you find particularly promising?

Let me run the risk of repeating myself; I don't consider any methods to be particularly 'mobile'. I have a fully pragmatic viewpoint on methods, which means that the relevant methods for mobilities researchers are the ones that they use because of their usefulness and not because they are defined as 'mobile methods'. So at times we go to the document archives and perform discourse analysis; at other times we immerse ourselves into the field through the use of ethnographic studies. So I don't think there are any particular 'mobile methods' and whatever works as a research method and documentation may qualify (provided it lives up to the same requirements for documentation and ethical concerns as any other method). In my own work I am engaged in exploring more technologically oriented methods as a supplement to the more 'classic' ones such as qualitative research interviews and ethnographic observations. In our '*Mobilities in Situ*' group at the *Center for Mobilities and Urban Studies* (C-MUS) we have recently explored a methodological set-up for studying mobile situations in airports and metros. Here we combine the research interview and ethnographic observation with thermal cameras and eye-trackers. We use the thermal cameras to make non-privacy evasive recordings of people in public spaces (we can see what people do, but not who they are on the thermal video footage) and we get maps of movement patterns, trajectories, and footage of movement and social interaction. The eye-tacking glasses are worn by mobile subjects and register their gaze patterns, the duration of a gaze and the orientation of for example wayfinding signage or other material props in the environment. We combine these four methods with the 'fifth method' of the design intervention. Here we make design interventions that mobile subjects interact with or which may modify their behaviour and practices. We record and interview people about these. This ongoing exploration of methods may fit the research design of a particular project such as the research we currently undertake in the Metro of Copenhagen and in Copenhagen airport. However, it may also touch upon on more basic research questions such as how people orient themselves when on the move; what the environmental queues they utilize are; and how they make sense of the material environment. This is interesting, for example in relation to the unquestioned status of state-of-the-art knowledge in planning and urban design by Kevin Lynch. Lynch coined the notion of 'wayfinding' in his seminal book *The Image of the City* (1960, MIT Press). He used students' mapping and field studies to support what has stood as the key insights about legibility and mobile orientation for decades. Now, I will not dispute the value of Lynch's concepts and I have worked with them extensively myself. However, as a researcher I would always be interested in verifying or falsifying statements that have been understood as the 'truth of the world'. Our research with eye-tracking glasses in mobile situations of actual transit environments holds the potential of verifying or falsifying key insights articulated by Lynch so many years ago. So to return to the final question: I find the combination of 'old' and well-known methods with new technological methods to be promising (and intellectually stimulating as well). In particular, I am interested in including methods whose data output are far from each other. If I can study the mobile situation on the basis of mobile trajectory maps, gaze pattern visualization, ethnographic observations, interview statements and design experiments I feel I have a very strong multi-method design that enables me to dive into a lot of interactional detail and knowledge of how mobile subjects may make sense of the world.

Design and creation

How do you see concrete artefacts, systems and technologies facilitating and affording mobilities? What is the role of design? How are the construction, making and institution of artefacts and material critical to a new mobilities agenda? Are there specific 'designerly ways of thinking' that may influence and form future mobilities research? If so, in what ways? How do you see a role for (design) experiments and 'speculative approaches' in future mobilities research?

The focus on design within the mobilities turn is but one of the newer directions that this field has taken. Obviously, not all will be interested in connecting to design. However, the choices of materials, the physical composition of spaces and infrastructural landscapes, and much more, lend themselves quite easily to a material mobilities design agenda. It seems an obvious theme of study to focus on how designed artefacts and spaces are affording particular mobilities (and conversely also often preventing others). So for me, the mobilities design research agenda is straightforwardly leading to a more material understanding. Furthermore, I see two important dimensions. One is the study of practices and objects of design. This is the most immediate link to the materialities agenda; we study stuff and how it interacts with mobile subjects. That is an immanently material focus. However, the other dimension is equally important. This is the turn to the design approaches and ways of thinking as method. Taking on the design practice's own methods for creating new ideas or challenging old ones seems to be a somewhat overlooked potential within the mobilities turn. Here we are looking at the design interventions and the physical 1:1 scale experiments. Something that the social sciences in particular has been lacking (a point made quite explicit by Nigel Thrift in the book *Urban Assemblages* edited by Farias and Bender (2010, Routledge). The ways in which a design intervention can facilitate a better and more detailed understanding of mobile situations is but one of the potentials. Another is the opportunity to engage with users and publics through the means of design interventions and co-creation processes. As argued in the book *Mobilities Design – urban design for mobile situations* I co-authored with Ditte Bendix Lanng (2017, Routledge) we may say that mobilities design is both a question of 'learning to see' familiar things in new and unfamiliar ways as well as being an 'invitation to act'. In our new research on a driverless bus inserted into a housing estate we are precisely trying to follow up on this second dimension. Furthermore, the design approach enables us to engage with the imaginary in ways often not seen in mainstream social science. Design is arguably about imagining futures in acts of 'world making' (here an important source of inspiration is Dunne and Raby's book *Speculative Everything: Design, Fiction, and Social Dreaming*, 2013, MIT Press). To imagine things marginally different from today is not so hard, but to connect to more radical utopian imaginaries and let them generate 'wild ideas' is one of the promises from engaging with design thinking (here inspiration is to be found in Ruth Levitas' *Utopia as Method*, 2013, Palgrave). Needless to say, a mobilities research agenda that stays in the thin air of a utopian imaginary is far from the kind of 'material pragmatism' (Jensen, 2016, see reference above) I prefer. To reference an ongoing and very fruitful dialogue I have had with another of the Interlude authors in this book, Monika Büscher, we may work with a double research strategy. One posing the utopian 'What if...?' question that opens up to critically creative speculations about possible futures. This is seconded by the just as important 'What now...?' question that brings matters 'down to earth' as it were, forcing us to ask questions about ethics, hard choices, policy dilemmas, and power. The really interesting material mobilities design research agenda is therefore one that juggles the creative 'What if...?' with the critical 'What now...?' question. So yes, there is a key role for designerly ways of thinking within material mobilities research.

Matters of concern and societal responsibilities

What are the critical issues of a public debate on material mobilities? What are the 'matters of concern'? How do you see mobilities research contributing to these agendas? How are the ethical responsibilities of material mobilities research emerging? Are there any inherent political dimensions of the research into material mobilities that we need to be observing? Are there any particular societal claims on the research? How do you see the interaction space between research and the public(s)?

Growing out of the 'What now…?' dimension of mobilities design research we might say that there are many critical issues of public importance to take on. There are many different ways into these. One might take point of departure in the Sustainable Development Goals of the UN or the Grand Challenges identified by the EU. Personally, I like to 'start in the situation' and see how some of these matters of concern (e.g. sustainable mobility or social exclusion) actually affect real people's real lives. There is no doubt that the global climate change agenda is going to shape much of our material mobilities research for the time to come. Moreover, the ways in which specific social groups are enabled or prevented to move and act within our infrastructural landscapes will be more and more important. Here it is vital to stop thinking about geographical scale as something static and stratified. For refugees and immigrants, the infrastructural landscapes of their mobility practices are as much 'global' as they are 'local'. The same goes for your daily commute afforded by global satellite communication and digital connectivity – they are equally beyond the dichotomy of local/global. Future material mobilities research needs to take on the relational understanding of places and the multi-scalar optics that we find in, for example, the thinking of Doreen Massey (e.g. *For Space*, 2005, Sage) and Steve Graham (e.g. *Vertical*, 2018, Verso). Future mobilities research must be attentive and sensitive to matters of concern that reach across spatial scales as well as human and non-human dimensions. It needs to 'research like it gives a damn' if I can paraphrase the title from Architecture for Humanities when they ask us to *Design Like You Give a Damn* (Architecture for Humanity (ed.), 2006, Thames & Hudson). In other words, we must explore unjust and socially exclusionary practices, systems, and interventions. The 'places' I personally find such themes best to investigate are the actual mobile situations (from commuting to refugee migration). Here we need to ask questions related to design and affordance in order to see the actual and pragmatic consequences of policies, designs, interventions and interactions. How we bring this research in better alignment with communities and publics is a real concern to me. Obviously one vital dimension of a public dissemination strategy is media appearance and ways of communicating that transgress the standard academic platforms of journals and publishing houses. At the moment this is something we discuss in some detail at my Department (and where blogs and social media appearance is a key theme). Moreover, it seems to me that the 'interventionist potential' of design thinking may be utilized to facilitate deliberations and discussions with wider publics; for example, using co-creation workshops around mobility plans and designs to bring research into the public. For some years C-MUS had a think-tank with a regional focus. We named it 'Mobility Challenges North Jutland' and had members from regional and city government as well as transport operators sitting around the table identifying matters of concern that they would like to have more knowledge about. The think-tank is now closed down but only to make way for a new initiative we term '*C-MUS Practice*' which has much of the same ambitions but now without a geographical delimitation. Moreover, '*C-MUS Practice*' is a network that has the potential to grow in more organic ways than the formal think-tank. If we move into the global arena I think it will be hard to underestimate the importance of the newly started '*Global Mobilities Network*'. The GMN grew out of the *Centre for Mobilities Research* (CeMoRe) established by the late John Urry at Lancaster University in the UK. Judged by the speed by which this network has taken on members from all continents, this strikes me as a very important platform for future mobilities research, and one that is bound to be shaped by the research community's discussion of matters of concern.

11 Moving *with*

Molecular mobilities and our connective tissue fascia

Doerte Weig

Introduction

Whether people are walking down the street or being transported in self-driving cars, movement is generated through and with bodies in space-time. The conceptual and practical levels of physicality, of bodiliness, in understanding movement and mobility, remain a central question raised by the movement paradigm now cutting across scientific disciplines and the field of mobility studies in particular; dichotomies of *stasis-mobility* and *body-mind* continue to dominate debate. In this chapter, I consider how the study of *fascia*, our bodily connective tissue, can inspire thinking through these issues and lead us into the molecular levels of moving-*with*. In this I draw on the distinction between 'molecular' and 'molar' mobilities, whereby molecular means those mobilities which are 'more fundamental and less easily perceptible, constituting life, the becoming of objects, and the unfolding of events'; and molar refers to mobilities which uphold the stasis-mobility binaries and 'assume [movements] occur *in* a spatial setting which is containing and static' (Merriman, 2012, p. 156).

Fascia, or the fascial system, is like a three-dimensional network inside the body, which forms both a bodily support structure and at the same time transmits information inside the body. It is not just one type of tissue but several, and learning about fascia's moving diversity is a way to get in touch with the incredible materialities that make up the human body. Fascia is central to our movement capabilities, which opens up new insights into what is human movement. Rethinking along sub-cutaneous lines is rethinking the relationship between depth and surface, inside and outside, self and other (Ahmed and Stacey, 2001, p. 4), as well as the intra-actions of mobilities and materialities. This approach is premised on a reading of the body not as a Cartesian fixed and bounded entity, but as ontogenetic, as permanently moving, sensing, vibrating. In this generative understanding of body-*ing*, there is no pre-existing entity, but the 'body continually transforms itself and is already not, at the moment when I speak of it, what it was a few seconds ago' (Laplantine, 2015, p. 13).[1]

Thinking through fascia also allows us to ask new questions about what it means to move *with* (others). There is vast diversity in human movement styles, as ways of bodily movement are socio-culturally distinct and gender specific

(Mauss, 1979 [1934]). We learn how to move in the socio-cultural environments of our childhood. As adults, we continue to live in on-going and multi-sensorial resonance to the organisation of physical space through architecture and infrastructure (Zardini, 2005), *and* to the socio-cultural diversity of people moving *with-in* it. Fascia is an adaptive and intelligent tissue, responding and recording the way we body through time in community. These responsive qualities of the fascial system combine issues around becoming bodies, materialities, temporalities and environmental affordances. We can examine what is going on at a molecular level whilst moving and encountering people in public spaces from the fascial perspective. Which are the different visible and invisible layers of socio-cultural engagement regarding community construction and cohesion, or negation of togetherness, in urban settings?

My argument is that fascia is not only good to think with in mobilities research, but more broadly relevant to designers, architects, geographers and policy-makers concerned with urban design and planning. Focusing on the human capability for movement, fascia takes us to the generative in-between of bodying, adding a molecular layer to the understanding that 'mobility is materially grounded' (Salazar and Jayaram, 2016, p. 3). It further seems possible to argue for a close link between the molecular movement in our bodies and the socio-cultural-temporal quality of moving bodies. Taking an interest in fascia can tie together different disciplines researching on sociality, mobility and biology, and open up to experimental methodologies. To make these arguments, this chapter is structured in three parts. First, I describe in detail fascia and its inspiring properties; how this connects to theoretical notions on *motility*, our capacity to move; and ideas of becoming from process philosophy and new materialism. Secondly, I draw on my workshop experiences to suggest how attuning to fascial properties can advance mobile methodologies. Thirdly, I propose how the fascial system can inspire mobilities thinking.

Allow me to take you on a journey of molecular surprise.

Inspirations: fascia, motility and becoming materialities

My thoughts on the ontogenetic capacity of moving-sensing bodying in community-time and space-time are strongly inspired by ideas of becoming from process philosophy (Whitehead, 1978 [1929]; Manning, 2016) and new materialism (Barad, 2007), in which material is understood as process. My own work into the temporalities of mobilities departs from the notion of *motility*, which is defined as the capacity or potential to move (Bauman, 2000). Researching on human movement with diverse groups, for example with Baka hunter-gatherers in Gabon (Weig, 2015a) or Sardana dancers and castellers (builders of human towers) in Catalonia (Weig, 2015b), led me to think about how different (bodily) mobilities have different viscosities, perceptibilities and segmentarities (Merriman, 2018, p. 3), and finally below the skin's surface to consider the molecular level of what is fascia, as I unfold in the following.

Fascia, or the fascial system

Fascia, or the fascial system, is our connective tissue which extends from the outer epidermis through all skin layers into the depths of tissue, enveloping muscles, organs, bones and nerves, and forming 'a continuous tensional network throughout the human body' (Schleip, 2012b, p. xv). Fascia is central to our movement capabilities, metabolism and perception. The fascial network develops before the bones in an embryo, and the shape of fascia in an adult is like an internal skeleton, an 'endoskeleton' (Myers, 2001). Together with the nervous system fascia forms a body-wide mechanosensitive integrating signalling system, and it is one of our richest sensory organs, as the fascial nerve receptors may be equal or superior to the retina (the light-sensitive layer in the eye) (Schleip, 2012a, p. 77).

Said simply, fascia is the tissue or white stuff in between layers of meat or the segments of citrus fruits. Fascia is vital to a person's sensing and movement capacities. Fascia absorbs, somatises, memorises everything that happens to us, and responds to the way a person lives and moves by becoming more or less permeable or solid. It is an organic and very alive tissue, but if it dehydrates, it becomes inert and stiff. It may be essential in novel treatments of, for example, back pains (Schleip, 2012b) or cancer (Langevin *et al.*, 2016).

In specialist terminology, it is relevant to *interoception*, the sensorial relationship people have with their own body, and *proprioception*, meaning that a person knows where his or her body is in space. Imagine wearing a piece of clothing that does not sit right and you attempt pulling it into the 'right' position; fascia layers attempt to do the same within your body. Envisage a fly alighting on a spider's web, whereby the change in weight and surface tension transmits this information throughout the web to the spider; the same happens with regard to communication along the fascial lines within the body. Applying pressure at one point of the body, say on your arm, creates a ripple and reaction throughout the fascial web.[2]

One of the most fascinating aspects of fascia, or the ECM – the extra-cellular matrix – as it is also known, are the different tissues, the diverse material layers and textures of the in-betweens which make up the ECM. The outermost level is the hypodermis or 'superficial fascia', which has a yellow colour and spongy quality. Next is the 'filmy, membranous fascia', which is like gauze and has stretchy, wet, slippery, gelatinous qualities. Finally, there is the 'deep, dense fascia', which is elastic, grid-like, stable, like strapping tape, white. All three levels are permanently moving, shifting and sliding when the fascial system is healthy; or sticking and like 'fuzz' if dry.[3] Attuning to this perpetual movement, the fascial system evidences how 'body' constantly composes itself with and within different material qualities and forces, temporal patterns and rhythmicities.

On some websites, fascination becomes 'fasci*a*nation' when referring to fascia's special qualities. In summary, these are, first, its multiple forms of network, continuum, fractal, and open (nerve) endings – forms of both structure and unbounded aliveness. Secondly, its diverse material layers and textures, which are all made up of collagen. Thirdly, the fascial system is central to our movement capacity, proprioception and interoception, and through its sensorial extensiveness receives more information from outside the body than the brain does through the commonly known five senses.[4] Fourthly, fascia is intelligent, in its embryological relevance and as a memory of life lived. Fifthly, it is adaptive and its viscosity allows for 'tensional responsiveness', providing both tension and support in the body and elasticity in movement. Finally, at sub-cutaneous and collagenous levels, it is part of the molecular materiality of our bodies.

Temporality and becoming: motility and process philosophy

The conceptual concerns with regard to levels of corporality, of bodiliness, in understanding movement and mobility, and the links to questions of temporality, reverberate in the concept of *motility*. Motility is defined as the capacity or potential to move or be mobile. Rather than just studying observable mobilities, such as walking, *motility* analyses the *before* of movement by considering the choices and limitations which *precede* movement (Kaufmann, 2002, pp. 37, my emphasis). It thereby addresses the lack of a temporal dimension in many mobility models and their critical limitation to questions of space and territoriality, ignoring, for example, the importance of motivation, imagination or desires in moving, which has been noted in archaeological, anthropological, sociological and geographical discussions (Kaufmann, 2002; Oetelaar, 2006; Salazar, 2010; Merriman, 2012; Weig, 2017).[5] *Motility* is also termed 'mobility capital' and understood as a form of capital that can be actively or passively exchanged with others (Kaufmann *et al.*, 2004; Kellerman, 2012).

Process philosophy and new materialism emphasise the temporal process of becoming over the state of being, and materiality as process rather than timeless substances. Reframing the body as *moving* entails that equally lived space is not conceived of as a given physical reality but an achieved structuring. Sociality is conceptualised as dialogical and molecular, where becomings and 'molar-molecular' multiplicities 'have replaced the world of the subject' (Bergson, 1911; Deleuze and Guattari, 1987, p. 162), moving us towards 'a new gentleness' and 'collective subjectivity' (Guattari, 1989, p. 139). Process philosophy has been advocated as an inspiration to resolve the binaries persisting in concepts of mobility around stasis-*mobility* and *mind-body* (Merriman, 2012, p. 7, 2018). By focusing on processes of continuity and rupture, on temporalities of gaps, intervals and breaks, not on the 'molar' but the 'molecular' of imperceptible becomings, this also addresses the central critique of *motility* as too deterministic regarding cause and effect (Urry, 2007).

In particular the (rather technical) concept of *prehension*, which can be divided into *positive* and *negative prehension*, can be instructive in this reading. A prehension is 'a process of appropriation of an element in its becoming of an actual entity' (Whitehead, 1978 [1929]). A negative prehension is the determinate and purposeful exclusion of elements in a process of becoming. The important dynamic of motility, of mobility potential, is to analyse any type of 'constraints of manoeuvres' (Kaufmann et al., 2004, p. 749). Constraints can refer to means of transportation, the accessibility of services and equipment, or the socio-economic position. Both prehension and motility share the lens of temporality and a notion of exclusion, of constraint. Process philosophy does not know a bounded subject, whereas the second main critique of motility is its identitarian focus. Combining a reading of motility with negative prehension could constitute a practical application of process philosophy in stimulating conceptualisations of mobility or socio-political transformation (Merriman, 2012, p. 8; Laplantine, 2015, p. 85), salvaging the concept of motility by asking what is the 'molecular' non-identitarian *before* of movement, in urban contexts.

Thinking about 'molecular mobilities' combines cultural, spatial and biological research questions and arguments. With support from current shifts in biomedicine towards a 'molecular configuration', which conceives body or organism as an open-ended network whose boundaries are in constant flux and negotiation with its environment (Sharon, 2014, p. 114), going 'molecular' here then refers not only to a temporal dynamic conceptualisation of the social and mobilities, but also to the sub-cutaneous physicality of the human body through fascia. This non-dichotomous thinking-with and working-with fascia extends existing approaches to movement and mobility by conceptually combining the temporality and materiality of ways of bodily movement. Fascia becomes theoretically and methodologically relevant to understanding how and what are mobility and the (re)production of sociality in urban environments.

Moving *with* fascia – working *with* fascia – methodological implications

To explore the relevance of fascia in mobilities research and methodologies, I have been offering 'sensorial awareness workshops', which combine a literature presentation with fascial movement exercises.[6] In the first part of the workshop, I present on movement philosophy and the new ways of relating opening up from movement-materialism, including notions such as that 'to human is a verb' (Ingold, 2015). The second part is concerned with biodynamic fascial and proprioceptive individual and group movement exercises. With the workshop participants, I have been exploring how a joint focus on sensorial awareness and social surroundings leads to integrated perceiving-thinking and new methodological applications. This highlights the researcher's positioning as key to grounding knowledge and how researchers need 'to be in and of the science' (Myers and Dumit, 2011; Barad, 2014, p. 158). Raising sensorial awareness emphasises how as researchers we are involved in on-going, co-creative processes of matter and meaning.

Not only philosophical or physicists' accounts of touch, but also fascia therapy, have shown that learning to feel the alterity within the self, in what is a 'testimony of self within self', enables you to feel the alterity of others in different ways (Bois and Austry, 2007). Studies with infants have shown that the capacity to move is related to the capacity to experience (Stern, 2010, pp. 7–8), and knowledge about fascia heightens physiological self-awareness. Applied to mobilities research, the first concern (in the workshops) is that feeling your own mobility differently entails feeling others' mobility differently. Fascia's intelligence connects with *kairos*, defined as the 'instant in which I begin to be disrupted and transformed by [others]' (Laplantine, 2015, p. 17) to become a Nietzschean perceiving-thinking-in-movement. With a specific view to methods of participant observation and sensation (Pink, 2010), the recently advocated CAKE technique of body therapists may be of interest.

CAKE stands for 'Constructive Anticipatory Kinaesthetic Empathy', and, rather than either emotionally merging with clients or keeping a distance as a therapist, focuses on a specific combination of self-sensing and kinaesthetic empathy (Schleip, 2009). Human biologist and leading fascia researcher Robert Schleip emphasises how this approach has positively impacted his therapy work, explaining the technique as follows:

> Before touching my client on a new place I ask myself: Where is this same place in my own body? How can I be more present there? And: am I able to anticipate kinesthetically in my own body the particular state of release (or warmth, letting go, vitality, postural integration, connectedness, wellness, etc.) that I hope to induce in my client in this area?
>
> (Ibid., p. 3)

Working at the level of CAKE is something that takes much practice for bodyworkers, and this kind of learning cannot simply be copied and applied by social scientists. However, the anticipatory molecular level and nature at which body treatment takes place may be an inspiration to mobilities researchers. If we can attune to this level of *before* in movement, to access this kind of temporality, of motility, we may be able to bring up more easily what deeply generates, co-creates and motivates human movement and the politics of mobilities. This may be one route for mobilities researchers and scientists in general to become *fascianated* embodied scientists.

An entry into such an approach is facilitated by and results in new vocabularies. The qualities of 'tensional-responsiveness' and 'wild multiple materialities' offer terms that are 'good to think with'. Recalling that we cannot see our thoughts, it is touch which often provides us with a sensation of our mental processes, and many words for thinking are tactile in basis, such as 'to grasp' (Classen, 2005). Fascia shares with touch that both rely on movement for their full expression, and that we cannot fully appreciate these movements visually. Thinking from within the fascial system brings us into contact with the materialities of bodying and what happens physiologically whilst movement occurs in various mobility settings.[7] Fascial sensing can teach us that tension need not relate to dichotomous poles of stasis-mobility, but can be 'tensional responsiveness', being in touch with the movement and responding to shifts in weight, pressure and other qualities. Appreciating the multiple molecularities that make up movement and mobility, tension can become con-joined to connectivity and response-ability. This applies regardless of the mode of transport, whether it is walking on foot, floating on a hover board, or sitting in an autonomous vehicle.

Thinking with fascia – an inspiration to theory?

By going molecularly in-depth to the fascial network, we can also sharpen and fine-tune the analytical lens of mobilities research. Purposefully engaging with *fascia* as an essential component of our human capability for movement, our *motility*, innovates and extends existing 'capacity-approaches'. Fasci*a*nated mobilities research can emphasise this link at the invisible level *before* movement takes place. It raises awareness of levels of corporality as it furthers the apprehension of 'other registers such as rhythm, sensation, experience, atmosphere and affect' (Merriman, 2012, p. 17), and questions how such a response to movement stimulus is or is not culturally specific. From these vantage points, I suggest that critical thinking about mobility itself must be in the bodying movement. Mobilities studies, in turn, can lead in the advance of understanding the materiality of what is body and the beauty of the interplay of 'movement' and 'body', neither of which are what we externally perceive them to be. Moving together in time forms the basis of our aesthetic thinking, but often alternative ways of moving through the world, for example by autists, are devalued (Manning, 2016).

Future thinking on cities and mobilities is predominantly guided by smart design arguments. With Donna Haraway, I argue that solutions to surviving in urban environments must be more than techno-fixes, rather aiming at perceptions of survival and moving *with*-ness (Haraway, 2016). From dance studies we know that people copy movements often without conscious volition as they are moved by 'kinetic empathy', meaning they 'experience instantaneous, corresponding sensory perception in [their] own bodies' whilst watching others move (Kolb, 2011, p. 8). Moreover, types and practices of sensory perception are socio-culturally distinct and cannot be understood or defined universally (Classen, 2012). This is an essential but underestimated dynamic in urban environments, as city walkways become interfaces for negotiation and confrontation of cultural difference and identity. What we think of as the 'stranger' is not in existence as ontologically prior, but is constructed through social relations and as part of self (Ahmed, 2000).

Fascia, as our largest sensory organ, can allow us to conceptually and actually experience otherness, strangeness inside our own bodies. What may at first seem like a rather outrageous proposition draws on related physical and philosophical concepts. First, physicist Karen Barad's work on the quantum theory of touching extends the idea that 'touch never ends' (Derrida, 2005). For Barad, 'ontological indeterminacy, a radical openness, an infinity of possibilities, is at the core of mattering' (Barad, 2014, p. 7). In this infinity of virtual and actual possibilities, holding your own hand, self-touching, becomes 'an encounter with the infinite alterity of the self', as 'all touching entails an infinite alterity, so that touching the other is touching all others, including the "self," and touching the "self" entails touching the strangers within' (Barad, 2014, p. 7). Combining Science and Technology Studies (STS) research on fascia with performance practices, Joe Dumit and Kevin O'Connor argue that this touching experience of alterity, getting in touch with your (fascial) self and sensing what goes on below the skin's surface, equates with the possibility of fascia even being understood and experienced as 'alien'. The term relates to the experience that body parts such as our stomach or sinews are not ours; they are 'of a different order of being', like aliens right inside our own bodies (Dumit and O'Connor, 2016, p. 23).

With regard to mobilities and urban design, this 'alien other' right inside our own bodies opens up new horizons. We know that cities or neighbourhoods with high levels of trust between inhabitants and strangers are happier and wealthier, and that positive encounters with strangers are good for building happiness and trust (Montgomery, 2013). So how can we design environments that foster trust, if the alterity starts within us? How can we organise cities in a way that encourages not only trust-building encounters with others, but with ourselves as a premise to growing happiness and trust? These types of questions connect motility to environmental affordances and move research and theorising away from the critical loftiness of the nomadic 'everything flows' debate which fails to 'identify the complex politics [and sensibilities] underpinning the production and regulation of mobilities' (Merriman, 2012, p. 5).

Walking, as the basic human transport mode, remains a central issue in questions on health and well-being, the development of sustainable societies, and ageing societies (in Europe). In examining pedestrian behaviour (and walking as a participatory method), the fascial lens offers another interesting insight. We have often learnt to walk and run with a strategy based on muscle power, but, for example, hurdling athletes are now training and retraining by adopting a fascial movement strategy (Earls, 2014; Kelsick, 2016). In this way, the ideas on sensorial extensiveness and feeling the alterity of self and others also connect to our most basic human way of moving, to walking. A socio-somatic reading of walking understands it not only as a mobility practice, as displacement related to geographical, socio-economic, or imaginary factors, but as being in (fascial) communication with others. Some urban designers are focusing on the walkability of post-automobile cities with 'urban cells' constructed around a 20-minute walking radius (Larson, 2012; Stibe *et al.*, 2016). We could take this one step further: city walkways could be covered by materials that are soft and responsive to our unique body movements. Tensionally responsive materials would prevent unnecessary physical wear and tear caused by hard, unresponsive surfaces, which would have an impact on national health costs. Softer surfaces may even impact levels of aggression, and inner-city neighbourhood violence.

Finally, a conceptual reading of the fascial system highlights that processes of co-creation and encounters themselves are ontologically prior to questions of ontology. The current status of scientific research on fascia has been described as 'pre-paradigmatic' (Dumit and O'Connor, 2016, p. 16). As I read fascia, it is good to think with, and it will be interesting to see what strength and inspirational

218 D. Weig

quality fascia as a paradigm can develop. However, it is important to remember that what make up fascia are living, vibrant materialities! Fascia may be the epitome of a keyword as 'something that never acquires a closed or final meaning' (Salazar and Jayaram, 2016, p. 4). Inherent in its ever-moving nature is that it is not to be used as a one-to-one model or metaphor, but that its pulsing vibrational qualities inspire us in a non-identitarian, processual way.[8]

Conclusion: allow yourself to become fasci*a*nated

Fascia, our connective tissue, opens up the body in movement from a theoretical and methodological perspective to access physiological and socio-cultural-political molecular levels of mobility, to the molecular moving-*with*. This combination of sociality, temporality and corporeality, addressed conceptually through *motility*, process philosophy and new materialism, and physiologically through *fascia*, advances conceptualisations of movement and mobility practices to correlate with corporeal realities. By taking the persevering dualistic models into the body and to a capacity level, thinking-tensionally-responsively-with-fascia extends understandings of body-*ing* and deepens current knowledge on how experiencing our environment and the people within it are bodily and multi-sensorial processes.

Moving *with* one another takes on new shapes in today's culturally blurred urban spaces, or our 'urban niche habitats' (Downey, 2016). Raising awareness on the socio-cultural, gendered and perceptive physicalities and politics of these mobilities questions how sharing or not sharing movement styles leads to conscious, or subconscious, social attraction or tension in ever-expanding urban contexts. Mobilising scientific research on fascia to the 'paradigmatic' stage, offers a new perspective on the links between culture, mobility and physicality in a city context, and contributes to establishing novel approaches in urban planning and smart or, hopefully, creative city learning in the twenty-first century.

The issues presented here concern our daily lives and immediate surroundings, how we enter into and interact in public spaces. They also refer to multi-species communication and multi-material attunement, to how we relate globally and with others in our environment in the Chuthulecene, as Haraway suggests terming our current epoch. A profound entry into our own body-ing vehicles in tensionally responsive co-creation of social relations affords us deeper capacities for response-ability, with which we may write what I call 'sensorial mobility narratives'. Let's write these new stories about how we want our urban environments to be, and how we want to move in, through and with them, through the tensional fascial network. Let's especially encourage those who are in a position to officially shape and design our urban spaces to 'go CAKE', to include new ways and levels of kinaesthetic empathy in mobilities policy-making.

Notes

1 This can be appreciated simply through attention to bodily systems such as breathing or digestion.

2 If you would like to try and feel your own fascia, imagine you are about to shake hands with somebody. As you begin raising your arm, the entire fascial web activates to prevent you from falling forward. This interplay between fascia and gravity also takes place when you take a step in walking. To learn more, you can also try out the practice on fascia in the *Somatics Toolkit* for scientific researchers at: http://somaticstoolkit.coventry.ac.uk/practice/.
3 How to define fascia is heavily debated, as different nomenclatures of fascia abound between body-workers, biologists, doctors, pathologists, dancers and scientific researchers (Adstrum *et al.*, 2016). I here adopt the three-level classification (Hedley, 2016), as it is most easy to grasp for the layman. In the latest comment on fascia nomenclatures, the terminology 'fascial system' is emphasised and how fascia 'interweaves' in the body (Stecco *et al.*, 2018). You can hear a podcast interview on the socio-economic relevance of fascia with Gil Hedley, an anatomist and ethics scholar who dedicates his life to discovering the mysteries of fascial layers, at http://somaticstoolkit.coventry.ac.uk/category/podcast/.
4 The five senses model dominant in Europe, Northern America and other parts of the world is not universal. For example, the Anlo-Ewe in Southern Ghana have a distinct 'sense of balance' and consider the five senses a 'folk model' (Geurts 2003).
5 The concept of *motility* and the idea of focusing on the *potential* to mobility has been applied variously, for example by the advocates of the 'new mobilities paradigm' (Sheller and Urry, 2006) or in sociology (Bauman, 2000) (see Weig, 2015a, p. 427 and Kaufmann, 2014, p. 9 for further details on applications).
6 For example in 2016, 'Critical Somatics: Movement and sensorial awareness in social dynamics' at the Conference "Disputed Futures", 2–4 June 2016, Coimbra, Portugal; and 'Tension and Connectivity: Sensorial awareness in processes of migration and mobilities' at "SIEF Migration and Mobility Working Group Meeting. Current Approaches to Migration and Mobility in Ethnology, Folklore and Anthropology", 11–13 September 2016, Institute for Cultural Anthropology and European Ethnology Basel, Switzerland. These two workshops were offered together with Joana Veiga, who is based in Lisbon and whose work combines anthropology, performance and art education.
7 Burgeoning research on animal locomotion and the microbiome may further contribute to these insights (Knight *et al.*, 2017).
8 When I first started work with fascia myself, there was a huge temptation to simply use fascia as a 'new model', but this must be resisted at all costs.

References

Adstrum, S., Hedley, G., Schleip, R., Stecco, C. and Yucesoy, C.A., 2016. Defining the fascial system. *Journal of Bodywork and Movement Therapies*, 21(1), pp. 173–177.
Ahmed, S., 2000. *Strange encounters: Embodied others in post-coloniality, Transformations*. Routledge: London, New York.
Ahmed, S. and Stacey, J., 2001. Introduction: Dermographies, in Ahmed, S. and Stacey, J. (Eds.), *Thinking through the skin: Transformations*. Routledge: London.
Barad, K.M., 2007. *Meeting the universe halfway: Quantum physics and the entanglement of matter and meaning*. Duke University Press: Durham, London.
Barad, K.M., 2014. On Touching – The Inhuman That Therefore I Am (V.1.1), in Witzgall, S. and Stakemeier, K. (Eds.), *Power of material/Politics of materiality, publication series of the Cx Centre For Interdisciplinary Studies at the Academy of Fine Arts Munich*, pp. 153–164.
Bauman, Z., 2000. *Liquid modernity*. Polity Press: Cambridge.
Bergson, H., 1911. *Creative evolution*. Macmillan & Co: London.

Bois, D. and Austry, D., 2007. Vers l'emergence du paradigme du Sensible. *Réciprocités*, No. 1, pp. 1–17.

Classen, C. (Ed.), 2005. *The book of touch.* Berg: Oxford, New York.

Classen, C., 2012. *The deepest sense: A cultural history of touch.* University of Illinois Press: Urbana.

Deleuze, G. and Guattari, F., 1987. *A thousand plateaus: Capitalism and schizophrenia.* University of Minnesota Press: Minneapolis.

Derrida, J., 2005. *On touching – Jean-Luc Nancy.* Stanford University Press: Stanford.

Downey, G., 2016. Being human in cities: phenotypic bias from urban niche construction. *Current Anthropology*, 57(S13), pp. S52–64.

Dumit, J. and O'Connor, K., 2016. The Senses and Sciences of Fascia: a Practice as Research Investigation by Joseph Dumit and Kevin, in Hunter, L., Krimmer, E. and Lichtenfels, P. (Eds.), *Sentient performativities of embodiment: Thinking alongside the human.* Lexington Books: Lanham, MD, pp. 35–54.

Earls, J., 2014. *Born to walk: Myofascial efficiency and the body in movement.* North Atlantic Books: Berkeley, CA.

Geurts, K.L., 2003. *Culture and the senses: Embodiment, identity, and well-being in an African community.* University of California Press: Berkeley.

Guattari, F., 1989. The three ecologies. *New Formations*, 8, pp. 131–147.

Haraway, D., 2016. *Staying with the trouble: Making kin in the Chthulucene.* Duke University Press: Durham.

Hedley, G., 2016. Fascial nomenclature. *Journal of Bodywork and Movement Therapies*, 20(1), pp. 141–143.

Ingold, T., 2015. *The life of lines.* Routledge: Abingdon.

Kaufmann, V., 2002. *Re-thinking mobility: Contemporary sociology, transport and society.* Ashgate: Aldershot.

Kaufmann, V., 2014. Mobility as a tool for sociology. *Sociologica*, 1, pp. 1–17.

Kaufmann, V., Bergman, M.M. and Joye, D., 2004. Motility: Mobility as capital. *International Journal of Urban and Regional Research*, 28(4), pp. 745–756.

Kellerman, A., 2012. Potential mobilities. *Mobilities*, 7(1), pp. 171–183.

Kelsick, W., 2016. *Fascia Training Principles.* Worcester: UK.

Knight, R., Callewaert, C., Marotz, C., Hyde, E.R., Debelius, J.W., McDonald, D. and Sogin, M.L., 2017. The microbiome and human biology. *Annual Review of Genomics and Human Genetics*, 18(1), pp. 65–86.

Kolb, A., 2011. Cross-Currents of Dance and Politics: An Introduction, in Kolb, A. (Ed.), *Dance and politics.* Peter Lang: Oxford, New York, pp. 1–36.

Langevin, H.M., Keely, P., Mao, J., Hodge, L.M., Schleip, R., Deng, G., Hinz, B., Swartz, M.A., Valois, B.A. de, Zick, S. and Findley, T., 2016. Connecting (t)issues: How research in fascia biology can impact integrative oncology, *Cancer Research*, 76(21), pp. 6159–6162.

Laplantine, F., 2015. *The life of the senses: Introduction to a modal anthropology.* Bloomsbury: London, New York.

Larson, K., 2012. Brilliant designs to fit more people in every city, available at: www.ted.com/talks/kent_larson_brilliant_designs_to_fit_more_people_in_every_city (Accessed 15 May 2014).

Manning, E., 2016. *The minor gesture, Thought in the act.* Duke University Press: Durham, NC.

Mauss, M., 1979 [1934], *Sociology and psychology: Essays. [Transl. by Ben Brewster]* Routledge & Kegan Paul: London.

Merriman, P., 2012. *Mobility, space, and culture (International Library of Sociology series)*. Routledge: New York, London.
Merriman, P., 2018. Molar and molecular mobilities: The politics of perceptible and imperceptible movements. *Environment and Planning D: Society and Space*, 106, pp. 1–18.
Montgomery, C., 2013. *Happy city: Transforming our lives through urban design*. Macmillan.
Myers, T.W., 2001. *Anatomy trains: Myofascial meridians for manual and movement therapists*. Churchill Livingstone: Edinburgh.
Myers, N. and Dumit, J., 2011. HAPTICS. Haptic Creativity and the Mid-embodiments of Experimental Life, in Mascia-Lees, F.E. (Ed.), *A companion to the anthropology of the body and embodiment*. Wiley-Blackwell: Chichester, pp. 239–261.
Oetelaar, G.A., 2006. Mobility and Territoriality on the Northwestern Plains of Alberta, Canada. A phenomenological approach, in Bressy, C. (Ed.), *Notions de territoire et de mobilité: Exemples de l'Europe et des premières nations en Amérique du Nord avant le contact européen actes de sessions* présentées au Xe congrès annuel de l'Association Européenne des Archéologues (EAA), Lyon, 8–11 septembre 2004, ERAUL, pp. 137–149.
Pink, S., 2010. The future of sensory anthropology/the anthropology of the senses. *Social Anthropology*, 18(3), pp. 331–340.
Salazar, N.B., 2010. *Envisioning Eden: Mobilizing imaginaries in tourism and beyond*. Berghahn Books: New York.
Salazar, N.B. and Jayaram, K. (Eds.), 2016. *Keywords of mobility: Critical engagements*. Berghahn Books: Oxford.
Schleip, R., 2009. How to build a strong and elastic fascial body; and how to guide your empathy with the CAKE technique. Excerpt from Self-Care for Rolfers, available at: www.somatics.de/artikel/for-professionals/2-article/13-self-care-for-rolfers (accessed 25 October 2016).
Schleip, R., 2012a. Fascia as an Organ of Communication, in Schleip, R., Findley, T., Chaitow, L. and Huijing, P. (Eds.), *Fascia: The tensional network of the human body*. Churchill Livingstone: Edinburgh, pp. 77–79.
Schleip, R., 2012b. Introduction, in Schleip, R., Findley, T., Chaitow, L. and Huijing, P. (Eds.), *Fascia: The tensional network of the human body*. Churchill Livingstone: Edinburgh, pp. xv–xviii.
Sharon, T., 2014. *Human nature in an age of biotechnology*. Springer Netherlands: Dordrecht.
Sheller, M. and Urry, J., 2006. The new mobilities paradigm. *Environment and Planning A*, 38(2), pp. 207–226.
Stecco, C., Adstrum, S., Hedley, G., Schleip, R. and Yucesoy, C.A., 2018. Update on fascial nomenclature, *Journal of Bodywork and Movement Therapies*, 22(2), p. 354.
Stern, D.N., 2010. *Forms of vitality: Exploring dynamic experience in psychology, the arts, psychotherapy, and development*. Oxford University Press: Oxford.
Stibe, A., Chatterjee, S., Schechtner, K., Wunsch, M., Millonig, A., Seer, S., Chin, R.C. and Larson, K., 2016. *Empowering Cities for Sustainable Wellbeing*, Short Paper. *Proceedings of the Workshop on Empowering Cities for Sustainable Wellbeing*. Adjunct to the 11th International Conference on Persuasive Technology. Salzburg, Austria, 5 April 2016.
Urry, J., 2007. *Mobilities*. Polity: Cambridge.
Weig, D., 2015a. From mobility to motility. Changes in Baka mobilities and sociality in north-eastern Gabon. *Hunter Gatherer Research*, 1(4), pp. 421–444.

Weig, D., 2015b. Sardana and castellers. Moving bodies and cultural politics in Catalonia. *Social Anthropology*, 23(4), pp. 435–449.

Weig, D., 2017. We descended the Ivindo: Baka Migration to Northeastern Gabon from the 1960s to Today. *African Study Monographs*, 38(2), pp. 63–96.

Whitehead, A.N., 1978 [1929]. *Process and reality: An essay in cosmology.* [Corrected edition by Griffin, D.R. and Sherburne, D.W., Gifford lectures.] Free Press: New York.

Zardini, M. (Ed.), 2005. *Sense of the city: An alternate approach to urbanism.* Lars Müller: Montréal, Baden.

12 Mobile work, space and processes of transition

Hanne Vesala and Seppo Tuomivaara

Introduction

Work has traditionally been bound by space, which ideally meant having one stable work location for which other locations would present exceptions. This ideal has been supported by the industrial work logic that is characterised by stability, predictability, planning and bureaucratic organisation (Kellogg *et al*, 2006; Kalleberg, 2009; Ellström, 2010). For some time now, this order has been challenged by developments such as network-based organisations, atypical employment relations and disappearing boundaries between work and leisure (Garsten, 1999; Bechky, 2006; Kellogg *et al.*, 2006; Koslowski *et al.*, 2017). Work is understood as becoming increasingly fluid and individualised (Garsten, 1999; Ibarra and Obodaru, 2016).

Working life has also become increasingly mobile, particularly in knowledge-intensive types of work. At the most elementary physical level, employees are moving away from individual offices to work in open offices, 'hot desks' or co-working spaces (Brown and O'Hara, 2003; Felstead *et al.*, 2005; Hirst, 2011; Spinuzzi, 2012). At the more functional level, workers operate in different networks as salaried employees or individual subcontractors. An entrepreneurial attitude is strongly encouraged. Although official telework frequency has not shown as remarkable an increase as may have been expected (Bergum, 2007; Pyöriä, 2011), 'unofficial' telework outside the boundaries of the working day has become a common phenomenon (Moen *et al.*, 2013; Cavazotte *et al.*, 2014).

There is an ongoing search for an alternative concept of work space which underlines mobility and aesthetic experience. While workers are opting for more mobile and fluid work practices and strategies, their sense of presence and absence, both physically and mentally, could be altering (Hetherington, 2004; Urry, 2004). This could further change what they perceive as relevant for both their work and life in general.

This chapter examines different approaches to mobile work in current literature and, in particular, an emerging approach that views mobile work as a transitional process. In previous studies, mobile work has typically been approached as a practical accomplishment and even as a potential burden (Brown and O'Hara, 2003; Laurier and Philo, 2003; Mark and Su, 2010;

Humphry, 2014). This chapter investigates the lived experience of mobility beneath the practical labour of finding one's way between different environments.

The chapter takes a Heideggerian phenomenological and existential approach in asking whether mobile work can become a transitional and 'authentic' experience that could disclose the workers' habitual practices and their inscribed values, which become taken for granted in a stable work environment. Furthermore, the chapter reflects on the space characteristics of this transition and on what role such space could have in contemporary working life, which demands increasing individual deliberation and decision-making. This chapter approaches these questions by analysing interview data collected from 32 creative professionals who were working in small- or micro-sized companies and who spent a short period of time working in the rural archipelago environment of southwestern Finland and Åland. The study finds that natural and 'lived' spaces (Lefebvre, 1991) can form a reflective space in which the experience of time becomes authentic (Heidegger, 1962 [1927]). To achieve such a reflective state, however, these spaces should be sufficiently different from the everyday environment to introduce a rupture to everyday habits.

This chapter begins by discussing the definition of mobile work and proceeds to examine how mobility may affect the personal–spatial experience. Next, three prevalent perspectives on mobile work in current literature are examined, with the third perspective being further elaborated on, i.e. mobile work as a transitional process, using Heidegger's idea of authentic temporality to assist the analysis. The chapter then continues by taking a look at the notion of 'lived space', theorised by Lefebvre, before moving on to describe the method and context of the study's empirical case. This is followed by an empirical analysis of the embodied temporal and spatial experiences arising during the rural archipelagic work period. The chapter closes by discussing the findings in the context of the changing contemporary (working) life.

Definitions of 'mobile work'

The term 'mobile work' originally referred to work that involves the physical movement of workers between various work locations such as main offices, side offices and clients' places (Vartiainen and Hyrkkänen, 2010). This movement can also occur within a singular workplace, as in the case of 'hot-desking', for example, where a worker has no fixed work site within the working environment but can occupy any desk that is available at the workplace location (Hirst, 2011). Recent trends in facility planning indicate an expansion of such mobility, together with an increase in open- and multi-space offices – a move that seeks to increase 'co-creation' and the exchange of ideas among workers in addition to lowering office rental costs (Dale and Burrell, 2008; Hirst, 2011).

'Telework' is a term that indicates a specific kind of mobility – work that is conducted outside the main workplace. In telework research, a consensus on one common definition of telework has not been achieved. Disagreements exist on whether it should be delimited to information and communications technology (ICT)-supported work, as the inclusion of the prefix 'tele' would indicate, or whether it should remain indifferent to the ICT involvement, as well as on whether it should cover both 'official' and 'unofficial' telework, and on whether telework refers solely to work at a fixed site or can include work that is conducted while one is, for instance, travelling (Sullivan, 2003; Haddon and Brynin, 2005). If understood in the broadest sense possible, telework could include a wide range of different work practices, many of them questioning the boundary between work and leisure. However, in telework research, empirical examples usually derive from home-based work (Hislop and Axtell, 2007). In fact, the two terms are commonly used interchangeably. Yet, due to the increase in mobile ICT tools and mobile working practices, the assumption that telework is work at a fixed site has grown increasingly outdated. In many ways, mobile work and telework overlap, with the former covering the latter, as some studies have indicated (Vartiainen and Hyrkkänen, 2010; Tremblay and Thomsin, 2012).

One more term that captures a particular dimension of mobile work practices is worth presenting here. Some researchers have opted to use the term 'flexible work', aiming to thus underline how working remotely can be just one among several tools used to adapt regular work to individual needs (Kelliher and Anderson, 2008, 2010; Peters et al., 2014; Putnam et al., 2014). These researchers have associated home-based work with other flexible work practices such as reduced working hours and job autonomy. This perspective does not concentrate extensively on the interrelation between new technology and work but rather on how the flexibility provided by working remotely can become a tool to support the workers' well-being, work–family balance and other individual needs.

These approaches show that mobile work is not only associated with ICT technology developments but also with the various processes related to the changing organisation of work. Vartiainen and Hyrkkänen (2010) suggest, following Kakihara and Sørensen (2004), that mobility in working life can be identified on at least three levels: (i) physical, (ii) virtual and (iii) operational mobility. While physical mobility refers to heightened spatial movement, virtually mobile workers can remain physically stationary but use diverse virtual work spaces. Operational mobility, on the other hand, refers to work that is based on diverse sources of income, such as freelancing and other independent work. It could be assumed that these dimensions further enforce one another, particularly in many of today's individualised, atypical careers (Kakihara and Sørensen, 2004).

These various ways of understanding work-related mobility indicate that this phenomenon already pervades much of contemporary working life – if not yet concretely, then at least as an emerging horizon of opportunity. For the present study, mobile work is understood broadly – as potentially involving intermittent periods of temporary stability for various reasons as well as a dynamic between movement and stability. It could even be constructive not to understand work-related mobility through external calculation of movement(s) but rather as a mental state that results from a situation in which the spatial arrangement of work has become fluid, contingent and open to change.

Mobility and the unbounded work space

Simultaneous with workplaces becoming physically unbounded, organisations have increasingly begun to appeal to workers as aesthetic consumers of different spatial atmospheres (Dale and Burrell, 2008). Consequently, this brings up the notion of distinctive mobile aesthetics, where the aesthetic sensitivity of workers is not expected to be cultivated in a personalised 'home' spot but through movement and serendipitous encounters in different spaces.

Mobility may involve virtual and imaginary travel, as much as the corporeal kind (Urry, 2004; Sheller and Urry, 2006), and current corporate design increasingly appeals to imaginary sensitivities (Dale and Burrell, 2008). The new, leisure-like and aestheticised organisational spaces invite workers to mentally travel away from toil and routine. Such multi-dimensional mobility emphasises individual, embodied experiences that are no longer systematically connected to any 'precise "here and now" of work and organisation' (de Vaujany et al., 2018, p. 1).

Latour (1999, cited in Urry, 2004) wisely reminds us that no space has ever been local as such, because its existence depends on a network of more distant connections. However, the development of ICT technology has potentially transformed the experience of presence/'real' and absence/'imaginary' as technology has diversified and enriched the ways in which virtual and imaginary worlds are inhabited. As a result, virtual ties to distant others may emotionally feel even closer than those in the physical proximity (Urry, 2004). What people perceive as 'present' or 'absent' may not be the same in their physical and mental existences, respectively.

The dynamics of presence and absence can also involve a more general way of managing the relations with others in terms of memories, traditions, past and future (Hetherington, 2004). What we hold as present is something that is considered to be culturally and socially relevant, whereas that which is absent and disposed of becomes marginalised. As Merleau-Ponty (2012 [1945]) emphasises, human perception is directed by how we are bodily situated in the world, in other words, by that which is 'present' to us. However, that which is put aside or is disposed of has never vanished completely but has the potential to renew its relevance as, for example, in the case of ruins becoming cultural heritage or trash being transformed into antiques (Hetherington, 2004). It could be said that what was made absent in these cases has constantly been growing a kind of latent meaning in the margins.

In movement, one may come across something normally absent that may feel surprising to one's habitualised perception, leading one to question the normalised social order (Douglas, 2003 [1966]). It is dubious whether mobility can diminish the distance between the margins and the centre completely, as has been suggested (e.g. see Cairncross, 1997). However, mobility may question and re-arrange this distance through a solicitation of encounters with new things which potentially merit the status of presence in one's perception, thus challenging what is valued as relevant in one's (working) life.

Three perspectives on mobile work

This chapter identifies three distinct approaches found in the scholarly studies of mobile work: (i) the practical perspective, (ii) the aesthetic and social perspective and (iii) an emerging transitional perspective, which is further elaborated on here. The most prevalent of the three perspectives has been the practical approach (Liegl, 2014). Studies on mobile work from this perspective have shed light on how work that does not have the support of a permanent physical environment becomes challenging and even burdensome to conduct (Brown and O'Hara, 2003; Laurier and Philo, 2003; Mark and Su, 2010; Vartiainen and Hyrkkänen, 2010; Humphry, 2014). The infrastructure is no longer invisible, as it would be in a habitual context, but becomes a practical concern for workers. When on the move, workers need to figure out which work activities they are able to perform in particular places with context-specific affordances (Brown and O'Hara, 2003). This perspective aims to describe the special dynamics between work, space and technology for those working on the move and how such work often escapes official work descriptions because things may not go as planned. The perspective further highlights how the flow of such work is always fragile and easily interrupted. However, mobile workers also develop special skills for adapting work activities to different and contingent environments (Felstead et al., 2005; Büscher, 2014).

Recently, a radically different perspective on mobile work has emerged. Liegl (2014) has shown that urban creative freelancers consider mobility not to be a burden but a resource and a useful tool for arranging their work. The creative freelancers he studied would have felt stuck in one work environment and be restlessly looking for new environments that would enable beautiful experiences, which, in turn, would inspire their work. What was found to be essential in this search for experiences is the variety of potential work spaces – the novelty of space, in particular, was the factor that enabled a strong experience. These workers also remarked that different spaces supported different types of work, and thus they used mobility to arrange their work tasks. From this perspective, work-related mobility does not appear as a mere necessity any longer but as a lifestyle choice (Czarniawska, 2014; Pigg, 2014; Henriksen and Tjora, 2018).

However, mobility may also be disruptive to existing cultural ideals about the organisation of work. Work has commonly been perceived as an everyday thing and industrial work logic has been associated with stability, hierarchy, rational planning and impersonality (Kellogg et al., 2006; Ellström, 2010). The successful accomplishment of work has depended on it being routinised. In the industrial work logic, individual, exceptional needs of workers would threaten the planned order of things.

The 'officiality' and impersonality of the workplace are signs of what type of behaviour is expected there (e.g. see Baldry, 1999). D'Adderio (2011) remarks that we read these signs from all kinds of artefacts in the workplace, which may not only be physical, such as furniture, office design and equipment, but also cognitive, including formal rules, regulations, software, codes of conduct and rules of thumb. Artefacts provide us with a certain way of looking at things and support a certain kind of habitual activity.

This habitual world becomes visible when it is interrupted (Large, 2008, p. 44) and it is this possibility that mobility entails. According to Heidegger (1962 [1927]), the familiarity with which we relate to our everyday environment hinders our ability to observe it from an outside point of view, unless the ordinary flow of events becomes broken. On the other hand, the ability to feel 'at home' is an ontological condition necessary for experiencing meaningfulness and significance in everyday activities. The way in which the everyday environment matters to us affects how we relate to the space around us, making it a necessary condition for any sensible activity (Heidegger, 1962 [1927]; Large, 2008). However, since we do not pay much conscious attention to the external characteristics of this space, being absorbed with whatever we are concerned about, we might lose sight of any other possibilities of existence that could feel authentically more as our own (Heidegger, 1962 [1927]). Paradoxically, to become aware of such possibilities may require entering a 'void', emptying one's life of everyday concerns (Ibid.).

Working outside the office signifies traversing through spaces that may not be specifically assigned to work, at least not with the specific rules and norms that the 'official' workplace involves. Working in a new environment has the potential to become a lived experience (Lefebvre, 1991) that enables the use of individual capabilities and experiences on a range that is wider than the normal 'official' environment allows. Simultaneously, those norms and rules that have become taken for granted in the everyday environment may be uncovered.

If mobile work initiates such a transitional process, it may be characterised as taking place in a liminal space, which is an ambiguous space in-between any known social positions and roles (van Gennep, 1960 [1909]; Turner, 1974). In organisation studies, liminality has often been viewed as a sort of anomaly in the organisational structure, although some studies have shown that liminality can also be a fluid, situational and momentary – one might say a phenomenological – achievement, enabling situated creativity and reflection (Sturdy et al., 2006; Iedema et al., 2010; Shortt, 2015). Daskalaki et al. (2016) have recognised liminal characteristics in work-related mobility. They found that translocal patterns of work challenged the dichotomies between place and non-place, oneself and others, as well as mobility and fixity, thus questioning the stability of identity and spurring situational identity reflection (Ibid.).

Heidegger (1962 [1927]) reminds that in one's everyday experience of time and place one does not simply calculate the moments or changes of place as they follow one another. Phenomenologically understood, each significant assignment of time and place represents a particular, meaningful 'then' and 'there', embedded in the general way we inhabit our familiar world. However, sometimes we experience a need for re-clarification of these meanings. According to Heidegger, there is a difference between drifting along in general habits and practices following clock time that is determined by the 'Others' and a more authentic sense of time – the 'moment of vision' (*Augenblick*) – which occurs when one becomes anxious about losing oneself in the generality of the public 'Others'. In a moment of vision, one recognises that things could be done otherwise and has the potential to make an individual 'decision' (*Entschluss*) about one's own life. This is when the succession of barely distinguishable events and occurrences is transformed into a 'situation' (Heidegger, 1962 [1927]; Large, 2008). Mobility at work, as a practical challenge, makes the time and place of work increasingly visible. Can it transform work from an everyday routine to a 'situation' and, if so, what could this mean?

Working in a 'lived space'

Before presenting the empirical case, the idea of a lived space versus an abstract space is discussed. According to Lefebvre's (1991) spatial theory, dominant places within the sphere of production and consumption, such as bureaucratic offices, are abstract and formal by their physical and symbolic design. These spaces seek to subsume any distinctions, the body and the sensual. However, even such spaces do not remain mere abstractions when their users appropriate them and reconstruct them in their everyday lived encounters. Thus, the contradiction between the abstract and the lived remains a constant (Lefebvre, 1991; Wilson, 2013).

Lefebvre (1991) associates lived spaces with the spheres of home, natural and historical spaces. These are all spaces that are distant from production and consumption as well as from abstract bureaucratic control; they are spaces in which people can experience social connectedness with others and with their cultural roots. Lived spaces are zones 'where people could spread out in comfort and enjoy those essential luxuries, time and space, to the full' (Ibid., p. 317). Working at home is an option that many prefer precisely because one can feel less external control there and can arrange one's own work more independently (Tremblay, 2003; Kelliher and Anderson, 2008). Yet, with the increasing power of rational, homogenised planning that is characteristic of abstract spaces and also prevalent in many urban residential areas, the authenticity with which people exhibit their social relations in lived spaces is, itself, at risk (Lefebvre, 1991, p. 314; Stanek, 2008).

We find lived spaces affective because they can reflect our inner states and memories (Bachelard, 1994 [1958]). These kinds of spaces are experienced as protective of one's inner world and enable it to grow. We often search for such comforting spaces in various forms of dwellings but research has shown that a pleasant natural environment can also provide comfort in the form of, for instance, stress recovery (Ulrich *et al.*, 1991), increased ability to focus attention (Kaplan and Kaplan, 1989), unburdening the mind from troubling issues (Korpela *et al.*, 2001; Korpela and Ylén, 2007) and learning as well as personal self-expression and community formation (Hale *et al.*, 2011). The natural environment has been shown to be a therapeutic environment for patients (Ulrich, 1984) and older people (Milligan *et al.*, 2004). Could it also be therapeutic for workers, and what kind of therapy would they need? This chapter now turns towards an examination of these questions through an analysis of the experiences of creative professionals during a working period in a Finnish rural archipelago environment.

The empirical context and the method

The empirical analysis of this chapter uses interview data collected in 2010–2011 from 32 creative professionals during a one-week experiment of flexible work in the south-western Finnish rural archipelago. The experiments were part of a study project that aimed to examine the benefits and challenges of working periodically in a rural environment and to learn about the experiences of the workers in order to develop rural service infrastructure for their specific needs. The archipelago area is geographically relatively isolated and has distinct characteristics both naturally and culturally. Its arid nature is, in parts, protected by UNESCO. The archipelago is a traditional residential area of the Swedish-speaking minority of Finland and a currently popular tourist destination. It is featured in many popular songs, novels and other cultural products in which the 'archipelago lifestyle' is typically depicted with an air of mysticism and romanticism as corresponding to a place where humans can experience the forces of nature. Being situated between the land and the sea, the archipelago could be seen as having liminal characteristics (Preston-Whyte, 2004).

The participating flexible workers were offered free working and lodging facilities by six municipalities during the work period. Voluntary participants, either in groups or as lone individuals, were recruited using advertisements. The participants spent the period in small groups of colleagues (2–4 persons) or alone (two cases). As participation was voluntary, it could be terminated at any moment if the participants thus chose. The participants themselves decided on the activities that they wished to carry out in the location, while the research project merely offered the use of facilities. They worked in small- or micro-level enterprises (less than 50 employees) and represented different creative professions, including journalism, design, research, mentoring and coaching, advertising, consulting and engineering. There were 17 female and 15 male participants, and all working-age groups were represented.

The facilities that the participants used bore distinct local characteristics, depending on the resources and personnel that were available in their municipality area to create the conditions necessary for this work experiment. Modern office hotels were used, along with traditional archipelago villas and homesteads that could serve as workspaces. In a rural community, the use of these workspaces was informal and the service providers were willing to accommodate any additional needs of the participating workers. The participants brought the mobile tools they needed for their work themselves.

The group participants were interviewed in groups at the end of the work period, while the lone participants were interviewed individually. Some of the interviews were carried out face-to-face and some by phone due to geographical distances. A thematic group interview was chosen as a method to encourage discussion and sense-making. In addition to their experiences during the experiment, the interviews dealt with the backgrounds of the participants, their work situations and reasons for participating in the experiment. After initial open coding, the analysis of the interviews was guided by Heidegger's (1962 [1927]) idea of authentic time and with an emphasis on a contextual and practical understanding of the 'body-in-place' (Jensen, 2016, p. 589).

Working time as authentic or forced upon

The interviews showed a distinctive contrast in the participants' use and experience of time during their stay in the archipelago in comparison to their everyday environment. The everyday environment was depicted as a hectic and potentially chaotic place in which concentration was often interrupted by external elements, such as demands from clients and colleagues, office noise, a tightly packed schedule, or, if working at home, by family needs. Furthermore, the participants noticed that interruptions were not only of external origin but that this restlessness had also in many cases become internalised – they had themselves developed a tendency to worry about other things while conducting their work tasks and to restlessly bounce between different work tasks. Such habits could lead to personal confusion about the order of work tasks, as this example depicts:

> I have felt this strange burden and worry that I am always doing the wrong thing, like when I am doing one thing, I realise that no, actually I should be marketing this, and when will I try to create new ideas as now I am carrying out this toil?
>
> (Male, ICT consultant)

Sometimes this lack of concentration and focus had made the workers feel exceedingly stressed and apathetic and unmotivated at other times. Viewed from the archipelago context, the everyday work environment emerged as a place in which the rhythm of work was not for the workers to decide. These descriptions resemble the Heideggerian notion of inauthentic temporality, which is dictated by the fluctuating interests of the 'Others' and which never delves deeply into any particular issue (Heidegger, 1962 [1927]).

> This somewhat sombre picture of the everyday work environment needs to be contextualised through the contrasting experience of the archipelago location. In the calm rural environment, some participants remarked how time seemed to go by faster and, sometimes, the passing of time was even forgotten. This experience was influenced not only by the rhythm of life in the rural environment itself but also by the way this dislocation transformed the connections to others, both near and distant. The participants had emptied their calendars of tasks that required contact with the 'outside world' as much as possible, partly for practical reasons and partly because they were orientated for the archipelagic work week to become something extraordinary:

> I have had to empty my calendar from all the small stuff because of this [period]. So there has not been pressure from other work tasks; I have been able to concentrate, in peace, for once, on one thing at a time.
>
> (Female, director and researcher)

Different degrees of the sense of isolation were experienced during the archipelagic period. Some participants decided to turn off their phones, others had instructed their colleagues not to try to reach them unless absolutely necessary, securing an uninterrupted work space for themselves in the archipelago. Other participants had given no such instructions but remarked, with satisfaction, about how the change in location had filtered away the less necessary interruptions. This is how one participant reflected on the changed pattern of communication with colleagues:

> It would be kind of weird, too, if one withdraws, teleworks, to conduct some long-span work task, and this is precisely the reason for wanting a peaceful environment, then wouldn't it be odd if the phone would ring all the time? That wouldn't be … well, it would, but really, some happy medium. Like you don't have to apologise for calling.
>
> (Female, journalist)

Thus, in the archipelago there were fewer external interruptions and demands on time. During the period, the participants favoured deciding flexibly and on an ad hoc basis about their use of time, negotiating within the archipelago work group when needed. This increased personal control of time affected their work orientation. The participants noticed that, unlike in their everyday environment in which work tended to be 'always on' at least mentally, in the archipelago they were better able to put work matters aside when they wanted and move on to other activities. Consider this example provided by a participant:

> At the time you dip into the sea after the working day, you really … [laughter], your mind gets refreshed considerably there. … You forget work and the free time gets started in a pretty nice way.
>
> (Female, marketing manager)

When the use of time could be locally decided upon, the participants adopted a playful and experimentative attitude towards their working arrangements (see also Vesala and Tuomivaara, 2018). They enjoyed the experience of having novel scenery viewable from the window and allowed themselves to have spontaneous breaks when their attention was attracted by the natural environment. Consequently, the participants became sensitised to their internal, bodily and mental, states and rhythms. In the words of a participant:

> You are in the middle of a different landscape, different rhythm; here the pulse is much slower than in the metropolitan area. Here you have nature and I am a visual person, I am very much affected by what I see …
>
> (Female, coach and consultant)

The calm, natural environment signified entering the realm of a more personal, inward-oriented rhythm, which could serve as a creative and exciting opening:

> Here you can break from routines and maybe discover new things, as you don't do things in the same way in the same place, but you go somewhere else. Then your inner clock starts ticking in a different way maybe. It is about giving yourself time and releasing your creativity.
>
> (Male, market researcher)

The participants were surprised by how they could conduct one task from beginning to end without any breaks, something that people tend to take as obvious in everyday life but which actually constituted a special experience for many of these workers, as it does for so many other knowledge professionals in the present day and age. The participants felt that they recovered the ability to mindfully concentrate on what they were carrying out in each moment.

Through this experience of the contrasts between the normal and the new environment, the participants began to reflect on how some elements of the everyday environment – schedules, office and city noise, phone calls and e-mails – thwarted taking hold of time. The normal environment encouraged staying busy, although the substance and meaning of this hastiness were sometimes lacking. Through such reflections, the participants became aware of these habitualised connections and began to envision different ways in which to construct their daily routines. For example, one participant found that the everyday environment resembled a world where 'everyone is walking at the same pace' but at the end of the week she had an emerging intuition of how to 'make use of it in a different way'.

The experiment also prompted the participants to reflect on their physical and social needs and on how their general work and lifestyles affected their wellbeing. These realisations could be connected to particular moments and places:

> I believe that here you realise, when you are sitting on a rock and taking a drag from a cigarette and then that cigarette gets thrown away halfway once you realise again that maybe you really shouldn't be smoking like that. For me, it is probably going to be like that, that I will realise many things here.
>
> (Male, manager in an advertising agency)

Novel workmates could also prompt insights and foster reflection. In many cases, the participants used the work period as an opportunity to spend time together with their colleagues from different offices or networks. The participants who worked in office hotels also met with local workers, who might represent very different occupations and working practices in comparison to their own. Such encounters could also be mind-opening as the following interview excerpt reveals:

> I have gained various things here, not necessarily all those that I anticipated but more like what these different people have given to me.
>
> (Female, coach and mental trainer)

The results suggest that the experience of time during the archipelago work period had characteristics of Heideggerian authentic temporality. First, the period, as a whole, had both importance and meaning for the participating individuals because they decided, of their own free will and as a result of their own interest, to break away from their everyday routines in order to participate in the experiment. By abandoning everyday routines, they chose to be open to a new environment and anything it might bring. During the archipelago period, the work rhythm was not experienced by the participants as if it was forced upon them or as restless and out of control – as it would be in the case of inauthentic temporality. Thus, time was allowed to orient inwards. In the archipelago environment, the participants could 'own' the time and apply situated creativity and resoluteness in their use of it. Second, time in the archipelago was personal and reflective. As a consequence of reviewing their own working and living habits in light of the new situation, the workers described having reflected about their future, which was something that their everyday hectic life rhythm did not support so well. This added a new, deeper dimension to working, as described by a participant:

> Here, work involves much more reflection and a kind of planning of things but, on the other hand, there is action too. It surely is much fuller [than in the everyday environment].
>
> (Female, toy designer)

Heideggerian future-oriented authentic temporality reaches towards the future through reviewing past experiences. Authentic temporality, as opposed to scientific clock time, is not preoccupied by the present moment. Rather, it is always oriented forward, to the future, simultaneously recognising its past and the potentialities that lie in the past and can be actualised in the future. In the authentic experience of time, the past, present and future become connected in their continuity. This convergence also resembles how time has been experienced in liminal spaces as being 'beyond or outside the time which measures secular processes and routines' (Turner, 1974, p. 57).

For some participants, past memories began to surface in a particularly vivid way and could also become a source of inspiration to them. For example, one participant described having experienced exceptional creativity in his work during the time in the archipelago, spurred by a re-emergence of old sources of inspiration from decades back:

> The kinds of drawings that I did in the beginning of the Nineties I have not done ever since, but during this week I have experienced a new renaissance. More than a dozen pieces of this kind of work and sketches have come into being during this past week.
>
> (Male, designer in catering services)

Sometimes, an environmental sensation has the potential to evoke emotional memories from the past, much like Proust depicts in his novel *In Search of Lost*

Time – where simply tasting a Madeleine cake brings the childhood world back to life once more for a character (Fuchs, 2018, p. 55). The change of work location can also engender imaginary travel back in time through personal history.

Conclusion

This chapter set out to explore whether mobile work could be a transitional experience and what kind of experience it would signify. The empirical study outlined above showed that mobility can, indeed, produce a 'situation' – a moment that stands out from the more insignificant everyday occurrences. According to Heidegger (1962 [1927], p. 463), as one loses oneself to the object of concern in everyday existence, one 'loses' one's time as well. In contrast, authentic existence 'always has time' because it has the character of a moment of vision: 'held in that future which is in the process of having-been' (Ibid.). During the archipelago experiment, the participants had time, in this sense, both for calm, concentrated work activity and for personal reflection about the past and the future. Yet, this experience was distinctively embodied because it was accompanied by sensitively 'tuning in' with the environment and following its attractions.

For mobile work to become a transformative experience, we suggest that it needs to be carried out in an environment that is distant from everyday mundane chores. An environment in which a person can feel 'at home' is essential for this experience. However, the environment also needs to be different in order to induce a rupture in everyday practices and shed light on their habitual structures. Absence from the everyday environment could enable the emotions that remain latent in the busy and largely reactive everyday life to surface and thus become 'present' to one's perception (e.g. see Hetherington, 2004). A lived space that is natural or historical (Lefebvre, 1991) can be assumed to support the experience of authenticity because such a place enables the feeling of connectedness to others and to one's personal thoughts. It has the potential to become a therapeutic environment (Hale *et al.*, 2011) that, in the context of current working life, could signify a space in which one could pull oneself 'together from the dispersion and disconnectedness of the very things that have "come to pass"' (Heidegger, 1962 [1927], pp. 441–442), i.e. the busy everyday dealings. The character of work conducted in such a space could provide a contrasting experience to that of work in the everyday environment, which may suddenly manifest in a very different and not altogether pleasant light. The reflection that authentic temporality encourages may not emerge without negative feelings. It may resemble the undefined liminal space 'in-between', which does not offer any known social roles but supports reflection and experimentation instead, processes that are both creative and potentially threatening (Van Gennep, 1960 [1909]; Turner, 1974; Thomassen, 2014).

Contemporary work is becoming increasingly mobile, which signifies that workers are expected to act in an increasingly self-directed, independent and entrepreneurial manner (Kalleberg, 2009). Furthermore, lifetime careers in a single organisation are becoming increasingly rare. The increased individual responsibility for working practices and one's career may be experienced not simply as empowering but also as threatening at times. Asking how individuals are able to utilise their personal life histories and experiences in the fullest possible manner when making important decisions, whether these decisions are about particular work problems or choices affecting their entire career, becomes increasingly important. Mobility may, accidentally or in anticipation, provide the resources for this individual deliberation and creativity. It may even engender therapeutic work environments that can serve as a useful resource for those workers who are lost and confused in the everyday struggle of their busy schedules and do not have the time to evaluate the direction of their career or their life. Further research on working in 'lived' and therapeutic spaces is needed, as well as research on how these spaces can support the execution of work tasks, community formation and the search for personal resources when navigating an increasingly complex working life.

References

Bachelard, G., 1994 [1958]. *The Poetics of Space: The Classic Book on How We Experience Intimate Places*. Boston: Beacon Press Books.
Baldry, C., 1999. Space – the final frontier. *Sociology*, 33(3), pp. 535–553.
Bechky, B. A., 2006. Gaffers, gofers, and grips: Role-based coordination in temporary organizations. *Organization Science*, 17(1), pp. 3–21.
Bergum, S., 2007. What has happened to telework? Failure, diffusion or modification? *The Journal of E-working*, 1(1), pp. 13–44.
Brown, B. and O'Hara, K., 2003. Place as a practical concern of mobile workers. *Environment and Planning A*, 35(9), pp. 1565–1587.
Büscher, M., 2014. Nomadic work: Romance and reality. A response to Barbara Czarniawska's 'Nomadic Work as Life-Story Plot'. *Computer Supported Cooperative Work*, 23(2), pp. 223–238.
Cairncross, F., 1997. *The Death of Distance*. London: Orion.
Cavazotte, F., Lemos, A. H. and Villadsen, K., 2014. Corporate smart phones: professionals' conscious engagement in escalating work connectivity. *New Technology, Work and Employment*, 29(1), pp. 72–87.
Czarniawska, B., 2014. Nomadic work as life-story plot. *Computer Supported Cooperative Work*, 23(2), pp. 205–221.
D'Adderio, L., 2011. Artifacts at the centre of routines: Performing the material turn in routines theory. *Journal of Institutional Economics*, 7(2), pp. 197–230.
Dale, K. and Burrell, G., 2008. *The Spaces of Organisation and the Organisation of Space: Power, Identity and Materiality at Work*. Basingstoke: Palgrave Macmillan.
Daskalaki, M., Butler, C. L. and Petrovic, J., 2016. Somewhere in-between: Narratives of place, identity, and translocal work. *Journal of Management Inquiry*, 25(2), pp. 184–198.
de Vaujany, F.-X., Dandoy, A., Grandazzi, A. and Faure, S., 2018. Experiencing a new place as an atmosphere: A focus on tours of collaborative spaces. *Scandinavian Journal of Management*. Advance online publication. https://doi.org/10.1016/j.scaman.2018.08.001.
Douglas, M., 2003 [1966]. *Purity and Danger: An Analysis of Concepts of Pollution and Taboo*. Abingdon, Oxon: Routledge.

Ellström, P.-E., 2010. Practice-based innovation: A learning perspective. *Journal of Workplace Learning*, 22(1), pp. 27–40.

Felstead, A., Jewson, N. and Walters, S., 2005. *Changing Places of Work*. Basingstoke: Palgrave MacMillan.

Fuchs, T., 2018. The cyclical time of the body and its relation to linear time. *Journal of Consciousness Studies*, 25(7–8), pp. 47–65.

Garsten, C., 1999. Betwixt and between: Temporary employees as liminal subjects in flexible organizations. *Organization Studies*, 20(4), pp. 601–617.

Haddon, L. and Brynin, M., 2005. The character of telework and the characteristics of teleworkers. *New Technology, Work and Employment*, 20(1), pp. 34–46.

Hale, J., Knapp, C., Bardwell, L., Buchenau, M., Marshall, J., Sancar, F. and Litt, J. S., 2011. Connecting food environments and health through the relational nature of aesthetics: Gaining insight through the community gardening experience. *Social Science & Medicine*, 72(11), pp. 1853–1863.

Heidegger, M., 1962 [1927]. *Being and Time*. Oxford: Blackwell Publishing.

Henriksen, I. M. and Tjora, A., 2018. Situational domestication and the origin of the café worker species. *Sociology*, 52(2), pp. 351–366.

Hetherington, K., 2004. Secondhandedness: Consumption, disposal, and absent presence. *Environment and Planning D: Society and Space*, 22(1), pp. 157–173.

Hirst, A., 2011. Settlers, vagrants and mutual indifference: Unintended consequences of hot-desking. *Journal of Organizational Change Management*, 24(6), pp. 767–788.

Hislop, D. and Axtell, C., 2007. The neglect of spatial mobility in contemporary studies of work: The case of telework. *New Technology, Work and Employment*, 22(1), pp. 34–51.

Humphry, J., 2014. Officing: Mediating time and the professional self in the support of nomadic work. *Computer Supported Cooperative Work*, 23(2), pp. 185–204.

Ibarra, H. and Obodaru, O., 2016. Betwixt and between identities: Liminal experience in contemporary careers. *Research in Organizational Behavior*, 36, pp. 47–64.

Iedema, R., Long, D. and Carroll, K., 2010. Corridor communication, spatial design and patient safety: Enacting and managing complexities. In: A. Van Marrewijk and D. Yanow, eds. *Organizational Spaces: Rematerializing the Workaday World*. Cheltenham: Edward Elgar, pp. 41–57.

Jensen, O. B., 2016. Of 'other' materialities: Why (mobilities) design is central to the future of mobilities research. *Mobilities*, 11(4), pp. 587–597.

Kakihara, M. and Sørensen, C., 2004. Practicing mobile professional work: Tales of locational, operational, and interactional mobility. *INFO*, 6(3), pp. 180–187.

Kalleberg, A. L., 2009. Precarious work, insecure workers: Employment relations in transition. *American Sociological Review*, 74(1), pp. 1–22.

Kaplan, R. and Kaplan, S. 1989. *The Experience of Nature: A Psychological Perspective*. Cambridge: Cambridge University Press.

Kelliher, C. and Anderson, D., 2008. For better or for worse? An analysis of how flexible working practices influence employees' perceptions of job quality. *The International Journal of Human Resource Management*, 19(3), pp. 419–431.

Kelliher, C. and Anderson, D., 2010. Doing more with less? Flexible working practices and the intensification of work. *Human Relations*, 63(1), pp. 83–106.

Kellogg, K. C., Orlikowski, W. J. and Yates, J. 2006. Life in the trading zone: Structuring coordination across boundaries in postbureaucratic organizations. *Organization Science*, 17(1), pp. 22–44.

Korpela, K. M. and Ylén, M. 2007. Perceived health is associated with visiting natural favourite places in the vicinity. *Health & Place*, 13(1), pp. 138–151.

Korpela K. M., Hartig, T., Kaiser, F. G. and Fuhrer, U., 2001. Restorative experience and self-regulation in favorite places. *Environment and Behavior*, 33(4), pp. 572–589.

Koslowski, N. C., Linehan, C. and Tietze, S., 2019. When is a bed not a bed? Exploring the interplay of the material and virtual in negotiating home-work boundaries. *Culture and Organization*, 25(3), 159–177.

Large, W., 2008. *Heidegger's Being and Time*. Edinburgh: Edinburgh University Press.

Latour, B., 1999. On recalling ANT. In: J. Law and J. Hassard, eds. *Actor-Network Theory and After*. Oxford: Blackwell Publishing, pp. 15–25.

Laurier, E. and Philo, C., 2003. The region in the boot: Mobilizing lone subjects and multiple objects. *Environment and Planning D: Society and Space*, 21(1), pp. 85–106.

Lefebvre, H., 1991. *The Production of Space*. Oxford: Blackwell Publishing.

Liegl, M., 2014. Nomadicity and the care of place – on the aesthetic and affective organization of space in freelance creative work. *Computer Supported Cooperative Work*, 23(2), pp. 163–183.

Mark, G. and Su, N. M., 2010. Making infrastructure visible for nomadic work. *Pervasive and Mobile Computing*, 6(3), pp. 312–323.

Merleau-Ponty, M., 2012 [1945]. *Phenomenology of Perception* [D. A. Landes, Trans.] London: Routledge.

Milligan, C., Gatrell, A. and Bingley, A., 2004. 'Cultivating health': Therapeutic landscapes and older people in northern England. *Social Science & Medicine*, 58(9), pp. 1781–1793.

Moen, P., Lam, J., Ammons, S. and Kelly, E. L., 2013. Time work by overworked professionals: Strategies in response to the stress of higher status. *Work and Occupations*, 40(2), pp. 79–114.

Peters, P., Poutsma, E., Van der Heijden, B., Bakker, A. B. and de Bruijn, T., 2014. Enjoying new ways to work: An HRM-process approach to study flow. *Human Resource Management*, 53(2), pp. 271–290.

Pigg, S., 2014. Coordinating constant invention: Social media's role in distributed work. *Technical Communication Quarterly*, 23(2), pp. 69–87.

Preston-Whyte, R., 2004. The beach as a liminal space. In: A. A. Lew, C. M. Hall and A. M. Williams, eds. *A Companion to Tourism*. Oxford: Blackwell Publishing, pp. 349–359.

Putnam, L. L., Myers, K. K. and Gailliard, B. M., 2014. Examining the tensions in workplace flexibility and exploring options for new directions. *Human Relations*, 67(4), pp. 413–440.

Pyöriä, P., 2011. Managing telework: Risks, fears and rules. *Management Research Review*, 34(4), pp. 386–399.

Sheller, M. and Urry, J., 2006. The new mobilities paradigm. *Environment and Planning A*, 38(2), pp. 207–226.

Shortt, H., 2015. Liminality, space and the importance of 'transitory dwelling places' at work. *Human Relations*, 68(4), pp. 633–658.

Spinuzzi, C., 2012. Working alone together: Coworking as emergent collaborative activity. *Journal of Business and Technical Communication*, 26(4), pp. 399–441.

Stanek, L., 2008. Space as concrete abstraction: Hegel, Marx and modern urbanism in Henri Lefebvre. In: K. Goonewardena, S. Kipfer, R. Milgrom and C. Schmid, eds. *Space, Difference, Everyday Life: Henri Lefebvre and Radical Politics*. New York: Routledge, pp. 62–79.

Sturdy, A., Schwarz, M. and Spicer, A., 2006. Guess who's coming to dinner? Structures and uses of liminality in strategic management consultancy. *Human Relations*, 59(7), pp. 929–960.

Sullivan, C., 2003. What's in a name? Definitions and conceptualisations of teleworking and homeworking. *New Technology, Work and Employment*, 18(3), pp. 158–165.

Thomassen, B., 2014. *Liminality and the Modern: Living Through the In-Between*. Farnham: Ashgate Publishing.

Tremblay, D.-G., 2003. Telework: A new mode of gendered segmentation? Results from a study in Canada. *Canadian Journal of Communication*, 28(4), pp. 461–478.

Tremblay, D.-G. and Thomsin, L., 2012. Telework and mobile working: Analysis of its benefits and drawbacks. *International Journal of Work Innovation*, 1(1), pp. 100–113.

Turner, V., 1974. Liminal to liminoid in play, flow, and ritual: An essay in comparative symbology. *Rice Institute Pamphlet – Rice University Studies*, 60(3), pp. 53–92.

Ulrich, R. S., 1984. View through a window may influence recovery from surgery. *Science*, 224(4647), pp. 420–421.

Ulrich, R. S., Simons, R. F., Losito, R. D., Fiorito, E., Miles, M. A. and Zelson, M., 1991. Stress recovery during exposure to natural and urban environments. *Journal of Environmental Psychology*, 11(3), pp. 201–230.

Urry, J., 2004. Connections. *Environment and Planning D: Society and Space*, 22, pp. 27–37.

Van Gennep, A., 1960 [1909]. *The Rites of Passage*. Chicago: University of Chicago Press.

Vartiainen, M. and Hyrkkänen, U., 2010. Changing requirements and mental workload factors in mobile multi-locational work. *New Technology, Work and Employment*, 25(2), pp. 117–135.

Vesala, H. and Tuomivaara, S., 2018. Experimenting with work practices in a liminal space: A working period in a rural archipelago. *Human Relations*, 71(10), pp. 1371–1394.

Wilson, J., 2013. 'The devastating conquest of the lived by the conceived': The concept of abstract space in the work of Henri Lefebvre. *Space and Culture*, 16(3), pp. 364–380.

13 Dwelling on the move

Cecilie Breinholm Christensen

Introduction: coherence vs. mobility?

> I didn't really want to go, I was tired and it was raining. However, already on the short trip with the connecting train I started to feel a small joy of being 'on the way' again. Totally unexpected. And just the act of boarding the IC3 fast train towards Odense woke the expectation of what would come – and I couldn't wait for the train to start going. I had actually missed it! The train and the train trip, the comfort of being transported, the sensation of the train's engine that starts, the train's silent puffing and the rhythmic sound from the tracks. I realised how I had missed going somewhere with a purpose, how being at work actually made me feel important to someone. Plus the train trip gave me a break and a distance, an opportunity to see other perspectives and horizons, which is exactly why I enjoy riding the train so much. The experience of reaching new understandings, new insight, get the world at a distance, feel transported and see the scenery rush by, while just being – without the option of being or going anywhere else. Just existing, right there on the train and feel alive, present. And just as much as I enjoy riding the train, I get just as disheartened when the train doesn't afford such an experience of existence, when I cannot get a window seat, when the other passengers are noisy, or when it's too uncomfortably warm.[1]

This chapter is motivated by the author's everyday commute by train between Copenhagen and Odense in Denmark for a period of slightly over one year, while at the same time embarking on further education part-time study in psychology. At the time I only had a vague idea of mobilities theory on the introductory level. Meeting mobilities theory with an architectural background that, in a Nordic tradition, emphasises 'sense of place', it had been puzzling me how to combine such a sense of place with a mobilities perspective. How can this phenomenological emphasis on coherence and contextuality be combined with an ontology of moving? This question extends further than mere design and architecture, however, since it fundamentally questions how it can be possible to maintain a coherent sense of self, in a psychological sense, while being 'on the move'. This question takes as its point of departure the presumption that personal and psychological coherence is important as a precondition to maintain mental wellbeing, which is based on a hermeneutic and phenomenological ontology of coherence and connection within the world of human existence (Brinkmann, 2012).

In the late modern world, the individual reflective identity has become a primary tool for maintaining such a coherent sense of self. Identity can be seen as a narrative that the individual must constantly keep going in order to keep oneself together across different contexts, experiences and encounters, and incorporate these in the individual's self-understanding (Giddens, 1991/1996). Maintaining a coherent sense of self in a psychological sense further implies that there should be an accordance between the different levels of the individual's self-interpretation, i.e. a continuity and coherence between the individual's understanding of self across time and space and in relation to social norms and values, among others (Rosa, 2004, 2014; Brinkmann, 2008, 2014).

However, forming and maintaining such a coherent sense of self seems to be ever more challenged in the present late modern world. Critical theorists and psychologists such as Rosa (2014), Honneth (2005) and Brinkmann (2008, 2014) point out how present-day social acceleration, individualisation and separation of time and space challenges identity formation. Though we live in a seemingly liberal and norm-free era, there is a constant pressure for self-development and performance because the individual has become an asset in a liberal market (Honneth, 2005; Brinkmann, 2008, 2014; Rosa, 2014). Furthermore, common moral values as interpretation resources have become unclear and disguised by a heavy individualisation, leaving it up to the individual to define a coherent sense of self (Honneth, 2005; Brinkmann, 2008). However, the hidden norms of self-development and performance create pressure, and the individual is thus pushed to constantly re-interpret him- or herself according to inexplicit moral norms and values (Brinkmann, 2008; Rosa, 2014). At the same time, it becomes more difficult to actually create and maintain accordance between the different levels of self-interpretation, since there is not enough time to integrate experience with the surroundings and understanding of self due to social acceleration (Rosa, 2004). This can then ultimately lead to a feeling of alienation, emptiness and exhaustion and thus challenge emotional wellbeing, which is, among other things, reflected in the increase in the number of people with psychiatric diagnoses like depression and stress (Brinkmann, 2008; Brinkmann and Petersen, 2015). In the above line of thought, identity formation is primarily viewed as a cognitive and emotional enterprise. However, identity formation is and should also be seen as a bodily practice, as something that is acted out on an everyday basis (e.g. Giddens (1991/1996), Brinkmann (2008) following Foucault, and Goffman (1959/1990, although he talked of 'self' rather than identity).

The question guiding this contribution is whether the increased everyday mobility of people that also characterises present social conditions further challenges the possibility to form and maintain a coherent sense of self, and thereby psychological wellbeing. Or put the other way around: how can it be possible to form and maintain personal and psychological coherence when commuting on an everyday basis – is there an opposition between being on the move and maintaining a coherent sense of self? Or is this just a false dichotomy? A further concern of mine as an architect is of course also the role of the designed material surroundings in this – whether they enable or prevent maintaining such a coherent sense of self.

Outline of chapter

First, the approach to answering the above questions will be outlined. The contribution builds on personal field notes from my train commute and uses Jensen's *Staging Mobilities*-framework (2013) to unfold observations and findings. Then the notion of 'dwelling' will be introduced as a conceptualisation of how personal and psychological coherence can be maintained as an everyday practice. Via empirical examples it will be demonstrated how the mobile situations observed during the train commute can be seen as ways of dwelling on the move. Focus will be on the role of the train's material environment in respectively enabling and preventing such a dwelling. In conclusion the chapter points out connections between the very design of the physical settings that frame mobile situations, the ability to dwell in these settings, and psychological wellbeing, thereby underlining the importance of the physical setting while being on the move on an everyday basis.

Methodological approach

To look into these questions I have taken as a point of departure my own commute between my home in Copenhagen and my work place in Odense from the middle of June 2015 until the end of July 2016. The commute is approximately one hour and 15 minutes by train, and two hours door to door – each way. With the direct 'fast train' there is only one stop on the way, approximately 10 minutes from Copenhagen Central Station. The train ride includes crossing the Great Belt bridge and train tunnel that connects the island of Funen in the south of Denmark, on which Odense is the biggest city, with Zealand where the Danish capital, Copenhagen, is situated on the far east of the island. The observations done here are based on the IC3 trains. These were put into service in the late 1980s, and despite closing in on their 30 years' life expectancy, they are still the most reliable trains of the Danish national rail service (McGhie, 2017). Furthermore, by popular opinion these are without doubt also more comfortable than the newer IC4 trains. However, this chapter will not elaborate further on comparative discussions of these two types of trains.

The findings are primarily based on classic observations and field notes from my own thoughts and experiences, but they also include observations of fellow commuters and non-commuters on the train and conversations with my fellow commuting colleagues, many of whom were commuting along the same route as myself. My own time on the train was spent on part-time psychology studies, among others, on an assignment that has formed the background for this chapter.[2] Thus, on the train I could easily maintain a role as a student, while at the same time being engaged in observations and taking field notes.

The *Staging Mobilities*-framework by Jensen (2013) has been used as an analytical tool to make sense of the observations. Consequently, the observations of what was going on in the train have been interpreted as situated mobilities manifested in, respectively, physical settings, material spaces and design; social interactions; and embodied performances (ibid., p. 6). In this perspective mobilities are viewed as embodied social practices that are acted out from below by individual social agents, as well as orchestrated from above by, for example, planning, design and social structures. Furthermore, a layer of personal experience has been added in order to complement the *Staging Mobilities*-framework with a psychological perspective. This is taken from Brinkmann (2012), who underlines the importance of including a phenomenological and personal aspect in qualitative studies of everyday life, not least when seen from a psychological perspective.

Thus; the overall methodical approach reflects a pragmatic focus on what can be called phronetic knowledge, i.e. knowledge that enables a more reflective and ethical practice (Flyvbjerg, 2001/2009). Such would be both the practice of commuting as well as that of architects, planners and decision-makers, who are responsible for the layout and design of the physical setting of, for example, train commutes.

Dwelling

The notion of 'dwelling' is not new in relation to mobilities studies, and the connection between movement and dwelling has been pointed out before, for example by Jensen (2012), Winther (2006) and Urry (2000, 2006, 2007). Here it will be used to conceptualise how maintaining a coherent sense of self can be seen as an everyday practise of dwelling and making oneself at home in the surrounding environment. In the following I will clarify my understanding of 'dwelling'.

First, from a phenomenological perspective, dwelling can be seen as human beings' primary existence, for example according to Heidegger (1951/2000). Humans build and therefore they dwell and exist as human beings on earth. From a more behaviouristic line of thought, dwelling can be seen as territorialising the physical surroundings in order to stay safe and ensure provision of food, mating and upbringing etc., and where distances between people mark different degrees of social relation (e.g. Hall, 1966/1990; Lawson, 2001). Dwelling can also be seen as an act of 'homing' and identifying with the surroundings, which come to represent one's understanding of oneself (Winther, 2006). Further, over time the dwelling becomes a bodily extension of the self through a bodily habituation of the dwelling, created by acting out rituals and routines within the dwelling (e.g. Pallasmaa, 1995; Vacher, 2011). Dwelling is also a social act, a personal territory defining social relations and distinguishing friend from enemy. A dwelling is for someone and not for others, either shared between several people or restricted to a single dweller (Pallasmaa, 1995). Finally, in a Western context the dwelling has become synonymous with home, as dwellings through history gradually have developed to become ultimately private and comfortable frames of family and home life (Rybczynski, 1986).

Dwelling can be seen as a process whereby an object, not necessarily but often a house, becomes bodily habituated and territorialised and ultimately an extension of the body, and with which a social and personal relation and sense of belonging and existence is formed. This object then becomes a place of identification, safety and security, in this way representing the individual dweller's identity and sense of self. In this sense, if one is able to dwell in and home the surroundings, then this can actually be a way to aid forming and maintaining a coherent sense of self in practice, thereby maintaining psychological wellbeing.

Empirical examples of dwelling on the move

What crystallised from my observations of the things people actually do on the train, myself included, was that the various mobile situations reflected sorts of dwelling on the move. This will be accounted for in this section through empirical examples. In accordance with the theme of this book, the focus will be on the role that the physical settings and material aspects play in this. The question is then, how and when material aspects of the train afford such a dwelling, and how and when they do not, when they prevent such a dwelling on the move.

Physical and material aspects: building a territory

First of all, referring to the above understanding of dwelling as territorialisation (Hall, 1966/1990; Lawson, 2001), people seem to build a physical territory on the train. This is in part supported by the physical layout of the seating, where the head and arm rests form a demarcation of the individual seat. The head rest protrudes a little, thereby offering a sense of visual privacy in addition to working as an actual head rest. The arm rest marks the individual couple of seats as a closed space. Furthermore the windows are kept within frames instead of forming one continuous surface for the whole coach, thereby offering a sense of shelter, covering the shoulder with the window frame rather than exposing it to the outside. Finally, the height of the seating offers visual privacy from passengers seated further down or behind in the coach, since there is no visual connection between the seats in this direction.

On top of the predefined layout of the seating it is possible to adjust the seat to fulfil one's own needs, thereby maintaining a sense of ownership and control. This is only to a certain degree, however, since people that differ to a large extent from the average size can have a hard time adjusting the seats to suit their needs. This especially concerns leg space, which is not abundant on the trains, and this points further to the role of fellow passengers. Since space is not abundant it is necessary to negotiate personal territory, leg space but also table space, for example in order to be able to work using a laptop, as the vignette below demonstrates.

I had gotten a window seat this morning (which I prefer – it makes it easier to just sit and look out and feel totally immersed in your own world, just yourself, a window and the landscape rushing past), so I was pretty satisfied. This morning I wanted to use my laptop, since I was writing down these observations. But the young woman opposite me apparently also wanted to use her laptop. Hers was a bit smaller than mine, maybe a 13″, mine being a 15″ so she needed the screen at a bit lower angle, whereas I needed mine a bit farther into the table for it not to tip over into my lap when typing. This meant that table space was scarce. To avoid 'clashing', I moved over to the aisle seat. For once there weren't that many on the train, and in this way I also had more leg space – and I wasn't going to sit and look out the window anyway. However, it was a brief respite. After 10 minutes, an older couple boarded the train in Høje Tåstrup, the one stop between Copenhagen and Odense, and they had of course reserved the two aisle seats in our four-seat arrangement. Well, then I just had to move back to the window again and negotiate the table space with the laptop opposite mine.

However, the layout of the seating varies. The above describes the standard seating layout, which affords territory-building very well, but in other parts of the train the seating layout differs, offering less visual and physical privacy as well as shielding, and less table space. In the quiet compartment, the table layout differs, offering foldable table space for each passenger of a four-seat group, thereby giving more leg space when the tables are not in use. These tables are much better for using a laptop as well, offering just enough table space for each seat to suit a laptop. On commuter trains, the quiet compartment is nevertheless often turned into first-class seating, making it unavailable for a daily commuter like me.

The physical territory is further marked by personal belongings and artefacts that people place around them. The standard passenger gear consists of a phone or other device to play music from, headphones, often with noise reduction, things to use for work like laptops, books, notebooks, pens, papers etc., tickets either in the form of printed tickets on paper, a commuter pass, student card or the Danish national 'travel card', and sometimes food and drinks, most typical on the morning train. The nature of the different artefacts tells a lot about the status of the individual passenger, whether it is an everyday commuter or not, a student or worker, someone on the way to the occasional meeting, perhaps with a group of colleagues, or someone travelling for leisure, e.g. for holidays.

The opportunity to build a personal territory on the train further depends heavily on the right to have a seat. This again depends on the status of the individual passenger, where commuters get a big discount on prebooked seats, as opposed to students for example. On a fully booked morning train this privilege as a commuter ensures working efficiency to be able to take full advantage of the time on the train, through the security of having a place to sit. However, the strictures around getting hold of 'seat tickets' make it quite a laborious affair, and why many of my colleagues often buy seat tickets for a couple of weeks at a time. Similarly, Jensen and colleagues identify seat reservations as one of the central aspects of the socio-material environment in staging interrail train travel (2016).

> As a commuter you get a reduced price for 'seat tickets', 10 kroner instead of 30 kroner. Still, it amounts to quite a significant amount if I were to buy a seat ticket for every trip, about 400 kroner per month. And that is on top of a commuter pass which is 4500 kroner per month. I quickly figured that I didn't need seat tickets. However, after a few weeks something happened which made me change my opinion on seat tickets radically. Before, you had to reserve the tickets by phoning DSB[3] or simply buy them in person at a station service desk. This meant having to spend extra time on the travel, leaving the office or home before planned. But now it became possible to buy commuter seat tickets in the app! The really smart thing about the app is that you can actually wait until you reach the platform to buy the ticket. In this way, you can evaluate whether the train will be crowded or not, and thereby the likelihood of conquering a seat without a seat ticket. I started to enjoy the right to a seat and, sometimes, I even bought a seat ticket before reaching the platform, especially in the morning, depending on my mood: whether I was in the mood for hunting seats in competition with the other seat hungry passengers, especially students, or whether I was in the mood for being able to quickly sit down somewhere, unpack my stuff, and get going with my studies. Oftenmost, my mood was for the latter…

Social aspects: connection and spatial negotiations

Social aspects include how to manage relations with other people on the train with individual needs for privacy and social connection. This refers back to dwelling as a social act (Pallasmaa, 1995; Vacher, 2011).

First of all, the above-mentioned layout of the seating on the train makes it difficult to maintain the minimum distance required in order to keep other people out of the individual's personal space (a distance of 1.2 m away from the individual according to Lawson, 2001). Instead, they come all the way into the intimate sphere (0.5 m away from the individual according to Lawson). In this way, it is impossible not to relate to the other people on the train in some way or other.

Thus, in order to maintain a sense of privacy in general, there are certain norms for social interaction on the train. These norms become especially evident when they are transgressed, for instance in the quiet compartment which only works if everybody knows and respects the rules. If not, the quiet compartment can work the other way around and actually prevent upholding a sense of territory and private space. The rules are also put out of gear when there is a train breakdown of some kind, and most notably when the train stops. It is as if the rules are only important when the train is running, in which case there is no way to escape. When the train has halted, a connection with the ground is re-established, and standard social rules apply instead of the train's social rules.

Dwelling on the move 247

For example it seems that both general noise and conversations are accepted in the quiet compartment as soon as there is a breakdown and the train has come to a standstill, as in the vignette below.

> Sometimes the rules of the quiet compartment are broken unanimously without anyone stubbornly maintaining the requirement of peace and silence. This happened one day on the way home from work, when the train suddenly stopped in Slagelse (which is normally not a stop for the fast train). There was no immediate reaction here in the quiet compartment, where I had found myself a seat as a rare exception – it is almost always full or reserved for first-class passengers. But after a speaker-call explained the standstill as being caused by a person being hit by the train and that there was consequently an up to two hours expected delay until the police and the paramedics had cleared the tracks, the rules about silence in the quiet compartment fell to the ground instantly. People started talking in a low voice to one another; one passenger asked in English if somebody could translate, several people sighed loudly, and yet others started making phone calls:
> 'Yes, see you at the Central Station when we get there; it could be up to two hours...'
> 'It just always happens!'
> 'Fuck, I just don't think I can make it; it might be up to two hours before we can leave from here ... it's just too bad, but there's just nothing to do about it...'
> 'I am in a quiet compartment, but I cannot really get out of my seat...'
> As time passed, people gradually quietened down again, but it was as if the rules ceased to function for as long as we were at a standstill. People kept talking in low voices together, asking if they could get out of their seats to stretch their legs, make phone calls, etc. When it was announced after about one and a half hours that the train was now ready to move forward again and we started going, there was however no sign of joy or relief from anyone at all. People passed the message on to the ones waiting at the other end and slowly surrendered themselves to whatever they were doing before. The quiet compartment gradually quietened down again, but was never as quiet as it had been before we stopped.

An efficient way to create a personal space and shut other people out is by the use of headphones, which are heavily used on the train, especially by commuters. Headphones can block out disturbing noise from others, and they become an excuse for actually ignoring others, even though you may be able to hear them. In this way they work just as much as a signal of privacy. This points back to the aspect of having colleagues on the same train. When you know people it becomes more difficult to shut them out, at least not without an explanation or excuse. And even though you excuse yourself, you cannot shut them out completely; you will have to relate to your colleagues no matter what, because they are already in your personal space and you already have a relation with them.

Again, this depends on individual preferences for either privacy or social relation and stimulation. Commuting with colleagues can also offer an opportunity to extend the working hours to the train, thereby leaving the office earlier than otherwise. And the time on the train can be an opportunity to discuss work-related things otherwise not possible in the office (also known as gossip). Further, commuting together with colleagues can create a sense of community and connection, where the colleagues become 'mobile withs' (Jensen, 2013). In the same way the other commuters on the train become 'mobile others' (ibid.), but over time they become known, which creates a sense of community, of being part of something and in the same situation as other people. In this sense the train can also be a meeting place, a place of unexpected social relations and an opportunity to encounter other perspectives on the world.

Furthermore, through internet and mobile connection it becomes possible to connect with and include other people not physically present in the individual personal space on the train. Thereby it becomes possible to maintain existing social relations, making it easy to uphold and preserve an already formed understanding of self through such relations. However, mobile and internet connections are not always optimal or possible, thus preventing such social connection, as shown in the following vignette.

> Usually it is on the train I get the chance, time and space to check my personal messages, mails, etc. As such I totally depend on having internet access on my phone on the train (which I normally have, except in the tunnel under the Great Belt). One Thursday on the way home from work (when I had bought a seat ticket via the app on my phone while walking to the station, and afterwards tucked the phone away in my coat pocket to save the trouble of opening my bag), I was unable to find my phone once on the train. I could find my work phone, however, which I had brought home with me, as I was going to work in Copenhagen the day after. When I wanted to access the train wi-fi I could also see my private phone as a network to connect to – but I could simply not recall where it might be. Anyway, I had some stuff to read for my studies, and I could access my Spotify account on my work phone, so I found my usual study-on-the-train-soundtrack and immersed myself in my studies. As we approached Copenhagen and I started getting ready for getting off, I finally found my phone in a coat pocket. It was a bit as if I had missed something on the train trip, both doing something which I normally did (check mails, messages – connect to the world and check up on what had been going on with my friends, family, in the news, etc.), but of course also having physically missed my phone.

Embodied performances: comfort and rhythms

Dwelling also depends on bodily comfort and habituation as pointed out in the above (Rybczynski, 1986), which again depends heavily on indoor climatic conditions such as temperature, smell, air quality, noise and light as well as ergonomic comfort. All of these aspects can disturb the ability to dwell, especially when they cannot be controlled or adjusted to fit individual needs. As mentioned above, the noise level can somehow be adjusted by use of headphones, or simply by shifting seats if this is possible. Light levels can be adjusted via individual lights in the panel above the seats as well as by the curtains. However, the curtains need to be negotiated with fellow passengers, thereby not always being possible to adjust individually. The temperature and air-quality conditions can be very poor on IC3 trains with often too-large temperature differences existing between the outside and inside and even between different coaches. The randomness and seeming difficulty of controlling these parameters, even for train personnel, make these conditions even harder to accept, whereby they pose an obstacle to the ability to make oneself comfortable on the train and thereby to dwell. The vignette below points to the importance of indoor climate for comfort.

> The train was full, as usual, and on a winter Monday morning, when the train gets stuffed with hundreds of people in a few minutes, all wearing heavy winter coats, boots, gloves, scarves, hats, bringing laptops, bags, headphones, coffee cups, breakfast bags, etc., etc.; the air promptly gets thick, heavy and queasy. It improves as the train starts rolling and the ventilation system begins to work, but it can be pretty unpleasant until then.

This aspect also relates to bodily habituation of the train ride, as Jensen has described in her study of train commuters (2012). Over time the train ride becomes a routinised practice unconsciously known by the body, including the sounds, smells, movements and rhythms of the trip. As a new commuter the trip is consciously organised and all activities during the trip are engaged in with full awareness: unpacking the necessary stuff for the trip, having your commuter pass ready to show, studying efficiently on the train, not wasting time, keeping track of time and packing down in order to be ready to get off, etc. But over time the body incorporates all the cues: the signs in the exterior surroundings, the shift in speed, the difference in light and darkness, and the activities disappear from consciousness and become routines, something you engage in without giving it a thought. This becomes extra-apparent when there is a breakdown of systems, and it is not possible to uphold the known routines. Then all activities come to consciousness again. The rhythms of the train also form part of this bodily habituation (ibid.). Different characteristics mark the different passages of the train ride, which over time take on certain meanings and invoke certain feelings. For example there is a great difference between departing and returning, and between crossing the Great Belt between Funen and Zealand from one side or the other, as the vignette below illustrates.

> Gradually as I've gotten accustomed to spend the train trip reading and working on my psychology studies in general, I have gotten myself a routine finely attuned to the train's rhythms between Copenhagen and

Odense. Time-wise there is appr. 10 min between the Central Station and Høje Tåstrup station, 50 min between Høje Tåstrup and the Great Belt and then another 15 min between the Great Belt and Odense. In this way, the journey both ways can be divided into three parts: the introduction, the main part and the ending. Besides, crossing the Great Belt bridge and tunnel can be seen as an intermezzo in two parts of appr. 5 min in total. Consequently, I have gradually established a routine in three parts corresponding to the three parts of the journey.

During the first part of the trip, I find my/a seat and put out my stuff (book, notebook, pens, phone, commuter pass, headphones depending on how much noise there is – most mornings it's actually not necessary despite the train being full, but most afternoons it's indeed necessary). In the morning, sometimes I get to check news, mails and stuff, and in the afternoon going home, I sometimes spend this time making short calls, e.g. to book a doctor's appointment or the like. As soon as we pass Høje Tåstrup (morning) or the Great Belt (afternoon), I instinctively take it as a sign that the main part of the journey has commenced, and I engage in my studies – reading, noticing, noting down, reflecting. Most of the journey is spent that way. When we get to the last part of the journey, I pack my study things away. Sometimes I also do it before, if I'm very tired and allow myself a little snooze (and sometimes I don't even get to put anything away and close my eyes with the book still in my hand). Otherwise, it is the last part of the journey which is reserved for relaxation. In the morning it's about listening to music and closing my eyes; in the afternoon I often feel a need to just sit and gaze into the air, doing nothing. This is also the time to check messages, mails, etc. And of course, to get ready to get off and go to work or home.

The different parts of the journey also have very different characters, with the passing of the Great Belt as something extraordinary, something very unique along the Danish train line. The contrast between the long dark break of connectivity with the rest of the world in the tunnel and the wide open surroundedness of sky and sea on the bridge is truly remarkable. It is like stepping into a cathedral, where the long prelude of the tunnel reinforces the liberating sense of openness on the bridge. And I rejoice over it every time. And every time I have to sit, just for a few seconds, breathe the air (though I know that I will not catch any sea breeze no matter how deep I suck the air into my lungs!) and feel surrounded by the sky and the big infinity to be seen. At least at those times where there's something to see. Some days it's pitch dark (during winter), and other days everything just fuses into a big grey lot, and then it doesn't matter. However, of course it works the exact opposite going the other way. The vast openness of the bridge being swallowed by the long dark tunnel. And I get sad every time. Not a very distinct sadness that affects whatever I'm doing, but a small sadness somewhere in the body, as if something has been turned off.

Personal experience: sense-making and meaning

Finally, the ability to dwell on the train ultimately depends on how well the train commute reflects and corresponds with the individual's understanding of self, as emphasised by Winther (2006), and the individual's ability to make sense of the train ride – in short, referring to Heidegger (1951/2000), how well one is able to exist on the train. If the train commute does not contribute in any meaningful way or fulfil any needs of the individual at all, it is not possible to identify with being on the train on an everyday basis, thereby preventing dwelling on the move.

In my own experience, the train ride is a welcome pause, an opportunity to just sit and watch the world fly by, have time to read or do nothing at all for a while. Also, the train commute offers an opportunity to spend time studying psychology on the train while having an interesting and meaningful job in Odense, and at the same time keeping my address in Copenhagen close to family and friends. In this way, the train commute makes a lot of sense and instead of posing an obstacle to engage in meaningful activities, it offers the opportunity to do exactly so. In the same way, it is very important for many of my commuting colleagues that they can spend their time on the train working, so that the commute does not become an obstacle to their family life and, for example, bringing children to daycare school and picking them up, which is illustrated in the following vignette.

> One afternoon, when I took the train home together with a new colleague, I casually asked her when she caught the train and stuff. She told me that she has a son in kindergarten and a husband who also works a bit outside of Copenhagen, so in order to make everyday life work out she gets the very early train from Copenhagen at 5.50 in order to get home in time to pick up her son. These days her husband brings him to kindergarten in the morning. Or, on other days, she brings him in the morning, and then she doesn't make it on the train until 7.50. These days she gets the train back home an hour later and leaves the picking up of her son to her husband – or her mom, who lives nearby.
>
> It's lovely to have her nearby, it's a great help in making everyday life work out.

Further, the importance of a reliable train service for these colleagues became evident during a long period of track maintenance works during the summer of 2016. During this time, the train service was replaced by buses on Funen, creating much longer and unpredictable travel times of sometimes up to five hours. Many of my colleagues simply stayed working in Copenhagen instead of embarking on the, now, long and exhaustive as well as unpredictable commute to Odense by both train and replacement buses. The difficulty of combining commuting with family life and parenthood has also been pointed out by studies of relations between fertility and commuting (Huinink and Feldhaus, 2012; Rüger and Viry, 2017). These studies show a tendency to lower fertility among, especially, female long-distance commuters – however, depending on national context (one of the studies compared commuters in four different European countries), i.e. national family policies, social norms and labour market structures.

The outdoor weather conditions also form part of the sense-making of train travel. During wintertime it is dark when being on the train, whereby the windows become mirrors of the interior, rather than an outlook to the exterior. Instead of offering a break, a time to reflect, the train feels more like a vacuum, like being cut off from the world. Consequently, during winter the train ride only makes sense for me as a time to study.

Furthermore, it is generally recognised among my colleagues that it can be hard work to keep oneself together when commuting a rather long distance to work every day. The commute is seen as a sacrifice made in order to get a meaningful job, and those of my colleagues who quit their job in Odense did so in favour of a job either closer to their home, or because the job in Odense lost value and meaning to them. This in turn has created a kind of snowball effect with fewer colleagues commuting, thus losing the community of fellow commuting colleagues, and the commute becomes more of an effort and less meaningful for the individual. In my own experience, even though I thought myself very well able to dwell on the move, I felt pronounced and unexpected relief when I finally moved to Odense in August 2016, and became able to control my own time and not having to depend on the train timetables anymore.

Conclusions

When viewing identity formation not only as a cognitive and emotional enterprise, but as something which is also acted out on an everyday basis, as a bodily practice, dwelling can be seen as a way to form and maintain a coherent sense of self while being on the move. By forming a personal territory on the train, fulfilling social needs of either privacy or connection, feeling comfortable and being able to make sense of the train ride it is possible to create a sense of dwelling, a sense of belonging and existence on the train. In this sense, everyday commuting does not necessarily challenge forming and maintaining a coherent sense of self, and thus, further, psychological wellbeing. There is not necessarily a dichotomy between commuting and maintaining personal and psychological coherence.

However, this depends on the individual commuter's ability to dwell on the move, and how well the individual commuter is able to stage the mobile situation from below and make sense of the everyday train ride, to make him- or herself at home, and to feel comfortable, safe and secure. Furthermore, this requires a lot of work – it can take quite an effort to maintain a coherent sense of self when commuting a long distance to work every day.

In addition, it also depends on how well the physical settings, material spaces and technology, among others, afford the possibility to dwell on the move. For example the layout of the seating, the table and leg space, fellow commuters, access to mobile and internet connection, opportunities to reserve a seat, indoor climate conditions, rail work, and outdoor weather conditions all influence and eventually pose obstacles to being able to dwell on the move. With reference to the *Staging Mobilities*-framework, this is part of what can be seen as staged from above, and consequently what designers, planners, engineers, social scientists, etc. can work with in the attempt to make improvements, thereby enhancing the possibilities of dwelling on the move and maintaining a coherent sense of self, and, thereby, psychological wellbeing.

Perspectives

Of course, personal and psychological wellbeing is more complex than that; it is not just a matter of being able to dwell on the move, and of course the physical settings, material spaces and design are not the *only* things that influence how well the individual is able to dwell on the move. As the empirical examples hint at, other aspects such as employment contracts that allow working on the train have an effect as well, as do wider social structures as pointed out in the previously mentioned studies of relations between fertility and commuting (Huinink and Feldhaus, 2012; Rüger and Viry, 2017).

Furthermore, a few delimitations of the above study should be mentioned. The above empirical examples and theoretical points are all based in a Western context with a Western understanding of dwelling and identity, which cannot be taken for granted across different cultural contexts (e.g. Hall, 1966/1990; Rybczynski, 1986). In addition, the study is based in a Danish context, Denmark being a small country with relatively short distances. Thus, the commute in question should be seen relative to Danish standards, where it is a rather long distance. Further, the study is focused on commuters for whom the commute is a deliberate choice in order to get a meaningful job. The empirical examples would probably have looked different if the study looked at commuters who do not have a choice of commuting, which would undoubtedly affect their ability to dwell on the move (e.g. Bissell, 2018). In relation to these delimitations, it would be interesting to look at examples where the commuter is *not* able to dwell on the move, when the physical settings prevent such or do not offer conditions as good as those of the Danish IC3 trains.

However, this study does point out connections between the very design of the physical settings that frame mobile situations, the ability to dwell in these settings and psychological wellbeing, thereby underlining the important role of physical settings when being on the move. In this sense, the notion of 'dwelling on the move' can be used as an analytical frame for the further understanding of such connections, specifically the personal and psychological consequences of being on the move. Linking the notion of 'dwelling' as an understanding of how people essentially inhabit and become familiarised with their surroundings as well as fundamentally exist in the world, to mobilities studies emphasises how commuting should not be seen as mere movements from point A to point B, but as a way of life itself – something which is also pointed out by Vannini in his study of ferry wayfaring on the Canadian west coast (2012). This, then, opens up the potential for a better understanding of complex relations between transport modes, and how well their physical settings enable or prevent 'dwelling on the move' and human wellbeing – a point which Urry (2006, 2007) for example, could have included in understanding why the automobile is so inhabitable, and how this could be explored in a transition to more sustainable alternatives that are equally attractive in terms of allowing for dwelling.

In closing, this chapter therefore suggests that the notion of 'dwelling on the move' acts as a framework for design guidelines for physical settings that frame not only everyday commuting, but forms of mobility of people in general. Creating physical settings that offer an opportunity to dwell when being on the move, then, supports mobile individuals in maintaining personal and psychological coherence, and thereby wellbeing, in a complex world of social acceleration and mobility.

Notes

1 An auto-ethnographic account from the author's field notes, partly previously published in Christensen (2017), but re-written for this chapter. All following vignettes are also from the author's field notes.
2 In addition, a short essay has previously been published (Christensen, 2017).
3 The Danish state railway company.

References

Bissell, D., 2018. *Transit Life: how commuting is transforming our cities*, Cambridge, MA: The MIT Press.
Brinkmann, S., 2008. *Identitet – Udfordringer i forbrugersamfundet*. Aarhus: Klim.
Brinkmann, S., 2012. *Kvalitativ udforskning af hverdagslivet*. Danish ed. Copenhagen: Hans Reitzels Forlag.
Brinkmann, S., 2014. *Stå fast – et opgør med tidens udviklingstvang*. Copenhagen: Gyldendal Business.
Brinkmann, S. and A. Petersen, eds., 2015. *Diagnoser – perspektiver, kritik og diskussion.* Aarhus: Klim.
Christensen, C.B., 2017. Dwelling on the move. In: D.B. Lanng and I.S.G. Lange (eds.), *Urban Design Kaleidoscope 2017: Celebrating 20 years of Urban Design at Aalborg University*, A&D Files, ISSN: 1603–6204, Vol. 112, Ch. 3.
Flyvbjerg, B., 2001/2009. *Samfundsvidenskab som virker*. Danish edn. Copenhagen: Akademisk Forlag.
Giddens, A., 1991/1996. *Modernitet og selvidentitet – Selvet og samfundet under senmoderniteten*. Copenhagen: Hans Reitzels Forlag.
Goffman, E., 1959/1990. *The Presentation of Self in Everyday Life*. Reprint. London: Penguin Books, originally Anchor Books 1959.
Hall, E.T., 1966/1990. *The Hidden Dimension*. Reprint. New York: Anchor Books.
Heidegger, M., 1951/2000. *Tænke Bygge Bo*. Danish edn., In: *Sproget og ordet*. Copenhagen: Hans Reitzels Forlag.
Honneth, A., 2005. Organiseret selvrealisering – individualiseringens paradokser. In: R. Willig and M. Østergaard, eds, *Sociale patologier*. Copenhagen: Hans Reitzels Forlag, pp. 41–60.

Huinink, J. and M. Feldhaus, 2012. Fertility and commuting behaviour in Germany. *Comparative Population Studies – Zeitschrift für Bevölkerungswissenschaft.* Vol. 37, Nos. 3–4, pp. 491–516.

Jensen, H.L., 2012. *Hverdagslivets kollektive mobilitet – om at pendle med tog og skabe et mobilt sted*, PhD dissertation. Roskilde University, Department of Environmental, Social and Spatial Change.

Jensen, M.T., S. Gyimothy and O.B. Jensen, 2016. Staging interrail mobilities. *Tourist Studies.* Vol. 15, No. 2, pp. 111–132.

Jensen, O.B., 2013. *Staging Mobilities.* London: Routledge.

Lawson, B., 2001. *The Language of Space.* Oxford: Architectural Press, Elsevier.

McGhie, S., 2017. IC3-togene skal renoveres for 385 millioner for at dække ind for IC4. Ingeniøren [online] 25 October. Available at https://ing.dk/artikel/ic3-togene-skal-renoveres-385-millioner-at-daekke-ind-ic4-207671 [Accessed 18 February 2019].

Pallasmaa, J., 1995. Identity, Intimacy and Domicile – Notes on the Phenomenology of Home. In: D. Benjamin (ed.), *The Home: Words, Interpretations, Meanings and Environments.* Farnham: Ashgate, pp. 131–150.

Rosa, H., 2004. Four levels of self-interpretation – A paradigm for interpretive social philosophy and political criticism. *Philosophy & Social Criticism,* Vol. 30, Nos. 5–6, pp. 691–720.

Rosa, H., 2014. *Fremmedgørelse og acceleration,* Danish edn. Copenhagen: Hans Reitzels Forlag.

Rüger, H. and G. Viry, 2017. Work-related travel over the life course and its link to fertility: A comparison between four European countries. *European Sociological Review,* Vol. 33, No. 5, pp. 645–660.

Rybczynski, W., 1986. *HOME – A Short History of an Idea.* London: Penguin Books.

Urry, J., 2000. *Sociology Beyond Societies – Mobilities for the Twenty-First Century.* London: Routledge.

Urry, J., 2006. Inhabiting the car. *Sociological Review,* Vol. 54, pp. 17–31.

Urry, J., 2007. *Mobilities.* Cambridge: Polity Press.

Vacher, M., 2011. An Exclamation Mark That Tells Me I Exist – An Anthropological Introduction to Dwelling. In: *Frontiers of Architecture III-IV: Living,* Humlebæk: Louisiana Museum of Modern Art, pp. 30–35.

Vannini, P., 2012. *Ferry Tales. Mobility, Place and Time on Canada's West Coast.* Oxon: Routledge.

Winther, I.W., 2006. *Hjemlighed – kulturfænomenologiske studier.* Copenhagen: Danmarks Pædagogiske Universitets Forlag.

Index

Page numbers in *italics* denote figures.

Actor-Network-Theory (ANT) 3, 50, 104, 142, 150, 166, 169; macro actor-networks 178, 180
air travel emissions 175
Alliance of Automobile Manufacturers, US 41–42
Amoroso, Nadia 122
anthropological mappings 193–195
anti-microbial resistance 51; with human mobilities 51
architectural practice, socio-material dimension of 143
architecture and experiential places: context-rich design 150; designing with narratives of 152–155; experience economy 151; materials mobilised in design meetings 155–161; NORRØN architects 151–152; research in design practices in 149–151; Yaneva's approach to 150
aroma wheel 130
assemblage ethnographies 143
automobile: congestion 35; cultural capital 38; exhibitions *see* motor shows; femininity 36; masculinity 36, 39; subjectivities, production of 37
automobility: components of imaginary 33; events related to 42; regime 33, 43; system of 42

Barad, Karen 216
Barthes, Roland 31, 33, 37, 40, 44–45
Basilica of Saint Peter, Vatican 34
bathhouse 153
Bennett, Jane 204
Berentz, Marco 151

Berlin public transport infrastructures *118*, 124–128
biological annihilation 50, 54
biometrics 79
black-boxing 'expert talk' 176–178
Blain, Patrick 41
Bloch, Ernst 102
'Blue Plateau' project, in Blåvand 153, 155
BMW 38
boarding school 102
Bourdieu, Pierre 18, 38
Braidotti, Rosi 52
brick-and-mortar (non-Internet) shopping 62
Britain From Above (2008) 50
Bus Rapid Transport systems 188

Calvin, John 34, 44–45
Camøno hiking trail 148
Caracas a pie (walking Caracas) case study 186, 188–195, 198; acupunctural mobilities design 196–198; city and urban mobilities 189–192; claiming of pedestrian mobility 196; experiencing mobilities and anthropological mappings 193–195; *Guía del Ocio* ('Leisure guide') 193; mobile ethnographies 195; Paseo Los Próceres 197; proclamation of urban mobilities change 192–193; 'sightseeing' guide 193; urban mobility 188–189
car-based planning schemes 188
carbon emissions 168–169, 171–172
carbon 'experts' 167
carbon innovations 167
carbon-intensive mobility systems 179
carbon inventories 179

carbon monoxide poisoning 40
carbon-neutrality: assembling the calculating device 175–176; black-boxing 'expert talk' 176–178; calculations of 170–171; 'carbon-neutral' destinations 175; carbon-neutrality network 176; 'carbon neutral' themes 174; C-Neutral certification network 170; Costa Rica's Carbon-Neutral campaign 173; deadline for reaching 171; goals of 12; growing material/non-material gap 171–175; methods to reach 171; National Voluntary Standard for Demonstrating Carbon Neutrality (Costa Rica) 170
carbon-neutral nations 11, 167, 170
carbon-neutral' tourism destinations 179
carbon-offsetting network 172, 176
carbon sink 169
car crashes 39–40, 45
car dealerships, collection of 33
Carse, Ashley 21
Carvajal, José 192–193, 195–197
Center for Mobilities and Urban Studies (C-MUS) 7, 205, 209
Centre for Mobilities Research (CeMoRe), Lancaster University 61, 209
Chatty Maps 130–133
Ciclovía ("bike path") initiative (Bogota) 188
city morphology 193
city planning 6, 188
civic and urban activism, social movements of 185
civil inattention 25
'civilizing march' of modernity 199
class society, enactment of 23
climate change 51, 177; mitigation for 174, 180–181
C-MUS *see* Center for Mobilities and Urban Studies (C-MUS)
C-Neutral certification network 170
coherence *versus* mobility 240–242
collective experimentation 51
combustion engine vehicles 173, 179
Comité des Constructeurs Français d'Automobiles 41–42
communicative travel 3
configuration of practices 21–23
connected situationalism 20
Constructive Anticipatory Kinaesthetic Empathy (CAKE) 215
consumer behaviours: affordances for 61, 74; materialities for 9; models of 62

consumer communities 167
consumer journeys 61; brick-and-mortar (non-Internet) shopping 62; decision-making process 62; movement during 62–63; online 62
consumer mobilities: affordances for information-gathering 59; cartographic Ordnance Survey maps 60; consumer journeys as a part of 61–62; Depthmap models 60; impact of movement on information-gathering 60; information and affordance when shopping 63–64; 'journey-by-foot' scale 60; mental accounting of travel distance 62; mental modelling of 60; modalities of movement 59–60; 'motorised-transportation' scale 60; participant mapping results 70–72; patterns of 70–72; phenomena of 'desire paths' 59; social dimensions of 61; in social practices 61; Space Syntax *see* Space Syntax
Corner, James 120, 122, 134; *Agency of Mapping, The* (1999) 121
corporeal travel of people 2
Cosgrove, Denis 119
Costa Rica: black-boxing 'expert talk' 176–178; carbon emission certification (C-Neutral) 168; Carbon-Neutral campaign 173; carbon-neutrality network 176, 179; carbon-offsetting network 172; 'climate change adaptation' measures 176; deadline for reaching 'carbon neutrality' 171; green technocracy 167; growing material/non-material gap 171–175; methods to reach carbon neutrality 171; Ministry of Environment and Energy (MINAE) 173; motorized fleet in 174; National Meteorological Institute 171; National Voluntary Standard for Demonstrating Carbon Neutrality 170; Quetzal bird 'research site' 169; urban design and planning 171
cross-country skiing: analysis of 80–96; body-mounted 'sports' video cameras 80; data collection 80; interactional mobility analysis 79–80; kick zone 79; making tracks for 87–96; micro-mobility practices 79; mobile 'active participant' ethnography 97; multimodal interactional approach to 79; practical infrastructure for learning to *91*;

cross-country skiing: analysis of *continued*
    practice of 82; qualities vital for 82;
    recreational 77; sensing snow as a
    polymorphous surface for movement
    82–87; skiers' feeling for snow 77; ski
    tracks 79; slippery condition of the snow
    82; as sociocultural spatial practice 78–79;
    symbolism of 79; testing of snow's
    slipperiness 85; video ethnography 97
cultural capital 38, 79
cultural dope, notion of 18
cyberspace 32

Danish national rail service 242
Davos Declaration (2007) 175
Debord, Guy 130–132
'de-carbonizing' economies, process of 12, 178
de Certeau, M. 103
decision-making processes: in contemporary societies 143; of mobilities systems 6, 62
de la Cruise, Poul Høiland 151
demolition of society 55
Depthmap 60, 65, 73; at global scale 67, 73; mapping workshop method overview 69; North Lancashire Depthmap models 66; at radius of 2 km 68; at scale of 5 km 67–68; at scale of 500 m 68
designerly ways of thinking 5, 12–13, 53, 143, 204, 206–207
designing mobilities, research agenda of 54, 199
design in use, Ehn's notion of 53, 148
design justice, notion of 4
desire paths, phenomena of 59
disaster risk management 52–53
distinct mobilities, materialization of 6
DIY alternatives, of dwelling and moving 186
Dresmé, Frank 130, 132–133
Dumit, Joe 217
dwelling: dwelling-in-motion 120, 244–252; embodied performances of 248–250; notion of 243–244, 253; personal experience 251–252; perspectives of 253–254; physical and material aspects 244–246; sense-making 251–252; social aspects of 246–248

'eco-concerned' tourists 174
e-commerce 62
economic capital 38
eco-products 174, 176

écriture, Derridean sense of 33
education: anthropological analyses of 101; asynchronicity in creation process 104–107; boarding school 102; conditions of mobility 102; and empirical study 103–104; for establishment of democratic society 101; in Greenland 101–102; language of instruction 102; 'more-than-human' perspective 104; multiple analyses of mobility in 104–113; as prerequisite for sustainable development 101; primary education 101; school dropouts 102; Science and Technology Studies (STS) 104; secondary education 101, 102; sensibility to mobile and educational research 103; socio-material practices in *see* filming, of socio-material practices in education; theoretical inspirations 103–104
El Nacional newspaper 193, 196
emergent relationships, process of 185
energy-intensive tourism 167
English Garden City planning 6
'environmentally efficient' technologies 173
'environmentally friendly' products 168; certification schemes for 168; eco-products 174, 176
Escobar, Arturo 205
European railway 22
experience economy 11, 147, 151–152, 163
'expert' knowledge 172, 177
extra-cellular matrix (ECM) 212

Facebook 32
FaceTime 10, 104, 107
familial social interaction 9, 77
fascia (fascial system) 210–211; as adaptive and intelligent tissue 211; and constraints of manoeuvres 214; Constructive Anticipatory Kinaesthetic Empathy (CAKE) 215; extra-cellular matrix (ECM) 212; fascial network 212–213; hypodermis 212; implications of working with 214–216; from inspiration to theory 216–218; kinetic empathy 216; mechanosensitive integrating signalling system 212; motility and becoming materialities 211–214; motility and process philosophy 213–214; Science and Technology Studies (STS) research on 217; shape of 212; superficial fascia

212; tensional responsiveness 213; trust-building encounters 217
fascial sensing 215
fascianated mobilities research 216
Fehmarn Belt Company 154
female long-distance commuters 252
feminist technoscience 50
ferry wayfaring 254
filming, of socio-material practices in education: asynchrone experiences 109–111; asynchronicity in the creation process of 104–107; ethnographic fieldwork 104; 'living the life' scene 111–113; mobile media technologies 104; "more-than-representational" text 107–113; theoretical and analytical perspectives of 104; virtual containing 107–109
flat ontologies: anti-reductionist 19; features of 18–21; posthumanist 19; relational 19
flexible work, empirical analysis of 230–231
focus-group interviews (FGIs) 74
Ford 38
Foucauldian automobility scholarship 37
freedom of movement 54, 185
freelancing 225
frictionless transportation, ideas of 6

garden city: Modernist urban planning 5; planning ideas 6; urbanization areas 192
Garfinkel, Harold 18
General Motors 38, 42
Geneva Motor Show (2018) 32, 34–41; automobile congestion 35; automobile desire 37; composition of the railway passengers 36; decontextualized automobiles 39–40; employees of 36; exhibition halls 34; exhibits of luxury cars and iconic sports cars 37; gendered automobility 36–37; Geneva Exhibition and Congress Centre 34; *La Cathédrale Saint-Pierre* (Gothic cathedral) 34; onsite parking 35; *Palais des Expositions et des Congrès de Genève* 34; Palexpo exhibition halls 34; public transportation 35–36; social class 37–39; as spectacle and celebration 41
geotagged social media 63
German society and culture 19
global de-carbonizing policies, materialization of 11
global financial markets 20

Global Mobilities Network (GMN) 209
Global South 50, 185; material mobilities in 199; social activism in 188
Goffman, Erving 25, 38
Good City Life project 130, 133
good life, idea of 4, 55
Gothic cathedrals 31, 34, 45; comparison to automobiles 31
GPS software 63
Graham, Steve 208
Grassroots Organisations (GROs) 55
'greener' society 11
greenhouse gas (GHG) emission 50, 168, 171, 174; Davos Declaration (2007) for reducing 175
'green' industries and markets 181
Greenland 9, 101–102, 104–105, 107, 109
'green' networks 12, 176
green technocracy 167
greenwashing, practices of 167–168, 176
Gross, Matthias 53
Guía del Ocio ('Leisure guide') 193

Hall of the Gods 157
Happy Maps 130
Haraway, Donna 52, 205, 216, 218
Harvey, Penny 24
heritage, societal traces of 163
home-based work 225
homesickness 10, 102, 104–105, 107, 109, 114
horse-drawn carriages 22–23
human and urban realities, commodification of 186
human–artefact relation 127
human exceptionalism 4, 205
human security 55
hydroelectric power production 175

iconic landmarks 153
iconic sports cars, exhibits of 37
Image of the City, The (1960) 206
imaginative travel 2
immobile material systems 1
impatient people, sociology for 19
inauthentic temporality, Heideggerian notion of 231, 234
in-depth interviews (IDIs) 74, 77
Indrio, Anna Maria 152
information and communications technology (ICT) 225; development of 226
information-gathering 59; affordances for 59; and affordance when shopping 63–64; consumers' mental modelling and 60;

information-gathering *continued*
  impact of movement on 60, 64;
  modalities of 9, 59
information morphogenesis 59
Ingold, Tim 204
In Search of Lost Time 234–235
Instagram 32
Institute for Social Futures (ISF), Lancaster University 61
International Organization of Motor Vehicle Manufacturers (OICA) 31, 41; membership of 41
intersituative connections 20
Italian sports cars 37, 39, 43

Jaguar 38
judgemental, notion of 18

Kaika, Maria 55
knowledge production 8, 53
Knox, Hannah 24
Kohl, Helmut 41

Lefebvre, Henri: notion of 'lived space' 224, 229; rhythm analysis 69; spatial theory 229
leisure and cycling activities 188
light rail projects 5–6
light rail scapes 5
lived space: *versus* abstract space 229; Lefebvre notion of 224, 229; notion of 224; social relations in 229; working in 229–230
luxury cars, exhibits of 37
Lynch, Kevin 206

McCurdy, David 41
mapping-in-motion, in Berlin 9, 120; analysis of 125–128; atmospheres 128; auto-ethnographic 124–125, 134; fieldwork experiment 124–128; S-Bahn journey 125–128; smells 126–127; sounds 126; Staging Mobilities model 125; travellers' behaviours 127–128
mass extinction 50
Massey, Doreen 208
mass photography 37
mass production automobiles, exhibits of 38
mass-transport systems 188
material mobilities: in global south 199; notion of 16, 26, 50
material sensitivity 5, 13, 178; within mobilities studies 9

material turn 140; affect on mobilities turn 4; within mobilities research 4–7, 16; new material turn 3–5, 50, 140, 204
Matup Tunuani (film) 103
mediation, relations of 20
Mercedes-Benz 38
metropolitan transit infrastructures, auto-ethnographic mapping of 123
micro-mobility practices 79
mobile assemblages 4
mobile ethnography 9
mobile media technologies 101, 104
mobile methods 9, 12, 21, 51, 54–55, 74, 205, 211
'Mobile Utopia 1851–2016' project 61
mobile work: definitions of 224–225; empirical analysis of 230–231; freelancing 225; inward-oriented rhythm 233; pattern of communication with colleagues 232; and sense of isolation 232; three perspectives on 227–229; translocal patterns of 228; work–family balance 225; working time 231–235; work space for *see* work space
'mobilises' critiques of humanism 51
mobilities design 4–5, 10, 12, 53, 120–121, 133, 186–189, 196, 199, 204, 207–208
mobilities paradigm 8–9, 50–51, 55, 60, 180; new mobilities paradigm 61, 69, 74, 166, 219
mobilities research, material turn within 4–7
mobilities transformation 55
mobilities turn 2–3, 4, 33, 103, 207; agenda of 5; materialities within 204–206; new mobilities turn 1, 178
mobility and immobility, practices of 16, 25
mobility capital 70, 213
Mobility Challenges North Jutland 209
mobility culture, aspects of 189, 193, 196
mobility inequalities 187
mobility justice: concepts of 187; debate on 185; theoretical and methodological frameworks of 187–188
modern urbanism, philosophy of 191
Mortensen, Erik 106
Moses, Robert 145
motility, concept of 213, 219n5
motorcycle-based transport 189
'motorised-transportation' scale 60
motor shows: automobile expositions 31; benefits of 39; Geneva Motor Show 32, 34–41; historical research on 31; Paris

Motor Show 37; Philadelphia International Auto Show 31; political economy of 41–43; *Salon de l'Automobile* (Paris 1955) 31; Sheller's research on 32; as spectacle and celebration 41; and system of automobility 33
moto-taxi 189–190
MVRDV's mapping projects 122

Naked City 130, 131–133
nature (s), constructing of 169–170
network-based organisations 223
New Urban Agenda 54
Nichols, Julie 122
Nishino, Sohei 122; *London Map Diorama* 122
no hierarchy, principles of 143
Non-governmental Organisations (NGOs) 55
Nonhuman Turn 3
non-place (s) 5, 228
Non-representational Theory (NRT) 3
NORRØN architects 147–149, 151–152; 'Blue Plateau' project, in Blåvand 153, 155; brainstorming potential activities 161; branding of 163; design-oriented perspective 160; design practices of 152–155, 162; First Houens Odde design meeting *157–159*; Hammershus Visitor Centre 159; legitimate peripheral participation 160; Rødby project 153–154; view of good architecture 153

Object-Oriented-Ontologies (OOO) 3
O'Connor, Kevin 217
OICA *see* International Organization of Motor Vehicle Manufacturers (OICA)
oil boom 191
Oldenburg, R. 61–62
ornamental automobile accessories 36

Paris Climate Accord (2015) 50
Paris Motor Show (1955) 31, 37
Parson's Structural Functionalism 17
passengering, notion of 25
pedestrian mobilities 186, 190, 195, 196, 198
pedestrian public spaces, reconstruction of 199
pedestrian scale of walkability 65
personal wellbeing 253
Philadelphia International Auto Show 31
photo diaries 77

photo registrations 193
Pintó, Juancho 192–193, 195
port town 6
'post-modern post-industrial' networks 166
prehension, concept of 213–214
private transport associations 190
product differentiators 174
Project 360 degrees 130, 131–133
psycho-geography, concept of 131–132
psychological wellbeing 241–242, 244, 252–253
public spaces, appropriation of 186
public spheres, features of 25
public transport 192–193; Geneva Motor Show (2018) 35–36; passengers in 25
public transportation infrastructure network 124

railways: class system of coaches 23; European railway 22; horse-drawn carriages 22; as main mode of transport 22; rise of 23; as symbol of societal hierarchies 23
Reckwitz, Andreas 17
reflexive practitioner 149
responsible research and innovation, concept of 51
Roberts, Les 122
Rødby project 153–154
Rolls-Royce exhibit 38
rules, Wittgenstein's notion of 17
rural service infrastructure 230

Sadler, Simon 132
Schatzki, Theodore 19, 25
Schleip, Robert 215
Science and Technology Studies (STS) research 104, 140, 150, 217
self-driving cars 210
self, sense of 241–242
self-touching 216–217
sense-making, methods of 79, 231, 251–252
sense of place 240
sensory perception, types and practices of 216
Sheller, Mimi 31–32
Situationist City, The (1998) 132
smart city sustainability 54
smellwalks 130
Smelly Maps 130–131
social class 19, 37–39, 41, 43, 186
social fact, Durkheim's notion of 17
social-material-political everyday life 52

social order 19; establishment of 20; problem of 26
social relations 10, 140–141, 216, 229, 243, 248; co-creation of 218; metaphors for 141
societal responsibilities, matters of 54–55, 144–145, 208–209
sociotechnical landscapes 166
sociotechnical regimes 167, 181
socio-technical transformations 53
Space Syntax 60; analysis of network structure 68; 'choice' measurement 66; core methods in 65; core principles of 64–65; methodology of 64; model of potential urban movement 64; network-mapping method based on 64; road-network model 60, 73; theory of 61; urban movements and social meanings 64–65
Spanish Platform for Mortgage Affected People (PAH) 55
spontaneous open-air terminals 189–190
sport emotions 36
sports science 79
'sports' video cameras, body-mounted 80
'Staging Mobilities' model 125, 242–243, 253
Star, Susan Leigh 21
stasis-mobility and body-mind, dichotomies of 210, 213, 215
street intersection 190
street maps 131
supra-structures: concept of 17, 21; notion of structure as 17; and praxeological critique 17–18
surface, notion of 78
sustainable development 167, 181; education as prerequisite for 101; Sustainable Development Goals 208
sustainable tourism 174; sites for 179
sustainable urbanism 177
Svinkløv, Martin 105
Swiss National Railways 35

tabula rasa 82
tactical urbanism 187
techno-scientific complexities 177, 181
telephone communication 20
telework 223–225, 232
tensional responsiveness 213; qualities of 13, 215
Terminal Town 7
territory-making process 78
touching, quantum theory of 216
touch never ends, idea of 216
trade show 33
traditional knowledge 78
traffic congestion 39, 188, 190
traffic-related modes of transport 186
transit infrastructures, mapping of: agency of 121–123; approaches towards master-planning 122; auto-ethnographic 123; Berlin public transport infrastructures *118*, 124–128; characteristic for 119; Chatty Maps 130–131; Corner's notion of 121–122; ecological agency of 121; elements of 118–120; extraction process 123; field, creation of 123; fieldwork experiment 124–128; Good City Life project 130; Happy Maps 130; mobilities design and 120–121; 'mobilization' and customization of 122; more-than-representational 122; MVRDV's mapping projects 122; Naked City 130, 131–133; operations of 123–124; plotting process 124; Project 360 degrees 130, 131–133; reflective expanse and customization of 120; 're-territorialization' of sites 124; Science and Technology Studies (STS) 120; sensorial impressions and atmospheres 128–133; Smelly Maps 130–131; state-controlled schemes for 122; variations on 128–133
transported travellers 120
transport energy 1
transport infrastructures 16; configuration of practices 21–23; disasters and accidents 25; flat ontologies 18–21; and infrastructuring 21–25; notion of 21–25; performative and relational dimension of 24; practice theory and relationality of 23–25; socio-material practices of 26; supra-structures 17–18; ubiquity and importance of 23
transport machine 5
transsituative connections 20
turn to the material 2, 3–4
Twitter 32

uneven mobilities: in Caracas 186; practices of 185; practices of everyday-life 186; socio-material dimensions of 186
United Nations World Tourism Organization (UNWTO): Davos Declaration (2007) 175
urban cells 217
urban configurations, mapping of 65–68, 192, 195

urban design: material conditions of 119; reflection and cross-verbalization of 123; site mapping of 119
urban development 5–6, 191
urban mobilities 12; in Caracas 188–192; challenges of 192; equal right to 187–188; modernist programming of 199; practices of 190; public debates of 193
urban model, of Lancashire 61
urban network: affordances for movement 60; cartographic Ordnance Survey maps 60; Depthmap models 60; materialities of 60; patterns of movement 65
urban niche habitats 218
urban pedestrians' practices 195
urban planning 5, 13, 142, 177–178, 218
urban resistance, to uneven socio-material mobilities 198
urban scents, influence on urban life 130
urban settlements 59
Urban Smell Dictionary 130
Urban smellscape taxonomy 130
urban sound: dictionary 131; taxonomy 131
urban spaces 7, 13, 59, 63–64, 69, 74, 123, 132, 177, 185, 189–190, 195–196, 204, 218

urban transformation 12, 186–187, 195
urban transit infrastructures 118, 120
urban zoning, strategies of 192
Urry, John 2–3, 33, 42, 44–45, 51, 173, 179, 209
utility infrastructures 123

video ethnography 9, 63, 77, 97
virtual travel 3
Volkswagen 38

wealth and income distribution 39
wild multiple materialities, qualities of 215
Wissmann, Matthias 41
working life, mobility of 148, 223–226, 235–236
working time, as authentic or forced upon 231–235
work-related mobility 225, 227–228
work space: aestheticised organisational spaces 226; aesthetic sensitivity of workers 226; concept of 223; mobility and the unbounded 226
World Economic Forum 41

Yaneva, Albena 10–11

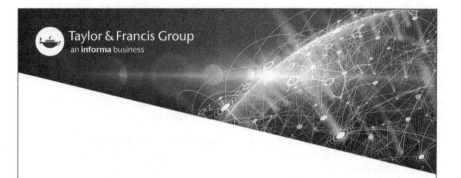